The History of the Jews in the Latin Kingdom of Jerusalem

The History of the Jews in the Latin Kingdom of Jerusalem

JOSHUA PRAWER

Clarendon Press, Oxford
1988

Oxford University Press, Walton Street, Oxford OX2 6DP
Oxford New York Toronto
Delhi Bombay Calcutta Madras Karachi
Petaling Jaya Singapore Hong Kong Tokyo
Nairobi Dar es Salaam Cape Town
Melbourne Auckland
and associated companies in
Berlin Ibadan

Oxford is a trade mark of Oxford University Press

Published in the United States
by Oxford University Press, New York

British Library Cataloguing in Publication Data
Prawer, Joshua
The history of the Jews in the Latin
Kingdom of Jerusalem.
1. Jews—Palestine—History—70–1789
I. Title
956.94'004924 DS124
ISBN 0–19–822557–1

Library of Congress Cataloging in Publication Data
Prawer, Joshua.
The history of the Jews in the Latin Kingdom of
Jerusalem.
Includes index.
1. Jews—Palestine—History. 2. Jerusalem—Latin
Kingdom, 1099–1244—Ethnic relations. I. Title.
DS124.P7 1988 956.94'4004924 87–23947
ISBN 0–19–822557–1

Set by Latimer Trend & Company Ltd, Plymouth
Printed in Great Britain
at the Alden Press, Oxford

PREFACE

THE history of the Jewish community in the Holy Land under Crusader rule has been sporadically treated, but has never merited a monographic study. It has been dealt with in the framework of Jewish history in the Near East, but overshadowed by the great centres of Babylon and Egypt. Such were the chapters devoted to the subject in the pioneering studies of S. Poznanski and the monumental works of Jacob Mann,[1] as well as in the numerous articles published in final form as seven studies in the collected papers of S. D. Goitein.[2] These pioneering and important studies opened new vistas and rewrote almost entirely unknown chapters in the history of Near Eastern Jewry. They were substantiated in masterly fashion by a massive publication of texts from the inexhaustible treasures of the Fusṭāṭ Genizah and their penetrating analysis. More recently a large quantity of references to partially published or still manuscript material was made in one of the most important works of our generation relating to the Near East, namely in Goitein's *Mediterranean Society*.[3] This was followed by M. Gil's publication of a monumental corpus of all available documents of the Cairo Genizah regarding Palestine in the early Muslim Period.[4] On our specific subject, a single attempt at a monograph was published in Hebrew over forty years ago.[5] And yet the story of the Jewish community

[1] S. Poznanaski, *Babylonische Geonim im nachgaonäischen Zeitalter* (Berlin 1914); Jacob Mann, *The Jews in Egypt and in Palestine under the Fāṭimid Caliphs*, 2 vols. (Oxford 1920–22; repr. with a supplement by S. D. Goitein, New York 1970); Id., *Texts and Studies in Jewish History and Literature*, 2 vols. (Cincinnati and Philadelphia 1931–5).

[2] S. D. Goitein, *Palestinian Jewry in Early Islamic and Crusader Times in the Light of the Geniza Documents* (H), ed. J. Hacker (Jerusalem 1980).

[3] Goitein, *Mediterranean Society*, 4 vols. so far (1967–83).

[4] M. Gil, *Palestine During the First Muslim Period (634–1099)*. Pt. i: *Studies* (H); Pts. ii–iii: *Cairo Geniza Documents* (Tel-Aviv 1983).

[5] J. Prawer, 'The Jews in the Latin Kingdom of Jerusalem' (H), *Zion*, 11 (1946), 35–82.

is a fascinating one, a part of the story of the conquered Syro-Palestinian population. As such it was viewed in the framework of research on the Crusader establishments in the East.[6]

Some years ago, writing a chapter on the 'minorities' (that is, the conquered population) in the Crusader states,[7] I became aware that a monographic study of Palestinian Jewry under Crusader rule would not only be an addition to Jewish history but also a very meaningful contribution to the study of the Crusader kingdom and society. The Jews, despite being a small minority amidst the conquered population, left far richer sources regarding their life and fate than the Oriental Christians, let alone the Muslims, who made up the bulk of the Palestinian population. This offers the possibility of a deeper insight and better understanding of what happened to at least some of the anonymous conquered population under Crusader rule.

The documentation at our disposal makes it possible to follow in detail the period of Crusader conquest with its massacres and ruin, and the subsequent process of reconstruction, temporarily interrupted by the Third Crusade, until we reach the period of the Second Kingdom, when the Jewish community, though no longer in Jerusalem, reached the peak of its development in the great Crusader trading centre at Acre. Better than for any other community we can follow the working of the community's internal organization in the framework of the Crusader kingdom's institutions. Here and there we also get glimpses of the attitude of the Jews to the Crusader conquerors as well as to neighbouring Muslim rulers. We also come across contacts between the rulers and the members of the community and, in rarer instances, cases of interfaith relations.

The salient characteristic is that of a closely knit community leading its own life with very little interference or contacts, but for the most practical purposes, with the outside. This seems to

[6] The second Hebrew edition of J. Prawer, *The Crusaders: A Colonial Society*, 250–330 (Jerusalem 1985).

[7] 'Social Classes in the Crusader States: The "Minorities"', in *History of the Crusades*, v. 59–117, ed. K. M. Setton, N. P. Zacour, and H. W. Hazard (Univ. of Wisconsin Press 1985).

have been the general tenor of interfaith relations. The same is also true in the realm of attitudes to the Holy Land. The pilgrims to the Holy Land—Christian, Muslim, Jew—often trod the same road but took not the slightest interest in the holy places of other religions unless they happened to be part of their own tradition. For the Jewish pilgrim, Nazareth and Bethlehem had nothing to do with the Annunciation and Nativity. He would have known nothing about a marriage in Cana of Galilee; the Jewish tradition knew the place as the burial-place of the prophet Jonah son of Amittai. The Jew had his own Jewish Palestine which was as much a religious as a national concept. Whoever was ruling it, his rule was ephemeral: part of the tenets of Jewish belief was that such rule was a transient event, a prologue that would end with the ushering in of the restoration of Israel.

In small communities in cities but also in villages, Palestinian Jewry as it was reconstructed in the twelfth and especially in the thirteenth century had some of the characteristics of the Frankish society. Created like the latter by a stream of immigration but added to an existing local nucleus, these communities presented a cross-section of the Jewish Diaspora. Oriental Jews from the Maghreb, Egypt, Yemen, Syria, and Iraq met and mingled with the Westerners who came from Spain, France, Italy, and Germany. Under the impact of these Westerners, the language of our sources changes from Arabic (albeit written in Hebrew characters) to Hebrew, the only common language of the Diasporas.

The newcomers brought with them their own attitudes to religion and philosophy, their preoccupations, and their academic traditions. But whereas the demographic picture reflects in some measure the general pattern of the Crusader kingdom, the similarity ceases at the level of intellectual life. Jewish Acre, though not as far as we can see a very creative centre, was clearly a centre of intellectual ferment and the meeting place of the various trends of Jewish thought, from Aristotelian rationalism harnessed to theology, through fundamentalism and pietism, to the borderlines of the mysteries of the different branches of the Kabbalah. An attack on the philosophical works of Maimonides spread from here and reverberated throughout the great centres of Judaism in the East and in the

West, coming to an end only with the disappearance of the Jewish community in the wake of the fall of Acre in 1291.

The story of the Jewish community in the Holy Land in any period cannot be treated without reference to the Jewish Diaspora. This is not only due to the physical fact that the Jewish Diaspora in every corner and in every age was the main reservoir supplying a fluctuating stream of pilgrims or eventual settlers in the Holy Land, but above all because the Land of Israel was the focal point of Jewish existence and its expectations of the future. This transcended the daily prayers for a return to Zion or the more solemn prayers of the Great Feasts. It influenced the Jews' way of thinking of themselves, the meaning of the Diaspora in the framework of history, and its picture of the blissful End. This stimulated writers, theologians, and philosophers and kept the awareness of the faraway Homeland alive throughout centuries. Pilgrimages and itineraries, philosophical treatises and exegesis, religious and secular poetry—their inspiration came in different degrees from the Holy Land. In our context the relation of the Diaspora to the Holy Land takes different turns whether in the poetry and in the treatises of Judah Halevy and in the reflections of Naḥmanides on the one hand or the earthly and religious pilgrimages to the Holy Land.

It is to be hoped that the following study will contribute to our knowledge of Jewish history but will also be a contribution to the history of the Crusader kingdom. Based on sources in Hebrew and studies written in the same language, and thus almost inaccessible except to a limited number of scholars, it should allow better insights into the story of a minority that linked its destiny in one way or another with that of the Holy Land under Crusader rule.

A few words should be added on the system of transcription of Oriental names. A large number, usually biblical and historical names, have been written according to common English usage. In others I have followed the transcriptions used in the studies of J. Mann and S. D. Goitein. Finally, names and quotations have been transcribed following the accepted diacritic signs. A particular problem was posed by the titles of books written in Hebrew which also have a title-page in one of the European languages. As a rule I have reproduced the latter in the way in which they are usually catalogued in libraries. As the books were printed in different countries at different periods the transcriptions vary and do not follow any systematic rules. Wherever possible I have indicated existing translations of sources and studies into European languages. Titles of books and articles written in Hebrew are usually given in English translation.

I should like to express here my thanks to friends and colleagues who read and commented on parts of the study. Among many let me single out Professors H. Beinart, B. Z. Kedar, J. Hacker, H. Soloveitchik of the Hebrew University and Dr Sylvia Schein of Haifa University. I owe a great debt to my assistant, Mr M. Sluchovsky, whose reliability and unceasing help were indispensable in writing the following study. And I should like to thank my assistant Mrs Sharon Roubach for her help in rechecking the text and in preparing the index.

Additionally I should like to express my thanks to Dumbarton Oaks and its former president Giles Constable, and to the Institute for Advanced Studies of the Hebrew University and its staff whose hospitality facilitated the writing of the following study.

J. PRAWER

The Hebrew University
Jerusalem, 1986

CONTENTS

	List of Maps	xii
	List of Abbreviations	xiii
1	On the Eve of the Crusades	1
2	The Conquest	19
3	Survival and Reconstruction	46
4	Rebuilding Jerusalem	64
5	The Jewish Community: Organization, Legal and Social Position	93
6	Pilgrimage, Immigration, and Settlement	128
7	The Hebrew Itineraries of the Crusader Period	169
8	The Thirteenth Century	251
	Epilogue	292
	Index	295

LIST OF MAPS

1 Jewish communities in the Holy Land under Crusader rule 112

2 The itinerary of the author of *Sefer Qabbalath Ṣadīqei Eretz Israel (Qivrei Avōth)* 179

3 The itinerary of the author of *Sefer Qabbalath Ṣadīqei Eretz Israel (Qivrei Avōth)*: The north (detail) 183

4 The itinerary of the anonymous pupil of Naḥmanides 238

5 The itinerary of the anonymous pupil of Nahmanides: The north (detail) 243

LIST OF ABBREVIATIONS

Assaf, *Sources*	S. Assaf, *Sources and Studies in Jewish History* (H) (Jerusalem 1946).
AOL	*Archives de l'Orient latin*, 2 vols. (Paris 1881–4).
Baron, *Social*	S. Baron, *A Social and Religious History of the Jews*, iv–v (New York 1957–8).
Barslavi (Braslavsky), *Studies* (H)	J. Barslavi, *L'Heger Artzenu* (Collected papers: *Studies in our country and its past*), Tel-Aviv 1954).
Benjamin of Tudela	*The Itinerary of Benjamin of Tudela*, ed. M. N. Adler (London 1907).
BJES	*Bulletin of the Jewish Exploration Society*.
Cathedra (H)	*Cathedra for History of Eretz Israel and its Yishūv* (Jerusalem 1976–).
Chronologie	H. Hagenmeyer, 'Chronologie de la première Croisade', *ROL*, vi (1896–).
Eretz Israel (H)	*Eretz Israel: Archeological, Historical and Geographical Studies* (Jerusalem 1951–).
Goitein, *Palestinian Jewry* (H)	S. D. Goitein, *Palestinian Jewry in Early Islamic and Crusader Times in the Light of the Geniza Documents*, ed. Joseph Hacker (Jerusalem 1980).
(H)	Hebrew.
JJS	*Journal of Jewish Studies* (1949–).

JQR	*Jewish Quarterly Review* (1888–).
Kaftor va-Pheraḥ (H)	Estori ha-Parchi, *Kaftor va-pherach*, ed. A. M. Luncz, 2 vols. (Jerusalem 1897–9).
Klein, *History* (H)	S. Klein, *Tōldōth ha-Yishūv ha-Yehūdi be-Eretz Israel* (History of the Jews in Eretz Israel) (Tel-Aviv 1935).
S. H. Kuk, *Studies* (H)	S. H. Kuk, ʻIyunim u-Meḥ-qarīm, 2 vols. (Jerusalem 1963).
Mann, i–ii	Jacob Mann, *The Jews in Egypt and in Palestine under the Fāṭimid Caliphs*. Preface and Readers' Guide by S. D. Goitein, 2 vols. in one (New York 1970). (First printing 1920.)
Mann, *Texts*	Jacob Mann, *Texts and Studies in Jewish History and Literature*, 2 vols. (Cincinatti and Philadel-phia 1931–5).
Mediterranean Society	S. D. Goitein, *A Mediterranean Society: The Jewish Communities of the Arab World as Portrayed in the Documents of the Cairo Geniza*. 4 vols. (Univ. of California Press 1967–83).
Outremer	*Outremer: Studies in the History of the Crusading Kingdom of Jerusalem* presented to Joshua Prawer, ed. B. Z. Kedar, H. E. Mayer, and R. C. Smail (Jerusalem 1982).
PL	Migne, *Patrologiae cursus completus: Series latina*, 221 vols. (Paris 1844–64).
PPTS	*Palestine Pilgrims' Text Society Library*, 13 vols. (London 1890–7).
Prawer, *Histoire*, i–ii	J. Prawer, *Histoire du royaume latin de Jérusalem*, 2 vols. (Paris 1969–70).

Prawer, *Latin Kingdom*	J. Prawer, *The Latin Kingdom of Jerusalem: European Colonialism in the Middle Ages* (London 1972).
REJ	*Revue des études juives* (Paris 1880–).
Responsa of Abraham Maimuni	ed. A. H. Freimann and S. D. Goitein (Jerusalem 1928).
Responsa of Maimonides	ed. A. H. Freimann (Jerusalem 1934); ed. J. Blau, 3 vols. (Jerusalem 1958–61).
RHC	*Recueil des historiens des Croisades*, 16 vols. (Paris 1841–1906).
HOcc.	*Historiens occidentaux*, i–v.
HOr.	*Historiens orientaux*, i–v.
ROL	*Revue de l'Orient latin*, 12 vols.
Sefer ha-Yishūv (H)	ed. S. Assaf and L. A. Meir, vol. ii (Jerusalem 1944).
Shalem (H)	*Shalem: Studies in the History of the Jews in Eretz Israel* (Jerusalem 1974–).
Taḥkemoni (H)	Juda al-Ḥarizi, *Taḥkemoni*, ed. A. Kaminka (Warsaw 1899).
Tombs of the Ancestors (H)	M. Ish-Shalom, Qivrei Avōth (Jerusalem 1948).
Urbach, *Tosafists* (H)	E. E. Urbach, *Baʿaley ha-Tosafot*, 2 vols. (Jerusalem 1980).
Voyages (H)	*Massaʿoth Eretz Israel*, ed. A. Yaʿari (Tel-Aviv 1946).
W.T.	William of Tyre

1

On the Eve of the Crusades

THE hosts of the First Crusade which penetrated northern Syria and made their way through Lebanon and the coastal plain of Palestine to Jerusalem moved through an area of political and religious dissent which had recently become the scene of bloody fighting. The traditional confrontation between the two great centres, Egypt and Mesopotamia, a three-thousand-year competition for the domination of the Near East was now represented by the Fāṭimid Shīʿā rulers of Egypt and the upholders of the Sunna, the new rulers of the North, the warrior-like Seljuk Turks. Having overrun Persia and Iraq they were accepted by the ʿAbbasid caliph of Baghdad, their conquests legitimized, and their commander, now boasting the new title of 'sultan', the 'wielder of power', was proclaimed and recognized as the secular arm of the Ruler of the Faithful. From the middle of the eleventh century the whole area between Mesopotamia and Egypt—that is, the coastal and mountainous parts of Syria, Lebanon, and Palestine—was thrown into political chaos which added to the misery wrought by the bedouin razzias and invasions.[1] Often local rulers navigated as best they could the dangerous and turbulent waters between the two giant opponents and tried to carve out lordships for themselves.[2] The Friday prayer in which the name of one or other of the contending caliphs was

[1] On the situation of Syria and Palestine between the Seljuk conquest and the Crusader invasion, see Y. Fraenkel, 'The Penetration of Bedouin into Eretz-Israel in the Fāṭimid Period (969–1096)' (H), *Cathedra* 11 (1979), 86–108; M. Gil, 'The Sixty Years War' (H), *Shalem* 3 (1981), 1–49; id., 'Additional Comments on the "Sixty Years War"' (H), *Cathedra* 20 (1981), 47–51. See also id. (below, n. 3), 328–76.

[2] The best example is that of the *qāḍī* ʿAin al-Daulah Abī ʿAqil, ruler of Tyre, who became independent in 1063 and remained so, with Seljuk help, despite the efforts of the Egyptian vizier Badr al-Jamālī, until 1089. The city was then captured by a Fāṭimid army, but its commander proclaimed his independence and held out until 1093. The city was then captured again by the Fāṭimids, but once more its commander proclaimed his independence.

proclaimed (*khutba*) was more often than not lip-service to the Sunnite ʿAbbasids or the Shīʿite Fāṭimids. Allegiances shifted and proclamations changed following the ascendancy of one or the other power in the area.

By the middle of the eleventh century, that is, a generation before the Seljuk invasion, the Holy Land was ruled by the Fāṭimids of Egypt, and under their generally benevolent attitude the Jewish communities in the Holy Land reached the peak of their development under Muslim domination.[3] The Islamic attitude to non-Muslims accorded the Jews, like all other 'minorities', the status of *dhimmis* (that is, the protected ones, or clients of the Muslim state), but ultimately and in everyday life the fate of individual communities depended on local conditions. The governor of the province, very often also his representative in the city or in the district, and the local *qāḍī* were the decisive factors in shaping the fate of the communities.

And yet political divisions were not the only factor to shape Jewish destinies. Individual communities and their larger groupings evolved independently. National legacies from previous periods sometimes mingled with legendary traditions. In some cases it was the particular position of a place or institution in the national and religious consciousness which was decisive in shaping the hierarchy of the nation's communities. Thus Palestinian Jewry, though numerically inferior to other Jewish centres and neither rich nor materially influential, claimed and often received recognition of its hegemony in certain matters throughout the Diaspora. As far as we can judge, eleventh-century Palestinian Jewry even at the peak of its development could not boast any great spiritual leader, and its cultural centres produced little which could compete with the great Jewish Academies of Babylon. Yet the Palestinian community claimed a particular standing in the nation, and that claim was based on the hallowed name of the Holy Land in general and that of the Holy City and its historical precedence in particu-

[3] See *The History of Eretz Israel*, vi: *Eretz Israel under Muslim and Crusader Rule, 634–1291*, ed. J. Prawer, pt. i: M. Gil, *Eretz Israel under Muslim Rule, 634–1099* (Jerusalem 1981), 130–51; id., *Palestine during the First Muslim Period (634–1099)*, i: *Studies* (Tel-Aviv 1983).

lar.[4] If such claims to hegemony were acknowledged (and this carried with it very often very practical material obligations for the party conceding such cognition)[5] this was a reflection not of any real balance of power but merely of some parts of the Diaspora being willing largely for historical and sentimental reasons (as in most claims there was very little of the religious) to acknowledge such claims.

Four authorities dominated Jewish life in the Near East under Muslim rule. The most prestigious, though not the most influential, was the 'Head of the Diaspora' (*rosh ha-gōla*), who claimed Davidic royal descent which was recognized by the Muslim caliphate in Baghdad. On a different level were the heads of the two great Babylonian Academies, those of Sura and Pumbedita, whose territorial competences stretched from their Iraqi centres into Persia in the east and to Syria in the West. The Palestinian Academy retained its authority in Palestine, in parts of Syria, and for a long period in Egypt. It is argued that the creation of the Fāṭimid caliphate, which included Palestine and Egypt assured more independence to the Palestinian Academy against the claims of the Babylonian centres especially at a time when the prestige of the latter was already waning.

The Palestinian Academy, Yeshivat Eretz Israel, also called Yeshivat Gaon Ya'aqov or Yeshivat Eretz ha-Tzvi, theoretically continued the old Sanhedrin tradition of the Talmudic (Roman and Byzantine) period. Owing to the Roman and then Christian–Byzantine prohibition of settling in Jerusalem, the Academy was located in Tiberias, the main settlement in Galilee, the most densely Jewish-populated part of the country. At an undetermined date but probably by the tenth century, the Academy moved to Jerusalem, despite the fact that the capital of the Muslim administration of the country was in Ramle; but even as late as the eleventh century, the head of the

[4] The most famous claim was that of the right to fix the calendar and the dates of festivities. The dispute between the Jewish great centres in Babylon and Palestine became a *cause célèbre* at the beginning of the tenth century (922) between the great luminary of the period R. Sa'adya Gaon, later the head of the Academy of Sura, and Aaron ben Meir, the son of the head of the Palestinian Academy.

[5] Such was the right to appoint *dayyanim* (judges) and some other community officers in Egypt. See ch. 5.

Palestinian Academy was sometimes known by the title of '*gaon* of Tiberias'.

The Academy was not only the place of study that its name suggests, but actually the most decisive element in the structure of Jewish autonomy recognized by the Muslim authorities. The head of the Academy bore the title 'gaon' and was the officially recognized representative of Palestinian Jewry in its dealings with the local government in the capital, Ramle, and in its dealings with the 'Abbasid caliphate in Baghdad, and from the middle of the tenth century, after the Fāṭimid conquest, with the authorities in Cairo. The Fāṭimid conquest brought in its wake a remarkable enlargement of the *gaon*'s role: the new rulers made him the official representative of the Jews (in theory, at least) in the whole Fāṭimid Empire. This was apparently to counteract the influence of the prestigious Academies in the 'Abbasid caliphate.[6] Officially, the *gaon* was nominated by the Fāṭimid caliph; in practice he was elected to his position by a delicate combination of promotion through merit, exalted genealogy, and pure nepotism. On his death he would be succeeded by his son, who would have served a long apprenticeship; where this was not the case he would sometimes serve another *gaon* before finally being promoted on the death of the latter. A text of nomination which has fortunately been preserved enumerates the *gaon*'s duties and competences as the head of the highest rabbinical court in the country. The main competence of the court was jurisdiction according to the *halakha* or official exegesis of the law; the head of the Academy also appointed *dayyanim* (local judges) and *ḥazanim*, who, in addition to the official tasks of readers of the Torah and cantors often fulfilled many other duties in smaller communities.[7]

The Academy often fulfilled the functions of a court of appeal, and generally speaking was entrusted with overseeing

[6] This view may be partially due to the fortuitous preservation of a document describing the *gaon*'s competences. See next note.

[7] S. D. Goitein, 'The Head of the Palestinian Yeshiva as Head of the Jews of the Fāṭimid Empire' (H), repr. in *Palestinian Jewry*, 70–82; id., 'On the History of the Palestinian Gaonate', ibid. 82–115; id., 'Government Installation of *gaons* and Jewish Judges' (enlarged earlier study), ibid. 70–82. Summarized, *Mediterranean Society*, ii. 1–40; M. Gil (above n. 3), 130–43; Mann, i. 153–202.

the behaviour of individuals and officials, and the functioning of the different communities. The court was composed of seven people, whose titles (in descending order) were: *gaon*, *ab ha-yeshiva* (also called *ab beit din*), *shlīshī be-yeshiva*—the Third in the Academy, and so forth to the last or Seventh in the Academy.

The Academy's revenues were assured from its property, which was regarded as a pious foundation paralleling the Muslim *waqf*, from donations, and from revenues deriving from taxation, as for example from the ritual slaughter of animals.

An alumnus of the Academy bore the title of Fellow of the Academy (*ḥaber ha-yeshiva*) and once appointed to a local community would keep up his link with his Alma Mater. Moreover Palestinian communities maintained their identities outside their native country; in the wave of migration into Syria and Egypt they kept alive their old connections and loyalties. They often gathered in their own synagogues and followed their own liturgies.

The seat of the Academy was in Jerusalem, but bowing to the importance of the great political and commercial centre of Ramle, the capital of Arab Palestine second in command in the hierarchy of the institution, the *ab beit dīn* usually resided there as the representative of the *gaon*. However, sometimes the *gaon* was represented in Ramle by another member of the hierarchy of the Academy.

In the middle of the eleventh century the authority of the *gaon* was challenged by the appearance of a descendant of the exilarch, the *rosh ha-gōla* from Babylon, who based his claim on his family of Babylonian *gaonim* and on his royal Davidic descent. The claimant, Daniel b. ʿAzarya, attempted to combine in his own person the office of *gaon* and the by now obsolete office of *nasi*, the official ruler of Palestinian Jewry in the second century CE. The competition developed into a sectarian quarrel which lasted a whole generation; the son of the claimant, David b. Daniel, who went to Egypt to mobilize the support of the local Jewry and the Egyptian government, proclaimed himself head of the Diaspora and tried to encroach on the competences of the Academy. The Seljuk invasion and expansion after 1071 facilitated this task, as he now gained the support of a Fāṭimid government anxious, it seems, to retain its authority in Palestine now overrun by the Seljuks.

Thus from the beginning of the second half of the eleventh century, the situation became chaotic. The Seljuk tribes led in the south by Atsiz, had since 1071 penetrated into Syria and Lebanon and were thrusting into Palestine. Generally speaking there was little opposition to the conquest of the interior. The cities in the hilly and mountainous area had, at best, only rudimentary defences. The struggle for the domination of the area had to be fought around great centres such as Damascus, Ramle, and Jerusalem, and along the coast and its large well-defended maritime ports. The Seljuks, an army of mounted archers, could do very little to besiege the maritime cities. Not only did the Turkish tribesmen lack a navy, but the Fāṭimids of Egypt, well aware of the imminent danger, could and did supply the cities of the coast by sea. It was often revolts in the cities which helped the Seljuks to gain the upper hand in the confrontation.

The confusion created by the Seljuks, who differed from the familiar Muslim population in appearance as well as in the method of warfare, had a shattering effect on the Jewish communities. As all great events in Jewish near-Eastern history this found its expression in a Jewish apocalypse, the *Prayer (Tefīla) of R. Simeon bar Yōḥai*. The latter was a second-century mystic and sage who hid in a cave for thirteen years during which time, according to tradition, the mysteries of the Holy Scriptures and the vicissitudes that would lead to the coming of the Messiah were revealed to him.[8] Thus, in the Prayer:

'And it shall come to pass on that day, that the Lord shall hiss for the fly that is in the uttermost part of the rivers of Egypt, and for the bee that is in the land of Assyria' [Isa. 7: 18]. God will hiss to the sons of Canaan [Canaan, the sons of Ḥam, are the Seljuks], and they will fight against the Ashkenazim.[9] And their first king leading them is a

[8] On R. Simeon bar Yōḥai see Y. Even Shmuel (Y. Kaufmann), *Midrashei Geūlah* (Tel-Aviv 1943), 167–8.

[9] According to Even Shmuel this refers to the European regiments in the service of the Emperor of Byzantium who fought the Seljuk invaders.

slave, who rebelled against his lord,[10] as it is written: 'Thus said the Lord . . . to whom man despiseth, to him whom the nation abhorreth, to a servant of rulers' [Isa. 49: 7]. Who is he whom the nation abhorreth? Clearly these are the sons of Canaan, who are the most horrible among the nations. 'The servant of rulers', that he will be a slave of rulers and will rebel against his lord and the people who rebelled against their lord will come to him and fight against the sons of Ishmael [the Egyptians], and they will kill their warriors and inherit their money and riches. And they are monstrously ugly and wear black garments,[11] and they are bitter and hasty, as it is written: 'I raise up the Chaldeans, that bitter and hasty nation' [Hab. 1: 6], and all of them are horsemen, as it is written: 'The horseman lifteth up the bright sword and the glittering spear' [Nahum 3: 3] and they come from far away lands 'to possess the dwelling places that are not theirs' [Hab. 1: 6]. And they climb the mountains, that is the mighty Mount of Israel, and they break into the Temple and put out the candles and throw open the portals.

The anonymous writer of the Apocalypse Prayer indicates quite clearly both the black banners of the ʿAbbasids and the most characteristic feature of the invading Turkish tribes, the mounted archer. What he expected is not clear. The Seljuks, horrible as they seemed to him,[12] were more than just part of an apocalyptic vision: for the Jewish communities in Palestine, who were on the whole sympathizers of the Fāṭimid regime, the appearance of the Seljuk hosts threatened the precarious peace of the beginning of the second half of the eleventh century. Thus Solomon b. Joseph Hakkohen, a member of the Palestinian family from which the *gaonim* were drawn, writing in Fusṭāṭ in 1077 on the deliverance from a Seljuk invasion of Egypt, described the invading Turks as follows:[13]

[10] *Midrashei Geŭlah*, 273–4. The text has: 'And the first being who leads them finds out that they rebelled against their Lord.' The amendment of the editor is based on the parallel text of the *Mysteries of R. Simeon bar Yoḥai*. According to the editor, the description fits the first Seljuk ruler.

[11] Black was the traditional colour of the ʿAbbasids, in whose name the Seljuks fought against the Fāṭimids of Egypt.

[12] His impression tallies with later European descriptions of the invading Mongols in the 13th cent.

[13] The letter was published and translated into English by J. H. Greenstone, 'The Turcoman Defeat at Cairo', *The American Journal of Semitic Languages and Literatures* 22 (1906), 144–73. The quotations are from ll. 40–9.

They were a strange and cruel people, wearing garments of many colours, armed and officered, chiefs among the terrible ones wearing helmets, black and red, with bow and spear and full quivers, and they trumpet like elephants and roar like the roaring waters, to terrify, to frighten those who oppose them ... They are mingled with Armenians, Arabs and Edomites[14] and Greeks and Franks,[15] Paphlagonians,[16] and Turks.

Actually there is much exaggeration in this description. The Seljuk commander Atsiz invaded Syria and Palestine in 1071, when he besieged the city of Tyre; he then attacked and captured Ramle, the Fāṭimid capital of Palestine, and then Jerusalem.[17] Atrocities seem to have been perpetrated during the unsuccessful Seljuk siege of Cairo as described by Solomon b. Joseph Hakkohen: 'They were like mortal foes, as those who are vindictive and revengeful; and they entered Fusṭāṭ, robbed and murdered; and ravished and pillaged the store houses.'[18] But despite the horrors described by our author Jerusalem did not suffer, and the conqueror tried to re-establish peace and civil life.[19] It was only when a revolt broke out in the city some four years later, in 1077, that Atsiz changed his policy, and the civilian population were massacred.[20] It was even argued that it was only the Muslims who revolted that suffered, whereas the Christians and Jews were spared. This is clearly contradicted by the author of our historical poem, who mentions two sieges, 'two times in two years';[21] and after the description of the destruction wrought around the city he says that they 'cut off the ears, and also the nose, and robbed the garments, leaving them stark naked ... and they had no mercy on widows,

[14] In Hebrew sources 'Edom' usually stands for Byzantium.

[15] This could mean Germans, but here it seems to mean Europeans in general.

[16] Heb. *rifatin*; see Greenstone, 'The Turcoman Defeat', n. 126. This strange enumeration of the different peoples might follow a Hebrew literary convention, which assigns to the expression *erev rav* (a mixture of people) a pejorative meaning.

[17] According to different Arab sources Jerusalem was captured either in 1071 or in 1073. The latter date seems more plausible. See M. Gil, 'The Scroll of Ebyatar', in *Jerusalem in the Middle Ages: Selected Papers*, ed. B. Z. Kedar and Z. Baras (Jerusalem 1979), 43 n. 10.

[18] Greenstone, above, n. 13, ll. 37–9.

[19] Ibid., ll. 61–92. The atrocities and destruction described here probably refer to later events (1077). See Prawer, *Histoire*, i. 115–17.

[20] Ibid.

[21] Greenstone, l. 63. Actually twice in four years.

neither did they pity orphans . . . they are robbers and thieves, they know only how to do evil'.[22]

Whatever the fate of the Jerusalem community during these troubled times, they certainly were not prosperous. The Academy of Jerusalem sought haven for some time in Tyre, the Phoenician capital, (*c.*1077), but some time later, probably in 1093, it moved to Ḥadrakh, probably a suburb of Damascus.[23]

The exile of the Palestinian Academy is symptomatic of the generation between the Seljuk and Crusader conquests. A cloud of silence descends on the whereabouts of the communities in the formerly important Jewish centres of Jerusalem, Ramle, and Tiberias. The mountainous part of the country was cut off from the coast, the former dominated by the Seljuks, the latter by the Fāṭimids, or as in the city of Tyre and some other coastal cities of Lebanon and Syria, by local rulers. Whatever information has survived originated on the coast. In Tyre in the north and as far south as Ascalon the Jewish communities continued to live under Fāṭimid rule to the eve of the Crusader conquest. Jewish communities must have also survived in the Seljuk-dominated areas, like Jerusalem or Galilee, but little of this transpires from the rich sources of the Egyptian Genizah, perhaps because communications were interrupted. This ominous silence is the opening chapter of the Crusader period.

By the end of 1096 or the beginning of 1097, more insistent rumours and ominous tidings of the movement of the Crusader hosts were reaching the East. The Messianic tension and upheaval which accompanied the beginning of the First Crusade in the Christian world were not entirely strange to the

[22] Greenstone ll. 75 ff. and *passim*. These events may perhaps explain the expression in a letter from Cairo in 1085: 'those Rabbanites who remain from Israel in Jerusalem', Mann, i. 192 n. 1, and M. Gil, *Documents of the Jewish Pious Foundations from the Cairo Geniza* (Leiden 1976), 213, l. 5.

[23] As to the date see Mann, i. 189. 'Ḥadrakh' is actually unknown in medieval sources. The name appears in Zech. 9: 1: 'in the land of Ḥadrakh and Damascus shall be the rest thereof'. The place referred to as the see of the exiled Palestinian Academy was, it seems, in a suburb of Damascus, and the identification goes back to Byzantine times. Cf. *Sifrei Deuteronomium*, ed. M. Friedmann (Vienna 1864; repr. Jerusalem 1978), 65, par. a: 'And said Joseph son of a Damascene . . . Heaven and Earth shall be my witness that I am from Damascus and there is a place there called Ḥadrakh.' Mann, i. 196 n. 1; J. Barslavy, 'On the Appointment of R. Ebyatar as Gaon during his Father's Lifetime and on the Cave of Makhpelah' (H), *Eretz-Israel* (1958), 220–3.

Jewish communities and were easily communicated to them. The millenary expectations, which characterized Christian Europe from the beginning of the eleventh century (or alternatively *c.*1034, following the computation of a thousand years after the crucifixion), were also current in the Jewish world. While generally restricted to small groups of visionaries, they represented a permanent current in Jewish existence and in propitious circumstances, they spread like wildfire from tightly knit circles of mystics to excite larger circles, whole communities, and at times great parts of the Jewish Diaspora.

By the middle of the eleventh century a tremor of great approaching events was felt in the Jewish world. The 'Computators of the End', as chiliastic visionaries were called, calculated the End of Days for the year 1068—that is, a thousand years after the traditional date (68 CE) of the destruction of the Temple (actually 70 CE). The famous Spanish Jewish poet, Solomon ibn Gabirol, raised his voice in protest to Providence in a moving poem: 'The stem of the Son of Jesse, until when will you remain buried [in the sense of 'hidden']? . . . Why should a slave rule the son of the nobles. It is a thousand years that I am enslaved.' The eternal question: 'How will the End be disclosed?' receives the traditional answer: 'And God ordered: this will remain mute and sealed.'[24] But the year passed uneventfully, though as Maimonides recalled three generations later in his famous *Epistle to Yemen* the computation sufficed to stir some kind of Messianic movement. 'A man rose at the time in one of the communities [Lyons in France or León in Spain] and in moonlit nights climbed to the tops of trees and flew from one to another to fulfil the Messianic prophecy of Daniel [7: 13]: "One like the son of man came with the clouds of heaven." '[25] The moonstruck Messiah was executed on the order of the rulers of *al-Ifranj*, as Maimonides calls the land with the mysterious city of 'Lenon' or 'Linon', and this put an end to the movement.[26]

The date of this movement is not clear, but it may have been connected with the expedition of a coalition of French and

[24] *Collected Poems of Ibn Gabirol*, ii., ed. Bialik-Ravnicki (Tel-Aviv 1925), 33.
[25] A. S. Halkin, *Epistle to Yemen* (H) (New York 1952), 103; Engl. p. xx.
[26] Cf. Baron, *Social*, v. 199 ff.

Aragonese knights against Barbastro in Spain in 1064.[27] However, there is also the possibility that this movement took place in the 1080s and thus falls into a chiliastic computation according to which the Messiah was expected to come in the time-span of 19 years of the cycle of 256 years—that is, between 1085 and 1104. This was based on the verse of Jeremiah (31: 7): 'Sing with gladness for Jacob . . . and say O Lord, save thy people, the remnant of Israel', the word 'sing' in Hebrew (*ranū*), having the numerical value of 256. When the greedy and bloodthirsty hordes of the Peasants' Crusade struck and massacred the Jewish communities in the Rhineland, a Jewish poet, R. Eliezer b. R. Nathan, bewailed the tragically shattered expectations: 'We awaited salvation at the fixed time of "Sing for Jacob". We hoped for peace but there is grief, we looked for redemption but there was terror.'[28] Whether such Messianic expectations were generally current among Jews at that period, or whether they were restricted to certain circles and invoked only in the aftermath of the horrible massacres in the Rhineland and the Danube valley, we have no way of knowing.[29]

The immediate reverberations of the great tragedy were actually felt even far away from the burned Jewish quarters in the West. Tidings of the massacres, rumours about the apocalyptic numbers of the Christian masses, must have reached the Near East by the end of 1096 or the beginning of 1097. The

[27] On the expedition of 1064 see M. Defourneaux, *Les Français en Espagne aux XIe et XIIe siècles* (Paris 1949), 136 ff. Another expedition from France to Spain in 1073 was led by Ebles of Roucy, whose sister was the mother of Peter I of Aragon. See F. Duncalf, 'The Councils of Piacenza and Clermont', *A History of the Crusades*, i (1969²), ed. M. W. Baldwin, 232.

[28] A. M. Habermann, *Persecutions in Germany and France* (H) (Jerusalem 1971). The phrase and interpretation is to be found in the works of two chronicles, Solomon b. Samson (p. 24) and Eliezer b. Nathan (p. 72). On the lunar cycle computation see Baron, *Social*, iv. 296–7 and viii. 189.

[29] A contemporary Muslim computation calculated the year 1107, that is, 500 years after the appearance of Muhammad, as the date of the End. This calculation influenced the Jews, but when the expectations were shattered a new computation was proposed, substituting the solar for the traditional lunar year. This pointed to the year 1122 (above n. 26), (Baron, *Social*, v. 201). This possibly influenced Jewish and Karaite pseudo-prophets like the converted Norman Obadyah and his Karaite interlocutor who met in that year on the frontier of the Crusader kingdom, in Banyās. Cf. J. Prawer, 'The Autobiography of Obadya the Norman a Convert to Judaism at the Time of the First Crusade', in *Studies in Medieval Jewish History and Literature*, ed. I. Twersky (Camb., Mass. 1979), 110–34.

Jewish communities, it seems, were no better informed, at least at that stage of events, than their Muslim or Byzantine neighbours as to the reasons for this stupendous movement. A singular epistle emanating from a Jewish community within the Byzantine Empire in the Balkans, or perhaps in Asia Minor, vividly reflects the atmosphere of the period and the reaction of a Jewish community to the shock-waves created by the advancing hosts of the First Crusade.[30] Its author, one Menaḥem b. Elijah, writing in all haste from a place on the Crusaders' route in his anxiety to let his correspondents have a summary of the rumours and events as quickly as possible, reports that he was on the point of leaving for Syria or Palestine (he uses the Arabic expression *al-Shām*, which can be applied to both), but decided against it: 'I saw the troops of the Westerners (*Ashkenazim*), moving in their masses and I do not know where they will turn.' News was pouring in from Salonika, Constantinople, Tripoli (in Syria), Abydos (at the entrance of the Dardanelles), and, as one would expect in such circumstances, from Khazaria.[31] Everything was in turmoil. A letter had been received in Constantinople from the community in *Franjan* (clearly, Western Europe) but its contents are unknown. The scattered scraps of news we have bear all the features of a Messianic upheaval. The letter from the West might have brought the bad tidings of the massacres in the Rhineland, but in all probability it too included the eternal question, asked whenever persecutions reached their peak, about the Signs of the Messiah. Actually, he writes, news had already arrived from Khazaria that seventeen communities were on the move into the desert to meet the Ten Lost Tribes, but nobody yet knew the outcome of the event. In these circumstances it is not surprising to hear that the prophet Elijah had already revealed himself in Abydos:[32] the local

[30] The letter was published in a critical edition by J. Mann in *Hatekufah* 23 (1925), 253 ff. Cf. A. Scharf, 'An Unknown Messiah of 1096 and the Emperor Alexius', *JJS* 7 (1966), 159–70.

[31] Possibly referring to the ancient Jewish state and now legendary Jewish communities in the Crimea; still, the writer might have used the expression to denote simply the Crimea. It was argued that he meant Khorasan. Obviously both were outside the routes of the Crusaders.

[32] In Jewish tradition Elijah is the precursor of the Messiah. Enoch and Elijah play the same role in the Christian apocalypse of the early Middle Ages. Cf. B. McGinn, *Visions of the End* (New York 1979), index s.v. Elijah.

community had announced it to the great community of Constantinople and to the community of the writer of our letter. Following the traditional response to almost every Messianic upheaval throughout the ages, the leaders of both communities excommunicated those of Abydos. But the shock-waves of the movement reached Tripoli in Syria, and the well-known head of the Palestinian Academy, the *gaon* Ebyatar b. Elijah Hakkohen (*gaon* from 1083 to 1150), who happened to be there, also wrote a letter to Constantinople on the subject.

The epicentre of this Messianic upheaval seems to have been Salonika. Here we witness patterns of behaviour which for centuries were to be the characteristic features of Jewish Messianic movements. The rich divided their property among the poor, people sold their businesses and stood in prayer and repentance awaiting the coming of the Messiah. 'They sit in their prayer shawls, they stopped working and we do not know what they are hoping for. And we are afraid that the thing might be revealed to the gentiles and they will kill us.' Strangely enough the author of this epistle mentions in the same breath that the Christians were gripped by excitement and the local bishop exhorted . . . the Jews to action! No wonder if in this atmosphere a Jew dreamed that 'all the communities of Romania [i.e. Byzantium] will assemble in Salonika and hence will go out [no doubt to the Holy Land]'. The dreamer would have been rebuked by the local Jewish authorities but for a letter which arrived from R. Tobias of Thebes, obviously a man whose name carried authority,[33] telling of what was happening in Salonika. Alas, we are left in the dark as to the contents of this letter.

As Elijah had already revealed himself, it was only a matter of time till the final events of history came about. That the time was approaching was also clear from the discussion with the Crusaders; the latter allegedly claimed that they had been forced to move to the East by a nation which sallied forth from beyond the Mountains of Darkness.[34] Thus, the mechanism ushering in the End was put in motion. Fittingly, the author of

[33] It has been suggested that this was R. Tobias of Thebes, the author of *Midrash Leqaḥ Tōv*; see Baron, *Social*, v. 383 n. 64.

[34] Obviously referring to Gog and Magog of the Jewish and Christian apocalyptic writings of the Middle Ages, based on Ezek. 38: 2 and Rev. 20: 8.

our epistle reflects upon the stupendous commotion and comes forward with what may be called a 'Jewish perspective' of the Crusades. Why should so many nations be moving to the Holy Land? Obviously they are not aware of God's counsel to gather them as sheaves on the threshing floor. 'And when the Westerners, all of them, will go to Eretz Israel, the threshing floor will fill up and then God will command: "Arise and thresh O daughter of Zion" [Mic. 4: 13].'

This is the only letter known today which originated in a Jewish community in the Levant during the First Crusade; more than two years were to pass before the siege and capture of Jerusalem by the Crusader hosts would bring new information on the vicissitudes of the Jewish communities in the Holy Land.

The hosts of the First Crusade, reaching first Lebanon and then Palestine in the spring of 1099, did not attempt to besiege or capture any of the well-fortified coastal cities. Rather, they accepted the bribes of money and provisions that the fearful Muslim city authorities offered them to vouchsafe their safety and continued to advance southwards beneath the city walls.

The Jewish communities, like their Muslim compatriots, must have been in mortal fear at the sight of the advancing hosts. In fact, with the news of the horrible massacres in Europe, the Jews knew even better than the Muslims what to expect from the appearance of the Crusaders. Accordingly, those in smaller places and unfortified townships sought asylum elsewhere, some actually going so far as to seek security in Egypt. In this they were followed by their neighbours and religious rivals, the Karaites. This Jewish sect, founded in the eighth century, joined the general movement looking for security and fled to Egypt to seek the support of the very wealthy Karaite community there. Such groups of Palestinian Jews and Karaites later helped in the rescue of Jews taken captive by the Crusaders. Although it is not clear where they settled, one has the impression that they concentrated in the eastern delta region of Egypt, possibly in Bilbais or Damietta.[35]

[35] From these groups emanated the detailed letter about the rescue of the Jews from Jerusalem through Ascalon to Egypt. The full text appears in Goitein, *Palestinian Jewry* (H), 240–50, with a partial text and English translation in *JJS* 3, 122. As to the authors, see below, ch. 2, p. 27.

The Crusader hosts proceeded from Lebanon southward along the coast to Caesarea and then inland to Ramle, the administrative centre of southern Palestine, the *Jund Filastin*. Flourishing communities of both Karaites and Rabbanites, as the Jews were sometimes called to distinguish them from the former, had probably existed here since the Muslim foundations of the city around 716. By the beginning of the eleventh century both communities reached the peak of their development in terms of numerical strength and prosperity.[36] The city suffered badly during the eleventh century from a series of earthquakes—in 1016, in 1033, and again in 1067. In the last, it is reported, 25,000 people were killed and only two houses remained. This coupled with the bedouin rebellion which brought about the establishment of the tribe of Banū Jarraḥ (1024) in the capital and the subsequent extortions wrought from the Rabbanite and Karaite communities, made the situation desperate. The Seljuk conquest also took its toll. The Jerusalemite Rabbinic court mentions in a decision written in 1070/1 (4831 of Creation): 'and Ramle was robbed and spoiled and the captives left there naked and hungry'.[37] The once-wealthy community which had supported the Jewish congregation and its institutions in a generally poverty-stricken Jerusalem was barely able to do so in the last quarter of the eleventh century.

The Muslim capital, though fortified, fell into Crusader hands without a fight on 2 June 1099. Abandoned by the (probably Seljuk) authorities and without a garrison, the local population—Muslims, Oriental Christians, and Jews—fled the city.[38] This was the end of the once-flourishing Jewish community in Ramle.[39] Neither during the Crusader period nor later did the city ever regain its earlier position, nor did a Jewish community of any importance settle there until our own times. A similar fate, we can conjecture, befell the Jewish

[36] *Sefer ha-Yishūv* (H), ii (Jerusalem 1944), ed. S. Asaf and L. A. Mayer, 19–21.

[37] Mann, ii. 462–3.

[38] When peace was established Ramle was resettled by its former Muslim and Christian population. See J. Prawer, *Crusader Institutions*, 112 ff.

[39] The last information regarding the Jewish community in Ramle before the Crusader conquest dates from 1094, when a Commentary on the Book of Ruth and the Song of Songs was copied in the city. MS Or. 2554. Cat. British Museum i (London 1894; repr. 1965), ed. G. Margaliouth, 224, quoted from *Sefer ha-Yishūv*, ii. 63 n. 42.

community in Jaffa. With the news of the advancing Christian armies the local Fāṭimid civil and military authorities simply fled, a fateful mistake which gave the Crusaders the first southern port of the future kingdom. The Jewish community must have left at the same time, moving in all probability either to strongly fortified Ascalon or to Jerusalem.[40] The urge to look for a fortified place of refuge must have been even stronger in smaller unfortified places.

Something of the mood and anxiety of these troubled times emerges from a letter, undated but very likely written at the approach of the Crusaders, from the community of Raffiyaḥ on the southern outskirts of the Holy Land, on the road leading from Palestine through Sinai to Egypt. The Jews there must have made a living by supplying the desert caravans entering or leaving the Sinai desert. One Joshua b. ʿAli, who bore the honorific title bestowed by the Academy of Jerusalem, *ḥaber*,[41] wrote to the highest Jewish dignitary in Egypt, a doctor at the court, the *nagid* Meborak,[42] requesting a letter of recommendation to the *qāḍī* of Raffiyaḥ:

We write this in the midst of great sorrow and suffering from deprivation and permanent fear that grows continually. And our soul is frightened and trembles because of the rumours which are reaching us. I therefore ask you that a letter should come from you to the *qāḍī* who is in Ḥaṣōr [Raffiyaḥ],[43] so that I will have a recommendation if

[40] The last information regarding the Jewish community before the Crusader conquest is an act of divorce passed before the Jewish court in 1077. *Sefer ha-Yishūv*, ii. 15 n. 3. Jaffa was abandoned at the same time as Ramle. On 17 June 1099 a Genoese fleet reached the empty port.

[41] *Ḥaber* means Fellow of the Academy and usually denotes a graduate holding a diploma therefrom and functioning as a *dayyan* (judge or head of the court). See Mann, i. 264 ff.

[42] The title *nagid* was bestowed by the Fāṭimid caliph on the official head of Egyptian Jewry. His authority extended over all territories ruled by the Fāṭimids, in our case Palestine. See ch. 5, p. 111–13.

[43] In the Middle Ages, Jews readily identified sites and places in the Holy Land with Biblical sites. Others carried Biblical names as a kind of courtesy. Two Ḥasōrs are known from the Bible, one in Galilee and one in the lands of the tribe of Benjamin. As Raffiyaḥ is not mentioned in the Bible the name Ḥaṣōr was applied to it because of its proximity to Gaza, as Deut. 2: 23 has it: 'And the Avims which dwelt in Haserim even into Gaza'. Cf. Klein, *History*, 108, and sources in next note. The same conclusion is reached by I. Ben Zvi, *The Book of the Samaritans* (H) (Jerusalem 1970) 125. M. Gil, *History* (above n. 3), vi, fol. 1, 74, identified the place with Caesarea. Although this is possible it seems very doubtful because Caesarea was strongly fortified. Moreover, the normal refuge from Caesarea would be the nearby Acre, not Ascalon.

I decide to go from Ḥaṣōr to Ascalon to stay there during these troubled times, because it is more fortified than Ḥaṣōr.[44]

If he really managed to move to Ascalon in time he was lucky as this southern city, of Herodian fame, was not captured by the Crusaders until two generations later, in 1154.

After a short rest in the now-empty city of Ramle the Crusader host made its way into the mountains of Judaea. Descending from the north, they reached a small hill (7 June 1099) which gave them their first view of the city of Jerusalem. This was the traditional place of the Tomb of the Prophet Samuel, Nebī Samwīl. The hill, on which later a Premonstratensian monastery was to be built, was baptized by the Crusaders as *Mons Gaudii*, Montjoye, to commemorate the joy of beholding Jerusalem.

In the evening of the same day Jerusalem was put under a siege which lasted for five weeks (7 June–15 July 1099). The city, which had been ruled since 1077 by the Seljuks, had suddenly been captured in the summer of 1098 after a forty-day siege by an Egyptian army part of a Fāṭimid effort under the vigorous Armenian vizier al-Afḍal, to stem the Seljuk penetration into Syria and Palestine. When the Crusaders besieged it the city was therefore ruled by the Fāṭimids.

The Fāṭimid commander, Iftikhār al-Daulah, had time enough to provision the city, and the whole population (which may well have swollen to some 20,000 or 25,000 inhabitants because of the influx from villages and smaller townships in the surrounding area) was called to arms, Jews included, to assist the Egyptian garrison. Following the common practice, inhabitants were called to defend the parts of the walls nearest their quarter, walls which they or their ancestors had probably built or repaired and which therefore protected their houses and families.[45] This was done, as one would imagine, partly to increase the population's incentive to fight. Fate decided that

[44] Mann, ii. 199–200; cf. ibid. i. 169–70 and E. J. Worman, 'Forms of Address in *Genizah* Letters', *JQR* 19 (1907), 728 n. 19.

[45] Thus when the walls of the city had to be restored in the middle of the eleventh century, the Christians had to repair the walls of their quarter. Cf. J. Prawer, 'The Patriarch's Lordship in Jerusalem', *Crusader Institutions*, 298.

the Jewish defenders found themselves opposing the Lotharingian host commanded by Godfrey of Bouillon.

The first Jewish Quarter had been created in the wake of the Muslim conquest of the city, that is after 638. With the end of Byzantine rule the prohibition, which for six hundred years had barred the Jews from living in the city was lifted. First decreed by the Emperor Hadrian after 137 or 138, it survived pagan Rome and was reinforced in the fourth century when the Empire became Christian but fell into abeyance or was officially abrogated with the Muslim conquest. The small, new community, linked with Tiberias and Galilee, settled near the recently built al-Aqṣā Mosque. It was soon augmented by the Samaritans who established their quarter, the *Samaritiké* nearby, and in the middle of the ninth century by the Karaites. These quarters probably continued to exist until the beginning of the eleventh century when the city, by now heavily reduced in comparison with its Byzantine zenith in the sixth century, had to adapt its crumbling defences to the actual needs of the city. By 1033 the southern and eastern line of walls begin to take their new course (which still exists), leaving the erstwhile Jewish Quarter outside the line of defences.[46] In the middle of the century, when the Christian Quarter was newly fortified in about 1063 with the help of the emperor of Byzantium, a new Jewish Quarter or concentration was created in the north-eastern part of the city, between Damascus Gate in the north and the Gate of Josaphat in the east. Even though the quarter was destroyed by the Crusaders, the area continued to be known as *Judearia* or *Juiverie* until late in the thirteenth century.[47]

It was on the wall of this quarter that in the summer of 1099 the Jewish community of Jerusalem played out its last hours.

[46] The earthquake which partially destroyed the walls of Jerusalem and wrought havoc in Ramle took place at the end of 1033 or beginning of 1034. The reconstruction of the walls by al Ẓahir may have begun before the earthquake but was completed later.

[47] See J. Prawer, 'The Vicissitudes of the Jewish Quarter in Jerusalem in the Arabic Period' (H), *Ẓion* 12 (1947), 136–48. On the siege and the Jewish Quarter: id., 'The Jerusalem the Crusaders Captured', in *Crusade and Settlement*, ed. P. H. Edbury (Cardiff 1985), 1–17. In contrast M. Gil, 'The Jewish Neighbourhood of Jerusalem during the First Muslim Period, 638–1099' (H), *Shalem* 2 (1978), 19 ff., argues the existence of the Jewish Quarter in the south of the city.

2

The Conquest

THE story of the siege of Jerusalem is too well known to be repeated.[1] The siege lasted five weeks, from 7 June to 15 July 1099, during which period the Crusaders changed their strategy from direct attack to siege. They also changed the deployment of their troops at least three times, looking for a weak spot in the city's defences.

In the last stage of the siege the attacks were concentrated in two areas, the eastern section of the north wall and the south-western sector of the walls. These stretches lacked natural defences like the valleys which surrounded the city on the other sides, being defended instead by an artificial moat and a barbican outside the main wall of the city. The northern wall was besieged by the hosts of Godfrey of Bouillon, Robert of Normandy, Robert of Flanders, and Tancred of Otranto. Only the western wall with the Jaffa Gate and citadel were patrolled, the combination of moat and natural valley near the citadel and the rising ground to the south making permanent siege in this area impracticable. It was only the south-western part of the city, on Mount Zion, that was permanently besieged by the Provençal host of Raymond of Saint Gilles, who moved his camp there after unsuccessful attempts to attack and besiege the city on the citadel side.[2]

Opposing the Crusader hosts was the Fāṭimid garrison of the city commanded by Iftikhār al-Daulah. The main stronghold was the citadel, but with the beginning of the siege the entire city was mobilized to man the three miles or more of city walls.

[1] See Prawer, *Histoire*, i. 223 ff; id., 'Jerusalem that the Crusaders Captured', in *Crusade and Settlement*, presented to R. C. Smail, ed. P. W. Edbury (Cardiff 1985), 1–17; R. Röhricht, *Geschichte des ersten Kreuzzuges* (Innsbruck 1901), 182–225.

[2] The final change in the deployment of the troops took place on the night of 9–10 July. The great siege-tower used against the northern wall was finally put in place on 12 July. The point attacked in the north was the weakest in the city's defences. See the maps of the siege in Prawer 'Jerusalem' (above, n. 1), 6, 8, 12.

The Fāṭimid contingent numbered several hundred men—Egyptians, Turks, and Sudanese. These were now distributed along the walls to reinforce the local defences and command the stone- and fire-throwing machines. By Thursday 14 July, the siege was drawing to a close. Fighting lasted the whole day but was inconclusive; the final, successful attack was launched on the morning of the next day, Friday 15 July, by the troops of Godfrey, at the Wādī al-Sāhira depression near the eastern corner of the northern wall of the city.

What happened to the Jewish community during the siege and the storming of the city can be reconstructed from Byzantine, Frankish, Arab, and Jewish sources, and though none of the writers was actually an eye-witness to the events, the sources corroborate each other fairly well and there is no reason to doubt their veracity. The most important source in our context is the Latin poem of Gilon of Toucy,[3] cleric of Paris, monk of Cluny, and finally cardinal bishop of Frascati. The poem was written in Paris some time before 1120, that is, soon after the time of the events.[4] After describing the Crusader march from Nicaea to Jerusalem and the preparatory organization for the siege of the city, Gilon goes on to describe the deployment of the besieging hosts during the first week of the siege. Then he describes the first general attack on the city on 13 June. The Crusaders succeeded in scaling and capturing the outer wall but failed to scale the main one. Gilon says:

> Mox gentilis adest, Judaeus, Turcus, Arabsque,
> Missilibus, jaculis obsistitur, igne, veneno.
> At nostri jaculis opponunt pectora nuda.[5]

Having described the construction of the great siege-tower by Godfrey of Bouillon on the eve of the final attack, Gilon goes on to characterize the night of 14–15 July, after the unsuccessful fighting on the 14th as the lull before the storm came to an

[3] *Historia Gilonis Cardinalis Episcopi De Via Hierosolymitana, RHC HOcc* v. 794 ff.
[4] On Gilon, ibid., pp. cxliii ff. He visited the Holy Land as papal legate in 1128.
[5] Gilon (above n. 3), 794, vv. 159–61. Cf. *Chronologie*, no. 389 (p. 466).

end, and describes how Godfrey's engineers brought their siege-tower up to the walls of the city:

Nox, quae Judaeis requiem transacta reliquit,
Lucida velabat tenebrosa sidera palla,
Cum Ducis artifices ad muros applicuerunt
Robora castelli minitantia solis ab ortu,
Nam levius poterant irrumpere solis ab ortu.[6]

This is followed by the description of the general assault on the city:

Occurrit suprema dies Gentilibus, illi
De bello fugiunt in bellum, lapsus ubique est,
A nullo ferrum revocatur, Turcus, Arabsque
Judaeique cadunt, horum de funere pugna.[7]

Gilon is the only Western source explicitly mentioning the Jews in action as defending the city of Jerusalem with their Muslim fellow-citizens. Other sources which describe the capture of the city, such as the anonymous *Gesta*, Tudebod, Raymond of Aguilers, and Robert the Monk, omit the Jews completely; there is no reasonable explanation for Gilon doing otherwise unless one ascribes it to particular perceptiveness on his part. Thus, Gilon indicates that the final assault on Jerusalem was made on a Friday:

Venerat illa dies, qua, mortificare magistrum
Gens Judaea Jhesum cupiens, se mortificavit.[8]

The descriptions themselves tally perfectly with what we know about the location of the Jewish Quarter on the eve of the Crusader attack on the city.[9] It was actually Godfrey's host that attacked the north-eastern walls of the city defending the

[6] Gilon, 797, vv. 261–5.
[7] Ibid. 798, vv. 305–8.
[8] Ibid. 797, vv. 272–3.
[9] See ch. 1, p. 18.

Jewish Quarter,[10] and as we have seen although the quarter itself was destroyed, the name was preserved in Crusader sources of the twelfth and thirteenth century as *Juiverie* or *Judearia.*[11]

The massacre of the native population—Muslims, Jews, and probably also some Oriental Christians, whom the Crusaders had difficulty in distinguishing from other Orientals—has been told many times in all its gruesomeness, but with the newly published Genizah material we can reconstruct some of the events in more detail. Godfrey's host burst into the city on the morning of 15 July and forced its way southwards, through the *Juiverie*, in the direction of the Temple Mount. The Muslim and Jewish defenders were forced to abandon the walls and retreat before the frenzied onslaught. It was then that the Jews shut themselves up in their prayer places and synagogues to which the conquerors then set fire. Anna Comnena in Constantinople heard about the massacre and wrote in her *Alexiade*: 'After a siege of a month the city [of Jerusalem] was captured, and they killed many of its Saracen and Hebrew inhabitants.'[12] A report from less far afield—Damascus—but some time later,

[10] The names *Juiverie* and *Judaria* are indicated in *Le Cartulaire du chapitre du Saint-Sépulcre de Jérusalem*, ed. G. Bresc-Bautier (Paris 1984), no. 169, p. 383; ed. Rozière, no. 185. *Ernoul, L'estat de la cité de Iherusalem* in *Itinéraires à Jérusalem et Descriptions de la Terre Sainte* (Geneva 1882), ed. H. Michelant and G. Raynaud, ch. 22, p. 49: 'Entre le Rue de Iosaffas et les murs de le cité, à main senestre, dusque à la Porte de Iosaffas, a rues ausi com une ville. La manoient li plus des Suriiens de Iherusalem. Et ces rues apeloit on le Iuerie.' Here he indicates the church of St Mary Magdalen. Cf. *Le Continateur Anonyme de Guillaume de Tyr dit de Rothelin*, 160: 'Et là manoient et demouroient li plus des Surienz dedenz la cité de Iherusalem. Et ces rues apeloit on la Giuverie.' In 1130 the name appears in a donation of William, prior of the Holy Sepulchre, to the church of St Mary in the Valley of Josaphat: 'in illa urbis parte ... que specialiter Judaearia nuncupatur', *Chartes de Terre Sainte provenant de l'abbaye de N.-D. de Josaphat*, ed. H.-F. Dalaborde (Paris 1880), no. 17, p. 43. There was also a *Ruga Surianorum*; see *Cartulaire de l'Ordre de Sain-Jean*, i. ed. Delaville le Roul (Paris 1894), no. 372, p. 255. On the settlements of Syrians in the former Jewish Quarter, see Prawer, *Crusader Institutions*, 87, 93.

[11] There is no reason to believe that there was still a Jewish Quarter in the southern part of the city, as suggested in Goitein, *Palestinian Jewry*, 233 n. 9. The later Jewish Quarter (from the middle of the 13th cent. and perhaps even a 100 years later; see ch. 8) near Zion Gate, although in the south of the city, could have had no connection with the former Jewish Quarter of the Arab period in the south beneath the Temple esplanade, which was by then outside the city walls.

[12] Anna Comnena, *Alexiade*, I. XI. i. 9; ed. B. Leib, ii (Paris 1945), 32.

by the Damascene historian Ibn al-Qalānisī, tells of the defenders abandoning the walls, and then: 'A number of the inhabitants fled to the sanctuary [of David] and a great host was killed. The Jews assembled in the synagogue, and the Franks set fire to it with them inside.'[13] This short description is also to be found in the account of other Arab historians like al-Athīmī, an anonymous Arab chronicler, and the Egyptian Christian writer Bōtrūs ibn al-Rāhab.[14] Another chronicler, Sibṭ ibn Jaūzi, had a rather confused description: 'The massacre was horrible; they assembled the Jews in their synagogue and put it to fire, then they destroyed the *mashhad* and the tomb of al-Khalīl [Friend of God]. Only the *miḥrab* of David was occupied by agreement.'[15] The '*miḥrab* [prayer-place] of David' certainly refers to the city citadel; as to the *mashhad* and 'tomb of al-Khalīl', the chronicler seems somehow to have confused his sources because the latter are in Hebron.[16] There is little doubt, then, that the Jews were burned in their prayer-places, though some chroniclers stress that the Crusaders assaulted the Jews in a synagogue; others state simply that the Jews were burned in their synagogue. It is rather difficult to believe that following the breaching of the walls and the fighting and massacre in the city the Crusaders could actually have assembled the Jews in a synagogue; it seems more probable that when hope of deliverance was abandoned, the Jews assembled in a synagogue, or several prayer-places, and prepared themselves for martyrdom.

Not all the community were massacred, however. Some Jews who escaped the general slaughter were captured and later employed, together with Muslim captives, to dispose of the horrible mountains of cadavers and disembowelled corpses which filled the squares and streets of the city. Six months later

[13] Ibn al-Qalānisī, *Dhail Tarīkh*, ed. Amedroz (Leiden 1908), 137, ll. 3–4. Engl. trans. H. A. R. Gibb, *The Damascus Chronicle of the Crusades* (London 1932), 48.

[14] Al-Athīmī, *Tarīkh*, a contemporary of Ibn al-Qalānisī, ed. Cl. Cahen in *Journal Asiatique* 1938, 373; *Anonyme Chronik*, ed. K. V. Zettersteen (Leiden 1919), 230; Bōtrūs ibn al-Rāhab (Beirut 1903), 72, ll. 13–19.

[15] 'Mirāt al-Zemān', in *RHC HOr*. iii. 520.

[16] *Khalīl*—'The Friend' (of God) refers to the Patriarch Abraham. The city of Hebron is often referred to by that name because of the Tomb of the Patriarch being there. Even the Jaffa Gate in Jerusalem is referred to as Bāb al-Khalīl.

the city still stank of dead bodies despite all the efforts to clean the city and burn the corpses.[17] An episode interpolated in the chronicle of Baldric, bishop of Dol in Brittany, has the following: 'Many Jews, however, were captured alive near the Temple, carrying corpses. But once they [the Jews] were identified [as such], they sold all of them; at the order of Tancred they were given [away] 30 for one piece of gold ... and many of those bought were taken overseas to Apulia; but some were drowned in the sea and others they beheaded.[18]

Baldric's interpolated text not only states facts but also indulges in anti-Jewish polemics. The interpolator would hardly have been aware that the actual price of a slave in the Near Eastern Muslim lands was $33\frac{1}{3}$ dinars,[19] so it was not this similarity which made him quote the price of Jewish captives as thirty Jews for one gold dinar. This was a legacy of the anti-Jewish polemic of the classical period which, repeated in the circumstance of a Christian conquest of Jerusalem, had particular irony: one may call it a 'literary' vengeance on those who were regarded, morally or physically, as descendants of the traitor Judas Iscariot, who received thirty pieces of silver for selling Jesus to the priests (Matt. 26: 14–16). In its earliest phase this 'vengeance' on the Jews took the form of a punishment inflicted on them by Titus. After the capture of Jerusalem he sold thirty Jewish captives for one piece of silver. The story seems to have originated[20] in the eighth century in the

[17] According to some sources, even poor Christians were employed (for payment) in the gruesome task. Some six months later the stench was still overwhelming, as noted by Fulk of Chartres, then visiting Jerusalem. *RHC HOcc.* iii. 366D. Ekkehard, ed. Hagenmeyer (Tübingen 1877), 200 n. 15. Cf. *Anonymi Gesta*, ed. Hagenmeyer (Heidelberg 1890), 476 nn. 4–6. Even later the outbreak of plague was linked to the contaminated air of the city.

[18] This interpolation (dating from the end of the 12th or the early 13th century) of Baldric of Dol, is to be found in the MS Paris 5513., Cod. G. *RHC HOcc.* iv. 103 n. 7: 'Multi etiam Judaei capti vivi circa templum fuerunt, qui similiter cadavera detulerunt. Hos cognitos omnes vendiderunt, et Tancredo jubente xxxta pro aureo nummo dederunt, et illos maxime deluxerunt, multosque emptos citra mare in Apuliam adduxerunt, quondam etiam in mare submerserunt, alios decollaverunt.'

[19] The $33\frac{1}{3}$ dinar as a price for Muslim, Christian, or Jewish captives is known from Egypt. See Mann, i. 87–90 and Goitein, *Palestinian Jewry*, 234 and ibid. n. 10. Obviously under given circumstances prices varied. So e.g. Saladin demanded as ransom for Christians in captured Jerusalem ten besants for a man, five for a woman, and three for a child.

[20] H. Lewy, 'Josephus the Physician: A Medieval Legend of the Destruction of Jerusalem', *Journal of the Warburg Institute* 1/3 (1938), 227–42.

Vindicta Salvatoris (one of the sources of the *Legenda Aurea*), and was then repeated by Walafrid Strabo in the ninth century, Wipo in the mid eleventh, Hugh of Fleuri and Cosmas of Prague at the beginning of the twelfth, and a century later in the *Schwabenspiegel* and by the Austrian Helbing. This list can be enlarged to include a number of sources from the twelfth century: the converted Jew Petrus Alphonsi; Peter of Blois, the anonymous author of *Li Estoire de Jérusalem et Antioch*, and the interpolator of Baldric of Dol.[21] All these texts repeat the story of the great mass of Jewish slaves whom the Romans sold at the derogatory price of thirty captives for one piece of silver. The story was rounded off, so to speak, in a rather unexpected way. 'The Crusaders found in the Holy Land . . . the place in which the thirty silver pieces were made'—thus a famous pilgrim Theodorich (*c.*1172) notes that on Mount Carmel (called Mount Caipha) there is a half-ruined tower of the same name (Caipha?) and 'herein it is said the 30 pieces of silver were made which were given to the traitor Judas as the price of the blood of Christ'. The same story is repeated but for a coastal site—a place called 'Capharnaum'—in two French itineraries of the thirteenth century.[22] Baldric's interpolator, telling the story of Jewish captives of the Crusaders, found it appropriate to introduce this disguised Iscariot episode into his narrative.[23]

As it turned out, the consequences of the massacre were not as terrible as feared. Once the massacre was over (it raged, as one would expect more vehemently on the day the Crusaders

[21] Petrus Alphonsi, *Dialogus ex Judeo Christiani, PL*, clvii, col. 571*c*; Petrus Blessensis, *Contra perfidiam Judeorum, PL*, ccvii, col. 851–3; ed. I. A. Giles, iii (Oxford 1856), 102–3. Peter of Blois even finds vengeance in the fact that the siege of Titus began at Passover, and so it was linked with the time of the passion of Christ. Additionally *Li Estoire, RHC HOcc.* v. 621 f.

[22] Theodoricus, *Libellus de locis sanctis*, ed. M.-L. Bulst and W. Bulst (Heidelberg 1976), ch. 39, p. 43; *Itinéraires* (see n. 10), 90, 180. On this strange 'Capharnaum' see ch. 7, p. 181.

[23] The 30 pieces of silver also entered anti-Jewish polemics in a different way. Judas is the prefiguration of the Jews, haters of Christians, argues St Augustine, *Enarratio in Psalmum CVIII, PL*, xxxvii, col. 1431–2; consequently whatever is said about him relates also to the Jews. In the 12th cent. Rupert of Deutz went even further: all the curses of Ps. 108, and their number is 30, are inflicted on the wretched nation of the Jews. Their number corresponds to the 30 dinars for which they killed the Messiah (*De Trinitate et operibus eius*, ii. cap. 6, *PL*, clxvii, col. 962; cf. col. 1222) and again in the Commentary on Zephania, *PL*, cliii, col. 654. The famous 15th-cent. pilgrim Felix Fabri saw the 30 pieces of silver in Rhodes and argued that they were struck by Terah the father of Abraham (H. Leclerque, *Dict. d'archéol. et de la liturgie chrétienne*, s.v. Judas).

broke the city's defences),[24] the Franks looted the city thoroughly and searched out captives for ransom. A letter written in Egypt, possibly from Damietta or Bilbais to Alexandria or Cairo, shortly after the events (summer 1100) by some Jews who had left Ascalon before the Crusader attack on Jerusalem summarizes the fate of the Jewish community in the city. It lists several groups of people who escaped the massacre but were victims of the conquest:

> Those who were saved from this event, or people who escaped on the second or third day after the battle and left with the *wālī* who received an *āmān* (safe conduct), or people who were captured by the *al-Ifranj* and remained with them for some time before escaping (but they are few), and the majority are those who were bought [ransomed], but to our sorrow a part of them passed away in various sufferings and persecutions.[25]

Each of the groups mentioned had its own story of sufferings which we can follow over several months from the summer of 1099. The news of the massacre in Jerusalem first reached Ascalon with the retreating Iftikhār al-Daulah, the former Fāṭimid commander of the citadel of the Holy City, who capitulated to Raymond of St Gilles when resistance became hopeless. On hearing of the tragedy, the *nagid* of Egypt, Meborak, performed the mourners' ritual of sitting on the floor, rending his garments, and weeping for the dead and the desecrated Scrolls of the Law.[26] It was from Ascalon that the first relief actions were organized to deal with the refugees who came with the commander. Urgent demands for help were dispatched to Egypt, to the great communities of Cairo and Alexandria. A collection was immediately proclaimed, and although both communities had been decimated by diseases during the previous four years, a month or so later the first sum of 123 gold dinars was dispatched with an emissary who had

[24] Albert of Aix (vi. 29) mentions that on the third day after the capture of the city (i.e. Sunday 17 July) a new massacre exterminated all the Muslims still alive. According to others the massacres lasted only 2 days. Cf. *Anonymi Gesta*, ed. H. Hagenmeyer, 38, p. 7 n. 43 (in fine on p. 475); id., *Chronologie*, 253.

[25] Goitein, *Palestinian Jewry*, 243 ff., ll. 25–8; and cf. 232 ff. Cf. id., 'Capture of Jerusalem by the Crusaders', *JJS* 3 (1952), 172, ll. 25–8.

[26] On the office of the *nagid* under the Fāṭimids, see Mann, i. 252 ff., and below ch. 5. On Nagid Meborak, who became influential at the court of Grand Vizier al-Afḍal, see ibid. 188 ff., 207 ff.

come from Ascalon[27] 'to redeem the Scrolls of the Torah and to [attend to] the ransoming of the people of God, who are in the captivity of the Kingdom of Evil, may God destroy it'.[28] This relief action was followed during the next few months by many similar ones.

The letter we have from emergency committees, if one may use this term, makes reference to an earlier action on behalf of the refugees. This could have been expected, since our letter was sent after Passover, in the spring of 1100, almost nine months after the Crusaders' capture of Jerusalem. Our letter, which emanated from a community in Egypt (possibly Karaite)[29] that had formerly lived in Ascalon has a most vivid description of the fate of the refugees from Jerusalem during the next nine months. As we have seen, unable to carry the burden of relief by themselves they applied for help to the great communities of Cairo and Alexandria. The appeal was sent by a special messenger to whom the money or letters of credit were to be entrusted. Even at the time of writing, we are told, news was arriving that 'some of those ransomed from the Franks and who remained in Ascalon are suffering from hunger, lack of cloth, and destitution. Some still remain prisoners while some of their number were killed in their presence, suffering death by many tortures to appease their [the Franks] wrath.'[30]

[27] All the details are preserved in a draft of an epistle written by the scribe of the rabbinical court Hillel ben 'Ali sent from Cairo to Ascalon. Goitein, *Palestinian Jewry*, 254–6; id., 'Geniza Sources from the Crusader Period', *Outremer*, 309–11.

[28] Goitein, *Palestinian Jewry*, 255–6, ll. 12–13, 16–17. The epistle is in Arabic but the last words are in Hebrew (*Outremer*, 310, ll. 12–13). The quotation is from the exhortation of the *nagid*.

[29] The assignment of this long and important letter to the Karaites rests on the expression *ha-maskīl* ('the enlightened one') in the signature. This was very common among Karaite scholars. Additionally the mention of the many Torah scrolls (which might represent the general loot of synagogues) and the presence of the Karaite family of Tustari (see below n. 33) make the assumption very plausible. Baron, *Social*, iv (1957), 110–15 also suggests the Karaites; so did Goitein (*JJS* 3. 171); cf. id. in *JQR* 45 (1954), 37 n. 11. I favoured a Rabbinic origin in *Latin Kingdom* (H), 268 n. 42. S. D. Goitein (who published the whole letter) assigned it definitely to a Karaite community but argued convincingly that the community rescue action was probably a common endeavour. This would explain why this Karaite letter found its way into the Genizah; see *Palestinian Jewry*, 238. For an excellent example of Rabbanite–Karaite co-operation in 11th-cent. Ascalon and Fusṭāṭ, see Mann, i. 169.

[30] Goitein, *Palestinian Jewry*, 242, ll. 9–11. For a full English translation, see 'Captive', *JJS* 3. 171, ll. 9–11.

Thus the community of Ascalon, still under Fāṭimid rule, organized the first relief action, ransoming whomever they could from the hands of the Franks. In fact, the rapid organization was due to the presence of an influential and wealthy man, Abū al-Faḍl Sahl b. Jōshʿa b. Shaʿaya, an agent (*mutaṣaraf*) of the sultan, whose words carried weight in Alexandria, who happened to be in Ascalon, and it was he who intervened and organized the relief action. Many were ransomed, but not all. Some were even taken captive to Antioch.[31] There was some consolation in the fact that the 'accursed Franks (*ashkenazim*)' did not violate the Jewish women captives.[32] Many a prisoner, despairing of his life or freedom, apostasized. Among the Jewish captives in Frankish hands was an eight-year-old boy of the Karaite Tustari family;[33] the Franks tried to induce him to apostasize and bring him up as a Christian priest, but he refused.

Few escaped from the capture of the Franks. As we have seen, the bulk of these were 'the men who ran away in the second and third day after the battle and came out with the *wālī* who received a safe-conduct [*āmān*]'.[34] These lines corroborate those Crusader sources that described the massacre in the city as lasting three days, and seem to confirm that although Iftikhār al-Daulah, commander of the city, had capitulated at the end of the first day of fighting, on Friday 15 July, he did not leave the city until two days later, that is, Sunday 17 July. He took with him the garrison,[35] and, as we now know, some

[31] Goitein, *Palestinian Jewry*, 243, l. 22 ('Captive', 172, l. 22).

[32] Ibid. 242, ll. 14–17; 243, ll. 23–5 ('Captive', ll. 14–17, 23–5).

[33] Ibid. 242, ll. 19–22; ('Captive', 172, ll. 19–22). On the Tustari family see M. Gil, *The Tustaris: The Family and the Sect* (H) (Tel-Aviv 1981).

[34] Goitein, *Palestinian Jewry*, 245, ll. 26–7 ('Captive', 172, ll. 267–7).

[35] According to Fulk of Chartres (*RHC HOcc.* iii. 261) the garrison numbered some 500 Turks, Arabs, and Abyssinians (probably Sudanese). On the date of capitulation and the leaving of the city the sources are not unanimous cf. *Gesta*, ed. Hagenmeyer, 477 n. 8. The author of the *Gesta* is not very specific (ed. Hagenmeyer, 38. 6, 39. 2), and the sources which used him are not better informed. Some fixed the date of capitulation and leaving of Jerusalem on the same day, 15 July (Alb. Aqu. vi, 28, *RHC HOcc.* iv, *Hist. belli sacri*, cap. 127, Petrus Tudebodus (Tudebodus imitatus), ed. J. H. and L. L. Hill (Paris 1977), 141. Bartolf de Nangeio, *RHC HOcc.* iii. 515; possibly Tudebodus *RHC HOcc.* iii. 109. Fulk of Chartres clearly implies that this happened on the third day after the capture of the city. The Arab chronicler Ibn al-Athīr (*RHC HOr.* i. 198) says that the garrison fought for 3 more days. The Genizah letter consequently corroborates Fulk of Chartres and vindicates the place of the episode in the narrative of the *Gesta*.

Jewish refugees, who succeeded in entering the citadel with the remnants of the garrison or joined the *wālī*'s column on its way to Ascalon.

Those who reached Ascalon were then transported with the caravans travelling across the desert to Egypt at the expense of the aforementioned benefactor, Abū al-Faḍl Sahl. Others tried to reach Egypt by sea. By land or sea, a large number died on the way from cold and hunger. Some who finally reached Egypt died there, being unaccustomed to the climate; others fell victim to plague that broke out there.[36]

Abū al-Faḍl Sahl even took a loan to redeem the Holy Scriptures which had been looted by the Crusaders: 230 codices of Pentateuch (*maṣḥaf*), 100 brochures (*daftar*) of the Books of the Prophets, and eight Scrolls of the Torah were all brought to Ascalon. Possibly other books were later redeemed by the Jewish communities. Thus, a Commentary on Isaiah by the great Saʿadya Gaon, which in 1030–31 was in the possession of one Joshiah b. Aaron in Acre and found its way to the Cairo Genizah, has a curious line written in Latin (and upside down in relation to the Hebrew text): *Interpretacio esaye prophete*, and it has been plausibly argued that this may have come from the loot of Jerusalem or some other place in the Holy Land during the Crusader conquest.[37] Whoever the Westerner who had the book, he was curious enough, for material or intellectual reasons, to inform himself of the contents or value of the book. Other books, some perhaps redeemed some time later, also found their way to Cairo. Thus a Scroll of Karaite origin indicates in a colophon that it was recovered by the *nasi* Solomon, who found favour in the eyes of

> Lord Baldwin, who ruled in the place of his brother, and he gave him what he wanted; he ordered his warriors, our brothers the sons of Esau, to return to us all our holy books and this Scroll of the Torah among them, and this is half a consolation. Therefore we gathered in the Synagogue of Rabbenu ʿAnan our *nasi* [the founder of the sect] and we blessed the king, may he live forever, today Friday, the day of Fast of the 10th of Ab, in the beginning of the year 1037 since the

[36] Goitein, *Palestinian Jewry*, 243, ll. 29–32 ('Captive', 172, ll. 29–32).

[37] B. Z. Kedar, 'A Commentary on the Book of Isaiah Ransomed by the Crusaders' (H), in *Jerusalem in the Middle Ages*, ed. B. Z. Kedar and Z. Baras (Jerusalem 1979), 107–12.

destruction of the Second Temple, 1417 of the Seleucid Era [1106] Amen.[38]

On the other hand, a Pentateuch left as a legacy to the Karaite community of Jerusalem which found its way to their synagogue in Egypt has the following Hebraeo-Arabic note: 'Was brought over from the ransom [books] of the spoils of the Holy City of Jerusalem to the community of Egypt, to the synagogue of the Jerusalemites',[39] and is in all probability an authentic example of Jewish books looted and then ransomed from the Crusaders.

Such redeeming of books probably took place later. In the year following the capture of Jerusalem, the ransom of lives was the most pressing preoccupation. More than nine months after the Conquest there were still some twenty ransomed prisoners in Ascalon waiting to be sent to Egypt. Money was badly needed for their sustenance and transport and to repay the debts for loans. The Cairo community was asked to congregate in the synagogue and read a letter of appeal and ask for voluntary donations for the liberation of prisoners. Moreover, pecuniary vows taken by the members of the congregation which had not yet been fulfilled or not earmarked were now being channelled to the ransom of the captives.[40]

It is impossible to calculate the numbers of Jews massacred

[38] The colophon was published by A. A. Harkavy in *Hazefirah* (1875), 47–8 and reprinted by Mann, i. 200 n. 1, who accepted it, though with some misgivings, as genuine, but later rejected it as a forgery (Mann, *Texts*, ii. 137 n. 2). The text was also declared genuine but somewhat dubious by Baron, *Social*, iv. 112. I very much doubt its authenticity. Expressions like 'our brothers the sons of Esau' or the prayer for Baldwin I in an Egyptian synagogue and a strange expression of blessing—'the king, may he live forever'—have a definite aura of forgery.

[39] P. E. Kahle, *The Cairo Genizah* (New York 1960), ii. 109. Some other books to be found in Egypt might be connected with Jerusalem. So e.g. in the list of books of the synagogue of the Jerusalemites in Cairo, which lists (AD 1186) some 50 codices, there is the famous *Maṣḥaf al-Tāj* (the full text of the Pentateuch) and another codex named 'The Brother of the Tāj'. The inventory was published by R. Gottheil, 'Tit Bits from the Genizah', *Jewish Studies in Memory of Israel Abrahams* (New York 1977), 160, 164; cf. S. D. Goitein, 'New Documents from the Cairo Geniza', *Homenaje a Millas-Vallicrosa* (Barcelona 1954), 719–20. Goitein suggested that this codex also came from Jerusalem; see *Palestinian Jewry*, 235.

[40] Goitein, *Palestinian Jewry*, 247, ll. 23–4.

or ransomed from Jerusalem. The sum of 500 dinars mentioned above was enough to ransom many, but we are in the dark as to other sums which might have been mentioned in other letters; we know that sums were spent by the Sultan's agent, and a debt of some 200 dinars was incurred for the sustenance of those ransomed in Ascalon and their transport to Egypt.[41] It is almost a miracle that the ransom was not set at the level customary for Jewish captives—three for a hundred dinars—otherwise the entire sum would have been spent on ransoming of a few alone.[42]

Despite the general picture of massacre and overwhelming suffering, one is nevertheless impressed by details, by particular cases to which one can append a name in the midst of atrocities against thousands of people. The Jewish prisoners who were not killed were mostly sent as slaves to Apulia, but nearer home we also hear of prisoners sent to Norman-held Antioch to await ransom. Among the latter was the eight-year-old boy mentioned earlier, and a man by the name of Abū Saʿad, son of 'the Tustari woman'. It is said that the Franks proposed that he apostasize and promised they would treat him well or even make him a priest. He, however, asked how he could ever become a Christian priest (*kohen* in the Arabic text). It seems that a part of the ransom had already been paid, but the man had not yet been set free.[43]

Elsewhere detail reminds one of special cases of piety. Among those who reached Ascalon was a venerable old man, Abī al-Kīr Mubārakh, who had taken an oath not to take advantage of public charity. A special ransom was therefore to be earmarked to save him alone.[44] The story of individuals is often very revealing in the midst of great calamities.

Particular experiences are also preserved in private correspondence. Such is a letter from a man from Maghreb or from Spain who started out in 1096 on a pilgrimage to Jerusalem and was caught in the whirlwind of insecurity, wars, and

[41] Ibid. 246, ll. 9–10 ('Captive', 174, ll. 9–10).
[42] Ibid. 244, ll. 44–6 ('Captive', 173, ll. 44–6).
[43] Ibid. 242–3, ll. 19–22 ('Captive', 172); the text is not clear at this point, but the general sense seems to be that the Jews had already paid a large part of the ransom and would certainly pay the rest. As to the Tustari family, see above, n. 33.
[44] Goitein, *Palestinian Jewry*, 247, ll. 11–14 ('Captive', 174, ll. 11–14).

Crusader conquest.[45] On reaching Alexandria it became clear to him that it would be impossible to continue, as the routes to the Holy Land both by land and by sea had become unsafe. Armies were fighting each other, and the bedouin tribes also took a hand in the fighting. A man who had come from Palestine had barely saved himself 'from the hosts, because there were so many to be found on the roads near . . . every city, and then the crossing of the desert inhabited by bedouin. Travellers barely escaping one fell into the hands of the other.'[46] There were revolts, he says, which reached even Alexandria. This clearly refers to the fighting between al-Malik al-Afḍal, the mighty vizier of Egypt, and the deposed pretender to the Fāṭimid caliphate, who had shut himself up in Alexandria. When peace was finally established, our pilgrim left Alexandria for Cairo, intending to continue to Jerusalem. His hopes rose when the Fāṭimids captured the city[47] from the Seljuks: 'and when God gave the blessed Jerusalem [*al-Quds al-Mubārakh*] into his [al-Afḍal's] hands. Alas this lasted but for a short while, which did not suffice for the voyage. The Franks arrived [June–July 1099] and killed its inhabitants from among the Ishmaelites and Israel, and most of those who remained were taken prisoner. Of those some were ransomed and there are some who are still now in captivity in all corners of the earth.'[48] The sentiments of the writer are clear. He hoped that the ruler of Egypt, al-Afḍal, whom he describes in glowing terms as the best of all kings 'who took from nobody neither a dirham nor anything else',[49] would go out against the Franks and expel them. The ruler, he says, had tried several times but had not succeeded 'but we still hope that God will give his enemies into his hands and it is inevitable that the hosts will clash this year. And if God will give us victory through him and Jerusalem is captured—and so it will be, *inshallāh*—I shall not tarry to go up to her to behold her.'[50] At this point our writer somewhat loses patience with Providence. If the story

[45] Goitein, *Palestinian Jewry*, 251–3, ('Captive', 175–7).
[46] Ibid. 251–2, ll. 14–17 ('Captive', 176, ll. 14–17).
[47] Jerusalem capitulated to the Fāṭimids after a 40-day siege in August 1098.
[48] Goitein, *Palestinian Jewry*, 252, ll. 24–8 ('Captive', 176).
[49] After the siege of Alexandria; ibid., ll. 21–2 ('Captive', 176).
[50] Ibid. 252, ll. 29–31; ('Captive', 176, ll. 29–33).

were to repeat itself, he says, he would rely on the mercy of God as life is too short to wait and tarry. He would then return home whether having seen Jerusalem or not—and both are possible.[51]

Fāṭimid Ascalon was the natural haven of the Jewish refugees from the southern part of the country in general and from Jerusalem in particular. In the north, it seems that a similar role was played by Tripoli or a smaller city in its vicinity.[52] The Lebanese capital had not been captured during the march of the hosts of the First Crusade to Jerusalem, and it is quite possible that Jewish prisoners from Antioch were held for ransom there. Our source in this case is a document assigned to the winter of 1099/1100, which would make it one of the earliest preserved letters after the calamity of Jerusalem, but the dating is precariously conjectural.[53] It was sent by Ṣadoq b. Josiah, a well-known figure of the Palestinian Academy whom we can trace back to the city of Tyre in 1094,[54] to a relative in Egypt asking for unspecified help from the *nagid* in Egypt. The writer was waiting in the place from which he wrote for the liberation of some captives in Antioch. A girl had already been liberated, some children were still in captivity, as was his son-in-law, a man of some standing in the community.[55] Possibly the letter refers to these troubled times of conquest, but its whole tenor seems to point to more relaxed and calmer times, even if problems of security were not altogether lacking.

Following the Crusader conquests, masses of people, freed captives and refugees, crowded the houses of relatives or

[51] Ibid. 253, ll. 37–8 ('Captive', 177, ll. 37–8).

[52] Ibid. 285. Actually the writer describes the place from which he writes as: *hād[h]ā al-balada*; for a larger city the noun *madīna* would have been expected.

[53] Ibid. 285–8. Goitein bases the dating on the conjecture that the children and a man mentioned as being in Crusader captivity in Antioch are the same as those mentioned above (text and n. 43) by the rescue committee from Ascalon. The identification of the writer's son-in-law in Crusader captivity is problematic as this would mean a very prominent Karaite had married the daughter of a prominent Rabbanite family. (Ṣadoq b. Josiah was a descendant of Ben Meir). See above, ch. 1, p. 3 n. 4), and below, n. 54.

[54] Mann, i. 189–90 suggested that he died in 1096. S. D. Goitein argues differently. If Mann is right then our letter was written before 1096 and has no connection with the Crusader conquest. There is no hint in the letter to the Franks.

[55] Goitein, *Palestinian Jewry*, 286, ll. 15–23.

schools and prayer places of the surviving communities, such as those of Ascalon, and probably also Tyre and Tripoli. The misery and the sufferings of victims are vividly described in some circular letters and poems but are perhaps most starkly evoked in a note whose very brevity communicates powerfully. Fate has preserved a letter of recommendation written by a community scribe for a woman refugee, an escaped or ransomed prisoner, who was now free but had to subsist, together with her little boy, in a world of insecurity, dependent on the charity of the congregation.[56] Opening with an appeal for charity (Isa. 56: 1) it continues: 'I make known to the holy community that I, a captive of the captives of Eretz Israel[57] came this week from Sunbat and I am naked without a cover and without a sleeping-mat and a little boy is with me, and I am helpless. And I pray to God and address myself to the community, may it be blessed that they should do for me what they do for all who pass through.' Was the destitute woman one of the refugees from Jerusalem? There is no way of knowing because for the next ten years the whole of the Holy Land was to become a battlefield with thousands of refugees from the cities captured by the Crusaders.[58] The fate of the Jewish communities in many places must be guessed; in only a few cases have we explicit information.

Jaffa was the first of the maritime cities in the Holy Land to be captured by the Crusaders, and this without a fight.[59] The conquest of the Fāṭimid-dominated shore and its fortified cities occupied the Crusaders during the first decade of their kingdom's existence because its present and future depended on safeguarding maritime communications with Europe. Thus Godfrey of Bouillon even intended to attack the major sea port of the country, Acre. An agreement was signed with the leaders of the Venetian fleet which appeared in the waters of the kingdom and dropped anchor in Jaffa. But the capture of well-

[56] Goitein, *Palestinian Jewry*, 289; id., *Mediterranean Society*, ii. 170.

[57] These words: '*shevūyah min shevūyey Eretz Israel*' (meaning, one of the people held captive there) are in Hebrew in the middle of the Arabic text. The expression must have become current because of its frequent use in that period.

[58] A register of paupers supported by the community in Fusṭāṭ drawn up by Hillel b. Eli *c*.1107 lists 12 families (from among 80) from the Holy Land. Goitein, *Mediterranean Society*, i. 57, and 405 n. 89.

[59] We have no information as to the fate of the Jewish community in Jaffa.

fortified Acre seems to have been too much for the meagre forces of the kingdom. Moreover, Godfrey of Bouillon took ill and died on 18 July 1100. It was therefore decided to capture the smaller port of Haifa, Acre's southern neighbour. Tancred and the energetic Pisan patriach, Daimbert, taking command of the army, sent word to the commanders of the Venetian navy, and the latter agreed to the change in plan.

Though smaller than Acre, Haifa was nevertheless a port of some importance. The port of that time was located at today's Bat Galim, in the narrow coastal strip at the foot of Mount Carmel. We know little about the city before the Crusader conquests[60] beyond that it might have been one of the coastal cities which the Ummayyads and 'Abbasids regarded as guardians of the marches of Islam against Byzantium. The settlers in these cities were generally Persians by origin,[61] although we know that in Tripoli in Lebanon many were Jewish.[62] We further know that until the middle of the eleventh century Haifa had been a small, rather obscure township. Its fortunes changed when the Fāṭimid caliph, al-Mustanṣīr (1035–95), decided to fortify some of the cities, both coastal and inland, to put an end to the insecurity in the area. It has been suggested that the fortifications were erected by Badr al-Jamāli, the future grand vizier of Egypt, several times governor of Damascus and at one time governor of Acre. After that Haifa appears as *Qaṣr Ḥaifa*, a name which we find at that period rendered in Hebrew as *Mivṣar Ḥaifa* and later in the Crusader period as *Castrum Cayphas* (with different Latin and French spellings). The Persian traveller Nasir-I-Khusrau mentions, in 1047, a shipyard in Haifa and a special type of ship known to the local population as *judi*.[63]

Once the attack on Haifa was decided, certain vested interests came to light in this connection. Thus Tancred who had by then carved out for himself a Galilean lordship based

[60] See A. Elad, 'Some Notes on Haifa under Medieval Arab Rule' (H), *Studies in the History of the Jewish People and Eretz Israel*, v (Univ. of Haifa 1980), 191–201.

[61] Id., 'the Coastal Cities of Palestine in the Arab period, 640–1099' (H), *Cathedra* 8 (1978), 161.

[62] Baladhuri, *Futūḥ al-Buldān*, ed. M. J. de Goeje (Leiden 1866), 127, quoted by Elad, ibid. 161 n. 28.

[63] Nasir-I-Khusrau, *Diary of a Journey through Syria and Palestine*, *PPTS* iv. 13, 19.

on Tiberias and its lake and the Golan Heights in the east, regarded Haifa in the west as the most natural maritime outlet for his Galilean principality, and assumed he would receive it as a result of this action. However, he was ultimately thwarted in his expectations as Godfrey promised the city to Galdemar Carpenel.

The siege of the city was directed by Daimbert and Tancred, while the city was blockaded from the sea by the Venetian fleet. The siege lasted almost a month (25 July–20 August 1100).

Although the capture of Haifa is mentioned in several chronicles, none is more detailed than the narrative of Albert of Aix extolling his hero Godfrey of Bouillon, or that of the anonymous Monk of Lido glorifying the Venetian expedition of 1100 to the Orient.[64] The role played by the Jews in the defence of Haifa is mentioned only by Albert, but the extremely curious description of the city's population in the Venetian chronicles might in some way relate to the events portrayed by Albert.

The decription by Albert of Aix, which as we have seen pays particular attention to the Jews, is rather unusual:

> And after approaching the walls with engines and machines, the men of Gaul attacked it strongly from all sides; and the citizens of Jewish origin who inhabited the place by a grant and consent of the king of Babylon [i.e. in Crusader usage, Egypt], against payment of taxes, rose armed on the walls, putting up a very strong resistance, until the Christian[s], pressed by different burdens during fifteen days, withdrew in almost total desperation from any further attack.[65]

Albert's narrative raises several questions. Did the Jews enjoy a particular standing in the town because of their connections with the shipyard? In eleventh-century Haifa we do find Jews engaged in maritime commerce,[66] a profession

[64] Alb. Aqu., l. vii, cap. 22 ff., *RHC HOcc.* iv. 1, 521 ff.; Monachus Littorensis, *Historia de Translatione Sanctorum*, cap. 40 ff.; *RHC HOcc.* v. 275 ff. One might expect some details in the *Gesta Tancredi*, cap. 139, *RHC HOcc.* iii. 704, but there are none.

[65] Ibid., l. vii, cap. 22, 521: 'Applicatis itaque muro ingeniis cum ingenti machina, et undique gravi assultu eam viris Galliae oppugnantibus, cives, ex genere Judaeorum, qui hanc inhabitabant dono et consensu regis Babyloniae in redditione tributorum, in moenibus armis exsurgentes, multum in defensione obstiterunt, quousque Christiani, variis plagis gravati per dies quindecim, prorsus diffisi manus suas ab omni assultu continuerunt.'

[66] Goitein, *Mediterranean Society*, i. 305, 476 n. 2, 305–8. Cf. Elad (above, n. 60), 199.

also exercised by their co-religionists in Crusader Tyre even a hundred years later.[67] There is no definite answer to that question.

The rather strange description of the privileged position of the Jews finds its parallel in the Monk of Lido's description of the Venetian participation in the siege. Haifa was 'the head of all the paynim and haughtiness', because of its fortifications and the exalted standing of its inhabitants.[68] The patriarch offered most generous conditions of capitulation: if the population were to surrender, 'they will not perform any service to any Christian prince, but for the payment which they paid yearly to the pagan princes'.[69] This is reminiscent of the yearly tribute paid by the Jewish community to the caliph of Egypt. The infidels of Haifa declared that neither Christ nor his apostles had ever entered the city; moreover, neither the sultan of Persia nor the emir of Egypt, despite frequent sieges and large armies, had ever captured the city. No god had ever subjugated the city to his religion. Their God differed from any other. They never obeyed any earthly ruler and they followed their laws of their own free will.[70] This sounds like a description

[67] *Benjamin of Tudela*, 30. There is nothing, however, to support the suggestion of B. Dinur, 'Notes on the History of the Jews during the Crusader Conquest' (H), *Zion* 2 (1927), 56–64, that the Jews formed the garrison of the city. This was followed by M. Ish-Shalom, *In the Shadow of Alien Rule* (H), (Tel-Aviv 1975), 180; id., *Christian Travels in the Holy Land* (H), (Tel-Aviv 1979), 91–3, who even argued for Jewish support for the Fāṭimid establishment in the Holy Land. The military character of such communities cannot be deduced from place names such as *Castrum Cayphas*, which represents, as already mentioned, the *Qaṣr Haifa*, and the Hebrew *Mivṣar Ḥaifa*. S. Runciman, *A History of the Crusaders*, i (Cambridge 1951), 316, wrote: 'Haifa was inhabited mostly by Jews, with a small Egyptian garrison.'

[68] Monachus (above n. 64, 275–6): 'Consilium est Caypham totius paganismi caput et superbiam obsidere . . . Et quia tota fiducia totaque paganismi superbia, partim pro loco ex inexpugnabili munitione, partimque pro civium insuperabili dignitate, ex illa civitate pendebat, fit consultum . . . istam ante alias expugnare.'

[69] Ibid. cap. 41: 'nulli christicolarum principi servitium aliquod exhiberent, nisi pecuniam, quam paganis principibus exsolvebant annis singulis, expugnatoribus Christianis adimplerent.'

[70] 'Crucifixus vester . . . in quem creditis nunquam urbem istam est ingressus, nec ipsius discipuli; sed nec vos eam virtute capietis, stultissimi homines et ignavi! quam soldanus Persidae vel ammirabilis Babyloniae, cum innumerabili multotiens manu obsidentes, nunquam vincere potuerunt, vos, numero pauci et a nostrae legis ritibus alieni, aliquando convincetis! Nos, nec Deus vester, nec alius Deus [*preferable reading to* nec estiam noster] potuit subjugare unquam suae legi; nos neque Deum quem alii colunt, colimus, nec terreno principi obedimus, neque legem nisi voluntariam observamus.' Ibid. cap. 41, 276–7.

of some extreme Shī'ite rite, a mysterious Baṭinite sect, which brings to mind the Persians who were settled there, but it is not impossible to read into it an echo of the existence of the Jewish community in this coastal city.

The siege seems to have concentrated at the city's citadel (*turris*); a huge siege-tower and seven *mangenae* (stone-throwing machines) were erected.[71] For fifteen days the attack continued without success, and we are told that it was repulsed by 'citizens of the Jewish race'.[72] The Christians removed the siege and, frustrated, were on the point of giving up, especially since dissent had broken out in the Christian camp. Tancred, who as we have seen was expecting to receive the city as part of his Galilean principality was thwarted by the dying Godfrey's promise to give the city to his *familiaris* Galdemar Carpenel, and retreated from action.[73] The patriarch did his best, trying every form of persuasion to assure Tancred's co-operation. 'How the city so valiantly defended by the Jews, should not remain undamaged to the utter confusion of the Christians, whose substantial part was already outworn.'[74] The Venetians, he pointed out, had already moved out to sea, out of reach of the city. The patriarch then proposed that the city should be captured and handed over to him by the faithful, who would then evaluate the amount of labour everybody had put into the siege so he could reward them accordingly. Whether the 'Jewish argument' or the hope of changing Godfrey's decision influenced Tancred we do not know; but we are told that in the name of Christ he put away all bitterness and 'sounded the trumpets, and having given the sign he exhorted the warriors that they should resume the interrupted attack on the city, should fight the Jews who had so valiantly defended the city'.[75]

[71] Alb. Aqu., l. vii, cap. 22: 'Obsederunt in machina mirae et procerae altitundinis et in tormentis lapidum septem quae vocant mangenas.' [72] See n. 65.

[73] Galdemar Carpenel belonged to the group of nobles led by chancellor Arnulf who sent for Baldwin to come to Jerusalem and claim his deceased brother's kingdom. Daimbert and Tancred, in Haifa, led the rival group which sent for Bohemond. Cf. Hagenmeyer, *Chronologie*, nos. 489, 491.

[74] Alb. Aqu., l. vii, cap. 23 (pp. 521–2): 'Quatenus civitas quae defensa fortiter a Judaeis habebatur, non tam viriliter in statu suo maneret ad confusionem Christianorum, quorum non modica pars attrita erat.'

[75] Ibid. l. vii, cap. 23 (p. 522): 'cornua sonuit, milites dato signo ammonuit quatenus assultum circa urbem intermissum repeterent, Judaeos expugnarent, qui urbem fortiter defensabant.'

The attack was launched against one of the city's strongholds in an attempt to penetrate the city from the siege-tower, with a Venetian soldier, three of Godfrey's, and twenty of Tancred's warriors making a desperate assault.[76] Using two-edged axes, hatchets, and iron mattocks they tried to breach the huge tower. But the Jewish citizens and the hosts of the Saracens faced them manfully without any hesitation, opposing them from the tower with oil, burning pitch, fire, and flaming flax. This burnt the Christian warriors in the siege-tower, 'and the city and its tower remained with its inhabitants invincible'.[77] An additional day and night of fighting brought no victory to the Franks. The next day, however, 'the Jews and Saracens, seeing that the Christians are invincible, nor can they be restrained by flames or arms from attacking the tower, suddenly abandoned the tower; as they were no longer able to hold it, they began to run away, and after them the whole city was also put to flight.'[78] The soldiers who penetrated the citadel opened the gates, and the Crusader host flocked into the city.[79] 'Whoever was found there was killed.'[80] The spoils, according to our chronicles, were immense: gold, silver, clothes, horses, mules, wheat, oil, and the like. The Venetians, who were out at sea, came back and took part in the massacre, but, adds our chronicler unctuously, they got no material reward for their pains.

[76] Alb. Aqu., vii, cap. 24 (p. 522): 'aut ex machina hac compositam [var. oppositam] turrim urbis penetrare, aut certe ante eandem turrim in eodem loco ville deperire'.

[77] Ibid. (pp. 522–3):'Quibus Judaei cives, commixtis Sarracenorum turmis, sine dilatione viriliter resistentes, a turri oleum, picem ferventem, ignem et stuppas opposuerunt; grande videlicet incendium, per quod christiani milites fumo et calore in machina exstinguerentur, et urbs ejusque turris invicta cum incolis suis remaneret.'

[78] Ibid. l. vii, cap. 25, (p. 523): 'Judaei et Sarraceni, videntes Christianos insuperabiles, nec suis flammis aut armis posse reprimi a turri et ejus assultu, ipsam turrim mox reliquentes, nec eam amplius retinere valentes, fugam inierunt; post quos universa civitas in fugam pariter conversa est.'

[79] The Monk of Lido adds some morally doubtful details to enhance the perspicacity of the patriarch. The inhabitants were ready to capitulate and asked the patriarch to mark the place of capitulation with a cross. The clever prelate put the cross in the lower city, and when the inhabitants came there looking for asylum they were massacred by the Christians. From what can be rescued from the description it seems that Haifa had a citadel which defended itself valiantly, and a township huddling around it.

[80] Ibid., 'Universis occisis in ea repertis.' The Monk of Lido (cap. 42) adds that the massacre was such that 'none could cross any street or square dryshod because of the blood and cadavers'.

The Crusader capture of the city and the massacre of its inhabitants put an end to the existence of the Jewish community therein. It is not clear whether a new community was ever established under Crusader rule; its flourishing neighbour Acre was obviously more attractive. Nevertheless it is probable that a small community was created later, at least to take care of the Jewish cemetery; this was much used during the Crusades and later periods, owing to a tradition which accorded Acre and the land to the north less sanctity than to Haifa.[81]

It is not very clear why Albert of Aix devoted such a detailed description to the capture of a relatively small place like Haifa. Moreover, though there is no reason to doubt his description, he is the only one to stress explicitly the importance of the Jewish community there. Albert took no part in the Crusade, so he must have relied on an oral witness or an *opusculum* that described the events. Actually among the Franks besieging Haifa there were not only the contingents of Daimbert and Tancred, but also those of Godfrey led by Galdemar Carpenel. It is possible that it was from the latter that Albert received his information on this subject[82] as well as about the role of the Jewish community in Haifa.

The strange sequel of the capture of Haifa was Galdemar Carpenel's taking possession of Hebron. Having tried in vain to take Haifa, which was firmly held by the troops of Tancred supported by the patriarch, he turned to the south, to Hebron, a city which had already been captured by Godfrey of Bouillon. A Jewish community which had existed there from earliest times had established a *modus vivendi* with the Muslim population as to the rights of entrance and prayer in the

[81] On the medieval Jewish cemetery and the 'boundary of the exiles of Babylon', see ch. 8 n. 3.

[82] B. Kugler, *Albert von Aachen* (Stuttgart 1885), 269 ff. Sources for the capture of Haifa in Hagenmeyer, *Chronologie*, *ROL* viii. 354–6. B. Dinur (above, n. 67), 62 n. 3, pointed out Albert's interest in the Jews during the Crusade. So e.g. he justifies the death of some Crusaders because of the massacre of the Jews in the Rhineland (1. i, cap. 69). The detailed descriptions of Albert are in glaring contradiction to the chronicler of Tancred, Radulf of Caen (cap. 139, *RHC HOcc*. iii. 704*B*). Even stranger is a version of Baldric of Dol, *RHC HOcc*. iv. 111. Tancred bypassed Caesarea, devastating the area he passed through, and reaching Haifa early one morning he suddenly invaded it. The inhabitants were unarmed and he took the larger part of the city that same day. The following night the Saracens ran away, some to Caesarea, some to Acre.

magnificent Herodian structure which sheltered the Tombs of the Patriarchs.[83] This was all the easier because in the beginning Islam was opposed to the veneration of the Holy Tombs. The Jewish community also built a new prayer-place here in the time of al-Afḍal, although it had to be presented as a regular house to the Muslim authorities.[84] The community must have owed its sustenance at least partially to Jewish pilgrims, as well as to the custom of sending bodies for burial there.[85] Some Jewish inhabitants even bore titles like Servant of the Patriarchs (*mesharet avōt ʿolam*), or that of *ḥaber*, that is, Fellow of the Palestinian Academy.[86] One can assume that with the approach of the Crusaders, the Jewish community left the unprotected town, but the place survived and flourished under Crusader rule, not least because of its veneration as a place of pilgrimage of all three religions. 'The Turks and the other Jews and Gentiles', we are told by Albert of Aix, 'venerate this fortification with great devotion, and it is held in no less fame and reverence by the Catholic faithful'.[87] It was wrongly argued on the basis of an abbreviated version of the *Tractatus de inventione Sanctorum Patriarcharum*[88] that the Jews were expelled by the Crusaders from Hebron. The original text actually refers to *c.*638, when the Jews showed the Muslims who captured Hebron from the Byzantines the entrance to the Tombs of the Patriarchs and were then granted the right to live in Hebron and build a synagogue there. But whereas the original chronicler wrote: 'Creator omnium et Redemptor universam regionem illam post multos annos incredulis illis praedictis [the Muslims] abstulerit et Latinis christianis reddiderit', the abbreviated text has: 'Postea vero, expulsis Sarracenis

[83] On one occasion the community even excommunicated some sectarians in the *meʿara* (the Cave), that is the Tombs of the Patriarchs. See a letter from the Palestinian *gaon* R. Solomon b. Yehuda (1025–51) to R. Ephraim b. Shemarya in *Sefer ha-Yishūw*, ii. 8 n. 7.

[84] Details in a letter sent from Hebron to the *nagid* in Fusṭāṭ; see *Sefer ha-Yishūv*, ii. 7 n. 6.

[85] On burial in Hebron see below, ch. 6 n. 4.

[86] Mann, ii. 203.

[87] Alb. Aqu., l. vii, cap. 26, *RHC HOcc.* iv. 254: 'Hoc praesidium Turci et ceteri Judaei ac Gentiles nimia devotione honorantes venerabantur, nec minori celebritate a catholicis cultoribus observatur et colitur.' *Gentiles* are obviously non-Turkish Muslims. The *praesidium* is the fortress-like Herodian sanctuary of the Patriarchs in Hebron.

[88] *RHC HOcc.* v. 309; Cf. *AOL* ii*a*. 421.

et Judeis, congregatus est in Ebron conventus clericorum etc.'[89] Clearly the abbreviator was misled by the beginning of the story and introduced the Jews in the wrong context.

The occurrences in Jerusalem and Haifa no doubt also befell Jewish communities in every other place that the Crusaders captured by force. One such place was the great port of Acre, which was captured after twenty days of siege on 26 May 1104 by Baldwin I with the help of Italian fleets. A Jewish merchant travelling along the coast who witnessed the siege later wrote to his mother: 'I arrived in Palestine before Acre was taken and thus witnessed the vicissitudes of the siege. We constantly faced danger of death, for we were near to them [the Crusaders] day and night, hearing their talk, and they heard ours; and our bread was coloured with blood.'[90] This is a moving but strange letter which ends with praises heaped on the writer's servant or slave, one Mubārak, who economized and saved expenses. We wish we knew more about the circumstances of writing. Clearly the letter was written after the capture of the city and thus we can assume that our merchant escaped the massacre which accompanied the event, though it can be argued that he witnessed the siege from the outside. Massacres happened in all the maritime cities of the kingdom (except, as we shall see, Tyre and Ascalon), and the Jewish communities were wiped out together with the Muslim inhabitants. This can be surmised and corroborated by more than simple circumstantial evidence, but as the dead were many and the ruin complete there were few survivors to tell the tale of woe.

This makes all the more precious a fragment of a letter recording the feelings of a man who escaped from a beleaguered city, the city of Beirut, at the last moment. Besieged since February 1110, the city was captured in May; and despite the explicit order of King Baldwin I, its inhabitants were massacred by an Italian contingent which took part in the siege and claimed a share in the spoils.[91] A letter, written probably in

[89] *RHC HOcc* v. 314.
[90] Goitein, *Mediterranean Society*, i. 132.
[91] Alb. Aqu., l. xi. 17; Cf. Prawer, *Histoire*, i. 275–6.

the last days of February 1100, and sent to Egypt[92] to a well-known personality, Dayyan Isaac b. Samuel the Spaniard (*ha-Sefardi*), to remind the *nagid* to intervene with a local *qāḍī* and *wālī* (place unknown, but possibly Tyre) on behalf of the writer,[93] ends with the following phrase: 'My heart stood still when a man from Beirut who had escaped at night arrived and told of 35 Jewish houses (*beit yehūdī*) there as well as foreign merchants who had stopped over there before continuing their travels. They were surprised by the siege and remained therein. *Barūkh dayyan ha-emeth*.'[94] Thus perished the Jewish community of the Lebanese coast in the general massacre.

When the city of Sidon was captured some time later part of the population was allowed to leave, which may have saved the lives of some of its Jewish inhabitants. Now only two cities on the Palestinian coast remained under Muslim domination: Tyre and Ascalon.

The decade of fighting (1099–1110) which created the Latin Kingdom left behind it, stormed, burned, and depopulated cities. Jews were wiped out together with their Muslim fellow citizens, and whole Jewish communities disappeared. The rich Genizah material regarding the Holy Land in the tenth and especially the eleventh century stops abruptly in the first decade of the twelfth century; one has the feeling that there were few people left to write, or even to ask for help. In some places, a decade or even two decades after the events survivors were still looking for members of their families taken prisoner by the Crusaders. Such may be the case of the writer of an undated letter sent from the Holy Land, probably to Egypt. To its author, the troubles, 'the activity and the dispersion of the captives in many lands',[95] seemed never-ending. The writer had managed to ransom his mother and small sister, but this had demanded much effort and travelling from place to place.

[92] According to Fulk of Chartres, *RHC HOcc* I. ii, cap. 42, Beirut fell on 13 May 1110; Alb. Aqu., xi. 17 has 27 May and W.T. has 27 April. As the siege lasted 75 days it must have begun in the last days of February. According to Albert the city capitulated but Bertrand of Tripoli and the Italians massacred those who stayed on in the city.

[93] Goitein, *Palestinian Jewry*, 295; id. in *Outremer*, 316–17.

[94] Ibid., ll.15–18. The letter is written, as customary, in Arabic in Hebrew letters. *Barūkh dayyan ha-emeth*—'Blessed be the True Judge'—is the traditional phrase pronounced on hearing of a death.

[95] Ibid. 292, ll. 26 ff.

And yet, he reports, there was still one female captive kept by the Franks, and no other way of saving her but by paying large sums of money. It is difficult to ascertain the date of this letter as the names of both writer and addressee are unknown. It has been argued that the letter may have been written during the period of the Crusader conquest.[96] No doubt other, similar letters, now lost, were in circulation at that time, with that same note of wistful envy expressed by our writer in referring to the recipient as one who lives in security: 'God knows that we are happy to hear that you are in peace. May God protect the kingdom in which you live.'[97] This letter, if it does actually belong to the period we are considering, is a sad echo of the fate of an individual family.[98]

The mood of doom and calamity also suffuses another contemporary letter, this time a letter of recommendation written by one R. Baruk b. Isaac, in all probability a rabbi from Aleppo. Through a heavy patina of biblical clichés pictures of real horrors emerge: the wails of the 'Daughter of Yeshurūn' (Israel) fill the road from which there is no return to her abode.

She was expelled from her life-giving heritage, and she became the despised one among the nations, trodden down in all the far corners of the world; she was captured like a wild bull, in a net. Naked in iron shackles, the boy is sold for money and the girl for a price. They were like nothing in the eyes of their captives, their beauty was trodden in the mud of the streets . . . The hoofs of the robbers were quicker than the eagles . . . The inhabitants of the navel [i.e. Jerusalem, the navel of the earth] were defiled and handed over to a foreign nation, whose language they did not hear in days gone by; their houses became the prey of the thiefs and there was nothing left not even a hovel when the sword was drawn from its scabbard . . . They fled one from a city

[96] This argument is put forward by S. D. Goitein, but it is not clear to me why the letter should be assigned to the Second Crusade. In my opinion it fits the First Crusade or some events of the 13th cent. better.

[97] Goitein, *Palestinian Jewry*, ll. 30 ff.

[98] An elegy (*qīnah*) published by S. Assaf tentatively assigned by him to the time of the First Crusade (*BJES* 7 (1939–40), 60–6, repr. in his *Sources* 17–19) was claimed by S. Klein to belong to the Byzantine period in the 4th cent. (ibid. 107–9) and by M. Azulai to the 7th cent. E. Fleischer has now definitely assigned it to the persecutions of Heraclius after the *reconquista* of Palestine from the Persians; see E. Fleischer, 'Lament on the Massacre of Palestinian Jews under Emperor Heraclius' (H), *Shalem*, v (1987), 209–27.

and two from a family, remnants of the survivors into the great world and they were thrown out from the holy place to deserted country in foreign lands. The haughty arm attacked and urged doom and destruction, and expelled all those who profess the unity of God from the orb of holiness without mercy and without attempt to console themselves in her stones [Ps. 102: 14].[99]

The period of Crusader conquests brought in its wake the strengthening of Palestinian communities abroad. This follows a well-known pattern of concentration of emigrants or refugees in a particular neighbourhood continuing their former cohesion by using particular prayer houses where they could follow their own liturgy and often establishing communal properties whose income was used for the benefit of the educational or ritual needs of the community. Thus we find people called 'Jerusalemites' (*Yerūshalmīm*) or 'people of Acco' (*'Akāwīm*) in Fāṭimid Egypt. Sometimes the eponymic was carried over to the second or third generation. Thus, neighbouring Muslim countries reverberated with names which for a time disappeared from the map of Jewish Palestine.

[99] Translated from the recent critical edition of N. Golb in *Studies in Genizah and Sephardi Heritage* presented to S. D. Goitein, ed. Sh. Morag and I. Ben-Ami (Jerusalem 1981), 103 ff. The quoted text is ll. 7–22.

3

Survival and Reconstruction

THE aftermath of the conquest was dozens of destroyed cities, fleeing populations, ruined economies. In the almost empty cities the conquerors tried to strike roots and settle. Here and there we hear that a quarter or neighbourhood of a city was taken over and then hastily fortified as there were not enough people to settle the whole area. Here and there, there was haggling over the ransoming of the captured prisoners. Jewish communities, mainly in Egypt, but also in Italy, as well as the local communities of Tyre and Ascalon mobilized their resources to rescue their brethren.

In the decade which followed the conquest, efforts were made to restore the once-flourishing cities. In some places we know that the new rulers pursued a deliberate policy of settlement, coming to the conclusion that there were policies more profitable than ruling empty cities. The best known example is that of Jerusalem.[1] Thus Oriental Christians, as well as Muslims and in some places Jews, who had escaped or survived the times of invasion and conquest returned to where they had lived before. There was, however, one place—and as far as we know, the only one—where Jews did not settle again, and this because they were barred from returning: Jerusalem. There is something obsessive in the prohibition instituted by the Crusaders, almost on the morrow of the conquest of Jerusalem, against Jews living in the Holy City, a prohibition which harks back for almost a thousand years, to a decree of the emperor Hadrian. Proclaimed in the pagan Roman Empire and renewed after two hundred years by Constantine the Great in the Christian Roman Empire, it was partially lifted with the Muslim conquest[2] and then fell into abeyance; but once the Holy City returned to Christian hands, the ancient

[1] See J. Prawer, 'The Latin Settlement of Jerusalem', *Speculum* 27 (1952), 490–503; id., *Crusader Institutions*, 85–101.

[2] See ch. 1.

prohibition was resuscitated. William, archbishop of Tyre, the great historian of the Latin Kingdom, introduces the story of Baldwin I's effort to colonize and settle the city of Jerusalem by organizing an immigration of Christians from Transjordan with the statement:

The Gentiles who were its [Jerusalem's] inhabitants were almost all put to the sword when their city was forcefully captured; but even if in some cases they escaped, no place was given to them to remain inside the city. The God-fearing princes regarded it as sacrilege to allow people who were not Christian to be in such a venerable place. Our own people, however, were so poor and few, that only with difficulty could they fill one of the quarters [of the city].[3]

William of Tyre's use of the generic expression 'gentiles' leaves little doubt that it was Muslims and Jews alike who were formally barred from living in Jerusalem. This is corroborated by several sources. Achard of Arrouaise, the prior of the new Austin monastery on the Temple Mount, the *Templum Domini*, says explicitly in his *Tractatus super Templo Salomonis*: 'The Lord who was born on earth without a sin, was killed by them [the Jews] for our sins. Since then the Jewish nation was dispersed and it is absent from this place.'[4] As the poem appears to be dedicated to Baldwin I (1100–18),[5] it bears witness to the contemporary scene. Two additional texts also corroborate

[3] W.T. xi. 27: 'Gentiles enim qui fuerant ejus habitores, urbe violenter effracta, pene omnes in gladio ceciderant; si qui autem casu evaserunt, iis non est datus locus intra urbem ad manendum. Instar enim sacrilegii videbatur Deo devotis principibus, si aliquos qui in christiana non censerentur professione, in tam venerabili loco esse permitterent habitatores.

[4] Achard d'Arrouaise, 'Tractatus super Templo Salomonis', ed. M. de Vogüé, in *AOL* i. 576 ff; ll. 408–10; a more complete edition is P. Lehmann, 'Die mittellateinischen Dichtungen des Priores des Tempels von Jerusalem Acardus und Gaufridus'. *Schriften der Monumenta Germaniae Historica* 6 (1946), 297 ff. ll. 708–10; 'Interfectus est ab eis pro nostris excessibus / Qui sine peccato natus est in terra Dominus / Et dispersa gens Iudea loco caret hactenus.'

[5] P. Lehmann (see n. 4 above), p. 300, thought the poem was dedicated to Baldwin II (the acrostic reads: *Baldvino regi*), but Baldwin I seems more plausible. Achard, prior of St Nicholas d'Arrouaisse (Pas-de-Calais), came to the Holy Land in 1108. One of the aims of his historical poem was to demand the return of property stolen from the Temple (Dome of the Rock); he says he knows by name the people who have it (308, l. 21: 'possem quidem quemque suo denotare nomine'). This fits Baldwin I's reign better than Baldwin II's, two decades after the sack of the Temple.

this. The Spaniard R. Abraham Ḥiyya, the author of *Sefer Megillat ha-Megalleh* (*c.*1120–29),[6] almost a contemporary of the prior Achard, summarizes the history of the Temple thus:

The Romans who ruined the Temple in the time of Titus, though they committed sacrileges, did not put any claim to the pure Temple [lit. pure house], as if they had in it any legacy or that it was worth establishing their prayer-house there. It is only when the wicked Constantine was converted that they came and presented such claims. And in the beginning when the Romans ruined it, they did not prevent the Jews from coming therein to pray. Similarly, the attitude of the kings of Ishmael was good and they allowed the Children of Israel to come to the House [i.e. Temple] and to build there a prayer-house and a school. The Jews from the neighbouring Diasporas used to make pilgrimage there in the Days of Festivity and pray there . . . And this was the custom as long as the kingdom of Ishmael lasted until in our own times the evil kingdom of Edom [Christians, here Crusaders] invaded the Temple . . . and since then they had profaned the Temple because they have made it their prayer-house and erected the monuments of their aberrations in it and have abolished the sacrifice,[7] as they prevented Israel from praying in the House . . . because since the day these sinners dominated the Temple they have not allowed Israel to enter it. Not even one Jew is to be found in Jerusalem in our own days.

This is also confirmed (*c.*1217) by the account of a Jewish poet from Spain, Judah al-Ḥarizi of his pilgrimage to Jerusalem, in which he quotes a Jewish inhabitant of the city telling that: 'The uncircumcised said that we killed their God and we caused them shame. Should they have found us in the city they would have eaten us alive.'[8] This situation is corroborated by Benjamin of Tudela, who visited the city around 1170 and found there only four Jewish dyers, near the Tower of David,[9] While Petaḥyah of Regensburg found only one Jew, a dyer, in

[6] Abraham bar Ḥiyya, *Sefer Megillat ha-Megalleh*, ed. A. Poznanski (Berlin 1924), 99–100.

[7] The *tamid* (i.e. permanent) sacrifice was replaced by the canonized ritual of prayer.

[8] *Taḥkemoni* (H), ch. 28; and see ch. 4 below on the restoration of the Jewish community in Jerusalem, pp. 67 ff.

[9] *Benjamin of Tudela*, 23. Petaḥyah of Regensburg, *Voyages*, 53.

the Holy City. A few years later all that remained of the former Jewish community was the use of the name of its ancient quarter, the *Juiverie*, for the north-eastern corner of the city.

Whereas we can assume with some degree of certainty that the Jewish population of cities captured during the first decade of Crusader rule perished, there were areas which suffered less or even escaped unscathed. The major military actions were directed at the conquest of cities, as there were actually very few castles to hinder the Crusader conquest and these were rather insignificant. It was the cities and their garrisons which ruled the countryside. Although Crusader foragings sometimes affected the villages and their inhabitants military expeditions were generally not directed at the rural countryside, and this probably explains why we find villages, especially in Galilee, with Jewish inhabitants or Jewish communities. The Jewish communities in Galilee, well attested for the Roman and Byzantine periods could often trace their origin to the period of the Second Temple. They had been strengthened by the influx of exiles or refugees from Judaea and the Hellenistic hostile cities of the coast after the Jewish revolt against Rome which culminated in the destruction of Jerusalem and in the subsequent revolt of Bar Kokhba, and later by the arrival of Jewish immigrants from neighbouring countries.

The Jewish communities of the two great centres of Ascalon and Tyre also fared better than the rest of their co-religionists. In both places the Jewish communities escaped destruction because the Crusaders captured the cities not by force but by capitulation. Moreover, the capitulation agreements were honoured by the Crusaders, which meant that the local population was not exterminated. In Ascalon, which played such an important role in the Jewish rescue operations after the fall of Jerusalem, we see the communal institutions functioning in 1145, eight years before the Crusader conquest.[10] In 1153 the city fell to the Crusaders; some time later, although we cannot date it exactly, a letter sent from Ascalon[11] seems to point

[10] On Sidon see above, end of ch. 2. On Ascalon, Mann, i. 202.

[11] See Goitein, *Palestinian Jewry*, 306–9.

clearly to the fact that the community did not disappear with the conquest. The letter is one of the rather rare documents of the Crusader period in which life in the country is seen through the eyes of the subjugated local population. It tells the story of a young girl taken prisoner or captured in unknown circumstances by a Frank who took her to Nablus.[12] Her brother, Musalam ben Abū Sahl, came to Ascalon and engaged the help of a fellow Jew, one Abū Saʿad ibn Janāīm, to go with him to Nablus. The ransom must have been enormous because after paying at least a half there still remained a debt of sixty dinars.[13] With the appropriate guarantees or securities presumably supplied by the Ascalonite, the girl was released and went with her brother to Cairo to try and collect the ransom still outstanding. We know from other sources that such collections were often made in the synagogue, the supplicant making a public appeal to the community for help.[14] But the date agreed for paying the remainder of the ransom passed, and the Frank appeared in Ascalon and presented his claim. The Ascalonite's situation was quite comfortable,[15] he could not afford such a sum, and although he was even prepared to mortgage his son as security for a loan he could find no taker. In our letter he therefore writes to his brother, Abū al-Bahā b. Janāīm, in Bilbais in Egypt, and asks him to find the man and urge him to send the money or the girl. Like all the letters we have of the preceding period the letter is written in Arabic using Hebrew letters, which in itself points to continuity with the earlier period. Moreover, the comparatively secure position of the writer and his good (or business) relations with the Frank of Nablus show the survival of the Jewish community in a city which had capitulated. Furthermore, a Christian influence

[12] Could she have been taken captive in a Crusader expedition to Egypt (Bilbais?) in 1168, when a good number of Jews were taken captive? Cf. Mann, ii. 317, and Goitein, *Palestinian Jewry*, 312–20.

[13] As already mentioned the normal rate of ransoming a captive was 33⅓ dinars. Goitein remarks that 60 dinars could cover the living expenses of a whole family for two and a half years (ibid. 306).

[14] Goitein, *Mediterranean Society*, ii. 170.

[15] He uses rather a strange expression: 'fī sitt ālāf ʿāfiyah min faḍal Allāh'—'in six thousand good states with God's grace.' (Goitein, *Palestinian Jewry*, 308, l. 4).

seems to be apparent, as 'mortgaging' children for the debts of their parents, although known in Talmudic times, was almost unknown in the Arab sphere of influence. Yet this is quite well attested for the Frankish period, with an *assise* of Baldwin III, based on Roman law, mentioning it explicitly.[16] As we have seen, however, in this instance the procedure was to no avail, and the writer of the letter had to turn elsewhere for help.

Evidence exists of the continued survival of the Jews of Ascalon as we know that *circa* 1170 Benjamin of Tudela found not only Jewish but also Karaite and Samaritan congregations there.[17] It is only in 1191 when the fortifications of the city were razed that these communities ceased to exist. Some of their number then moved to Jerusalem, which until that time had no Jewish population.[18]

Far more important than Ascalon, which never regained its Herodian glory, was the Jewish community in Tyre. Here too the city capitulated (1124), and the population could choose whether to stay on or leave. One can imagine that the local Muslim aristocracy and religious dignitaries left the city, but many, if not the bulk of the population, remained.[19] Although we have no direct proof, it seems that most of the Jewish community also probably remained. This tallies with the fact that nothing is heard of Tyrian Jews in Syria or Egypt, as we hear about Jews from Acre and Jerusalem who settled in these countries. Moreover, the description of Benjamin of Tudela (though some thirty years had elapsed between the capitulation of the city in 1124 and his visit *c.*1170) rather strengthens the feeling of continuity in the life of the community. The

[16] See J. Prawer, 'Roman Law and Crusader Legislation', *Crusader Institutions* (Oxford 1980), 444. Cf. id., 'Notes on the History of the Jews in the Latin Kingdom of Jerusalem' (H), *Shalem* 2 (1976), 103–5, Engl. trans. in *Immanuel* 9 (1979), 81–7.

[17] *Benjamin of Tudela*, 28.

[18] See ch. 4, pp. 71–2.

[19] The Muslim chronicler Ibn al-Athīr, *RHC HOr.* i. 359, says that only the poor and the sick remained. This is certainly a biased exaggeration. Other sources confirm that Muslims stayed on in the northern coastal cities which remained to a great extent Muslim. See 'Imād al-Dīn in *RHC HOr.* iv. 309, ii. 383, and additional sources quoted by Prawer, *Latin Kingdom*, 51.

importance of the community is also clear from the fact that together with the far greater and more famous cities of Damascus and Acre it took an active part in ransoming or helping co-religionists from abroad; their help was so generous that there was apparently no need to seek help from Egypt.[20]

Whatever the size of the Tyrian community immediately after the Crusader conquest, it was strengthened by renewed Jewish immigration. Benjamin of Tudela found in Tyre Dayyan Ephraim of Fusṭāṭ,[21] R. Meir of Carcasonne from southern France, and Abraham the *rosh ha-qahal*, that is, head of the community.[22] On this basis one would assume the existence of two or even three congregations in the city, a phenomenon quite well known in Jewish history which was to become increasingly common in the Crusader period because of the continued immigration of Jews from different countries. The title 'Head of the Community' could perhaps indicate, though there is no definite proof, some kind of overall organization to represent the community officially to the ruling authorities. Benjamin indicates a congregation of some significance both in terms of size—400 to 500 households—and stature: he commends their '500 Jews learned in the Talmud', the highest praise a Jew can bestow on the intellectual and religious quality of his co-religionists.[23] Wary as we are of medieval statistics, a community of three congregations was obviously an important one. Some time after the visit of Benjamin of Tudela we find the scholars of the community of Tyre corresponding with the great Jewish luminary Maimonides in Egypt. A number of his *responsa* were answers to questions put forward by R. Ephraim of Tyre, who can be

[20] Goitein, *Palestinian Jewry*, 266, l. 16. The letter (discussed on p. 58 n. 57) was written *c.*1174–87. However, despite the evident importance of Tyre, there is no historical basis for the legendary account of the visit of the great poet Yehuda Halevy. See Ch. Shirman, 'The Life of Yehuda Halevy' (H), *Tarbiz* 9 (1938), 229. Note also that one of the Hebrew itineraries locates his tomb in Kabrī.

[21] The name is given as Ephraim Miṣri. Miṣr is Egypt, but was commonly used for Fusṭāṭ, or Old Cairo. Cf. below, n. 24. There is a confused tradition, probably based on a misreading, that he was a pupil of R. Anatoli of Lunel; see Mann, ii. 325 n. 7, commenting on the chronicle of Sambari, ed. A. Neubauer, *Mediaeval Jewish Chronicles* i (Oxford 1895; repr. Jerusalem 1967), 133.

[22] *Benjamin of Tudela*, 30 (H).

[23] The number is expressed by the numerical value of letters: 'about *TQ*', that is 500; whereas Asher's text has *in extenso* 'about four hundred'.

identified with R. Ephraim, the head of the community who was mentioned by Benjamin of Tudela.[24] Although Maimonides' view of the intellectual centres of Palestinian Jewry was none too flattering (see Ch. 5, p. 111–13), he still addressed its leader in Tyre, as 'the great scholar from among the scholars of Israel, and I refer to the whole of Eretz Israel and its neighbouring countries, because of your dwelling therein, "the Lord has not left you this day without next of kin" [Ruth 4: 14]'.[25] This same R. Ephraim can be identified with the R. Ephraim of Fusṭāṭ, who played such an important role when Maimonides organized the ransoming of Jews from Bilbais taken captive in the Crusader invasion of Egypt in 1168. A circular letter emanating from Maimonides sent in 1169 to Jewish communities[26] to collect money for the ransom read: 'We, all the *dayyanim*, the elders and the scholars all of us make the rounds night and day and urge people in synagogues and the market places and at the gates of the houses, until we get something for this great work.'[27] Two special emissaries, writes Maimonides, were sent to collect money and ensure that money promised was actually delivered. Some time later Maimonides extended this rescue operation to Palestine.[28] The Cairo community, we learn, had already collected a large amount of money, despite the fact that Fusṭāṭ (that is, Old Cairo) had

[24] *Responsa of Maimonides*, ed. Freimann, no. 105. Freimann argued that we are dealing with two different persons (ibid., Introd. xli–xlii). The name of Maimonides' correspondent in Tyre is spelled *mṣr* in one place, which can be read *miṣr[i]*, i.e. from Egypt, or '*mi-ṣ[ō]r*', i.e. from Tyre.

[25] That is to say that the future of learning is assured. This *responsum* (ed. Blau, no. 75; ed. Freimann, no. 312), must have been sent to Tyre as there was at that time no other intellectual centre of prominence in the Holy Land.

[26] The letter has been published several times; cf. S. H. Margulies, 'Zwei autographische Urkunden von Moses und Abraham Maimuni', *Monatschrift für Geschichte und Wissenschaft des Judentums*, 44 (1900), 8–13; N. Bentwich, *Solomon Schechter: A Biography* (Philadelphia 1931), 143; and Goitein, *Palestinian Jewry*, 312–14. Two similar letters addressed to the smaller communities in Egypt (in the Rīf) and in small towns like Damirah, Jaujār, Samanūd, Damsīs, and Sunbāṭ, were probably sent on the same occasion (Mann, i. 244, ii. 317). One of the letters is dated Tamūz 1173 (ibid. 316). The chronology of these circulars needs more explanation. The letter just quoted was dated differently by Margulies (Tamūz 1484 Seleucid era = 1173) and by Bentwich 1172, but Goitein, p. 312, with a different reading, dated the letter 1169.

[27] Ibid. 312, ll. 8–11.

[28] Ibid. 312 n. 1. Goitein suggested that Maimonides acted in his capacity as the *raīs al-Yahūd*, the official head of Fāṭimid Jewry, but this (like the dates) is not explicitly stated in the document.

been burnt down by the Franks in 1168. He calls on other communities to do likewise. Moreover:

I have already written to the *dayyanim* in Palestine [*al-Shām*], to the two venerable dignitaries, the righteous *dayyanim* R. Ḥayyim the Dayyan and R. Ephraim the Dayyan . . . that they should contact the captives and . . . deal with their deliverance and should appoint a man who would liberate them according to an agreement on the ransom of those unhappy people. The man should come here and receive the sum of money against signature.[29]

This circular letter was to be made public in the different communities by one Aaron Halevy, whom we meet on several similar occasions as Maimonides' emissary for charitable fund-raising.[30]

Ephraim of Fusṭāṭ, the *dayyan* of Tyre, who as we have seen probably lived in Egypt before moving to Tyre, must have been a man of some learning if he is the subject of the rather extraordinary eulogy by Maimonides 'Rabbenu Ephraim the enlightened *dayyan*, the wonderful, the great Sage, the father of wisdom, the man of intellect'—such titles did not customarily flow from Maimonides' pen.[31] At his death, R. Ephraim's disciples continued their master's tradition and kept up the correspondence with Maimonides. Two among them, R. Meir and R. Ḥiyyā,[32] are known to have corresponded with Maimonides' pupil Saʿadya b. Berakhya the teacher (*ha-melamed*) as late as 1201.[33]

Another area where as we have seen the Jews were hardly affected by the Crusader conquest was the Principality of Galilee. Here we witness the existence of a dozen or so Jewish communities not in cities but in villages, a feature which we do not find on the coast or in Judaea or Samaria. Although our documentation dates only from the beginning of the thirteenth century, clearly it cannot be assumed that these were new

[29] Goitein, *Palestinian Jewry*, 314, ll. 7–13; cf. S. Goitein, 'Moses Maimonides, Man of Action, a Revision of the Master's Biography', in *Hommage à G. Vajda*, ed. G. Nahon and Ch. Touati (Louvain 1980), 158.

[30] Goitein, *Palestinian Jewry*, 316–18, in a letter of 1170 sent to Jewish communities in rural areas.

[31] Ibid. 314, ll. 8–9. Goitein accepted this identification in *Outremer*, 322.

[32] *Responsa of Maimonides*, A. Freimann, Introd. xl.

[33] Ibid., no. 138 and note to l. 13; Mann, ii. 316

settlements and that the Jewish village communities were created in that century; they certainly existed under Crusader rule a century earlier, and many existed, as we know, under Arab domination and were even flourishing in the late Roman or Byzantine period. The Jewish pilgrim from Europe, Samuel b. Samson, who came to the Holy Land with one of the great waves of migration *c.*1209–14,[34] has left a description of his pilgrimage in 1210 which contains a detailed list of these settlements. As a newcomer and stranger, he took advantage of the presence of the exilarch David b. Zakkai the Second of Mosul[35] and joined his company, following an itinerary prescribed by the location of the Jewish communities and Holy Tombs. Coming to Galilee, he noted the following:[36]

> From here (the village Lod) [the name is a copyist's error] in Galilee we went to Safad ... and I myself and the exilarch went to Kfar Par'am[37] ... wherefrom we came to Kfar 'Amino [corr. 'Amūqah] ... wherefrom we came to Kfar Nabartā and we returned to Safad where we celebrated the Sabbath. And in all these places there are communities in which there are more than five *minyanim*.[38] From here we went to Gūsh Ḥalav and on our way we found a township[39] by the name of Qismā ... and from here we climbed to Kfar Moran [corr. Meron] ... wherefrom we went to Gūsh Ḥalav where we celebrated Purim. There are there good people, full of charity. And in each place we came—more than two *minyanim* came to receive us[40] to honour the exilarch.

If our pilgrim and narrator is to be relied upon not only as to the names of places visited but also their size, then we are dealing with substantial communities compared to the contem-

[34] See below, ch. 7, pp. 214ff.

[35] The Spanish Jewish poet al-Ḥarizi met the exilarch *rosh gōla* in Mosul. (*Taḥkemoni*, 368). On his pilgrimage, the exilarch carried with him a letter of recommendation, probably from the caliph or some other Muslim dignitary, which enabled him to enter the Tomb of the Patriarchs in Hebron.

[36] Sh. Schulz (ed.), *R. Schmuel Ben R. Shimshon* (Weizen 1929), 10–12; *Hameamer* 3 (1920), 32, repr. *Voyages*, 80–1. Cf. below, ch. 7, pp. 213ff.

[37] The text has 'Kfar Bar'am', which is mentioned later. Because of topographical considerations the correction 'Kfar Par'am' was proposed by A. L. Sukenik, 'Notes on Itineraries to the Holy Land in the Middle Ages' (H), *Meassef Ẓion* 2 (1927), 109.

[38] *Minyan* denotes the 10 males necessary for public (as distinct from individual) prayer.

[39] *'Ir* is translated here as township since under Arab influence, the Hebrew term *medīna* was usually used for a city.

[40] The Hebrew may also mean 'will accompany us' or 'will leave us', but the translation suggested in the text seems more logical.

porary size of other Palestinian rural communities.[41] Some of these are also known from other sources: Gūsh Ḥalav, in which Benjamin of Tudela found some twenty families,[42] and ʿAlma, in which he counted fifty families and observed the existence of a large Jewish cemetery.[43] Other communities are known from other sources. We know, for example, of Banyās (Paneas, biblical Dan), which in the eleventh century boasted two congregations, and in 1120 witnessed the dramatic meeting of two false Messiahs.[44] A letter from the thirteenth century sent in all probability to a *nagid*[45] bears the signatures of a number of people holding office in Galilean settlements clustering around Safad: Bīrya, ʿAin al-Zeitūn,[46] ʿAlma, al-ʿAlawiya in the vicinity of Gūsh Ḥalav, and Al-Jīsh, i.e. Gūsh Ḥalav.[47] In all probability there were also Jewish communities in Kfar Ḥananya[48] and Daltōn (Arab. Dalātah).[49]

[41] In the vicinity of the nearby Lebanese lordship of Tyre the average village numbered about 20 households (Prawer, *Crusader Institutions*, 162); the same around Ascalon and Beit Jibrin (ibid. 177 n. 133).

[42] Generally speaking, the Jews preserved the ancient biblical and Talmudic Hebrew toponymy, though sometimes Hebrew sources would indicate the current (Arabic) name and identify it with its biblical forerunner. Gūsh Ḥalav, which became famous through Josephus and following him in Christian sources as Giscala, was correctly identified by the first Jewish scholar of Palestinology, Ishtori ha-Parḥi, *Kaftor va-Pheraḥ*, 295: 'Gūsh Ḥalav, which is called Jīsh.' *Benjamin of Tudela*, 30 in the ver. of Mss Epstein and Casanatense: 'between Timnath Seraḥ and Miron; whence [sc. from Timnata] one day to Gūsh, which is Gūsh Ḥalav and there are some 200 Jews' (not trans. in the Engl. version).

[43] Ibid. 30.

[44] Mann, ii. 202–3. The description: 'two congregations in the fortress of Dan' probably means a Babylonian and a Palestinian community, but could also refer to a Rabbanite and Karaite community. On the two pretenders see J. Prawer, 'The Autobiography of Obadiah the Norman, a Convert to Judaism at the Time of the First Crusade', in *Studies in Medieval Jewish History and Literature*, ed. I. Twersky (Cambridge Mass. 1979), 110–34.

[45] Mann, ii. 204.

[46] The name of that well-known place was given as ʿAqāl Zeitūn, but should be ʿAin al-Zeitūn. J. Barslavi, *BJES* 6 (1939), 48, and Klein, *History*, 121.

[47] A better reading and interpretation of these signatures was proposed by J. Barslavi, *BJES* 9 (1942), 55–60; id., *Studies*, 63–6.

[48] Hence the name al-ʿAnani. Barslavi, ibid. 78, opposed Mann's interpretation. A list of poor people in Egypt supported by the community mentions a man from Kefar Ḥananya; see Barslavi, *Studies* (H), 75–83; and a letter written between 1187 and 1214 and published in S. Goitein, *The Yemenites* (H) (Jerusalem 1983), 132, l. 26, mentions a man 'from among the wealthy' (*baʿalei batīm*'—lit. house proprietors) who got into a dangerous situation in Kfar Ḥanan before reaching Jerusalem.

[49] The Jewish community in Dalton is well documented for the 11th cent. (*Sefer ha-Yishūv*, ii. 6). Among the memorable events was the burial of the *gaon* Elijah b. Solomon Hakkohen in the coastal city of Tyre in 1083: 'and all of Israel carried him on their

All in all, some fifteen villages with Jewish communities clustering around Tiberias are mentioned in the twelfth century, and the castle and city of Safad in the thirteenth. The story of the latter before the Crusader period is obscure, and the Crusader data are contradictory and confusing.[50] From a Genizah letter we know now that Safad existed in the beginning of the eleventh century.[51] The place did not play any major role in the twelfth century but acquired great importance in the thirteenth.[52]

In the twelfth century, however, it was Tiberias, the capital of the Crusader Principality of Galilee, that assumed the central role. In fact, a Jewish community had existed in Tiberias throughout the Roman, Byzantine, and Arab periods. Let us recall that it was Tiberias which led the Jewish revolt against the hated Byzantium and collaborated with the invading Persians in 614, and Tiberias which sent the first contingent of Jews to settle in Jerusalem after the Muslim conquest.[53] Known by its ancient name Raqat, it was a flourishing community with its own special commercial centre, the *Sūq al-Yahūd*, the Jewish market. Jews settled here even from far away Khaibar in the Arabian peninsula,[54] and its thermal baths and their medicinal properties attracted people from afar. A centre of Jewish learning, its tradition of copying the Scriptures was known throughout the Jewish world.[55]

In 1099 Tiberias capitulated to Tancred without resistance. It is therefore reasonable to assume that the community which existed in the preceding period continued to exist under Crusader rule. Whatever the case, in the second half of the

shoulders and not on horses a distance of three days to the Mount of Galilee to Daltōn for burial, to the summit of the mountain next to Yossi ha-Galīli, and nearby Jonathan b. ʻUziel, Hillel and Shammai, Elʻazar b. ʻArakh, Elʻazar b. ʻAzaryah, his ancestor and all the Just ones.' *Megillat Ebyatar*, new edn. by M. Gil in *Jerusalem in the Middle Ages*, ed. B. Z. Kedar and Z. Baras (Jerusalem 1979), 86, text, 2, ll. 23–5; cf. *Tombs of the Ancestors*, 123.

50 Crusader data mention as foundation dates 1102 and 1142. See J. Prawer, *Histoire*, i. 332 n. 29.

51 In 1023–4 a deed of sale was written for a young boy, Mūsi b. Habba b. Salomon of Safad (ha-Ṣfati); see J. Barslavi, *BJES* 9 (1942), 55–6 and id., *Studies*, 62–3.

52 On Safad, see ch. 8, text and n. 111.

53 See ch. 1 and n. 66 below.

54 Barslavi, *Studies*, 44, 67.

55 Abraham ibn ʻEzra quotes from the ʻSages of Tiberias' in his Commentary on Exodus. Cf. H. Graetz, *Geschichte der Juden*, vi (Leipzig 1894), 382.

twelfth century we find Jews in contact with the Princess Eschive of Galilee, wife of Raymond of Tripoli. It transpires that a man by the name of Abū al-Ḥusein b. Abū al-Kīr from Acre was in debt to the wife of the *qūmiṣ* (*Comes*) and the Lady of Tiberias *al-sīt Ṣāḥibat Ṭabariyah*), and the rulers of Tiberias put his relatives into prison to extract the money. A sum of 21 dinars would have satisfied the immediate demands, but the total sum demanded was greater. As Abū al-Ḥusein could not raise the money he went to Egypt, like so many other Palestinian Jews, to try his luck there. But he left behind a wife and children, and the writer of the letter which has come down to us, probably his father-in-law or uncle, had grave doubts about his long absence which had already lasted far more than a year. We wish we knew more about how Abū al-Ḥusein came to be in debt to the rulers of Tiberias. It was definitely not because of regular taxes, but it could have been the outcome of some unlucky business in which the Frankish rulers had a share.[56] In the 1170s Benjamin of Tudela found a sizeable community of some fifty households here,[57] and he mentions by name the community leaders R. Abraham the Visionary,[58] R. Mukhtar, and R. Isaac. An almost contemporary itinerary written in Hebrew, that of R. Jacob b. Nathanel, confirms the existence of a Jewish community there.[59] An interesting reference to the community of Tiberias is also to be found in the incompetently abridged and very confused description by Petaḥyah of Regensburg.[60] He mentions in the city a R. Nehōrai and his son R. Judah who keep a written genealogy going back to 'Rabbi', that is Rabbi Judah Hanassi, the great exilarch of the second century CE. By profession R. Nehōrai was a physician, also an apothecary and spice merchant.[61] He and his son sat in the

[56] Goitein, *Palestinian Jewry*, 259–67. The same letter mentions another Palestinian Jew by the name of Saʿad who went to Egypt. He lived in utter poverty in order to save the money needed to return to his family. Abū al-Ḥusein came from Acre; Goitein's suggestion that he lived in Tiberias or the vicinity is not warranted by the text.

[57] *Benjamin of Tudela*, 29.

[58] Heb. *ha-ḥōze*, a name used in the Bible for a particular class of prophets.

[59] Ed. Grünhut, as an appendix to *Sibūv of Rabbi Petaḥya of Regensburg*, 96; see below, ch. 7.

[60] *Voyages*, 51.

[61] Heb. *besamim* can mean spices, medicaments, and perfumes; in this case probably spices used in pharmacy.

market place (perhaps the ancient *Sūq al-Yahūd*) with covered faces, we are told, and pursued an ascetic way of life.

The number of communities surrounding Tiberias was probably greater than our sources ostensibly indicate. The basis of his assumption is the large number of Jewish Holy Tombs that appear to be located in Galilee. While this was partially because tombs commemorating the Sages of the Mishnaic and Talmudic period (that is, Roman and Byzantine times) were usually identified with places known from their heroes' activity, which were for the most part in Galilee because after the Roman destruction of the Second Temple and the laying waste of Judaea Jewish life found refuge in Galilee, such traditions could not have survived unless there were communities which assured their survival. The existence of a Holy Tomb does not necessarily confirm the existence of a Jewish congregation in the immediate locality, but it does suggest that there were Jewish communities in the vicinity that contributed to the continuity of traditions and in all probability to the care of the monuments.[62]

The presence of a fairly dense map of Jewish settlements explains an otherwise enigmatic colophon dating from the fourteenth century.[63] It is a genealogical tree of a family and counts seven generations. It begins with 'Rabbenu [i.e. our master] Ezekiel Hakkohen the Galilean' and continues with 'Rabbenu Ḥananya, the great rabbi, the head of the Academy,[64] who judged Israel in Upper and Lower Galilee for fifty years'. It is difficult to calculate the date the colophon refers to, but it certainly brings us near the end of the twelfth century or possibly to the first half of the thirteenth. In the first case the colophon would probably refer to Tiberias, in the latter to Safad.

Seeing the number of the Jewish communities in Galilee, one wonders if there might be some truth in a rather enigmatic statement of the English chronicle known as that of Benedict of Peterborough referring to the Third Crusade. The saviour of

[62] The Jewish itineraries very often mention a dome (*kīpah*) or similar structure on the tombs; in other places they simply mention the existence of Jewish cemeteries. See ch. 7.

[63] Mann, ii. 204 n. 5.

[64] In the Aramaic, *beit-midrashā*.

the city of Tyre, Conrad of Montferrat, closed the gates of this royal city in the face of the unlucky king of Jerusalem, Guy of Lusignan. King Guy was camped with a small retinue outside the city walls: 'and Templars and Hospitallers and all the Christians which were dispersed in that region began to flock to him and adhered to him as to their lord and king, because of the danger of the Jews and Pagans'.[65] This calls to mind similar events in the same region five hundred years earlier, when 'The Jews from Tiberias, the mountains of Galilee, Nazareth, and their vicinity' rose against Byzantium, joining the victorious Chosroes of Persia.[66]

Whereas the Jewish communities of Galilee, including Tiberias, as well as of Ascalon and Tyre survived the Crusader conquest, in other places Jewish communities were re-established, once the Crusader kingdom entered a phase of stabilization. In some places, Jews who had fled before the Crusaders and found a temporary refuge elsewhere now came back to their former settlements; in others it was newcomers from neighbouring countries in the Levant or immigrants from Europe who created new communities in old centres. A good example is furnished by Acre. The city was captured in May 1104 by Baldwin I, aided by a Genoese and Pisan fleet. The Muslim commander capitulated in return for a free exit, but the Genoese, unhappy about the peaceful capitulation, prevented the garrison and the inhabitants from leaving the city with their belongings. The departing exiles were attacked, plundered, and killed, and the Frankish army joined in the action. Four thousand people were reported to have perished, and their property, which was immense, became spoils of the attackers.[67] A very short time later, however, some time

[65] 'Benedict of Peterborough', *Gesta regis Henrici II et Ricardi I*, ed. W. Stubbs (London 1867), 93: 'Confluebant ergo ad eum Templarii et Hospitales et omnes Christiani qui dispersi erant in regione illa propter metum Judaeorum et Paganorum et adhaerebant ei sicut domino et regi suo.' As we know today this is actually the first draft of Roger of Hoveden. In the final version, however, this phrase is missing. Cf. B. Z. Kedar, 'Jews and Samaritans in the Latin Kingdom of Jerusalem' (H), *Tarbiz* 53 (1984), 392 n. 20.

[66] The Christian chronicler Ibn Batriq (Eutyches) quoted by M. Ish-Shalom, *Christian Travels in the Holy Land* (H), (Tel-Aviv 1979), 68–9.

[67] The most detailed description is in Albert of Aix-la-Chapelle, *RHC HOcc*. iv, cap. 27–9; cf. R. Röhricht, *Geschichte des Königreichs Jerusalem* (Innsbruck 1898), 47.

between the capture of the city in 1104 and 1111, a Jew from Acre wrote a letter to Egypt[68] asking the recipient, himself formerly from Acre, to seek the intervention of the *nagid*, the head of Egyptian Jewry, on his behalf. It seems that the father of the writer had settled in Acre before 1094 with a group of people from Tiberias. We do not know what happened in the intervening years, but the person to whom the letter was addressed had left Acre, perhaps before the Crusader conquest of 1104.[69] The writer, with a family of ten, remained and had difficulty in eking out a living as a *shōḥet* (a ritual slaughterer) and cantor—both occupations that imply the existence of a Jewish community. In fact the letter explicitly mentions the existence of a *qahal*, an organized Jewish community which pays the salaries of its officials. Another sign of stability, rather unexpectedly, is the mention of Jewish oyster fishers from Alexandria whose misbehaviour in local inns of doubtful reputation is censured by our writer with all the solemnity of a communal official.

The city of Acre, which had already enjoyed some prominence in the previous Arab period, was destined to become, economically and later on politically, the most important city in the kingdom, second only to Jerusalem in international fame. With its cosmopolitan population and great economic possibilities, Acre was to become the most important Jewish centre under Crusader rule, although we must wait almost fifty years to hear about this. The little we have is connected with Maimonides' landing and short stay there *circa* 1165.[70] A very short time later, when Benjamin of Tudela came to Acre, he found that it was already one of the largest Jewish communities in the country, 'around 200' families headed by the community leaders, R. Ṣadōq, R. Yefet, and R. Jonah.[71] Despite its size we

[68] The text that follows is based on Goitein, *Palestinian Jewry*, 302–5.

[69] People bearing the patronymic 'Akāwī, i.e. originally from Acre, are often to be found among the Jews of Egypt. See *Sefer ha-Yishūv*, ii. 50 n. 13 and Barslavi, 'Genizah Fragments on the Maritime Cities 'Acco and Gebal [Jubail]' (H), *Eretz-Israel* i. (1951), 153–7; *Studies*, 84–91. The term *min āhl 'Akah*, ('from the people of Acre') probably points to the existence of a congregation in Cairo originating from Acre (Barslavi, p. 85).

[70] See ch. 6, pp. 141–2.

[71] *Benjamin of Tudela*, 91. R. Yefet is possibly the son of Elijah Dayyan, to whom Maimonides sent an interesting letter. See *Responsa of Maimonides*, ed. A. L. Lichtenberg, ii. (Leipzig 1859), 37, col. 3.

hear relatively little about the community, though it is referred to by Petaḥyah of Regensburg,[72] and we know from a *responsum* of Maimonides that it had an organized rabbinical court which functioned on the customary lines of such institutions.[73] Yet though Acre was already an important centre in the twelfth century, it was only after the second quarter of the thirteenth century that it played a major role in Jewish life.

A similar process probably unfolded in such places as Sidon and Caesarea on the coast and Beirut to the north, which we last heard of as being besieged by the Crusaders. Benjamin of Tudela found Jewish communities in all these places.[74] Inland, again according to Benjamin of Tudela, Jewish communities were found in Lydda, Beit Nūba, Zarʿin, and—rather unexpectedly—in Bethlehem.[75] The small community known to have existed in Beit Jibrin may have had different origins, perhaps in connection with the colonizing enterprise of the order of St John.[76] It is also conceivable that the Jewish community which existed in Nablus in the thirteenth century[77] had already existed there in the twelfth century.

Two sources are sometimes referred to as proving the existence of Jewish communities in other places, but actually there is no such proof. A Petrus Judeus is mentioned among the inhabitants of Mahumeria (al-Bīrah),[78] but clearly a man who had taken the oath to the canons of the Holy Sepulchre in the name of the Holy Trinity in order to receive land was not Jewish. Another confused reference occurs in the itinerary of John of Wirzburg who mentions 'a great Jewish village across the Dead Sea called Ein Gedi',[79] but this is simply taken from Eusebius.[80] Finally, there is some confusion regarding the small Templar fortress *Toronum militum* or Latrun, which Benjamin of Tudela correctly calls in his native Spanish *Toron de los*

[72] Ed. A. Benish (London 1856), 54; L. Grünhut (Jerusalem 1904), 30.

[73] *Responsa of Maimonides*, ed. A. Freimann, 159, 156–7.

[74] *Benjamin of Tudela*, 19, 21.

[75] Ibid. 26, 28, 29.

[76] Ibid. 27. On the settlement of the place see J. Prawer, *Crusader Institutions*, 117–26.

[77] On Nablus, see ch. 8 n. 1.

[78] *Cartulaire de l'Église du Saint Sépulcre*, ed. E. Rozière (Paris 1849), 241; ed. G. Bresc-Bautier, 238; cf. ibid. index, s.v. Petrus Judeus.

[79] *Descriptiones Terrae Sanctae*, ed. T. Tobler (Leipzig 1874), ch. 10; cf. *PPTS* v. (1896), 57–8.

[80] Ed. Klostermann (Leipzig 1904), 428.

Caballeros. The number of Jewish inhabitants indicated in some manuscripts is patently wrong.[81]

Thus, reviewing the period from 1099 to 1187, the First Kingdom of Jerusalem, one has the impression that the Jewish communities partially succeeded in re-establishing themselves in the main cities of the kingdom. As we have seen the only exception, but a significant one, was the capital, Jerusalem.

[81] Ed. Adler, 23 (H), Engl. trans. 22. The number 200 in some MSS is the result of the copyist misreading the letter *dalet* as *reish*; the former represent the number four, the latter two hundred. One MS indicates 300, another states that there are no Jews there.

4

Rebuilding Jerusalem

CRUSADER rule in Syria and Palestine lasted no more than eighty-eight years (1099–1187). In the middle of the twelfth century the Latin establishments in the Levant reached the zenith of their power and their greatest territorial expansion. But in the meantime calls for a *jihād* as well as the actual consolidation of Muslim power when Saladin succeeded in adding Syria and parts of Iraq to his Egyptian domain, began to threaten the security of the kingdom. The situation reached its climax when the Crusaders entered into a fateful campaign against Saladin which led to the disastrous battle of Hattin (July 1187). The bulk of the Crusader military power, including the contingents of the Military Orders, was massacred or taken captive. Saladin crowned his victory by a triumphal march through the kingdom, Crusader castles and cities opening their gates almost without resistance. Even the capital, holy Jerusalem, capitulated after a short and unheroic resistance. Saladin guaranteed safety to everybody everywhere and the right to move to places still in Christian hands (actually, the city of Tyre). It was only in Jerusalem that Saladin exacted vengeance for the Crusader massacre of 1099, but even here he ultimately agreed to ransom its inhabitants. Yesterday's rulers, now refugees, started on the long march from the Holy City to Tyre, which was miraculously saved from capitulating to the Muslims. Some smaller castles, like Safad and Belvoir in Galilee, continued to withstand Saladin's attacks, but even they were to surrender during the following year.

The promise of free retreat with whatever possessions one could carry certainly proved attractive. Secular and ecclesiastical lords preferred to save themselves, temporarily at least, than fight in hopeless conditions. Moreover, and this may have a direct bearing on our subject, Saladin tried to win over the Oriental Christians in Crusader cities. As early as 1136, Zengi attempted to give his campaigns against the Crusaders the image of a war to restore the *status quo ante*. Thus, former landowners were allowed to claim possession of land which had been in Crusader hands for almost two generations, and for this purpose they could have recourse to the archives in the capital of Muslim Syria. Saladin followed the same policy. Thus after the capitulation of Nablus, we are told by a Muslim chronicler, Saladin's cousin, who received Nablus from his uncle, 'made peace with a part of the inhabitants [obviously, Oriental Christians] and against the payment of a poll tax (*jizya*), which they obligated themselves to pay in the future, he left them the right to use their lands and buildings'.[1] Saladin had reason enough to believe that, with rare exceptions, the Oriental Christians were not over fond of the Crusaders and felt no particular loyalty to them.[2] Things went so far that the Crusaders actually suspected the Oriental Christians of having been bribed by Saladin, or even having invited him to invade the Crusader kingdom.[3] One may doubt the truth of these allegations, but their existence and diffusion prove that Saladin's policy of sowing dissension among the Christians was successful. At the same time we should bear in mind that in many cities the Oriental Christians represented a significant part of the population,[4] and the results of such a benevolent attitude did not fail to impress them.

[1] On the policy of restoration of Zengi in Maʿarat al-Nuʿmān in 1136, see Ibn al-Athīr, *RHC HOr*. i. 423. On Nablus see ʿImād al-Dīn quoted by Abū Shāma, *RHC HOr*. iv. 301–2. In Jerusalem after its capitulation Saladin allowed the Oriental Christians to stay in return for payment of the *jizya*: 'thousands remained therein and in her vicinity. They turned to work planting vineyards and soon harvested fruits and vegetables', ibid. 340.

[2] On the relations of the Crusaders with the native Christians, see Prawer, *Latin Kingdom*, 214 ff., and id., 'The Minorities in the Latin Kingdom', in *History of the Crusades*, ed. K. M. Setton *et al.*, v. 59 ff.

[3] On the accusations of connivance with Saladin see letters from the Holy Land sent by the Order of St John in *Chronicon Magni Presbyteri* (*Mon. Ger. Hist. SS*, xviii. 508), and letters sent by the Genoese in R. Röhricht, *Regesta Regni Hierosolymitani*, nos. 661, 664*a*. The accusation against the Greek Orthodox Christians originated among the Copts, the monophysite enemies of the Chalcedonian Greeks. Cf. Sawīrus ibn al-Mukaffaʿ, *History of the Patriarchs of the Egyptian Church*, iii. pt. 2, ed. A. Khater and O. H. B. Khs. Burmester, (Cairo 1970), 131–3.

[4] See e.g. ʿImād al-Dīn: 'The majority of the population of Sidon, Beirut and Jubaīl were Muslims, pitiful men living in the vicinity of the Franks.' *RHC HOr*. iv. 309. In Jabalah and Laodicea many of the population were Syrian and Armenians (ibid. 352–3, 358, 362). In Jerusalem the north-eastern quarter of the city, the so-called *Juiverie*, was inhabited by Christian Syrians. See above, ch. 2. Large communities of Oriental Christians were to be found in Acre.

There are no direct testimonies to Saladin's attitude to the Jews in the Holy Land, but it is plausible to assume that basically they benefited from the policy of restoring the status quo. An anecdote told by the great Jacobite scholar and historian of Jewish origin, Bar Hebraeus, about Saladin's behaviour during the siege of Acre is indicative of Saladin's attitude to the Jews—and hence of the Jews' attitude to him. A Damascene Jew, we are told, a merchant, brought twenty measures of sugar from Alexandria by sea. On approaching the port of Acre he was arrested and his property confiscated on the pretext that he was a heretic. The Jew appealed to Saladin, who ordered the immediate restoration of the confiscated property.[5] Saladin's behaviour in this case as well as in other instances did not go beyond strict adherence to Muslim law, but there can be little doubt that he was warmly regarded by the Jews. Forgeries which circulated in the Jewish world even credited him with willingly accepting the idea of Jewish sovereignty over Jerusalem once the city was captured from the Crusaders! His expected and wished-for victories over the Christians were even linked with the Day of Salvation.[6]

Saladin's victories stirred and revived hopes in the Jewish communities in the Holy Land and in the neighbouring countries. Messianic speculations were rife everywhere. It seems quite probable that they started in the Jewish Quarter around 1179 and eventually spilled over into the Christian and Muslim populations.[7] These speculations predicted great events for as early as the year 1186. The fall of Jerusalem to

[5] *The Chronology of Bar Hebraeus*, trans. E. A. W. Budge, i (Oxford 1932), 396 (Engl. trans. 342).

[6] On the attitude of Saladin to Egyptian Jewry see E. Ashtor-Strauss, 'Saladin and the Jews', *Hebrew Union College Annual* 27 (1956), 305–26. Cf. the forged letter assigned to Maimonides, publ. A. Neubauer, 'Une pseudo-épigraphie de Moïse Maimonide', in *REJ* 4 (1882), esp. 173 ff., which supposedly reached the Jews in Fez on 20 Aug. 1187 (Jerusalem was in Christian hands until 2 Oct. 1187). Cf. F. Baer (below n. 7), 151. In that forged epistle Saladin says that he will be victorious over the Crusaders but ultimately the king of the Jews will rule in Jerusalem. He will take over the rule in peace and perhaps he (i.e. Saladin) 'will find grace in his eyes'. In 1185, two years before the fateful expedition to Hattin, a Jewish teacher, one Mauhūb, dreamt that the Egyptians would shed Christian blood in 1186, and this would be the beginning of redemption. Mann, *Texts*, i. 548.

[7] The original text of the apocalyptic prophecy was in Hebrew and then spread in the West (Spain) as well as in Byzantium, Egypt, and Persia. See J. Baer, 'Eine jüdische

Saladin in 1187 and the European reaction which mobilized Christendom for the Third Crusade in a vain attempt to recapture the Holy City were anxiously watched by the Jewish Diaspora, and the meagre results of the Crusade added to the glamour of Saladin and explain the speed with which a legend was created crediting him with restoring the Jewish community in Jerusalem.

It is this story which in a sense opens the second chapter of the history of the Jews in the Latin Kingdom. The often-repeated but basically legendary story of the restoration of the Jewish community in Jerusalem by a proclamation of Saladin originated with the Spanish-born Hebrew poet al-Ḥarizi in his *Taḥkemoni*. Here he noted, among other things, in verse and in prose, his impressions of a voyage to the Holy Land (*c.*1217). Coming to Jerusalem he asked an inhabitant of the city:

'When did the Jews come to this city?' 'Since the Ishmaelites captured it, the Jews settled it, he answered.' 'And why did they not live in it when in the hands of the uncircumcised?' He said: 'Because they said that we killed their God and we put them to shame. Should they have found us, they would have eaten us alive.' 'So how did it happen that you are in this place?' He answered: 'God was zealous for his name and had pity on his nation. It is not good', he said 'that the sons of Esau [i.e. Christians] should be heirs to the Temple of the Holy of Holies, whereas the sons of Jacob should be exiled from it. Otherwise the Gentiles will be likely to say in envy: "God abandoned in wrath his firstborn . . ." '

And God stirred the spirit of the king of the Ishmaelites in the year four thousand nine hundred and fifty of Creation, and the spirit of wisdom and bravery rested upon him; and he and all the hosts of Egypt went up and put siege to Jerusalem and God delivered her into his hands. And he ordered that a proclamation should be made in every city, to old and young, namely: 'Speak ye on the heart of

Messiasprophetie auf das Jahr 1186 und der dritte Kreuzzug', *Monatschrift für Geschichte und Wissenschaft des Judentums* 70 (1926), 113–22, 155–65. But cf. the very plausible interpretation of B. Lewis, 'An Apocalyptic Vision of Islamic History', *Bulletin of the School of Oriental and African Studies* 13 (1951), 308–38, which assigns the last part of the apocalypse to the First Crusade. Cf. E. Ashtor-Strauss (above, n. 6), p. 319, and other sources quoted there. It seems also that a fragment of a Jewish apocalypse which prophesied that 'the Jews will not be [henceforth] expelled from the Temple' relates to Saladin and the siege of Acre 1189–91, and not, as argued by Ginzberg, to the Crusader siege of the city in 1104. *Genizah Studies in Memory of S. Schechter*, i. *Midrash and Haggadah* (NY 1928), par. 32: 'The Vision of the Last War', 310–12.

Jerusalem, whoever is from the seed of Ephraim, whether in Assyria or in Egypt, and those forsaken at the ends of the horizon, those who are willing should ingather from all the world's corners and dwell inside her boundaries. And now we are settled here in the shadow of sweet peace . . .'[8]

This famous dialogue, important as it is as an historical source, is no less important in describing what may be called the Jewish view of the Crusades. During the First Crusade the Jews expressed their protest against Providence and history for allowing the Crusaders to capture and dominate Jerusalem. In a climate of heightened messianic expectations they glossed over the fact that the city was captured from the Muslims, who had ruled it for more than four hundred years, and not from the Jews. This approach found its complement in the letter of a contemporary of the First Crusade in Byzantium. Its anonymous author affirms that the Crusade was a God-willed movement whose main purpose was to gather the gentiles in Jerusalem for the hour of doom and vengeance.[9] Al-Ḥarizi's narrative is true to the same tradition. Saladin's expedition against the Crusaders and his capture of Jerusalem are part of the divine plan to restore the Jews to their homeland and capital. No other reason is known or adduced.

In form and substance, al-Ḥarizi clearly and consciously imitated or paraphrased the declaration of Cyrus of Persia which called on the Jews to return from Babylon and settle in Jerusalem.[10] There is, however, no other source to confirm the issue of such a proclamation by Saladin in the year 4950 of Creation—that is, 14 September 1189–3 September 1190—or at any other time. The total absence of sources, even of Jewish

[8] Ed. A. Kaminka (Warsaw 1899), *The Twenty-eighth Gate*, 245; *Voyages*, 67–8. Cf. the beautiful but not always exact translation, *The Taḥkemoni of Judah al-Ḥarizi*, by V. E. Reichert, ii (Jerusalem 1973), 146–9. Al-Ḥarizi indicated the date of his visit in Jerusalem in *maqāmah* xxviii as: 'One thousand, one hundred and forty-eight years since she was exiled from her abode'. Medieval Jewry fixed the year of the destruction of Jerusalem by Titus in 68 or 69 CE. Depending on the calculation this would correspond to 1216 or 1217.

[9] See ch. 1, pp. 13–14.

[10] Cf. Ezra 1: 1–4; 2 Chr. 36: 22–3.

sources close to Saladin,[11] throws very serious doubts on the existence of such a proclamation. And yet the information gathered by al-Ḥarizi from the Jews in Jerusalem had a solid core of historical truth, namely the annulment of the Crusader prohibition which barred the Jews from settling in Jerusalem. Whether or not this was done by an official proclamation cannot be ascertained. It seems more likely, however, that Saladin's policy of restoring in Jerusalem and everywhere else the status quo allowed the Jews to flock back to Jerusalem along with new Muslim settlers.[12] The lapse of the Crusader prohibition, an infamous descendant of pagan Rome and Christian Byzantium, was interpreted by the Jewish community that al-Ḥarizi found a generation later as a renewal of Cyrus's proclamation. Obviously it was al-Ḥarizi who contributed the historical reminiscences and the literary form in which the events have come down to us, but there is no doubt that with the Muslim conquest of the city a new Jewish community was able to strike roots in its ancient capital.

In another famous *maqāmah*, al-Ḥarizi tells us more about the composition of the Jerusalem community. There he met 'the saints of the Most High who came from France . . . there is also a distinguished community from Ascalon . . . [and] there is also a notable and excellent community from the Maghreb'.[13] This *maqāmah* is preserved in another Hebrew version and in a later Arabic translation made by al-Ḥarizi himself. The Hebrew version has a shortened description of the author's journey to Jerusalem and makes no mention at all of the new Jewish community there.[14] But the Arabic translation, which closely follows our first Hebrew text of the *maqāmah*, reads as follows: 'I came to Jerusalem in which there were at that time

[11] See the letters of a Jewish physician in the court of al-Malik al-'Azīz 'Uthmān, the son of Saladin, below pp. 81 ff.

[12] The possibility that Saladin actually wanted to attract Jewish settlers to Jerusalem should not be discarded outright. A parallel case is that of Nūr al-Dīn, who after the capture of Edessa from the Crusaders in 1149 settled 300 Jewish families there. Cf. A. S. Tritton and H. A. R. Gibb, 'The First and Second Crusades from an Anonymous Syrian chronicle'. *Journal of the Royal Asiatic Society* (1933), 291. Cf. R. Grousset, *Histoire des croisades*, ii (Paris 1935), 822 and Ashtor-Strauss (above n. 6), 326.

[13] *Taḥkemoni, maqāmah* xlvi.

[14] S. M. Stern, 'An Unpublished *Maqāma* by Al-Ḥarizi', *Papers of the Institute of Jewish Studies London*, i (Jerusalem 1964), 186–201. On Jerusalem in this new Hebrew version, see ibid. 205, l. 22 ff.

three Jewish communities: first a Frankish community, second, a Maghrebi community, and third, a Palestinian (*shāmi*) community.'[15] This tripartite division of the newly established Jewish community in Jerusalem tells in a nutshell the story of its establishment and restoration. The Third Crusade and the vicissitudes of war had far-reaching effects on the restoration and structure of the Jewish community in Jerusalem. In a sense they were an accidental by-product of Saladin's scorched-earth strategy in his confrontation with the Christian hosts, which aimed at the total destruction of all cities and castles captured from the Crusaders.[16] Behind this policy was the logical assumption that once their strongholds were physically destroyed, the Crusaders would not be able to muster anew enough manpower and financial resources for their reconstruction. In the peace treaty which ended the Third Crusade, Saladin even succeeded in forcing the Crusaders to accept 'the condition that the destroyed fortifications of cities should not be rebuilt.[17]

Among the first victims of this policy was the city of Ascalon. The city surrendered to Saladin on 4 September 1187, after thirty-five years of Christian rule. The Crusaders received forty days of grace to evacuate the city which then remained under Muslim domination for the next four years, until it was threatened by the hosts of the Third Crusade. Saladin was ready to pay any price to ensure that the city would not fall to Richard the Lionheart and become a Crusader bastion again on the main road from Syria and Palestine to Egypt. To prevent this, Saladin ordered the razing of its fortifications. The protests of the native population and the hardships suddenly heaped upon them did not change his decision and between 12 and 23 September 1191 the fortifications were systematically destroyed. The population, afraid to stay in an unfortified city in the face of the Crusader threat, moved out, Muslim and Jew alike seeking refuge in Egypt or in other parts of Palestine and Syria (*al-Shām*), fleeing on foot when beasts

[15] The Arabic version, ibid. 190–1. Cf. Y. Ratzaby, 'An Arabic Maqāma by Alharizi' (H), *Criticism and Interpretation*, xv (Bar Ilan Univ., Ramat Gan 1980), 18–19.

[16] J. Prawer, *Crusader Institutions*, 483; cf. id., *Histoire*, ii. 83 ff; this was systematically continued by al-Malik al-Mu'aẓẓam, ibid. 154–5.

[17] Id., *Histoire*, ii. 90, 98–9.

were not available.[18] It was these Jewish refugees from Ascalon who laid the foundations of the Ascalonite community which al-Ḥarizi found in Jerusalem.[19]

The new Ascalonite settlement probably merged easily into the Palestinian congregation (hence the name Shāmi in the Arabic version of al-Ḥarizi) which would have been formed four years earlier, immediately after the capture of Jerusalem by Saladin. The Ascalonite Jews had close relations with the nearest Jewish community in Egypt, namely the community of Bilbais across the Sinai desert, which was now strengthened by the exodus from Ascalon, and the Ascalonites in Bilbais likewise remained in contact with their relatives and friends who settled in Jerusalem. Later on we hear of Jews from Bilbais migrating to Jerusalem, and Jerusalemites moving to Bilbais.[20]

Bilbais was not only 'near the land of Goshen', as it is described in one of our letters,[21] but also on the main road from Egypt to Palestine. Consequently we also find here Jews who made their way from the Maghreb in the west through Egypt to the Holy Land; there were always some, it seems, who stopped in Bilbais instead of continuing their journey. Thus, Bilbais had close links with two congregations: with the Jews from Maghreb, through those of their number who stayed on in Bilbais; and with the former Ascalonites now living in Jerusalem. From a letter of 1214 we learn that the community in Bilbais took upon itself the task of collecting money for the different congregations in Jerusalem. The collection, as was the custom, was announced in the synagogue; it is clear from the letter that this was not the first time; similar collections were sent to the congregations even before 1214. The writers stipulated that the money collected was to be distributed to 'the synagogue of Ben al-Yamani' and the 'Rabbanites'. These

[18] Behā al-Dīn, *RHC HOr.* iii. 263–5.

[19] I suggested this interpretation in *Zion* 11 (1946), 48 ff. This was accepted by B. Dinur, *Israel in the Diaspora* (H), ii. 450 n. 33 and by others.

[20] Goitein's assumption that the Ascalonite Jews settled in Bilbais in the wake of the capture of their city by the Crusaders in 1153 seems plausible; those Ascalonites, however, who corresponded with their former fellow citizens in Jerusalem almost three generations later in 1214 were hardly any relations of the former. A letter previously assigned to an uncertain date after 1153 now proves to have been written earlier, *c.*1127–38. Cf. Goitein, *Palestinian Jewry*, 299, 333.

[21] Ibid. 298.

definitions are rather confusing: the first literally means the synagogue of the 'son of the Yemenite; while the other is even more baffling, as it is doubtful that there was a Karaite community at that time in Jerusalem (which would have made the expression 'Rabbanites' meaningful).[22] The writer of the letter asked that the recipient, who was to go with the collected money to Ascalon,[23] inform him of his return and confirm that the money had been received by 'the community of Jerusalem'[24] and distributed as agreed upon. The letter ends with greetings to one Abū Sa'id al-Kutnāni, to R. Elijah al-Raīs, and to the sheikhs of Ascalon and Maghreb. The French congregation, which will be mentioned three years later by al-Ḥarizi is indicated by the use of the term *rabbanim*, that is, the scholars from France.

We can easily identify R. Elijah al-Rāis of our letter with the head of the Maghrebi congregation mentioned by al-Ḥarizi; we learn from the Arabic version of the *maqāmah* that his full name was R. Elijah b. 'Aqnīn. He must have been a rather controversial personality: whereas al-Ḥarizi accuses him in Arabic of exceeding pride, in Hebrew he is described as a man of compassion showing great charity to the needy. Yet there is much slander against him, we are told, and rumours of misdoings and bad deeds; God alone knows the hidden truth.[25] These suspicions might relate to the distribution of the financial aid coming from abroad and would explain the precaution taken in asking the emissary who went to Jerusalem to bring back 'a letter from the community of Jerusalem so that the community [of Bilbais] should know that you arrived and

[22] Goitein, *Palestinian Jewry*, 298 ff. The text reads (ll. 5–6): al-dhahab al-mandhūr likanīsat ibn al-Yamani wa al-dhahab al-mandhūr lilrabbānīm'. Goitein assumed that the 'rabbanim' of this text refer to the rabbis of the different congregations. I suggest that, following the Jewish Oriental usage, it refers to European scholars. See below, text and nn. 38, 53, 66. Note that three years later al-Ḥarizi mentions the presence of a French community.

[23] This the writer learned from a letter which was addressed to his father; ibid. l. 5.

[24] Ibid., l. 8: 'al-jamā'ah mīn al-Quds'.

[25] Goitein identified this R. Elijah with the *raīs* Elijah mentioned in a letter from one Abū al-Raḍḍā Hakkohen from Tiberias. Ibid. 299. *Taḥkemoni, maqāmah* lvi. The full name R. Elijah b. 'Aqnīn is known from the Arabic version of the *maqāmah*. Cf. M. Stern (above, n. 14), 101. Ratzaby (above, n. 15), 19: 'a man of knowledge and morals. These he partly inherited from his ancestors and partly acquired by himself. But he is possessed by exceeding pride and people avert their eyes from him.'

distributed the money according to what was written in the agreement with him'.[26] The writer adds that until now there had been no problems, but 'a man has one friend and ten enemies who want to hurt him'.

There is, however, another possibility, based on a rumour recorded in a scurrilous *maqāmah* of al-Ḥarizi 'about a man of Jerusalem of whom there were slanderous reports'. 'The man was appointed in Mount Zion as the Head (*rosh*) of Holiness', but far from being saintly he seems to have been accused of promiscuity with a Muslim lady who infected him with a skin disease. As a result he was called not by his title of Head of Holiness but by the pejorative nickname, 'Head of Peʿor'.[27]

Despite internal quarrels, the Maghreb congregation was, by al-Ḥarizi's testimony, 'good and important'. It was a newly established congregation, and it has been suggested that the pilgrimage to Jerusalem from far-away Maghreb was the result of anti-Jewish persecutions. These, known in Hebrew sources as 'dress persecutions', were the result of the discriminatory legislation of the Almohad rulers Abū Yūssuf Yaʿaqūb al-Manṣūr and his son Muḥammed al-Nāṣir which began in 1198/9 and continued for several years.[28] It is not impossible, however, to assume that the Jewish immigration from Maghreb was influenced by a Muslim pietist movement. The Muslim immigrants from Maghreb came to Jerusalem after its capture by Saladin. They settled in a Maghrebi Quarter which became a pious foundation (*waqf*) during the rule of al-Afḍal ʿAli, Saladin's son, in Damascus.[29]

In addition to the Ascalonite and Maghrebi congregations mentioned in the letter, we also learn of the existence of a previously unknown Yemenite congregation in Jerusalem. The story of its establishment is rather obscure. According to al-Ḥarizi, the head of the Ascalonite or Palestinian congregation was one Saʿadya *Ish Yemīni*, which in simple literary usage

[26] Goitein, *Palestinian Jewry*, 300, ll. 8–12.

[27] The slanderous poem, *Taḥkemoni*, *maqāmah* ciii. The 'Head of Peʿor' is a pun on *Baʿal Peʿor*, the Moabite God whose cult promoted promiscuous relations with Medianite women and caused the outbreak of a plague. Cf. Num. 25: 1–9.

[28] J. M. Toledano, *Ner Maʿaravi: Hist. of the Jews in Morocco* (H), (Jerusalem 1911), 34 ff.; B. Dinur, *Israel in the Diaspora* (H), ii. 329–33. Cf. *Enc. of Islam*², i. col. 166.

[29] Mujir al-Dīn al-Ḥanbali, *Al-ins al-Jalīl bi-taʾrīkh al-Quds wa al-Ḥalīl* (Būlāq, AH 1283), 396–7.

(based on Esther 2: 5) means Sa'adya the righteous man or the important man. It has been suggested, however, that the epithet refers to the man's origin, namely, that he was a Yemenite Jew, but judging by the ethnic jealousies so common amidst thirteenth-century Palestinian Jewry, I am rather hesitant to accept this explanation.[30] There is also the question of the name: in the Arabic version the head of the Palestinian congregation is called Mufaḍḍal b. al-Yamani. Though it was quite common to have a Hebrew and an Arabic name, this adds to the obscurity of the problem.[31]

Whatever the case, it is clear that by 1214 a Yemenite synagogue existed in the city, and some Genizah documents help to elucidate its origin. The story begins with a Yemenite, one R. Solomon, who migrated from Yemen to Fusṭāṭ in Egypt. His son Abraham settled in Jerusalem after it was captured by Saladin. He founded a synagogue known as 'Kenisah ben al-Yamani' which is referred to by the leaders of the congregation of Bilbais. Abraham spent some time both in Fusṭāṭ and in Bilbais and married, or rather remarried, there. His wife followed him to Jerusalem but he divorced her when the news came that his sons from a former marriage had left Yemen and had already reached Qūṣ on the Red Sea with the intention of joining him in the Holy City.[32] As the letter mentioning the arrival of the children in Qūṣ is dated 1196, Abraham the Yemenite must have reached Jerusalem not long after its capture by Saladin.[33]

The scattered information we have about the Yemenites in Jerusalem can be summarized as follows. The first mention we

[30] Goitein suggested that *Ish Yemīni* indicates Sa'adya's Yemenite origin. In *Palestinian Jewry*, 321, 332, he argued that the man was of Yemenite descent but born in Ascalon.

[31] A *ra'īs* Mufaḍḍal is mentioned in another letter (TS 20. 172), *Palestinian Jewry*, 334, ll. 11–12, sent by Abū al-Raḍḍā Hakkohen from Tiberias.

[32] The details are from a letter of Abraham b. Solomon printed in Goitein, *Palestinian Jewry*, 325.

[33] The letter, which mentions the siege of Damascus (1196), was sent from Jerusalem by Abū Zikhrī, the Jewish physician of al-Malik al-Mu'azzam and of al-Malik al-'Azīz, the son and the nephew respectively of Saladin; see Goitein, *Palestinian Jewry*, 325. Cf. id., 'Parents and Children: A Genizah Study on the Medieval Jewish Family', *Graetz College Annual of Jewish Studies* 4 (1975), 47–68.

have of a Yemenite is of R. Abraham in 1196. In 1211 we learn from a letter sent from Alexandria that money was collected in the community for paying off a loan from the *wālī* (governor of the city of Jerusalem), for the restoration of an 'old synagogue known as that of R. Saʿadya Hakkohen, known as the son of the Yemenite of blessed memory'.[34] If any money remained it was to serve as an 'Alexandrian fund', which probably means that it should be at that community's disposal. The senders demand that the payment of the debt should be made in the presence of three people,[35] R. Saʿadya, a R. Kaleb, and the *al-raʾīs* the Yemenite.[36] In 1214 we are on surer ground because, as we have seen, a Yemenite synagogue is explicitly mentioned in the correspondence from Bilbais.

In addition to mentioning the congregation of Ascalonites, the Maghrebis and the Yemenites, al-Ḥarizi also cites a newly established congregation, that of immigrants from France led by 'saints of the Most High, who came from France to settle in Zion', headed by R. Baruk and his brothers, R. Meir and R. Joseph. The presence of this European community is linked with the great wave of Jewish immigration from Europe. The victories of Saladin and the tremendous effort made by Europe to launch the Third Crusade had their effect on the Diaspora: in their wake and during the whole of the thirteenth century we witness not only the immigration of individuals but collective immigrations to the Holy Land headed by some of the spiritual leaders of European Jewry.[37] The earliest, which started, it seems, *circa* 1209, is described by the sixteenth-century chronicler Ibn Verga as follows:

[In] the year [4]971 [of Creation, i.e. 1211], God stirred the rabbis of France and the rabbis of Angleterre [*sic*] to go to Jerusalem; and they

[34] Goitein, *Palestinian Jewry*, 333–5, 334, ll. 7–8: 'al-kanīsah al-ʿatīqah al-maʿrūfa br. Saʿadya al-Kohen al-maʿrūf bibn al-Yamanī'. Saʿadya is mentioned here (1211) as dead, and consequently cannot be identified with the head of the Ascalonite congregation mentioned by al-Ḥarizi.

[35] Ibid. 334, ll. 11–12.

[36] It is not impossible that the messenger, also entitled *raʾīs*, was himself a Yemenite.

[37] Cf. J. Prawer, 'The "Lovers of Zion" in the Middle Ages' (H), *The XIX Archaeological Convention* (Jerusalem 1965), 128 ff.; and see below, ch. 7.

were more than three hundred. And the king honoured them greatly and they built for themselves prayer-houses and places of study (*batei midrashōth*). Our rabbi, the Great Priest (*hakkohen haggadol*), our master Jonathan Hakkohen also went there. And a miracle happened to them: they prayed for rain and they were answered and they sanctified the name of heaven.[38]

Even from this late and certainly abridged text it is obvious that the original source referred not to an ordinary pilgrimage such as those constantly under way to the Holy Land, but to an extraordinary movement.

No doubt the establishment of the Crusader kingdom, once the period of conquest was over, favoured the flow of Jewish pilgrimages from Europe because of the facility of transport and communication. In this case, however, we witness a new phenomenon on a larger scale, almost mass immigration. Moreover, there is a new element in it, namely, the participation of the spiritual leaders of the communities. As indicated by Ibn Verga, the immigrants came from France and *Angleterre* but perhaps the latter meant Plantagenet territories in south-western France (after 1204) rather than England.

Such a large-scale movement did not pass unnoticed, and the traces left in a number of contemporary writings complete our picture. The sources at our disposal point to a large movement which continued unabated for several years, and then sporadically for almost a whole century. The earliest started *circa* 1209 or at the latest in 1210.[39] In that first group was R. Jonathan b. David Hakkohen of Lunel, one of the great rabbinical personalities of the period. With him were R. Samuel b. Samson, Saʿadya, and Tobiah. Their pilgrimage is known to us

[38] This note added by Joseph Ibn Verga to the chronicles written by Solomon and Don Judah ibn Verga (late 15th cent.) indicates that he used an ancient source which was in the hands of R. Shem Tob Sansolo. Cf. *Shalem* 2 (1976), 105, and J. Hacker's explanation in n. 11 ibid. Ibn Verga, *Shevet Yehuda* (The rod of Judah), ed. A. Shohet (Jerusalem 1947), 147 and cf. below, ch. 7. I assume that Ibn Verga used an Oriental source, where according to custom *rabbanim* would mean European scholars.

[39] I have suggested that there were two immigrations (*Zion* (1946), 18); my friend and colleague E. E. Urbach, in *The Tosafists* (H) (Jerusalem 1954), 230, reached the same conclusion. Different interpretations are put forward by S. Krauss, 'L'émigration de 300 rabbins en Palestine en l'an 1211', *REJ* 82 (1926), 333–53, and H. J. Zimmels, 'Erez Israel in der Responsen-Litteratur des späteren Mittelalters', *Monatschrift für die Geschichte und Wissenschaft des Judentums* 74 (1930), 46.

in detail because one of the participants, Samuel, left a written itinerary.[40] The date can be assumed with some certitude as autumn 1209,[41] and the immigrants probably left from a port in southern France near Lunel. Samuel b. Samson certainly returned to Europe but possibly made another pilgrimage to the Holy Land later. He is otherwise unknown, but it has been suggested that he may be the son of the great Tosafist R. Samson of Sens.[42] This is not impossible, but in this first group participants from southern France would have been more likely. The way in which the itinerary is signed indicates that it was concluded after the pilgrimage had been accomplished and probably in Europe, although possibly it was written in Acre. Unfortunately, the itinerary suffered at the hands of its copyists, and in consequence its descriptions are rather confused.[43]

This pilgrimage or immigration was, as already indicated, the first of a larger movement which continued through the whole of the thirteenth century. Though we can assume its ideological background with some measure of certainty,[44] it is more difficult to be certain why it started towards the end of the first decade of the thirteenth century. Perhaps the presence of R. Jonathan of Lunel, a great admirer of Maimonides may point to a solution: in the original Arabic text of his famous *Epistle to Yemen*, Maimonides, despite his opposition to millenarian calculations, states his family tradition that the gift of prophecy, the precursor of the Messiah, will return in the year (4)970. This corresponds to 1 September 1209–22 August 1210. His tradition was not an isolated one. A commentary of the Pentateuch of one Avigdor (Qara?) has the following calculation: 'From the creation of the world until the death of Moses

[40] Ed. F. Schulcz (Weitzen 1929), repr. in *Hazofeh* 14 (Budapest 1930), 69–81, 375–8. Repr. in *Voyages*, 75–83. See below, ch. 7.

[41] The author signed his itinerary in the following way: 'Samuel b. Samson who comes from Jerusalem and from Galilee in the year [4]970 of Creation'. F. Schulcz (above n. 40), 6.

[42] This was suggested by M. Steinschneider in *Cat. Bodl.* nos. 2480, 2641, and was noted by R. Röhricht, *Bibliotheca Geographica Palaestinae* (Berlin 1890), 45. Mr N. Schorr kindly drew my attention to this entry. Cf. *Magazin für die Wissenschaft des Judentums* 3 (1887), 157–9. This is accepted by Urbach (above, n. 39), 277.

[43] See ch. 7, 214 ff.

[44] See ch. 6, 156 ff.

2486 years ... From the death of Moses to the coming of the Messiah 2486 years. In all 4972.'[45] This year corresponds to 1212. It is just possible that these messianic calculations are linked with the early waves of migration.

Another group was led by very prominent personalities of that age, the French Tosafist R. Samson b. Abraham of Sens and his brother Isaac, and R. Joseph b. Baruk and his brother R. Meir from Clisson in Brittany. There were at least two separate groups in this pilgrimage. One landed in Egypt, where it met with Abraham the son of Maimonides, and included R. Joseph and probably also his brother R. Meir. These were the leaders of the French community in Jerusalem described five years later by al-Ḥarizi. About this group we are told by Abraham Maimuni (the son of Maimonides):

> When the sages of France came to this land [Egypt], the great master R. Joseph of blessed memory and his other brother ... of blessed memory, as well as the venerable R. Abraham, the father of R. Gershom of blessed memory, R. Joseph and the venerable R. David and other sages of blessed memory, we saw that they were men of wisdom, intelligence, and piety. We rejoiced in them and they were happy with us and we did in their honour as we were required to do.[46]

The R. Joseph mentioned here belonged to the northern French circle of the Tosafists,[47] and his emigration to Jerusalem is prominently stressed in the *Tosafot*, where his name appears as 'R. Joseph from Jerusalem', 'the Jerusalemite', 'from Eretz ha-Tsevi',[48] or 'R. Joseph from Eretz Israel'. His grandson noted his ancestry as follows: 'I the youngest [an expression of humility] Joseph, the son of R. Nathanel, the grandson of our

[45] *Epistle to Yemen* in the original Arabic, ed. R. J. Kafih (Jerusalem 1972), 49, and A. S. Halkin's English trans. (New York 1952), p. xvi. The commentary on the Pentateuch in the *Cat. of the Hebrew MSS in the Bodleian Library*, ed. Ad. Neubauer (Oxford 1886), no. 2273, 789–90. Text quoted by A. Kupfer in *Tarbiz* 42 (1973), 118 n. 23.

[46] Abraham b. Maimon, *The Wars of the Lord*, ed. R. Margoliot (H) *Milḥamōth ha-Shem*, Jerusalem 1953), 53. I have translated from this critical edition. In earlier editions the names and titles are often garbled.

[47] Cf. H. Gross, *Gallia Judaica* (Paris 1897), 595–6. Cf. Urbach, *Tosafists*, 266.

[48] Cf. H. Gross in *REJ* 6 (1883), 178 n. 3. *Eretz ha-Tzevi*—lit. the land of the gazelle—is one of the titles of the Holy Land as the land of beauty based on Dan. 11: 16.

master R. Joseph Clisson the Jerusalemite who went to Eretz ha-Tsevi.'[49] Abraham Maimuni mentions that R. Joseph and R. Meir were very happy with al-Ḥarizi's translation of Maimonides' *Guide of the Perplexed* into Hebrew.[50] And, as we have seen, al-Ḥarizi met both of them in Jerusalem.

Not much later, R. Samson of Sens and his brother Isaac migrated to the Holy Land. They obviously took a different route to Acre, for as Abraham Maimuni wrote: 'and we heard about master R. Samson of blessed memory of the Tosafists that he was in Acre, as we did not see him because on his way he did not pass us'.

Ibn Verga's ancient source was clearly referring to an extraordinary type of mass migration, but historians, rightly cautious, had many misgivings as to the number of rabbis (three hundred!) mentioned in the text. Obviously this could not actually refer to the religious leaders of the Jewish communities. Is there any sense in the number, even if we understand it as denoting a large number of people who took part in the migration? This was doubted until a recently discovered letter from the Genizah made the number not only possible but even plausible. The information is included in an exchange of letters between two cantors (*ḥazzanim*) of the communities of Alexandria and Cairo dated (4)173 of Creation, that is, 1213.[51] Having dealt with personal matters, such as the exchange of copies of *Seliḥoth*[52] the Alexandrian cantor transmits family news: your mother is fine, the money you sent arrived safely, your brother Saʿīd quarrelled with his wife and left her and nobody knows where he is. And then unexpectedly:

[49] Colophon of a Hebrew MS. Cf. *Catalogue of Hebrew Manuscripts in the Collection of Elkan Adler* (Cambridge 1921), no. 1444, 25. Cf. S. H. Kuk, 'R. Joseph Clisson the Jerusalemite' (H), *Jubilee Volume of J. L. Fishman* (Jerusalem 1926), 69–71; Repr. *Collected Papers*, ii. 258–62, and M. Ish-Shalom, in *BJES* 8 (1940), 12–13.

[50] Maimuni's statement is somewhat confusing as it could be understood as if al-Ḥarizi had translated the book for the two brothers in Jerusalem. Clearly he only showed them the translation. Both brothers are mentioned as dead by al-Ḥarizi, one in Damascus at the latest in 1221 as al-Ḥarizi visited Egypt after the Fifth Crusade; see M. Stern (above n. 14), 194–5. Thus the attempt to connect R. Meir of Clisson with a R. Meir whose tomb was shown in Giscala cannot be upheld. On the tomb in Giscala see *Tombs of the Ancestors*, 167–8.

[51] The sender was Judah b. Aaron al-ʿAmmāni (cf. Mann, i. 241) and the addressee Abū al-Majd Meir ben Yakhīn, Abraham Maimuni's factotum. The letter (TS 12. 299) was published and analysed by Goitein, *Palestinian Jewry*, 338–40.

[52] *Seliḥot* are penitential prayers composed of religious poetry, *piyūtim* (poems).

and during the night when I write to you, my lord, these lines, seven of the *rabbanim* reached us,[53] great scholars and they are accompanied by a hundred souls, men, women, and children, looking for bread, as if we did not have enough beggars of our own. We have around 40.[54] The majority of the community is in trouble because of lack of livelihood. And here such great expenses are burdening them. We shall see how things work out.[55]

Clearly, as we have already seen from other sources we are dealing with a mass movement which in this case disembarked in Alexandria on its way to the Holy Land. It is a remarkably large group and this movement which started *circa* 1209 continued for the next three or even four years (our letter must have been written at the beginning of 4173, just after the New Year, that is, autumn 1213).

Despite much zeal and effort, not all of these French immigrants managed to settle in Jerusalem. Others, surrendering to economic needs, left Jerusalem for Acre. This is what happened, for example, to R. Samson of Sens; he intended to go to Jerusalem but settled in Acre, a city in which later on we also find his son and family.[56] This probably also happened to the two brothers, R. Joseph and R. Meir of Clisson, one of whom died in Damascus.[57]

As already mentioned, the size and the particular composition of this immigration differed from that of the foregoing and following periods. Moreover, we can assume that the actual numbers were even greater but have not survived in our documentation.[58] At the same time, immigration from neighbouring countries continued. The facility with which Jews moved freely between Cairo, Jerusalem, Damascus, and even

[53] Clearly Egyptian Jews (perhaps all Oriental Jews) used the expression *rabbanim* to describe the leaders or sages of Ashkenazi Jews. In the text, 342, l. 16: 'waṣal ilaynā sab'ah min al-rabbanīm al-'ulamā al-kibār'. Cf. above n. 22 and text at n. 67.

[54] Goitein remarked that the writer Yehuda b. al-'Ammāni, being the court scribe of Alexandria, would know the list of the needy ones probably supported in and by the community (ibid. 340 n. 18).

[55] Ibid. 340, ll. 16 ff. and margin.

[56] His tomb (near Haifa, where Jews from Acre buried their dead) is indicated by an anonymous pupil of Naḥmanides (1270–91) in *Toṣōth Eretz Israel*, ed. S. Assaf, *Sources*, 76.

[57] See n. 50.

[58] On the other hand, an alleged immigration from Provence in that period did not take place. Cf. J. Ta-Shma', 'The Immigration of the Scholars from Provence to the Holy Land' (H), *Tarbiz* 38 (1969), 398–9.

Crusader Acre is remarkable. Good fortune has preserved the correspondence of a family which was probably characteristic of the period and deserves our attention. Almost contemporary with the forced exodus of the community from Ascalon and its establishment in Jerusalem, we find a Jewish family from Egypt which tried to settle in Jerusalem and partially succeeded. The vicissitudes of that family also give us a glimpse of the attitude of the Jews to the Holy City at that period.

The father of the family, Dayyan Elijah b. Zekarya,[59] was a physician and the son of a physician; it has been suggested that it was his father, Abū'l-Faraj, who was himself the son of the 'physican of Alexandria', who settled in the Holy Land.[60] After the capture of Jerusalem by Saladin the family lived in Jerusalem, and it seems that they were befriended by the governor or some other Muslim high official in the city. It is quite possible that Elijah served the governor of the city in a professional capacity. For reasons unknown he left Jerusalem and went to Egypt. After that he made several journeys to Jerusalem. On one of them he wrote a letter to his son Abū Zikrī, who continued in the physician's profession and was soon employed by the Ayyūbid princes, probably thanks to the help and connections of his father, as an ophthalmologist. It is a particularly moving letter. The writer, an observant Jew, leaves the caravan with which he crossed the Sinai peninsula on its way from Palestine to Egypt, in order to observe the Sabbath. Although the caravan is already close to Bilbais, Dayyan Elijah stops at al-Muṭaīlib with two hired bedouins to guide and accompany him on the caravan route to Egypt after the Sabbath.

The relations of the family with the Ayyūbid court must have been quite close, as Dayyan Elijah was able to send a letter to his son (probably in Jerusalem) with a messenger of the sultan (*rasūl al-sultān*) passing through the oasis. He was to

[59] A. L. Motzkin, 'Elijah b. Zechariah, a Member of Abraham Maimuni's Court: a Geniza Portrait', *REJ* 128 (1969), 339–48. Id., 'A Thirteenth-century Jewish Physician in Jerusalem', *Muslim World* 69 (1970), 344–9.

[60] Goitein, *Palestinian Jewry*, 327. The extant signature in the Arabic written address is: 'Ben Abū 'l Faraj known as Ibn al-Rāis', 331.

give the letter to Emir Nūr al-Daulah,[61] presumably a governor or high official of the city, who would then pass it on to the writer's son. The relations between Dayyan Elijah and this Muslim personality must have been quite cordial, as he asks his son to tell him that they are 'of his family'.[62] One has the impression that at the time of the voyage Dayyan Elijah thought he was leaving the city only for a while; he asked his son to 'pray for us that God should not take away his grace from us and will return us to you in peace, after I accomplish what I have undertaken to do'.[63] At that time three brothers, Raḍī, Abū Zikrī, and Solomon Abū 'l-Barakāt stayed on or met in Palestine.[64] During their stay in Jerusalem they developed good relations not only with the governor of the city but even with the *imām*, the man responsible for the mosques and public prayer, as well as with an Oriental Christian, al-As'ad, and a Muslim with the title *al-amīn* (the trustworthy) with whom they had some financial dealings.[65] Of the three brothers, we know that Abū Zikrī was already married, whereas Raḍī who was a man of tempestuous and quarrelsome character, must have been somewhat younger. The youngest, Solomon, still had a teacher, a R. Peraḥyah, who is gently exhorted to teach the youngster and told that he will be adequately recompensed for this. Their father admonished the brothers not to quarrel and generally to behave themselves and protect the family name. The letter also contains the expression—'and Shalom and to all the *rabbanim*, let their peace be augmented'—the same title which as we have seen appeared a few years later in a letter dealing with a collection of money in Bilbais, and applied to the French immigrants who founded a congregation in the Holy City.[66]

The family was split up, and Abū Zikrī spent a brief time in Cairo,[67] and irregular periods in Jerusalem. Once he went there

[61] Goitein, *Palestinian Jewry*, 328, l. 12. The same man is called 'the magnificent *emir* (al-Amir al-Agal) Nūr al-Daula', 330, l. 12.

[62] Ibid. 330, l. 13.

[63] Ibid. 328, ll. 14–15.

[64] Ibid. 329 n. 40.

[65] Ibid. 330, l. 5; p. 331, ll. 14–16.

[66] See n. 22.

[67] This explains why he left his medicaments, the instruments of his trade and some cloth in Egypt and had to ask his father to send them to Jerusalem; ibid. 323.

with his wife, then again alone. As a court physician he must have been close to the ruling class of the city, even in the absence of his exalted Ayyūbid protectors. Court life or city life had their effect on him and Abū Zikrī took a Muslim lady as his mistress. This obviously caused some scandal in the Jewish community, and the news reached Cairo. It seems that his younger brother, Solomon, was sent by his father to Jerusalem to ascertain the facts and preach morals to the straying brother. Preaching or time had their effect, and the affair is not mentioned again.[68] Letters written shortly after his father's journey to Egypt,[69] in the autumn of 1195, tells us that he fell sick in Jerusalem and was afraid to spend the winter in the city as his benefactors the Ayyūbid princes al-Malik al-ʿAzīz and al-Malik al-Muʿaẓẓam laid siege to Damascus, then in the hands of al-Afḍal, another son of Saladin.[70] Despite his illness, which he says sometimes made him feel he was going to die, he still frequented the sultan's palace (*dār al-sulṭān*), to keep up relations.[71] Then tragedy struck the family: Raḍī, who had left Jerusalem and like many others settled in Acre, the great flourishing city of Crusader Palestine, suddenly died. Following the Jewish custom of Acre, he was buried in the cemetery near Mount Carmel.[72]

At this time the family—which seems to have been constantly on the move between Egypt and the Holy Land, and there between Jerusalem and Acre (the facility of movement between the Muslim and Christian cities is worth mentioning)—was widely dispersed. Abū Zikrī was with the court in Egypt, whereas his father and mother and a young sister were in the Holy Land,[73] and it was from there that the father

[68] Motzkin, 'Jewish Physician in Jerusalem', 344–6. On another case of promiscuous relations in Jerusalem, see above, n. 27.

[69] Ibid. 323, ll. 10–11. He probably refers to that when writing 'since the day you journeyed from here I did not have a healthy body even one day'. Obviously this could be an exaggeration, but it would rather point to a recent departure.

[70] As the city fell in July 1196, the letter must have been written in the autumn of 1195.

[71] Motzkin, 'Jewish Physician in Jerusalem', 324.

[72] Sick for three months in Acre, he ordered that he should be buried in Haifa (272, ll. 7–11). On the difference in 'sanctity' between Haifa (which was inside the boundaries of the land settled by those who returned from the Babylonian exile) and Acre (which was regarded as being outside these boundaries), see below, ch. 8 n. 3.

[73] Goitein, *Palestinian Jewry*, 275, l. 11.

announced the bad news to his son. Abū Zikrī's reaction is expressed in a strange letter,[74] where real grief and an attempt to console his father is mingled with a jarring note of self-importance when he lists the high court officials who came to console him.[75] Rather unexpectedly this court physician, so proud of his courtly acquaintances, adds in a rather incongruous way: 'and I say that anybody who changes his mind about living in Jerusalem will not see any good . . . and whoever leaves there brings calamity on himself and his children'. And in another phrase he expresses the wish that God should bring the whole family together again.[76] Some time later the other son, Solomon, who did not follow the family tradition of medicine but served as a teacher in Bilbais and elsewhere, echoed the same sentiment in a letter to his father: 'I pray to God that he gathers our family in Jerusalem and will not disperse us among the lands.[77]

The Jewish community restored in Jerusalem after 1187 was thus an extremely heterogeneous body, a melée of various congregations differing in customs, native language, and liturgy. It was in the nature of things that tensions arose, and al-Ḥarizi, who spent a month in the city, was very much aware of their intensity. Such a situation, as we shall see, characterized the Jewish community not only in Jerusalem but in the Holy Land as a whole during the thirteenth century. The basic tension, if not to say polarization, was that between Oriental Jewry and the relative newcomers from the West. Some of the Oriental Jews appear to have taken an aggressive posture. A generation after the immigration from France, the exilarch Hodaya b. Yesse 'called all those from France heretics, bent on gross anthropomorphism'. Abraham Maimuni, who at that time fought against the slanderers of his great father, stated explicitly: 'he cursed by name real orthodox people . . . and

[74] Goitein, *Palestinian Jewry*, 268 ff. When first published in 'Letters from Eretz Israel in the Crusader Period' (H), *Yerushalaim* ii–v (1945), 59 ff., the letter was assigned to another Jewish physician, Abū 'l-Barakā ibn al-Quḍāʿi. About the real identity of the writer and his family, see Goitein, *Palestinian Jewry*, 321 ff.

[75] Ibid. 270, l. 43. When the Muslim dignitaries came to console him he was with Ibn al-Yamani.

[76] Ibid. 272, ll. 16–17.

[77] Quoted by Goitein, ibid. 332 n. 51, from an unpublished letter (Camb. ULC. Or 1080 J 124).

moved irresponsibly and without compunction against you [i.e. against R. Joseph b. Gershom Ṣarfatī], as well as against all the people from France, because you are from France'.[78]

As we have seen, despite the fact that the original destination of the pilgrims was Jerusalem, not all immigrants succeeded in settling there. Some, after trying in vain to strike roots, left Jerusalem and moved on to the great Crusader commercial centre and capital of the Second Kingdom, Acre. Here they found themselves in Christian surroundings, more similar to their native Europe and speaking a familiar vernacular, French. Moreover, being at the crossroads of international commerce and with direct links with Europe, Acre was more prosperous than Jerusalem. Some of the immigrants, however, decided to leave the country entirely and move to Egypt, though they were not always easily integrated. A man like Anatoli b. Joseph of Lunel was appointed *dayyan* in Alexandria, then in Fusṭāṭ.[79] On the other hand, we find Jews bent on migrating to the Holy Land who did not make it further than Egypt; however, such immigrants preserved their ethnic identity for some time and kept up a correspondence with their relatives and friends in the Holy Land. The French Jews are thus to be found in the great Egyptian cities, in Alexandria and Fusṭāṭ, but also in the easternmost city of Bilbais where we have already found Ascalonites and Maghrebis.

The new Jewish community in Jerusalem, created amidst fervour and excitement, did not last even one generation. It is often argued that the circumstances of its disappearance were the result of economic difficulties. There is little doubt that it was hard to make a living in Jerusalem, but the total disappearance of the community and its three or four congregations was probably connected with other factors. The single and most important was the order issued in February 1219 by the ruler of Damascus and Jerusalem, the ʿAyyūbid prince al-Malik al-Muʿaẓẓam to demolish the walls of Jerusalem. This momentous decision was taken to prevent the Crusaders, at that time

[78] Mann, i. 175; ii. 371–3. *Responsa of Abraham Maimuni*, 15, 17. On R. Joseph b. Gershom see below, ch. 8, pp. 269 ff.

[79] J. Barslavi (below, n. 81) argued that the name appears in the list of people entitled to free lodging paid for by the community in that city. The argument, however, is not conclusive.

victorious in Damietta and directly menacing Cairo, from reconquering Jerusalem. The reaction of the terrified and outraged city population is recorded by Muslim chroniclers. The emirs of Banyās and Salkhad, we are told, who had to execute the order, were reluctant to do so, and it needed the personal appearance of al-Muʿaẓẓam to persuade them to demolish the fortifications. The work of destruction went on for more than three months (March–June 1219). An Oriental Christian source indicates that when the work was accomplished, only the citadel remained. The Muslim population, deprived of defences and in fear of a Crusader onslaught, evacuated the city,[80] and it is obvious that the Jewish populations would have left too. Clearly, if the Crusaders were ever to come back neither Muslim nor Jew would have much chance of survival. This fear, exacerbated by the destruction of the city walls explains why the community created by the immigration of the Jews after its capture by Saladin was so short-lived.

After the initial panic, however, when it became clear that the Crusaders were bogged down in the floods of the Nile and in any case were in no position to endanger the Holy City, some of those who had fled began to return. It is to this period, roughly between 1221 (the Crusaders' defeat in Egypt) and 1229 (the Crusaders' return to Jerusalem), that a number of letters emanating from Jerusalem should be assigned. The writer certainly belonged to the group of French immigrants. He signs his letters 'Yeḥiel b. Isaac of blessed memory, ha-Ṣarfati Yerūshalmi'.[81] The earliest surviving letter was written, probably to Egypt, very soon after his arrival in the Holy Land.[82] One of his teachers, it seems, was a personality of

[80] On the destruction of Jerusalem in 1219 and for other details see *Extrait de l'histoire des patriarches d'Alexandrie relatifs au siège de Damiette*, trans. E. Blochet, in *ROL* xi (1908), 251–2, and Oliverus, *Historia Damiatina: Die Schriften des Domscholasters*, ed. Hoogeweg (Tübingen 1894), 203. Another destruction wrought by the same al-Muʿaẓẓam in 1220 is recorded in *Hist. Damiatina*, 254. Cf. Prawer, *Histoire*, ii. 153, 164. Cf. details in Prawer, 'Notes on the History of the Jews in the Latin Kingdom', *Shalem* 2 (1976), 103–12. A shortened English version is in *Immanuel* 9 (1979), 81–6.

[81] Mann, i. 240–1; ii. 304; id. *Hebrew Union College Annual* 3 (1926), 299 ff. The signature quoted is ibid. 229. Additional material was published by J. Barslavi, 'Genizah Fragments Concerning Scholars from France and Germany in Eretz Israel and Egypt at the time of Maimonides and his Son' (H), *Eretz Israel* (1956), iv. 156.

[82] *Hebrew Union College Annual* 3 (1926), 299: 'We came safely to the holy city of Jerusalem, and peace be upon you . . . from Yeḥiel b. Isaac of blessed memory ha-Ṣarfatī Yerūshalmi.'

strong principles which brought him into conflict with the establishment of his time: there is a mention in one of the letters sent by Yeḥiel to Bilbais which reads: 'Joseph b. Gerson of blessed memory, the Ashkenazi his pupil R. Yeḥiel Ṣarfatī here in Jerusalem.'[83] This teacher of R. Yeḥiel, as well as his teacher's father, belonged to the group of immigrants who came from France in 1209 and after. Abraham Maimuni mentioned him among the French scholars who passed through Egypt and visited him: 'The old R. Abraham the father of R. Gershom of blessed memory and R. Joseph and R. David and other scholars.'[84] It is not clear whether the Joseph and David mentioned here were the sons of R. Gershon, but clearly the latter was the father of a Joseph who was the teacher of R. Yeḥiel Ṣarfatī.

Circa 1236, when Abraham Maimuni wrote *The Wars of the Lord*, R. Gershon was no longer alive; we do not even know if he participated in the immigration of 1209 or came later. On the other hand, we have some details about R. Joseph b. Gershon Ashkenazi, the teacher of R. Yeḥiel, although the chronological sequence is none too clear. As we find him in Egypt it may be that his migration to the Holy Land might not have been very successful, but it is possible that he went to Egypt before going to the Holy Land, or that he left the Holy Land for Egypt. At that time he was a well established scholar, and Abraham Maimuni addressed him in rather unusual terms of reverence: 'My lord the great scholar, the *dayyan*, the fortress and bastion.'[85] He served as *dayyan* in Alexandria, where he became involved in an acrimonious quarrel with the exilarch Hodaya b. Jesse who tried to arrogate to himself religious competences in the community of Alexandria. Joseph b. Gershon opposed him bitterly, pointing out that claims based on prerogatives of genealogy like Davidic descent were no longer valid; the autonomy of the scholars was based on their scholarly authority and the independence of their congregations rather than on historical tradition. This dispute over principles quickly turned into an inter-congregational quarrel when the

[83] Barslavi (above, n. 81), 158.

[84] See n. 46.

[85] *Responsa of Abraham Maimuni*, no. 17; ibid. 193, 196; and cf. Urbach, *Tosafists*, ii. 318–19 and n. 2.

exilarch Hodaya b. Jesse accused the European and Italian[86] scholars of gross anthropomorphism.[87] In the midst of the discussion Joseph left Egypt and settled in the Holy Land, and in 1233/4 we find him in Acre.[88]

R. Yeḥiel b. Isaac Ṣarfati, as we know was this scholar's pupil, possibly in Egypt, where R. Yeḥiel resided for some time. During his stay in Egypt R. Yeḥiel married, and we learn from one of his letters sent from Jerusalem, that he was related to the well-known R. Anatoli b. Joseph whose daughter was the sister-in-law of R. Yeḥiel.[89] Sometime after 1221 R. Yeḥiel was officially invited by one Ḥanīna b. Juda to come and settle in Jerusalem, to assure leadership for the Jewish community which was coming into being but which was divided by internal quarrels.[90] The invitation was couched in most flattering terms. The writer was requested (probably by the elders of the community) 'to ask him until he will consent to bend his steps to the Holy City of Jerusalem'.[91]

R. Yeḥiel's letters depict a very sad and difficult situation. Nothing remained, as far as we can see, of the three or four congregations described by al-Ḥarizi. The new community was poor and heavily dependent on Egyptian support.[92] A benefactor from Egypt, who seems to have also been a man of scholarly disposition,[93] donated money for the building of a ritual bath (*miqveh*), but there were internal squabbles. They do not need it, R. Yeḥiel wrote bitterly. There are no rains and the pools are empty and the gentiles do not allow the Jews to use the Siloam pool for ablutions. But 'I made for them a *miqveh* in my home and there is no other but that one.' Moreover, in this ritual bath his wife taught the other ladies the strict precepts of ritual immersion. He then suggested that the terms of the pious foundation (*heqdesh*) should be changed, and turned to other purposes.

[86] The text has 'Rōmī', which can also mean Byzantine, but in our context it is doubtful. The accusation was launched against European scholars.

[87] *Responsa of Abraham Maimuni*, 13–18.

[88] On the community of Acre, see ch. 8.

[89] Barslavi (above, n. 81), *Eretz Israel*, iv. 159.

[90] Mann, ii. 304, wrongly identified him with Yeḥiel b. Elyaqīm, *dayyan* of Aleppo. Cf. B. Dinur, *Israel in the Diaspora* (H), ii. 519 and 548 n. 77.

[91] Ibid. ii. 304, ll. 5–6.

[92] Ibid. ii. 304 n. 3.

[93] Yeḥiel calls him: 'my lord master the Rav', ibid., l. 7.

The poverty of the community exacerbated their relations. The pious foundation just mentioned gave rise to a quarrel between R. Yeḥiel and one Dayyan Solomon.[94] Fifty dirhams, we learn, were sent from Egypt to Solomon and one Isaac for the building of the *miqveh*. The letter confirming the donation was brought to the court but in the meantime the money had been misappropriated.[95] The result was that in protest R. Yeḥiel ceased his customary teaching and preaching on the Sabbath. He also abstained from rabbinical decisions. As he wrote: 'I sit and study at home and they remain without any study [*Torah*], without a priest and without a teacher.' Quarrels broke out in the synagogue despite the fact that an anathema threatened anybody who stirred up quarrels in the synagogue. At the bottom of all these scandals was this Solomon whom he calls 'Solomon of Mashreqah' (Gen. 36: 36—the successor of Hadad). This nickname may have had more literal meaning in this connection: *mashriq* in Arabic means 'Oriental', and Yeḥiel might have been referring to the inter-congregational tensions in the community. The quarrel went so far that it brought about the intervention of the Muslim authorities, who meted out corporal punishments. It is worth noting that though the community of Jerusalem was still of mixed European and Oriental origin, correspondence was in Hebrew and not in the usual Arabic, possibly because R. Yeḥiel did not know the language.

At this point our information about Jerusalem dwindles and then ceases.[96] A single document which might belong to this period, however, affords us a glimpse into the life of a community which is poor and disintegrating but still has its pride. The document deals with the case of a woman who appoints a representative to pursue her claim to inheritance; the authorization is not directed to a Jewish court in the city in the customary manner, but in general terms to 'the nobles of

[94] Mann in *Hebrew Union College Annual* 3 (1926), 299–300.

[95] One of the trustees argued: 'the money was eaten by the wife', ibid.

[96] It seems plausible that R. Yeḥiel was the correspondent of Abraham Maimuni's follower Judah b. Aaron. A fragment of a letter by Judah is extant (Mann, ii. 305, par. 4), in which he expresses his wish to see his friend. Judah b. Aaron al-ʿAmmāni was the man who described the immigrants from France rather pejoratively. See above, n. 51.

the community Yeshūrun, the splendid, the exalted, the revered community of Jerusalem, the holy city'.[97]

The last echo of this precarious life in a destroyed city comes from a letter almost contemporary with its loss to the Crusaders. In faraway Egypt, a former inhabitant of the city, one Joshua b. Solomon, required a formal statement from the former inhabitants of Jerusalem, that he was actually a Levi and that they saw him as such being called to the reading of the Torah.[98] The letter is preserved as a Hebrew draft, and the final Arabic form had to be taken by the claimiant to prove that he belonged to the Levites. The letter was written in April–May 1229—that is, following the dramatic signing of the peace treaty between al-Malik al-Kāmil, sultan of Egypt, and Emperor Frederick II (February 1229) by which Jerusalem (excluding the Temple Mount) was handed over to the Crusaders.[99]

We know about the violent reaction against al-Malik al-Kāmil in the Muslim world in general and in Jerusalem in particular. 'It was proclaimed in the city of Jerusalem; wrote the Muslim chronicler Baibars, 'that the Muslims have to leave the city and that it will be handed over to the Franks. The Muslims took to the road cursing al-Kāmil, full of sadness and bitterness for the loss of the Holy City.'[100] As we have seen, there can be little doubt that the Jews joined the exodus of their Muslim fellow citizens.

The Franks rebuilt some of the city's fortifications, but the Jews, who were allowed to live freely in all the other Crusader cities of the kingdom, were now excluded from Jerusalem. Pilgrimage to the Holy City was officially allowed, but in effect it was restricted because the prohibition on Jewish habitation meant there was nowhere a Jewish pilgrim could stay in the city.

[97] Goitein, *Palestinian Jewry*, 230 and n. 2.

[98] The reading of the Torah in the synagogue follows a hierarchic order of *kohen*, *levy*, and *israel*.

[99] Ibid. 336. Goitein's dating raises some questions. In the Hebrew text the witnesses state: 'when we were in Jerusalem', whereas in the Arabic form: 'when we were in ruined (*al-makhrūbah*) Jerusalem'. As the letter was written Apr.–May 1229 it obviously follows the handing over of Jerusalem to the Christians in Mar. 1229.

[100] J. Prawer, *Histoire*, ii. 198 ff.

A lonely fragment of a letter from that period bears witness to the new situation and to Jewish attempts to gain a foothold in the city. The story is told in a letter from an Egyptian Jew from Bilbais living in Tiberias to a relative who intended to go on pilgrimage to Jerusalem.[101] He reports that during a business trip to Jerusalem he met the *jāndār*—in all probability the viscount, that is, the civil governor of the city, at that time Gerald of Sais—and the lord (*al-ṣāḥib*) of the city, probably the castellan Baldwin of Picquigny, and they talked about 'the prohibition of entrance of the Jews into the city'. This resulted in an agreement to allow the Jews to go on pilgrimage (*al-zayāra*) to the city and to allow a Jewish dyer to settle there. This would have been of tremendous importance in that it would probably have facilitated Jewish pilgrimage to Jerusalem.

The peace treaty between al-Malik al-Kāmil and Frederick II lasted for some fifteen years. The Crusaders were then expelled from Jerusalem, and in 1240 the city was captured by the ruler of Transjordan. Soon restored to the Crusaders by the Egyptians, it remained in their hands for a short time, during which period (1244) they ruled even the Temple Mount, which until that time had been under Muslim domination.[102]

However, the situation in Jerusalem was precarious. The city was only partially inhabited, and its fortifications, but for the citadel, were in ruin. The inhabitants settled round the citadel and around some fortified places near the Damascus Gate and Zion Gate. The threat of a razzia, especially of the Muslim inhabitants from the Hebron mountains, was present. In case of attack the Crusaders had to alert their forces in Acre, two or three days' distance from Jerusalem, to come to their rescue. In the event, in 1244 the Khwarezmians captured Jerusalem and put an end to the Christian domination of the city.

During the fifteen years of Crusader domination of the Holy City (1229–1244) no Jewish community had developed, but in

[101] Goitein, *Palestinian Jewry*, 300 ff. Cf. B. Z. Kedar, 'The Jews in Jerusalem 1187–1267 and the Role of Naḥmanides in the Re-establishment of their Community', in *Jerusalem in the Middle Ages: Selected Papers*, ed. B. Z. Kedar and Z. Baras (Jerusalem 1979), 122–37.

[102] Prawer, *Histoire*, ii. 278, 308.

the generation which followed the expulsion of the Crusaders in 1244 a new community began to appear. Its origins, like those of the great community of Acre, were linked to a great revival of Jewish immigration to the Holy Land.

5

The Jewish Community: Organization, Legal and Social Position

THE major period of conquest came to an end around 1110 when the entire seaboard from Beirut to the desert frontier of Sinai, with the exception of Ascalon in the south and Tyre in the north, fell into Crusader hands. A new chapter now opened in the history of the country, a chapter which was to last some three generations until the disaster of Hattin (1187) put an end to the First Kingdom. It was during this period that the political regime and the social system were developed, and patterns of economy adapted to the new circumstances. In one way or another these patterns were to survive for a full century more, until the fall of the last Crusader establishments in the East in 1291.

Once the kingdom had reached a degree of stability, some time during the first quarter of the twelfth century, the Jewish communities sprang to life again. Some, as we have seen, had escaped destruction, while some were reconstructed when the turmoils of war abated and their former inhabitants returned: others again were newly created with the influx of immigration.

This new period was ushered in by a change in Crusader policy. As early as the capitulation of Beirut in May 1110, the leaders of the besieging host had tried to implement the capitulation agreement and to restrain their fighting men, especially from among the poorer classes. But they failed, and the Italian contingents sacked the city. This first attempt to preserve the population was followed by a similar one in Sidon (December 1110), and finally by the orderly capitulations of Tyre (1124) and Ascalon (1153).[1] In each case the city's

[1] Cf. J. Prawer, *Crusader Institutions* (Oxford 1980), 85–6.

population was spared and given the choice to leave or to stay on. The major part of the population, we are told by a Muslim chronicler, preferred to leave rather than live under Crusader domination.[2]

One of the results of this change in Crusader policy was that two major Jewish communities were saved from destruction: the communities of Ascalon and of Tyre. The former, which had played such an important role in redeeming the captives from Jerusalem in 1099 and was to function for another fifty years under Fāṭimid rule, seems to have undergone the change of ruler without major disasters;[3] the same is also true for the community at Tyre. Together with the Jewish communities in the rural areas, especially in Galilee, which were hardly the object of the conquest and consequently had not suffered during the fighting, they were to constitute the nucleus of the Jewish community under Crusader rule in the Holy Land.

There was very little in Crusader policy directed specifically towards the Jews. Like many a colonial power in more recent times, the Crusaders followed a general policy towards the whole of the conquered population. This large framework included Jews, *de jure* if perhaps not always *de facto*. Crusader laws directly affecting Jews are very few, and mostly relate at the same time to other religious 'minorities' even if the Jews are expressly mentioned. Only in one case, as far as we can see, does Crusader legislation relate to Jews and Muslims only. This is the law already mentioned which barred Jews and Muslims from settling and living in Jerusalem. Although the date of that law is not recorded it seems very likely that it belongs to the earliest phase of Crusader rule immediately follow-

[2] On the events in Sidon, see Ibn al-Athīr, *Kamel Altevarykh* (al-Tawārikh) AH 504, *RHC HOr.* i, pt. 2, 276. After the capitulation some of the population left; those who remained had to pay 20,000 dinars, a fine which impoverished them. On the events in Tyre, AH 518, ibid. 358–9. The population left with whatever they could carry, and only the sick remained in the city.

[3] When Ascalon capitulated in Aug. 1153 the Muslim inhabitants were allowed to leave for Egypt. This was probably what the inhabitants wanted, but one can also understand the Crusaders' interest in ridding a major frontier city of its Muslim population. The same interest did not necessarily hold for the Jewish population; and in fact, a short time after the Crusader conquest, we find proof of the existence of a Jewish community there. See above, ch. 3.

ing the capture of Jerusalem from the Muslims, possibly to the summer of 1099. And this law, let us remember, related to no other city but Jerusalem.

All other Crusader legislative acts listed the Jews with other minorities. It can be safely stated that the Jews, who in the previous period had been classified among the *dhimmis*, that is the protected population of the Muslim state, continued to enjoy a similar status under Crusader rule. In this legal position they found themselves now joined by the former ruling Muslims, now demoted in their turn by the conquest to the class of *dhimmis*. This was obviously the greatest social and legal change which came in the wake of the Crusader conquest. A new stratum of second-class citizens was created, which now included the numerical majority of the population, a new 'minority' in the sociological meaning of the expression. But what was in a sense in the nature of things took on a different character when the Oriental Christians did not fare very much better than their former rulers. As far as official law is concerned, it was the same legislation which affected the whole non-Latin population.[4] A detailed definition of its ethnic scope is given in a Crusader law, probably passed in 1192, immediately after the Crusader capture of Acre from Saladin. This law, an *assise*[5] as it is called in the legal Crusader vocabulary, fixed particular quarters, and consequently the use of particular markets in Acre, for the non-Frankish population. As distinct from the Franks, whether native Poulains (that is, Crusader children born in the Holy Land) or newly arrived Europeans, all the 'minorities' were relegated to the northern quarter of the city, Mount Musard.[6] This particular *assise*, was proclaimed a hundred years after the conquest of the Holy Land, but other laws, some promulgated very early, also refer to the whole non-Frankish population. Thus, one of the ancient laws which fixed the customs to be paid in the kingdom

[4] See J. Prawer, 'Social Classes in the Crusader States: The "Minorities"' in *A History of the Crusades*, v, ed. K. M. Setton, N. P. Zacour, and H. W. Hazard (Univ. of Wisconsin Press 1985), 59–117.

[5] *Livre des assises des bourgeois*, ed. H. Kausler (Stuttgart 1839), ch. 238, 282; ed. Beugnot, *Lois* ii (Paris 1843), ch. 243, p. 178.

[6] For a detailed analysis, see ch. 8, text and nn. 21–7.

spelt out in one breath 'and it has to be understood that this custom should be paid by Saracens and all kinds of Syrians who come with their merchandise on the land of the kingdom'.[7]

The uniformity of this system found its expression in the judicial procedure of the kingdom as well. The *wergild* of a non-Frank is half that of a Frank. From this rule derives the system of *amendes*, payments or fines to be paid to the offended party. This is already clearly expressed in one of the most ancient *assises*.[8] A knight who causes grave injury to another knight and avows it pays a 100 besants to the lord of the knight and 100 shillings to the claimant. But 'if the claimant is from another nation than that of the law of Rome', the lord receives 50 besants and the claimant only 50 shillings.[9] The legal distinction is here quite clear between those who are of the 'Law of Rome', that is, Latins, and all the others who are not. The Crusaders seem to have adopted very early such basic legal rules which referred to all non-Franks. Although the Jews were perhaps not originally envisaged, the evolution of these rules was finally applied to all non-Franks.

Crusader society as it developed in the beginning of the twelfth century was based on the social and legal distinction between nobles and non-nobles, called in the kingdom 'burgesses', an expression which corresponds roughly to the English 'commoners' more than that of burgesses in medieval usage.[10] This meant different jurisdictions and different codes of law *ratione personae*. The development of these jurisdictions is outside the scope of this study, but a parallel development, although based on different premisses relating to non-Latins, took place in the early days of the kingdom. According to an ancient and

[7] *Livre des assises*, ed. Kausler, ch. 237, p. 276: 'et ses dest on entendre que ceste droiture devent paier Sarasins et de manieres de Suriens qui vienent o marchandise en le terre dou reaume.' Ed. Beugnot, 174.

[8] This *assise* deals with what is termed *cop aparant*, i.e. open wound, which was probably promulgated by Baldwin III (1143–62). Cf. Prawer, *Crusader Institutions*, 465–8. A different dating is argued by J. Riley-Smith in *Crusader and Settlement*, ed. P. W. Edbury (Univ. Cardiff Press 1985), 176–81.

[9] Jean d'Ibelin, *Assises de la Haute Cour*, ch. 114, *Lois* i. 186–7: 'Et se le clamant est d'autre nassion que de la lei de Rome', etc.; and see below, n. 21.

[10] Cf. Prawer, *Crusader Institutions*, 250 ff. and index s.v. burgesses.

venerable tradition, the 'Syrians' (an expression which in this case means, in all probability, the Oriental Christians following the Greek rite, although it may also refer to the Jacobites) asked for and were granted judicial autonomy, that is, their own courts and the use of their own laws.[11]

The autonomy granted to the Oriental Christians, the Court of the Raīs, was no Crusader innovation. Such autonomy had existed earlier under Muslim rule, and once the Crusader conquest became more established, the Oriental Christians asked for and received, recognition of their own institutions. The same policy was pursued in relation to the Jews. They had their autonomous courts and community institutions under Muslim rule, and these continued under Crusader rule.[12] The whole realm of matrimony and its ramifications like divorce, alimony, family property, wills, and inheritance remained under the jurisdiction of the respective native clergies, and among them Jewish rabbinical courts which were recognized as competent and solely competent in such cases. Rabbinical courts under Crusader rule are specifically documented for Tyre and Acre[13] (but there were also contemporary rabbinical courts in Muslim-dominated Jerusalem and Safad), and it is almost inconceivable that there were Jewish communities of any size without a rabbinical court. (Obviously, very small settlements would depend on the rabbinical courts of larger settlements.)

It was a standing rule among the Jews never to have recourse to alien powers or jurisdictions. The notion *'arkaōth shel gōyim*,

[11] Jean d'Ibelin, *Assises de la Haute Cour*, ch. 4, and *Livre des assises des bourgeois*, ed. H. Kausler, ch. 236. Cf. J. Prawer, *The Latin Kingdom of Jerusalem*, 152 ff., and H. Mayer, 'Latins, Muslims and Greeks in the Latin Kingdom of Jerusalem', *History* 63 (1978), 175 ff., esp. 185.

[12] The scope and functioning of Jewish autonomous courts and jurisdiction are tellingly described in Goitein's classic 'Interfaith Relations, Communal Autonomy, and Government Control', in *Mediterranean Society*, ii. *The Community* (Univ. of California Press 1971), 311–411. For Christian autonomy in the particular case of Jerusalem, see J. Prawer, 'The Patriarch's Lordship in Jerusalem', *Crusader Institutions*, 296–315. Cf. A. Fattal, *Le Statut légal des non-Musulmans en pays d'Islam* (Beyrouth 1958), esp. 344–50.

[13] e.g., a Jewish court in Acre decided *c.*1170 as to the status of a woman whose husband had disappeared. There was a Christian witness to the fact that he was murdered. The matter was referred for an opinion to Maimonides in Egypt; see *Responsa of Maimonides*, ed. Freimann, par. 159. The *dayyanim* (members of the court) of Tyre corresponded with Maimonides, see above, ch. 3, text and n. 30.

that is, the jurisdictions or state power of the gentiles,[14] is psychologically related to *malshīnūth*, to informing and the treacherous informer, or invoking the gentiles (whether Muslims or Christians) to intervene or gain a foothold in Jewish affairs. Quarrels and litigations between the members of the same community had to be settled according to Jewish law, the *halakha*, consequently excluding any alien intervention.

A separate mechanism, however, applied for disputes with non-Jews. Thus when the Court of Raīs was merged with the Court of the Market (*Cour de la fonde*),[15] the situation changed somewhat. This particular court, which functioned, as its name suggests, in the market, was composed, as appropriate for the type of cases likely to come before it, of two Franks (certainly burgesses) and four Syrians,[16] presided over by a Frankish bailiff. The court was competent in civil suits (the *Livre des assises des bourgeois* specifies debts, lost or spoiled mortgages, renting of houses) to the amount of 1 mark of silver, whereas higher amounts and jurisdiction involving loss of life or limb were brought before the Court of Burgesses. Obviously, the Court of the Market was appropriate for mixed cases, that is, where plaintiff and defendant belonged to different communities. This was an attempt to apply, albeit not very rigorously, the rule of judgment by peers which was followed in the judicial structure of the kingdom.

How did the existence of the Court of the Market affect the legal position of the Jewish community? Clearly it did not infringe on its autonomy—an autonomy which had existed before the Crusader conquest—just as it did not interfere with the autonomy of the communities of the Oriental Christians. The Court of the Market was used only in mixed cases, that is, when an Oriental Christian, Muslim, or Jew was a claimant or

[14] *'Arkaōth* derives from the Greek *arché* or *archeion*. It was only in cases deemed to be of extreme necessity or in the most bitter disputes that Jews would invoke state or even ecclesiastical intervention. This happened, it seems, in Montpellier during the first anti-Maimonides dispute, *c.*1235, and possibly again *c.*1284. Nearer to the time under discussion the exilarch of Damascus, Jesse b. Hezekiah, called on 'the powers of the nations of the world' against Solomon Petit, see *Responsa of Maimonides*, ed. A. L. Lichtenberg, iii (Leipzig 1859), 22. An interesting case of a Jew pronounced delinquent by a Jewish court in Egypt (1134) in which the Jewish authorities invoked the state power to arrest him is reported in Goitein, *Mediterranean Society*, ii. 35 and n. 57.

[15] *Livres des assises des bourgeois* (above, n. 11), ch. 236.

[16] There is no indication as to the denomination of these Oriental Christians.

defendant against a member of another religious community. Obviously there was some disadvantage in the fact that the jurors were only Franks and Oriental Christians. This is one of the few instances in which Oriental Christians were more favourably treated than Muslims and Jews. Not only Jews, however, but the vast majority of the population, the Muslims, were not represented among the jurors of the court.

The procedure followed in the court was based on an attempt to assure some measure of equity. As the judgments relied on witnesses, and witnesses only, there was the general rule that the witness had to be of the community of the defendant. 'The reason [or law] commands thus that in all lawsuits in which one claims from another in the [Court of the] Market, it is necessary that he [the claimant] should have witnesses from the same religion to which the defendant belongs. It is the law that other witnesses will not be valid.'[17] If the claimant cannot produce the right witnesses then the defendant takes an oath that he is innocent on his holy Scriptures and thereby he is acquitted. Thus, 'the Jews should swear on the Torah of his religion (*la Tore de sa lei*)'. The lawyer who wrote the *Livre* is careful to indicate that the Samaritans will take an oath 'on the five books of Moses which they hold', whereas the Muslim takes an oath on the Qoran, the Armenian, Syrian (clearly now Jacobite), and the Greek take their oath on the Holy Cross and the Evangels 'written in their alphabet'.

This seemed to be such an equitable rule that the author of the *Livre des assises des bourgeois* broke into a short passage of self-praise: 'Because even if they are Syrians and Greeks, or Jews or Samaritans, or Nestorians or Saracens—they are men like the Franks'. This praiseworthy maxim is then spoilt by the addition: 'and they are obliged to pay and render that which shall be adjudicated, exactly as it is established in the Court of Burgesses'.[18] Despite the Jewish aversion to invoking official

[17] *Livre des assises des bourgeois* (above, n. 11), ch. 236: 'Bien coumande la raison que de toutes les autres leis don l un se clame de l autre en la fonde, si est mestier qu il ait garantie de cele meysme lei don celuy est de qui il se claime; car ce est dreis, que autres garanties ne li deivent valeir.'

[18] Ibid.: 'Car encore soient il Suriens et Grifons ou Judes, ou Samaritans, ou Nestourins, ou Sarasins, si sont il auci homes come les Frans, et sont tenus de paier et de paier et de rendre ce qui iugé leur sera, tout auci come est establi en la cort des borgeis.'

authorities in their internal affairs, an aversion common to all minorities, such events were not unknown. In such cases—that is in suits between Jews, or Syrians, or Muslims and the like between themselves—witnesses of any community were acceptable.[19]

The same rules of procedure are discussed in another chapter of the *Livre des assises des bourgeois*, which basically repeats the foregoing but also relates to another possibility, namely, that an agreement or transaction has been made in court between the two parties. Whereas in a litigation the claimant needed two witnesses of the same community, there was no such need in the latter case, presumably because the transaction in court was carried out before witnesses.[20]

It must have mattered very little to the minority communities that their testimony was not admissible in the *Haute Cour*, the royal High Court, as none of their members ever had any direct interest or business to transact in the High Court. This discrimination included all the 'people who are not obedient to Rome',[21] and it must have been of little meaning that they were legally classified together with perjurers, traitors, bastards, fornicators, or apostates. Their testimony, however, was acceptable in proving age or descent (genealogy). So also when a noble had dire need to prove that he was unable to attend a convocation of the court, he could call upon witnesses from the 'minorities', if Roman Catholics were not available.[22]

Thus the official legislation was a tolerable one and compares favourably with conditions in contemporary Europe. This, as has been said, was not the result of a particularly tolerant policy on the part of the Crusaders, but resulted from their following a rule later to be followed by all colonial powers, namely that of strict segregation on the one hand and of non-interference in the communal or religious matters of the subject population on the other.

[19] *Livres des assises des bourgeois*, *in fine*: 'n i deit aver devision es garens, ou soit qu il soient de lor lei ou d autre lei'.

[20] Ibid. ch. 63.

[21] Jean d'Ibelin, *Assises de la Haute Cour*, ch. 71; *Lois* i. 114. The quoted expression: 'genz de tel nassion qui ne sont obeissans a Rome'.

[22] Jean d'Ibelin, *Assises de la Haute Cour*, ch. 9; *Lois* i. 98–9.

The description of the strict legal position, however, does not tell us the reality of the social position of the Jews under Crusader rule. Obviously they were barred from holding fiefs, and it seems that they were also excluded from acquiring burgage tenures, basically city property,[23] as Crusader law excluded from such holdings 'persons outside the Catholic faith, idolaters, Jews and Saracens'. The reason given is that they cannot perform 'the usages, customs and assizes' followed in the procedure of acquisition. For different reasons, knights and noblemen, priests, and the Military Order were also barred.[24] As to the latter, their exclusion was usually stated in acts of transaction in this type of property carried out before the court. How far these rules were implemented is difficult to say. There is proof enough, for example, that Oriental Christians did possess city property such as houses and land. The same is true for Oriental Christian priests, who should have been disqualified on both ethnic and occupational grounds. It is therefore not entirely impossible that the Jews held city property, although the list of cases to be judged before the Court of the Market includes renting of city property but not its possession.[25] Still, this could simply imply that property transactions did not come before the Court of the Market.

A description of the position of the Jews beyond the legal status is not easy. One can assume that the Crusader rulers and nobles were not that interested in legal definitions as long as they were not needed for practical purposes. Thus, the legal position of the Jewish inhabitants of some dozen or so villages in Galilee is unknown. Were they regarded as *villani*, serfs of the lords of these villages, and therefore subject to the obligations of the inhabitants of the rural areas of the kingdom?[26] This might have depended not only on where they lived but

[23] Cf. Prawer, *Crusader Institutions*, 250–62.

[24] The quotations are from the *Abregé du Livre des Assises des Bourgeois*, ch. 24, *Lois* ii. 254–5, written in Cyprus, at the beginning of the 14th century but reflecting the situation in the Kingdom of Jerusalem.

[25] See above, p. 98 and n. 15.

[26] On the problem in general, see J. Prawer, 'Serfs, Slaves, and Bedouin', *Crusader Institutions*, 201–17.

also on their profession. Whatever the case, the Jewish inhabitants of the Crusader cities were hardly regarded as serfs. We see them engaged in urban or predominantly urban professions, which in practice precluded bondage.

Yet we find some curious cases, all of them in the northern principalities, where some non-Latins, including Jews, were treated as if they were serfs. Thus in 1175 a Syrian, Ben Mussar, is given by Bohemond III to the Order of St John in Jubail 'with his children and all their rights and possessions', and in Laodicea a Jew, Garinus, is alienated in the same way. Again in Laodicea, in 1183, Bohemond III gives the same Order 6 Greeks, 5 Armenians, and 7 Jews. The text of the last donation adds the following: 'All those men mentioned above, Latins as well as Greeks, and Armenians and Jews, will belong to the House of Hospitallers who will hold them and possess them in perpetuity, in peace, and without appeal, free and liberated from any *tallea*.'[27]

Beyond the legal framework which we have tried to describe, the most important feature influencing the position of the Jewish communities is the fact that the Jews, like all other minorities, were not directly dependent on the Crown. If such a situation was ever envisaged, thus continuing a European tradition which can be followed back to the Carolingian Empire, it did not leave any trace. Only the bedouin were regarded as the king's property, and he could and did on occasion transfer some of their tribes to one or another nobleman of the kingdom. One of the reasons for this situation was that the bedouin tribes did not live in one territory, but were found in different areas, very often on the frontiers of the kingdom, moving with their herds from place to place.[28] The non-Latins, however, including the Jews, were directly dependent on the territorial quasi-sovereign powers, that is, on the lords of lordships, city lords, and, with the growing tendency towards decentralization, on the lords of the autonomous city

[27] The cases quoted are from Delaville le Roulx, *Cartulaire de l'Ordre de St. Jean*, i (Paris 1894), 324, 436–7. A tentative explanation is given in Prawer, *Crusader Institutions*, 213.

[28] Cf. J. Prawer, 'Serfs, Slaves, and Bedouin', *Crusader Institutions*, 201–14, esp. 214.

quarters, whether the Italian and other maritime communities or the Military Orders.

The external mark of dependence was the particular tax of their class paid to the territorial power. With their Muslim and Oriental Christian fellow-citizens the Jews paid a *capitatio*, a descendant of the Muslim *jizya* (paid under Islam by all non-Muslims), to the overlord of the city. In places where the overlordship was divided between the king, the Frankish lord and the Italian communities, the Jews paid their *capitatio* and were under the jurisdiction of the respective powers. Such a situation is clearly the case for the Venetian lordship (the Venetian 'third', as it was legally termed in Tyre,[29] the Genoese part of the same city,[30] and for the royal and Venetian quarters of Acre respectively. In Acre the *ruga Judaeorum*[31] was located in the new suburb of Mount Musard, whereas the Venetian Quarter was in the Old City. A decree of the Maggior Consiglio of Venice of August 1271 revoked an earlier (not chronologically specified) decree which ordered the Jews under Venetian jurisdiction to concentrate in the Venetian Quarter.[32] The advantages, material and in prestige, of having people under a given jurisdiction concentrated in legally well defined areas are self-evident. The Jewish subjects of Venice, however, refused to comply, and the Venetian authorities gave in to their demand.[33] These Jewish Venetian subjects, it was plausibly argued, might have migrated to Acre from one of the Venetian colonies in the Aegean, or they might have been successful

[29] See ch. 8 n. 12.

[30] Prawer, *Crusader Institution*, p. 7.

[31] Ibid. n. 31.

[32] *Deliberazioni del Maggior Consiglio di Venezia*, ii. ed. R. Cessi (Bologna 1931), 352: 'De revocatione facta de consilio quod Iudei de Accon stare debeant intra rugam Veneciarum, in tantum quod stare debeant sicut prius.' D. Jacoby, 'L'expansion occidentale dans le Levant: les Vénitiens à Acre dans la seconde moitié du treizième siécle', *Journal of Medieval History* 3 (1977), 261 n. 110, argues, it seems, that 'sicut prius' should mean that they can stay on as before the decree. This is possible, but obviously it can also suggest that they lived in the quarter before. This is more plausible because we can assume that on being accepted as Venetian 'burgenses', that is, subjects of Venice, they originally settled in the Venetian Quarter. We do not know when the original decision was taken nor how long elapsed between the original decision and its revocation.

[33] D. Jacoby, ibid. 258 n. 39, argues that another decree in July 1272, which compelled 20 of the most important Venetians who lived in Acre to stay in the Venetian Quarter excepting knights and *iudices* (Cessi (above, n. 32) 354–5, par. 12), really refers to Jews, as the compendium *iud'* should mean *Iudei* and not *iudices*.

businessmen on whom the Venetian *baiulo* bestowed the status of Venetian subjects.[34] A curious Venetian document from the end of Crusader domination (29 September 1290) comes from Tyre. In this northern commercial centre the Venetians, as we know, owned their own autonomous quarter. A decision taken by the Maggior Consiglio regarding fraudulent commerce to avoid taxation specifically excludes the Jews from Tyre from the newly proclaimed decision.[35]

The situation of the Jews as it appears from the juridical treatises and scanty other information seems on the whole rather favourable under Crusader rule. Remarkably, the anti-Jewish legislation of the third Lateran Council of 1179 and of the Fourth Lateran Council of 1215 appear not to have been applied in the kingdom. The former decreed that Christian witnesses should be allowed to testify against Jewish defendants, but this was never followed and, as we have seen, ran contrary to the rules in the kingdom. The latter, which imposed the wearing of a degrading Jewish badge, is simply not mentioned in the legal or narrative sources of the kingdom.[36] This is all the more symptomatic, because dress regulations discriminating against 'minorities'—Christians, Jews, and Samaritans—had a long tradition in the Muslim east. Starting some time at the beginning of the eighth century, they were proclaimed and enforced time and again until by the end of

[34] This right was bestowed on the Venetian baiulo in Acre in 1256. Cessi, (above, n. 32), ii. 352. The right was conceived in general terms and did not specify any particular group (D. Jacoby, 245). There is no actual proof regarding Jews, but the mention in the Venetian documents in 1271, as compared with their absence in the report of Marsiglio Zorzi in 1244, would certainly indicate the appearance of Jewish Venetian subjects there.

[35] Cessi (above, n. 32), iii. 283: 'quod quicumque de cetero tansabit [*sic*] comerclum solvendo per nostros Judeos perdat medietatem haveris sic tanxati . . . et de solutione dicti comercli non intelliguntur Judei de Tyro.' Cf. E. Ashtor, 'Gli inizi delle communita ebraica a Venezia', *Rassegna mensile di Israel*, 49 (1978), 685, reprinted in his *The Jews and the Mediterranean Commerce* (Variorum: London 1973), no. 4.

[36] *Sacrorum Conciliorum Nova et Amplissima Collectio*, ed. J. D. Mansi, xxii. (Florence 1759; rep. Graz 1961), col. 231, and ibid. 1156. The only case which could be interpreted as a particular example of discrimination is to be deduced from a letter apparently written from Acre soon after its capture by the Crusaders in 1105 and before 1111. A Jew writes from Acre to Cairo: 'the uncircumcised do not allow us to slaughter'; see Goitein, *Palestinian Jewry*, 304, l. 39. As the letter is a complaint against a local adversary we are reluctant to accept it at its face value. The fact remains that no other document mentions such a prohibition during the Crusader period.

the thirteenth century they had become the general rule. Under these regulations (which were compounded by other degrading regulations, like the prohibition to ride horses or the obligation to wear humiliating signs, even in bathhouses), white and black dress were reserved for believers, while yellow, blue, and red were reserved for Jews, Christians, and Samaritans respectively.[37] It is therefore rather surprising that the Crusaders, who took over so much from the previous rulers in their relations with the native population, did not renew or enforce any discriminatory dress regulations. Things developed on different lines. In 1120 the Council of Nablus proclaimed a strong warning against Muslims attempting to wear Frankish dress. Whoever broke this prohibition would be at the mercy of the king.[38] Like many other prohibitions proclaimed on the same occasion, this clearly aimed at keeping the conquered population segregated from the conquering minority. Although the aim was not dissimilar from that of dress discrimination in Muslim countries, the legislation differed entirely. There were no humiliating badges or prescribed colours: the prohibition was against imitating Frankish dress. But the lack of discrimination in dress gives only part of the picture of the Jews' status: it is even more surprising to learn that in the last quarter of the thirteenth century Jews in Acre possessed Muslim slave-girls, and possibly sometimes even non-Muslim slaves.[39]

One also has the impression of security. This can be deduced from the freedom with which Benjamin of Tudela, Petaḥyah of Regensburg, and other Jewish pilgrims roamed the country. A letter was sent to Maimonides in Egypt from Crusader Tyre, asking whether or not one is allowed to teach a Christian the performance of religious precepts (*miṣvōth*). His *responsum*: 'Religious precepts and their rightful explanation may be taught to Christians, but not to Muslims', because 'if one explains to them [the Christians] the right meaning perhaps

[37] A. Fattal (above, n. 12), 96 ff. Cf. Goitein, *Mediterranean Society*, ii. 288.

[38] J. Mansi, *Concilia*, xxi, col. 261 ff. Cf. Prawer, *Latin Kingdom*, 519. Note also that the Franks abhorred the use of Muslim dress. Cf. Prawer, *Latin Kingdom*, 250.

[39] *Responsa of Rashba* (*R. Solomon b. Adret*), i. (rep. of Bnei-Braq, 1958), nos. 53, 68. The *Responsa* were sent from Spain to R. Elijah of Acre. It can be argued, however, that this was a purely academic question discussed in the school of Acre. The *responsum* is one of a group of 25 sent by Rashba to Acre.

they will return to Judaism',[40] suggests that it was not merely an academic question. We even have proof that a number of Muslims and Christians *were* converted to Judaism in the Crusader-dominated Holy Land[41]—proof not only of the vitality of the Jewish community but also of a social framework which made such events possible. An *assise* which dates back to the first half of the twelfth century, to King Baldwin III, based on the Provençal *Lo Codi* but ultimately going back to the famous *Novella* 115 of Justinian, enumerates as one of the reasons for permitting children to disinherit their parents the case of Christians going to Muslim lands to become Jews or Muslims (in Justinian, Jews or Samaritans). This is made even more significant by the fact that this 'reason' is not in *Lo Codi* or in any other related text.[42]

There can be little doubt that the Jews had freedom of religion and their own, probably inconspicuous, prayer-places. The appearance of *dayyanim* and heads of communities (*rosh qahal*), in the descriptions of Benjamin of Tudela, as well as the communal organization that we know to have existed in the first half of the thirteenth century in Acre, leave little doubt on this account.[43] Equally important as evidence are the numerous Tombs of the Just (*qivrei ṣadīqīm*) in the different itineraries. Many of them are domed structures, the very conspicuousness of this feature indicating a context of relative security. Elsewhere we hear about prayer-places or synagogues; some are mentioned in the Hebrew descriptions of the Holy Land,[44] and

[40] *Responsa of Maimonides*, ed. Freimann, no. 364.

[41] Cf. B. Z. Kedar in *Tarbiz* 53 (1984), 402–5. A famous *responsum* of Maimonides written after 1177 (ed. Freimann, no. 345, pp. 309–10) is clearly written to a converted Christian. Cf. ibid., p. xlvi.

[42] J. Prawer, 'Roman Law and Crusader Legislation: The *Assise* on Confiscation and Disinheritance', in *Crusader Institutions*, ch. 17. The relevant text is ibid. 449.

[43] I feel that my friend H. E. Mayer's view regarding the religious discrimination against Muslims is rather too harsh; see H. E. Mayer, 'Latins, Muslims, and Greeks in the Latin Kingdom of Jerusalem', *History* 63 (1978), 175–92, esp. 185–6. Mosques were confiscated in places in which there was a major concentration of Frankish population, that is in the major cities of the kingdom, but probably not elsewhere.

[44] e.g., *Tōṣōth Eretz Israel* mentions the synagogue in Tyre. On this source, see pp. 232 ff. A prayer-place in Acre is mentioned between 1104 and 1111 (Goitein, above, n. 36, at the end). A large number of prayer-places and *yeshivōt* (Academies) existed in Acre in the thirteenth cent. See ch. 8, passim.

they certainly existed in all major congregations. The generally favourable social framework is also proved by the migration to the Holy Land, to be discussed later, and by the growing number of Jewish pilgrimages.

Most remarkable, however, is the fact that at the time when every Crusade was accompanied in Europe by anti-Jewish pogroms—one can even postulate that anti-Jewish pogroms became a part of the Crusader rite—there was no anti-Jewish pogrom in the Levant in the two hundred years of Crusader domination. This can probably be explained by the difference between a mass movement (but only the first Crusade bore this character) and the situation in an ethnically and religiously heterogenous state with its own rules of conduct and behaviour. Whatever the reason, there is a marked difference between the Latin Kingdom and Europe at a time of anti-Jewish persecutions. Common everywhere on the local level in the twelfth century they became more severe in the thirteenth, thus ushering in the first great expulsions from England and France at the turn of the century. Nothing of this kind took place in the Latin Kingdom. In fact Jews settled in the Christian part of the country rather than in the Muslim-dominated interior not only because economic conditions made it imperative, but probably also because of the general conditions of security.[45]

Whatever the general situation, however, the Promised Land was certainly no earthly paradise for the Jewish community. Despite formal legislation there was a strong current of anti-Semitic feeling. The most important historian of the kingdom, the Jerusalem-born William, later archbishop of Tyre, strongly censured King Baldwin III, who like many other members of the Frankish nobility put his faith and health in the hands of an Oriental physician: 'For our Eastern princes, through the influence of their women, scorn the medicines and practice of our Latin physicians and believe only in the Jews, Samaritans, Syrians, and Saracens. Most recklessly they put themselves under the care of such practitioners and trust their

[45] Strauss's view, in *History of the Jews in Egypt and Syria* (H), ii (Jerusalem 1951), 31 ff., that the general situation of the Jews under Crusader rule was less favourable than under Islam cannot be substantiated.

lives to people who are ignorant of the science of medicine.'[46] It is enough to read what an enlightened Muslim emir like Usama ibn Munkidh had to say about Frankish medicine to understand the Frankish princes without invoking their womenfolk.[47] By the middle of the thirteenth century the author of the *Livre des assises des bourgeois* states that nobody has the right to exercise the profession of a physician unless he has passed an examination before the physician of the place and has been confirmed in his profession by the bishop of the city.[48] This could have had a detrimental influence on the exercise of the profession by the Jews, but one may doubt its implementation. A special degree was even issued by a church council held in Jaffa in 1251 prohibiting Christians from being treated or receiving medicaments from Saracens or Jews. This is against the canon law, argued the church prelates. Moreover, as Jews and Saracens do not have recourse to Christian physicians, it brings the Christian religion into disrepute.[49] This decreee had hardly any effect, and we find Jewish physicians in the twelfth as well as in the thirteenth century. Thus Petaḥyah of Regensburg met in Tiberias one R. Nehōrai the physician, who also sold herbs.[50] According to a Muslim physician, Maimonides was in all probability offered the position of a physician to Amalric, count of Jaffa–Ascalon;[51] and, in 1283 we find Samouel le Miege, the physician Samuel, heading the Jewish delegation which welcomed the king of Cyprus and Jerusalem in Tyre.[52] One may doubt if these people followed the rules

[46] W.T., l. xviii, ch. 34. R. Ch. Schwinges, *Kreuzzugsideologie und Toleranz. Studien zu Wilhelm von Tyrus* (Stuttgart 1927), 295–7, makes William of Tyre (or the Crusaders) far too tolerant in their relation to Oriental Christians and Jews.

[47] Usama ibn Munkidh, *Autobiography: An Arab-Syrian Gentleman of the Crusades*, trans. P. Hitti (New York 1929), 162–3.

[48] Ed. Beugnot, ch. 238, *Lois* ii. 169.

[49] *Sacrorum Concilorum Nova et Amplissima Collectio*, ed. J. D. Mansi, xxvi (Florence, 1784), cols. 328–9. This is probably the origin of a similar decision taken in Cyprus in the fifties of the 13th cent. Ibid., col. 314 CD. Cf. B. Z. Kedar in *Tarbiz* 53 (1984), 404. This prohibition was repeated in Europe time and again throughout the centuries but to no avail.

[50] L. Grünhut (ed.), *Die Rundreise des R. Petachjah aus Regensburg* (Jerusalem and Frankfurt 1905), 29.

[51] According to a Muslim source the Count of Ascalon (Amalric?) invited Maimonides to serve as his physician. Al-Qifṭī, *Tārikh al-Ḥakmā*, quoted by Dinur ii. 4, 330. Chwolson, *Literaturblatt d. Orients* (1846), 341. On the community of Tyre see ch. 8 below. Cf. Abū Zikrī the 'Ayyūbi physician, ch. 4, p. 82.

[52] *Les Gestes de Chiprois*, ed. G. Raynaud (Geneva 1887), 214, par. 419.

prescribed by Crusader law that a new physician had to pass an examination before the local physicians and then be confirmed by the bishop.[53]

It was not only the bishop of Tyre who found the employment of Jews as physicians unacceptable. An anonymous description of the Holy Land composed *circa* 1168–87, that is, contemporary with William of Tyre, contains a succinct summary of the author's attitude toward the Jews: 'They are obstinate, weak like women, everywhere slaves [or serfs], they are afflicted by menstruation, they follow the Old Testament according to the letter, and use the Hebrew alphabet.'

These pearls of acute observation were later on used by the fire-spitting bishop of Acre, James of Vitry:

> The Saracens, among whom they dwell hate and despise them more than the Christians; for whereas the abominable avarice of Christian princes tolerates them for the sake of worldly profit, allows them to hold Christian men in bondage, and suffers Christians to be plundered by them by their intolerable usury, among the Saracens they work with their own hands at the vilest and roughest trades, they are the serfs and slaves of the Infidels, and are only suffered to dwell among them in the lowest station of life. This condemned nation is scattered all over the world . . . being everywhere slaves and tributaries.

He continues to inform us that they are frightened and weak like women 'and they have a flux of blood every month'.[54]

This stereotype of the Jews was not born in the Crusader kingdom; it is clearly a part of the Christian European perception of the Jews. There is a repetition of European *loci communes* such as one finds in Peter the Venerable three generations earlier.[55] This, however, hardly corresponded to

[53] *Livre des assises des bourgeois*, ch. 238; *Lois*, ii. 169.

[54] 'Tractatus de locis et statu sancte terre ierosolymitane', ed. G. M. Thomas in *Sitzungsberichte der Bayerischen Akademie der Wissenschaften, philos.-philol. Classe* ii (Munich 1865) 144–60. The text was analysed and relevant items reprinted by B. Z. Kedar in *Tarbiz* 53 (1984), 390–4, 408. Jacobus de Vitriaco, *Hist. Iherosolymitana*, cap. 131 in Bongars, *Gesta Dei per Francos* i (Hanau 1611), 1096. Engl. trans. A. Stewart in *PPTS* v (London 1896), 87.

[55] James of Vitry goes on to describe the Jews as eternal exiles bearing the sign of Cain on their heads, not to be killed because they are witnesses of the truth of the Christian faith. Since the end of Antiquity this has been the stock in trade of anti-Jewish polemics. Cf. Y. Baer, 'Eretz Israel and the Diaspora in the Eyes of the Middle Ages' (H), *Meassef Zion* 6 (1924), 149–71.

the position or occupations of Jews in the neighbouring Muslim countries, and usury, though practised in the Holy Land, was by no means a Jewish monopoly—in the land of Italian banking and Templar establishments, this would have been very unlikely. The outburst of James of Vitry seems likely to be a part of his general hatred of the Jews (combined, to be sure, with the hatred of almost everybody else), and was similar to such other outbursts as an anti-Semitic poem composed at the time of the Third Crusade, perhaps in Jerusalem, calling on the Christian princes to expel the Jews from their kingdoms.[56] The fact still remains, however, that there is no record of anti-Jewish pogroms, let alone expulsion of Jews from the kingdom.

Yet despite fairly stable conditions and the fact that Jews settled in Christian-dominated parts of the country rather than in Muslim ones, Jewish sentiments were definitely pro-Muslim and anti-Crusader. Suffice it to quote a letter written at the end of the twelfth century in which a Jew heaps praise on the ʿAyyūbid rulers, or a Jewish apocalypse which predicted the victory of Saladin over the Christians. We have already noted the eulogy of Saladin as a latter-day Cyrus who called the Jews to settle in Jerusalem.[57] It is in the same vein that al-Ḥarizi, who visited Cairo after the failure of the Fifth Crusade, described the ʿAyyūbids in glowing terms in an Arabic *maqāmah* as 'the Kings of Islam who were assisted by Divine help, and given the victory by His infinite assistance . . . through whom all were saved'. He compares this miraculous event with the division of the Red Sea and the saving of the people. 'All that through the happy star of the kings of the son of ʿAyyūb, who appeared like suns of good fortune in the highest heaven, and through whom God protected religion and the world. May he lengthen their days in the shadow of happiness, give victory to their standards, and raise their feet above the necks of kings.'[58]

It was in the framework of the existing legal and social situation that the Jewish communities translated the basic rules

[56] *Anonymi de nova via novae civitatis*, ed. H. Hagenmayer, in *AOL* ii. 580 ff. Hagenmayer had some doubts where the poem was written, despite the line: 'huius urbis [Jerusalem] nos summus incole'—although this might have had a metaphorical meaning.

[57] See ch. 4, n. 6.

[58] S. M. Stern (above, ch. 4, n. 14) 194–5 and ibid. n. 15.

of autonomy granted by the Crusader authorities into a series of institutions whose main purpose was to safeguard the existence of their nation and traditional Jewish way of life. These institutions were partly local (that is, related to a specific community), and partly transcended the boundaries of local communities.

In the previous period, that is under Islamic rule, it was the 'Yeshiva of the Holy Land', that is, the Academy of Jerusalem with its head, the *gaon*, which exercised a decisive role in regulating the functioning of the local community. The heads of the local communities, the judges (*dayyanim*) and a large number of sundry officials, were appointed with the consent, as a rule, of the local community by the central organ. As we have seen, the title *ḥaber* (i.e. Associate or Fellow of the Academy) was bestowed on the man appointed by the *gaon* to the highest community office. The Jerusalem Academy also appointed its graduates to the Palestinian communities in Egypt after competing there with the great Academies of Babylon, Sura and Pumbedita. (Egypt traditionally belonged to the Jerusalem Gaonate.)

This system of self-government—which has recently been described as based on a dual principle, ecumenical and territorial—was already breaking down at the end of the eleventh century. The Academy of Jerusalem left the Holy City for Tyre, then moved to Damascus, and, in 1127, to Cairo.[59] The situation is clearly expressed by Maimonides in the last quarter of the twelfth century:

There are titles known in Eretz Israel and in the West [i.e. Egypt], such as calling some people 'Head of the Academy' (*rosh yeshiva*), and others 'President of the Court' (*ab beit dīn*) and they make a distinction between the 'Head of the Academy Gaon Ya'akov'[60] and the 'Heads of the Academy of the Diaspora' (*roshei yeshiva shel gōlah*) and this is addressed to people who were never seen as presiding over any Academy, sometimes they use other titles. All these, however, are vainglorious expressions, intended to flatter, and people strive for the titles and boast about their ancestries. And I myself saw in Eretz Israel, people titled 'ḥaberim' [i.e. Fellows of the Academy] and in

[59] Goitein, *Mediterranean Society*, ii. 12. The first Palestinian *gaon* in Egypt was Maṣlīaḥ b. Solomon Hakkohen (1127–39); ibid. 26.

[60] That is, the head of the Jerusalem Academy.

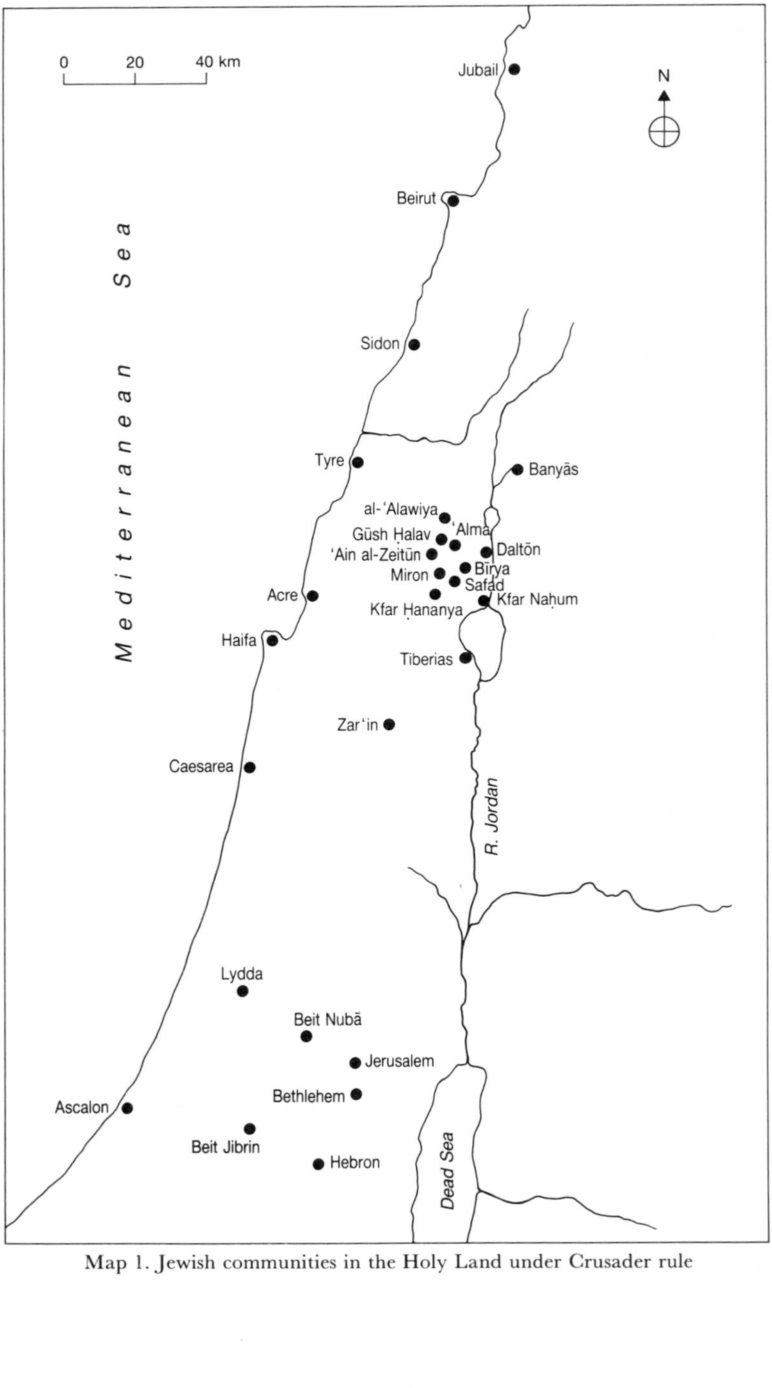

Map 1. Jewish communities in the Holy Land under Crusader rule

other places called 'Head of the Academy' (*rosh ha-yeshiva*) and they knew less than a student who had studied for only one day.[61]

During the whole period of Crusader domination we find no instance of the Egypt-based *gaon* intervening in the affairs of the Holy Land. Although it could be argued that this might reflect the state of our documentation rather than reality, it seems that such intervention did in fact cease in this period. However, from time to time we do see interventions of the exilarchs (*roshei gōlah*) in Palestinian affairs, for example by David b. Daniel of Mosul, Jesse b. Hezekyah (the *nasi* of Damascus), and Samuel Hakkohen b. David, head of the Academy of the Diaspora in Baghdad.[62] Their interventions, however, were brief, and can be explained in the context of the anti-Maimonides dispute rather than on an institutional basis.

On the other hand, Palestinian Jewry under Crusader rule remained in contact with the great scholars of the period, like Maimonides and Solomon b. Adret. In some cases the contacts were purely scholarly, in others it was a matter of seeking practical advice regarding religious law. In Palestine and elsewhere, the standing of the great scholars and their relations with local heads of communities, who were often scholars in their own right, defied legal definitions. Such relations exemplify the extraterritorial cohesion of the Jewish Diaspora based on the community of faith and religion. Great scholars accepted as the legitimate and authentic expounders of the religious law ruling Israel did not (barring exceptions) perform any communal function; or such functions as they did perform had nothing to do with their standing as a supra-territorial authority in the life of the nation.

A particular case is that of the *nagid*, an office which sprang up, in Egypt at least, in the last quarter of the eleventh century, as the highest authority of Egyptian Jewry and at the same time its official representative *vis-à-vis* the Fāṭimid authorities.[63] The *nagid* appears on our scene on two particular occasions. In the first it was Abraham, son of Maimonides in Fusṭāṭ, who

[61] Maimonides' Commentary on Tractate *Bekhoroth*, ch. 4, p. 5. On the confusion and proliferation of exaggerated titles, see Mann, ii. 312 and above p. 52.

[62] All of them intervened during the later dispute over the philosophical works of Maimonides. See ch. 8, pp. 285 ff.

[63] Goitein, *Mediterranean Society*, ii. 30 ff.

was asked for a basic decision regarding the competences of an exilarch. Following his decision, sent to Alexandria, the community of Acre promulgated its own statute opposing the exilarch's claims. The moving spirit behind this legislation was a French scholar, Joseph b. Gershom, appointed by the *nagid* Abraham Maimuni as a judge (*or beit-dīn*) in Alexandria, who later settled in Acre.[64] Technically speaking, the *nagid* did not intervene directly, but as the scholars of Acre stated: 'After we saw the statute (*taqanah*) and the consent (*haskamah*) . . . which was promulgated and decreed by the consent of the scholars of Egypt and the members of his Court [*yeshiva*] with R. Abraham b. Moses, we arrived at the conclusion that what they said was truthful, right, and correct . . . and therefore we also agreed to establish the same statute.'[65] It is therefore the example of the proceedings of the *nagid* and his Cairene court and not any formal competence they exercised in the kingdom of Jerusalem which was invoked in this case.

A different situation prevailed in the 1280s, during the anti-Maimonides dispute. The *nagid* David b. Abraham Maimuni, temporarily deprived of his office in Egypt, exiled himself to Acre where he could rely on the support of a part of the community. When the dispute broke out, accompanied by written declarations of scholars from Europe, mainly Germany, and mutual excommunications, the *nasi* of Damascus, Jesse b. Hezekyah, decreed that all anti-Maimonides letters and their like should be handed over to David b. Abraham. A thundering excommunication by the exilarch David b. Daniel stated that only David b. Abraham would be allowed to absolve from the excommunication.[66] Clearly, again, such proceedings spring not from the office of *nagid* (from which David b. Abraham was in any case temporarily deposed) but rather from the personal involvement of David as Maimonides' grandson.

In these circumstances it is rather unexpected to find two dignitaries styled '*nagid* of Eretz Israel and Yehūda'—the first, 'Obadya b. 'Ulah, in the last quarter of the twelfth century,

[64] *Responsa of Abraham Maimuni*, 15–16. Cf. ch. 8, text and n. 55.

[65] Ed. A. H. Freimann in *Aluma* 1 (1936), 31. (See below, ch. 8 n. 55.)

[66] On the excommunication of Jesse b. Hezekyah see *Kerem Hemed* 3, 169–72; on that of David b. Daniel see *Ginzei Nistarōt* 3 (1865), ed. J. Kabak, 117–24.

and Hillel b. Moses in the thirteenth. The former, whose Arabic name seems to have been al-Raīs Abū'l Ridha,[67] must have belonged to an important family as he could trace his genealogy for five generations, counting among his ancestors 'candidates' (that is students of the *yeshiva*) and members of the Egyptian court. The genealogy of Hillel b. Moses extends to ten generations.[68] It was suggested that the office of '*nagid* of Eretz Israel and Yehūda' was created after the conquests of Saladin. The office bore the Arabic title of *Raīs al-Yahūd bil-Shām*, the last geographical name comprising Syria and the Holy Land.[69]

Tempting as the theory might be, it needs more proof to substantiate it, and at the moment does not seem very plausible. The major Jewish communities in the Holy Land, excepting Jerusalem, were on the coast captured by Saladin (excepting Tyre) after the disaster of Hattin in 1187, but they did not remain under Saladin's domination for more than a very short period, and even this was the time of battles and sieges during the Third Crusade. By 1192—that, is five years later—the coast was again in Crusader hands, and Jerusalem fell in 1229. At that time Abraham Maimuni was *nagid* of Egyptian Jewry. It is thus not very plausible to assume that Saladin felt any special need to have a particular *nagid*, as distinct from that of Egypt, for the Holy Land, or even for Syria, which he partly dominated after 1174 with the death of his benefactor and later competitor Nūr al-Dīn.[70]

All in all, then, the Jewish communities in the Crusader kingdom, although they maintained contacts with bearers of

[67] Mann, i. 243, 257. The genealogy of 'Obadya was published by S. Schechter, *Saadyana: Geniza Fragments of Writings of Saadya Gaon and Others* (Cambridge 1903), 82 n. 4. For another version, see Mann, ii. 313, l. 3.

[68] Hillel b. Moses' genealogy of Abū'l-Najam family, publ. S. Poznanski, 'Deux listes commémoratives de la Geniza', *REJ* 66 (1913), 60–74.

[69] The text of appointment in Qalqashandi, publ. R. J. H. Gottheil in *JQR* 19 (1907), 534. 'Al-Shām' was the usual name for Syria and Palestine even in Hebrew sources. Cf. Mann, i. 257 n. 1. A Damascus-based *nagid* for Syria and Palestine is argued by E. Strauss (above, n. 45) 240–1. Sources for the existence of a vice-*nagid* in Jerusalem are from the end of the 14th cent. See J. Hacker in *Zion* 45 (1980), 127–8.

[70] Perhaps these titles, strange for that period, both taken from bits of genealogies, should be regarded only as honorific titles already denounced by Maimonides (above, n. 61). One wonders if they do not paraphrase the title of the famous and controversial David b. Daniel of the second half of the 11th cent.: *Nasi Eretz Israel ve-Yehūda*.

important titles in their immediate neighbourhood—and perhaps Syria and even Iraq—were in no way dependent on them. So far as we can see there was no Jewish central institution in the kingdom, either as an organ of autonomy or representation. In this respect the Jewish communities differed from the communities of the Oriental Christians where bishops and, in some cases, patriarchs, fulfilled such functions.

It was, therefore the local community, and the local community only, without any superstructure, which was the carrier of Jewish autonomy. Such a traditional territorial institution as the Jerusalem Academy was only a memory, and its twelfth-century namesakes in Egypt had no contact with, let alone influence on, the Jewish communities under Crusader rule.

We have also to bear in mind that the political structure of the Latin Kingdom did not encourage any central Jewish institutions. Unlike the previous period, the Jewish communities had no central government but depended on semi-autonomous feudal or communal lordships. There was no place for official representation of the kingdom's Jewry—relations and representation were on a local level.

The basic unit of autonomy was the local community, the *qahal*. Glimpses of its functioning emerge from the rather scanty documentation at our disposal. Benjamin of Tudela's itinerary, which we shall examine later, takes us from community to community and records the same type of organization everywhere. He does not explain this specifically but the fact is that for every community, after evaluating the number of Jewish families (or inhabitants), he uses the expression *ūvrōsham*—'headed by' or 'led by'—and gives the name of the leaders. So the 20 families in Antioch are headed by R. Mordecai, R. Ḥayyim, and R. Samuel; Latakiah (Laodicea), a community of 100 Jews, was headed by R. Ḥayyim and R. Joseph; Byblos with 200 Jews (elsewhere he indicates 150 Jews there) was headed by R. Meir, R. Jacob, and R. Simḥa; 50 Jews in Beirut were headed by R. Solomon, R. 'Obadya, and R. Joseph. In Sidon he mentions 20 Jews but no names of leaders. Acre had a community of some 200 Jews headed by R. Ṣadōq, R. Yefet, and R. Jonah. The leaders of Caesarea, with 200 Jews, are not mentioned; nor are the heads of the community in Ramle because a community of three Jewish families would not need leadership.[71] Ascalon, with 300 Rabbanite Jews, is headed by R. Ṣemaḥ, R. Aharon, and R. Solomon (there were also 40 Karaites and 300 Samaritans); the 50 Jews of Tiberias are headed by R. Abraham the Seer (*ha-Ḥōze*), R. Mukhtar, and R. Isaac. The leadership of ʿAlma in Galilee with 50 Jews is not mentioned. At the head of the community of Damascus, which numbered some 3,000 Jews (Petaḥyah of Regensburg some years later wrote 10,000), was R. ʿAzaryah (or ʿEzra), the 'head of the Academy of the Holy Land'. Little can be learned from Petaḥyah's itinerary, mutilated by unqualified copyists, except the bare facts of the existence of organized communities. After mentioning the *qehīla* of Tiberias, he adds: 'and in Eretz Israel also there are communities (*qehīlōth*), but they do not contain more than a hundred, or two or three hundred [members]'.[72]

Only in one place, in the great community of Tyre, a community of some 500 Jews, did Benjamin of Tudela note more details: 'and among them scholars of the Talmud and at their head R. Ephraim Miṣri the *dayyan* and R. Meir of Carcasonne and R. Abraham the head of the community (*rosh ha-qahal*).[73] Although we find here the distinct expressions of *dayyan* and *rosh ha-qahal*, it is probably an oversight that community officials are not mentioned in other places; Benjamin would clearly have taken their existence for granted, as being customary in any fully-fledged Jewish community. His description of Tyre, however, points to the emergence of a particular community problem: one of the *dayyanim* is from Egypt, another from Carcasonne. R. Ephraim, who came from Cairo and who, as we have suggested, had close relations with Maimonides,[74] might have received his licence from the court of Cairo, whereas R. Meir of Carcasonne was probably an alumnus of a rabbinical school in France. Moreover, it is also conceivable that in a large community like Tyre, and possibly in the two major cities of the kingdom, different

[71] One source indicates a Palestinian population of *c*.300, but actually there were only 3 families. The difference in numbers is the result of a different reading of an abbreviation. Cf. Benjamin of Tudela (Eng. trans.), 27 n. 4.

[72] *Voyages*, 51.

[73] *Benjamin of Tudela*, 18.

[74] On R. Ephraim of Tyre and his relations with Maimonides, see pp. 52–3.

congregations within the community had different leaders. We know that such a situation existed after the reconstruction of the Jewish community in Jerusalem following Saladin's conquest. Al-Ḥarizi found three congregations there around 1217, each of which he calls *qehīla*—these were the congregations of Ascalon, of France, and of Maghreb. One can almost certainly assume that there were different prayer-places to accommodate the different liturgies, as well as particular leaders brought over from their place of origin by the respective communities. A similar situation no doubt existed in Acre, at least after the middle of the thirteenth century. Whether they were based on origin and particular liturgies or on different schools of study, the Jewish community of Acre comprised a large number of congregations.

We wish we knew more about the functioning of these Palestinian communities under Crusader rule but the Genizah, so rich for Palestinian affairs to the last quarter of the eleventh century, dries up almost entirely. This is due not so much to the general impoverishment of the Palestinian communities during the next two hundred years of Jewish history, which can hardly be argued, but to a change in their demographic composition which brought them culturally closer to Europe than to the Levant. Still, we are not entirely in the dark. As we have seen, a Jewish court resided and functioned in Acre *circa* 1104–11 and again in the 1170s. Approximately at the same time, about 1177, a Palestinian community, probably of Tyre or Acre, used the dreaded weapon of excommunication to assure the observance of *ḥol ha-moʿed* (the intermediate days of Passover). The excommunication was to be proclaimed in the synagogue, which obviously made it a community affair. Maimonides, answering a Palestinian query, felt very strongly about it. 'Such things should not be done in Israel', writes Maimonides, 'and especially in a place which has a great scholar [i.e. like yourself] among the scholars of Israel.'[75] Another *responsum* which also might have been of more than academic interest points in the same direction. The query, which came from R. Ephraim, now residing in Tyre, dealt with the participation of

[75] *Responsa of Maimonides*, ed. Freimann, no. 72. The eulogy of his correspondent sharply contrasts with Maimonides' rather poor opinion of the state of scholarship in the Levant (see text above and n. 61).

scholars in paying taxes. To judge by the phrasing of the *responsum*, the question reflected an actual situation. The Talmudic rule exempted scholars from taxes, and actually forbade the community to impose taxes on scholars. Maimonides upheld the ancient custom and ruled accordingly.[76]

More details about community organization reach us from Acre in the 1230s. The events will be discussed in some detail below,[77] but in this context the important feature is the resistance of the autonomous community to interference from an outsider, a high-ranking notable. The *bnei qahal 'Acco* (sons of the community of Acre) reacted by promulgating their own statute (*taqanah*). Its operative parts prohibited any single person from excommunicating any other member of the community. This could only be carried out by 'three important members of the community (*shlōsha ḥashūvey ha-'edah*) in every city'.[78] This was quite a common procedure, though the number varied and we often find 'seven important men of the community', or even 'ten important men of the community'. Although not exceptional, the legislators used the expression *'edah*, whose connotation is the *'adath qedōshim*, that is, the holy community. If we read the text correctly, the proclaiming of an excommunication cannot be a general one, but must be done in each city individually (*bekhol 'ir va-'ir*). The inquiry is carried out by three notables, and the absolution can only be given by a scholar of standing imposing a fine on the delinquent. The fine, it is expressly stated, was not to profit the excommunicated but the needy or the synagogue. Here we have an excellent example of the community and its autonomous functioning. Yet, one should note that there is some obscurity as to the standing of the 'notables of the city' and the scholars. Obviously the former might have included scholars, although the expression seems to refer more to the lay members of the community.

We have already noted that a city could have more than one congregation, and as we have seen such was the case in Jerusalem after the re-establishment of the Jewish community

[76] Ibid. no. 105. Maimonides designates the demand as outright robbery (*gezel*).
[77] See ch. 8.
[78] Text publ. Freiman in *Aluma* 1 (Jerusalem 1936), 31.

there, following Saladin's conquest. A similar situation must have existed in Acre, at least after the middle of the thirteenth century. It seems likely that the school which continued the traditions of the French and Ashkenazi Tosafists, the schools which followed the early teachings of the Kabbalah, and those which followed the traditions of the rationalizing philosophy of Spain and Provence had particular congregations. There might have even been questions of a common language, and the different groups centred round their *yeshivot* and prayer-houses spoke French and Arabic among themselves. Their common language might have been Hebrew, as we know it was in fifteenth-century Jerusalem.[79]

This type of multi-congregational community seems to have been in the nature of things, but although we know of some schools like that of Solomon Petit (of whom more later) and the dissents which split the community on intellectual lines, we have little direct proof as to the situation on the organizational level.

A particular problem which arose in the thirteenth century was the validity of rabbinical titles or licences. The Palestinian Academy had left its native soil long ago and the links with neighbouring communities in Egypt or Syria were rather lax. Moreover, to judge by many indications, the Jewish communities in the thirteenth century were overwhelmingly of European origin. True, some of the scholars who migrated to the Holy Land went through Egypt and were licensed by the Cairo court. A good example is that of R. Gershom b. Joseph, who was appointed to the rabbinical court by Abraham Maimuni before settling in Acre.[80] But few others claimed such appointment (*minūy* or *smīkhūt*), owing their scholarly standing (and in many cases their rabbinical licences) to the schools of Europe. Thus, the two brothers mentioned earlier who came from Clisson in Brittany in the beginning of the thirteenth century, or the Tosafists who came with the wave of migration after

[79] Bernhard von Breydenbach, *Beschreibung der Rheyse*, 1483, repr. in H. Meissner-Röhricht, *Deutsche Pilgerreisen* (Berlin 1880), 163; cf. M. Ish-Shalom, *Christian Travels in the Holy Land* (H) (Tel-Aviv 1979²), 261; and *The Pilgrimage of Arnold von Harff* (1498–9), trans. from German by M. Letts (London 1946), 217–20; cf. Ish-Shalom, ibid. 272–5.

[80] R. Gershom mentions it in his letter to Abraham Maimuni, *Responsa of Abraham Maimuni*, 14–15.

1209, brought their scholarly qualifications from Europe. It seems very plausible that their descendants and later emigrants were educated in the schools they established in the Holy Land, like those of Naḥmanides in Jerusalem and later in Acre, or those of the 'Parisian Academy of Acre'. Thus the autonomy of the Jewish communities was, as it were, rounded off by their own schools and alumni.

Despite many lacunae a general picture of the position of the Jewish communities under Crusader rule emerges that is very often far more detailed and clear than it is possible to draw for the numerically far more important Oriental Christian or Muslim communities. It is more difficult, however, to draw a picture of their economic position and occupations.

At the end of the tenth century, the Jerusalem-born Muslim geographer al-Muqaddasi, describing *al-Shām*, wrote: 'The majority of the money changers and dyers, bankers, and tanners in this district are Jews and the majority of physicians and scribes—Christians.'[81] Be that as it may, very few of these occupations appear in the twelfth- and thirteenth-century documentation.

It remains a matter of conjecture what kinds of profession were pursued by the Jews who inhabited a dozen or so Galilean villages. Some, like the village of ʿAlma, had, according to Benjamin of Tudela, a substantial Jewish community, about fifty Jews;[82] as to other villages, we are told by a thirteenth-century traveller: 'and in all those places there are communities (*qehīlōth*) which count more than five minyanīm [that is, more than fifty adults].'[83] One is tempted to assume that in these village communities, Jews were engaged in agriculture. Though this seems plausible, there is no direct proof that this was really the case. Some of them could have pursued crafts, but bearing in mind the usually small size of Palestinian villages of the Crusader period it is difficult to imagine that all the Jews were craftsmen, or that they were middlemen. Some

[81] Ed. M. J. de Goeje (Leiden 1906), 183, ll. 6–8. The rather rich Genizah documentation of the period fails to substantiate this statement.

[82] *Benjamin of Tudela*, 45.

[83] The itinerary of R. Samuel b. R. Samson; see ch. 6.

rabbinical sources may be helpful in this connection. The *responsa* of Maimonides, however, are not easy to interpret, as when he is asked to rule on payment of tithes and the laws of *shevi'it* (the sabbatical year) 'from what is sown by the gentiles in Syria and in the Land of Israel'.[84] Neither are a number of other queries any more conclusive.[85] Still, the preoccupation with agriculture and the religious laws connected with it and incumbent on the inhabitants of the Holy Land, which would culminate at the beginning of the fourteenth century in *Kaftor va-Pheraḥ*,[86] lead us to assume the existence of Jewish agriculture. If the Galilean Jews were not only peasants living entirely off the land, then they were often at least partially engaged in agriculture.

The general impression one has of Jewish occupations would assign a fairly large place to craftsmen. Some of them, probably the lowest class, were wandering craftsmen. Thus describing the Druze population in the mountainous area east of Sidon, Benjamin of Tudela notes: 'there are no Jews among them, but craftsmen and dyers come among them for the sake of their trade and then return to their homes and they like the Jews'.[87] A similar impression is given by a *responsum* of Maimonides from almost the same time about a murdered Jew who used to peddle wares, probably produced by himself, in the villages near Acre.[88]

Among the Jewish craftsmen, a large number were dyers. This occupation had long been traditional among the Jews, with Jewish dyers known to have been active in the Byzantine Empire,[89] as well as in other parts of the Mediterranean such as Naples and Sicily.[90] Under the rule of Islam dyeing was an extremely important profession in view of the inhabitants'

[84] *Responsa of Maimonides*, ed. Freimann, no. 132. If the sowing were done by Jews, the tithes and *shevi'it* would be automatically obligatory in the Holy Land.

[85] Ibid. nos. 133, 135, 141.

[86] *Kaftor va-Pheraḥ* was written in 1320 in Betsan by a Spanish Jew who signed his name as *Ishtori ha-Parḥi*. Among other problems, he also tried to identify the biblical and Talmudic flora and fauna of the country, using Arab vocabulary.

[87] *Benjamin of Tudela*, 29.

[88] *Responsa of Maimonides*, ed. Freimann, no. 159

[89] G. Caro, *Sozial- und Wirtschaftsgeschichte der Juden*, i (Leipzig 1908), 254 ff.

[90] Ibid. 248–51, 489.

passion for colour.[91] The large number of people engaged in the profession was also the result of specialization, but nevertheless it seems that the profession was neither lucrative nor honourable. A calculation of expenses for dyeing a given quantity of cloth shows the payment of the dyer to be only one-quarter of the price of the pigments.[92] Moreover, Byzantine tradition made the dyers dependent on the state, which partly controlled the textile industry. On the other hand, let us remember that people with the *ongle bleu* had hardly any part in the city government in northern Europe. In the East we find no direct reference to their social position, but a fourth-century Hebrew text classified them definitively as belonging to a lower social class.[93] In the Latin Kingdom the dyeing trade seems to have been a seignorial monopoly, and the Jews engaged in it bought the right to exercise their trade from the king or lord of the place. For the city of Jerusalem, it is clearly stated by Benjamin of Tudela that four Jews who lived opposite the citadel and the royal palace 'were buying the dyeing installation (*beit ṣevi'a*) from the king'.[94] Some years later, Petaḥyah of Regensburg found only one Jew in Jerusalem, R. Abraham the dyer, 'and he pays a large tax (*mas*) to the king to leave him in the place'.[95] As late as 1235 when the plea of a Jewish merchant persuaded the Crusader authorities to allow a Jew to settle in Jerusalem and thus facilitate Jewish pilgrimages to the Holy City; the man's profession was that of a dyer.[96] Here again it is plausible to assume a seignorial monopoly of the trade. It is probably from the Latin Kingdom that the institution was transferred to Cyprus, where dyeing, though not a monopoly, was strictly supervised by the authorities.[97]

[91] Cf. the fascinating description in Goitein, *Mediterranean Society*, i. 105 ff.

[92] Goitein, *Mediterranean Society*, 107.

[93] *Midrash Tanḥūma*, Nasa 8: 'Let us be instructed whether a handicapped priest (*cohen*) is allowed to raise his hands [in the special blessing of the priests given on particular occasions during prayer]. So we were taught by our masters: *cohen* who has a deformity (*mūm*) in his hands should not raise his hands in blessing. R. Hōshaya taught: if the majority of the inhabitants of the city are engaged in such trade then he is allowed to raise his hands, so for example there are townships in the south where they are engaged in purple (*argaman*) dyeing and their hands are stained.'

[94] *Benjamin of Tudela*, 23.

[95] Ed. E. Grünhut, 32.

[96] S. D. Goitein, 'Genizah Sources from the Crusader period', *Outremer*, 320–1.

[97] *RHC*, *Lois* ii. Ordonnances, ch. 9. Obviously it could have been a remnant of a Byzantine control.

Another profession with which Jews were associated was that of glassmaker, especially of the famous glass of Tyre[98] which was exported to Europe. Glassmaking had a venerable ancestry in this area, and even its birthplace was attributed to the particular qualities of the sand in the neighbourhood of Acre. Jewish glassmaking was already widely known in Gaul in the seventh century, and by the beginning of the eleventh century (1011) Jewish glassmakers were exporting their wares in huge quantities from Tyre and Beirut.[99]

It is in the same city of Tyre that we find Jewish shipowners. 'And the Jews have there ships in the sea', wrote Benjamin of Tudela.[100] This is a unique testimony and may represent the declining remnant of an occupation which was quite common among Mediterranean communities until the twelfth century and even more in the marine commerce of the Indian Ocean.[101] One can assume that these Jewish vessels plied the coasts of the Levant, Egypt, and North Africa. The scope for employing the ships in European trade seems negligible. The mighty commercial fleets of the Italian and later also Provençal maritime cities with their monopolistic privileges made the life of any competitor, and a non-Christian to boot, impossible. Not even the Crusaders were able to build their own commercial fleets.

Little more can be learned from the documentation at our disposal regarding Jewish occupations, yet we shall certainly not err in assuming that the Jews took part in the commercial life of the great Crusader trading centres such as Tyre or Acre. Their origin and contacts in the European West and direct links with the Jewish communities in the Levant made them perfectly suited as intermediaries in the export, import, and transport business. Unfortunately, our information comes from outside; that is, we have indications of Jewish merchants from abroad dealing with merchants, no doubt Jews, in the kingdom, but information originating in the kingdom proper

[98] *Benjamin of Tudela*, 30. One of the versions (ed. A. Asher, 2 vols. London 1840–1, 30) does not mention the Jews and reads: 'And there are glassmakers of the good glass known as Tyrian which is famous [important] in all the lands.'

[99] Goitein, *Mediterranean Society*, i. 109–10 and nn. 64 ff.

[100] *Benjamin of Tudela*, 30.

[101] Goitein, *Mediterranean Society*, i. 311.

has yet to emerge. Thus, the famous archives of the Manduels and the notary Amalric lists a number of Marseillais Jewish merchants who traded with Acre.[102] Benaciat b. Bonfils Destour (de Turribus) receives a *commenda* of saffron from Guillaume Gros when travelling to Acre in the ship St Antony belonging to Bernard of Narbonne (6 April 1248); Bonnat b. Bonfils received from Pierre Viadier a *commenda*—a load of 'amenlons'—for Acre in the same ship (8 April 1248); Moses b. Astruc, who gives a *commenda* of 108⅔ besants to be carried by Pierre Gilles to Acre on the St Esprit (22 March 1248); Profact son of the deceased Moses makes a *commenda* of mixed merchandise worth £50 with Pierre Bellaygue bound for Acre (24 March 1248) and of 51 besants for Acre (30 March 1248); Saure Rimous, citizen of Marseilles, son of Davin Rimous, makes a *commenda* of almonds and spices for Sicily and Acre (28 March 1278); Vidal (or Vital) Negrel negotiates a *commenda* of mixed merchandise with R. Deners for Acre (19 March 1248).[103] There is one record of a Jew of Acre engaging in trade, one Moses of Acre, a citizen of Marseilles who was engaged in trade with Sicily.[104] Note that there was no distinguishing characteristic to the Jewish participation in commerce with Crusader states: the sums involved are quite modest and certainly smaller than similar investments by Christians.[105]

Scanty information also comes from other places in the Mediterranean. Thus a Jewish family from Barcelona, the Ascandranis, settled in Alexandria and continued their relations with Spain. Related to them was a member of a wealthy Jewish family, Isaac Cap, who spent a few years as banker in Acre. In 1280 he absconded from the city with money deposited with him by Jews and Christians, and a mighty coalition was set up to impound the merchandise of Aragonese Jews trading in the eastern Mediterranean, as reprisal. No lesser powers than the Orders of St John and the Templars, the consuls of Venice and Pisa, and the representatives

[102] I. Loeb, 'Les Négociants juifs à Marseille au milieu du XIIIᵉ siècle', *REJ* 14 (1888), 73–83. Cf. J. Pryor, *Business Contracts of Medieval Provence* (Toronto 1981), 86–8.

[103] L. Blancard, *Documents inédits sur le commerce de Marseille au moyen âge*, i (Marseilles 1884), ii (ibid. 1885): ii. 16, no. 388; ii. 27, no. 411; i. 317, no. 127; i. 322, no. 140 and i. 328, no. 277; ii. 415, no. 15; i. 289, no. 65.

[104] 23 Apr. 1248, ibid. ii. 105, no. 576.

[105] Loeb (above, n. 102), 81.

of the king of Cyprus participated in the reprisal. This forced King Pedro III of Aragon to intervene to save his Jewish subjects. Strangely enough, a few years later Isaac b. Samuel Cap was again among the leaders of the Jewish community in Barcelona.[106]

Genoa is probably a good example of the disappearance of 'Easterners' from a maritime trade now taken over by the local merchant class. Archetypal Oriental merchants like the Syrian Ribaldo di Sarephia and the Jew Blancardo appear now in association with new merchants like the famous della Volta and others, but theirs is a losing battle: in the period of the Crusades they are unable to compete with the Christian shipowners.[107]

The fact that Jews were, as far as we can see, little represented in maritime traffic does not mean that they did not take part in the commercial life of the maritime cities. As we know, their places of origin, knowledge of languages, and contacts with their co-religionists in the Levant made them most suited for the task. The Italian banking houses, however, played a major role in finances which included loans on interest. As is well known, there was no other trade where loans brought in as high a rate of interest as maritime commerce, a fact explained by the risks that commerce runs against the forces of nature and the piracy of man. Jews engaged in making loans are to be found in two cases only. In 1274 the Lady Agnes of Scandalion (a small lordship between Acre and Tyre—Iskanderūna) requested and received a loan of the rather large sum of 2,000 gold besants from a Jew, Elijah; six years later in 1280 it was her son Joscelin, the new lord of Scandalion, who received another loan of 1,700 besants from a number of Jews in association with bankers from Sienna. In

[106] Y. Baer, *A History of the Jews in Christian Spain*, i (Philadelphia 1966²), 210. The letters of Pedro III of July 1290 to the two orders and the consuls of Pisa and Venice and the lieutenant of the king of Cyprus are in J. Régné, *History of the Jews in Aragon: Regesta and Documents, 1213–1327* (Jerusalem 1978—reprint of studies published in *REJ*), no. 804. The king argues that Isaac Cap has not resided in the lands of Aragon for many years because of the threats of his debtors (!). In Dec. 1280, however, King Pedro III states that Isaac Cap is allowed to stay for 2 months in the land of Aragon, as he is now ready to make good his obligations to his overseas debtors (ibid. 857).

[107] See E. H. Byrne, 'Easterners in Genoa', *Journal of the American Oriental Society* 38 (1918), 176–87. Id., 'Genoese Trade with Syria in the XIIth Century', *American Historical Review*, 25 (1919–20), 198–9.

both cases it was the Teutonic Order which guaranteed the loans, with the lords of Scandalion pledging their landed property as security.[108]

Here our description must end. The information at our disposal on the economic position of the Jews is unfortunately too scanty to allow us to draw a more detailed overall picture of their occupations in the framework of their social position and communal organization.

[108] H. Prutz, 'Elf Deutschordensurkunden aus Venedig und Malta', *Altpreussische Monatsschrift* 20 (1883), 8–9, 393–4, 394–6. R. Röhricht, *Regesta Regni Hierosolimitani* (Innsbruck 1893), nos. 1398, 1435. The second deed speaks about the Order which tried to find the necessary money: 'a Iudeis et mercatoribus Senensibus sub gravibus usuris' (ibid. 395). The sum was 1,700 besants of Saracen gold and 460 besants and 8 caroubles.

6

Pilgrimage, Immigration, and Settlement

THE destruction and the restoration of the Jewish communities in the Holy Land followed the rhythm of Crusader warfare. The Crusader conquest, the Muslim attempts at a *reconquista*, the warring between the branches of the Ayyūbid dynasty and their Mameluk successors wrought havoc along the Syro-Palestinian coast—the urbanized part of the country, the area of Jewish communities. The inland cities, but for Jerusalem, suffered less, being seldom defended; and the same was true of the villages in the rural areas. Time and again the destroyed communities rose from the ruins, but it seems that their restoration was only partially due to survivors. It was mainly the result of an influx of newcomers, some from less devastated areas of the Holy Land, the majority pilgrims and immigrants who came from abroad braving dangerous roads and stormy seas—dangers ever compounded for the Jews by the latent enmity of their surroundings.

For generation after generation, pilgrims came to the Land of Israel. Some, relatively few, remained; others returned to their native lands. Economic motives played only a secondary role in the migrations; nor can the long list of persecutions or expulsions in Europe, the Near East, and North Africa account for the movement. The Holy Land was seldom, if ever, a haven of peace and tranquility, and it could offer migrants little or no improvement in their economic position or status in life. These pilgrimages, which in the thirteenth century turned into a movement of immigration and settlement must be explained by an entirely different set of premisses. The Holy Land—Eretz Israel (in the Hebrew sources the expressions are interchangeable) was always present in the minds of medieval

Jewry. For the overwhelming majority it was an object of faith, an aim never to be attained at the present time. The repetition of the name of Zion in daily prayers became routinized and with time lost its messianic tension, retaining instead a message of a better morrow in an undefined future. There were, however, individuals, groups, and trends which nurtured a different perspective: the Holy Land obviously loomed large for some circles of visionaries, and it played an important role in every messianic speculation and upheaval, which in Judaism as in the more popular trends of Christianity were not only spiritually but also physically linked to the Holy Land. Thus, outbursts of messianic activism kept alive and sharpened the perception of the Holy Land. So did great events, which seemed to decide the destiny of the Land of Israel. Such periods, however, intensive as they sometimes were (for example, at the beginning of the twelfth century), were only one of the causes of Jewish pilgrimage to the Holy Land.

The pilgrimage to Jerusalem as a religious commandment fell into abeyance some time after the destruction of the Temple; although some pilgrims may have had a feeling of fulfilling a religious duty, this was not theologically warranted. And the concept of pilgrimage as atonement for sin was seldom practised before the end of the Middle Ages, and when it was the atonement was linked more to the fact of voluntary exile from home and family than to the physical or geographical goals of the pilgrimage.

Judaism never knew indulgence and the cult of Holy Places as these developed in Christianity. The Land of Israel is holy; it is the Holy Land; Jerusalem is holy and so is the Temple Mount, which even in ruin remained imbued with its ancient sanctity and thereby restricted the right of the Faithful, unable to preserve purity, to enter its holy precincts. The cult of Holy Places as it developed in Christendom as early as the fourth century, reaching its peak as a ritualistic by-product of Crusader piety and European greed for relics, was unknown in Judaism until relatively very modern times and even then was held (and is still held) in suspicion and even contempt by some orthodox Jews. Despite the lack of such basic premisses, however, medieval Judaism was not lacking in miracles wrought in Holy Places or Holy Tombs. Tales of miraculous events, heavenly interventions to prevent or punish sacrilege, edifying events which extolled the effectiveness of Jewish prayers to prevent climatic disaster, or to prove the superiority of Judaism over other religions, fill the pages of the Hebrew itineraries.[1] This contrasts quite strongly with the lack of any cult of relics in Judaism; though some of the Christian pilgrims' enthusiasm rubbed off on the Jews, this particular aspect never played an important role in Jewish life. The only place in which medieval Judaism approached the Christian cult of Holy Places was in the Tombs of the Patriarchs in Hebron. The tradition was an old one, and a legend in the Talmud has it that Caleb b. Jephunneh, one of the twelve spies sent out to explore the Holy Land, prostrated himself on the Tombs of the Patriarchs. The prayer at the burial place of the Patriarchs was probably intended to implore the Forefathers for intercession.[2] Even Maimonides went on a pilgrimage and prayed at the Tombs of the Patriarchs. As far as we know, there was no particular ritual to be performed on such an occasion. The reaction was spontaneous. The pilgrim prostrated himself on the Tomb or nearby and prayed for God's help and mercy.[3] The Hebron tradition was strengthened in memory and practice by the creation of one of the oldest Muslim pious foundations (*waqf*).

Just as the devotional acts practised at the Tombs of the

[1] See e.g. the miracle at the Tomb of David, where a storm drove out Christian diggers, *Benjamin of Tudela*, 39. A similar miracle in Hebron is recounted by Jacob b. Nathanel Hakkohen, ed. E. H. Grünhut, 11. A wind or storm preventing gentiles from sacrilege recurs constantly in Jewish itineraries. For many other instances, see ch. 7, *passim*.

[2] Tractate *Sotah* 34*b*, Engl. trans. I. Epstein (London 1936), 169. The concept of intercession as well as merits of the Forefathers (*zekhūt avōth*) from which descendants could benefit were hardly accepted. Talmudic Sages argued that these merits came to an end at the time of the ancient kings of Judah (Tractate *Shabbath* 55*a*). Tractate *Sanhedrin* 104*a* has: 'a son imputes merit to a father, whereas a father does not impute merit to a son'. *Ta'anith* 16*a*, however, mentions a controversy regarding the custom of visiting cemeteries. One of the parties argues that 'the departed will intercede for mercy on behalf of the living'—a statement which was denounced in many quarters. Cf. below, n. 12.

[3] None the less a prayer from the Fāṭimid period seems to refer to a liturgy written in Zippori (Sepphoris) 'the burial place of our holy Rabbi [the exilarch Judah]'. It included prayers, possibly connected with mourning, on the hallowed tomb of the great codifier of the Mishnah (early 3rd cent.). Mann, ii. 357.

Patriarchs were rather exceptional, so was the custom that developed of burying the dead or rather their bones near or sometimes inside the complex of buildings that comprise the Tombs of the Patriarchs.[4] Strangely enough, a place which seemed almost predestined to play such a role—namely, the Tomb of Rachel—does not figure prominently in the medieval inventory of the Holy Places.[5] Pilgrims passing by would inscribe their name on the tombstone, but it does not seem that a more particular value was attached to the place.[6]

The only sites which enjoyed a particular status were the Mount of Olives and the area around the Temple Mount, including sections of walls and specific gates. The major and almost unique goal of pilgrimages to the Holy Land was always Jerusalem. For the tenth and eleventh centuries, when the

[4] *Benjamin of Tudela*, 41, mentions barrels full of bones of the deceased, but adds that this was done 'in the time of Israel', and that the bones are still there. However, an early 12th-cent. commentary by Solomon b. ha-Yatōm to Tractate *Mashqin* (*Mō'ed qatan*), ed. H. P. Chayes (Berlin 1909), 17 and n. 3, mentions the burial of bones in Hebron as a contemporary custom. Despite dangers the practice continued under Crusader rule and was sanctioned by Maimonides, who regarded it as a meritorious act to bring the bones of parents to the Holy Land for burial if they expressed such a wish during their lifetime (*Responsa of Maimonides*, ed. Blau, no. 116).

[5] As the Mother of the Nation, Rachel is seen as mourning over the fate of her children. Her burial place is indicated in the Bible as Efrat, that is Bethlehem (Gen. 35: 16, 35: 19), but also as Zelzah (correctly, Ṣelṣaḥ) (1 Sam. 10: 2), on the border between the tribe of Judah and the tribe of Benjamin. It was the former tradition which was transmitted to the Christians and became dominant. Naḥmanides, who finished his Commentary on the Bible in Jerusalem (*c.*1267), commenting on Gen. 35: 15 and explaining the noun *kibrath* (AV 'a little way') as denoting a distance, adds: 'And now that I was found worthy and came to Jerusalem, praised by the good and benevolent God, I saw myself that between the burial place of Rachel and Bethlehem there is not even a mile . . . and I saw clearly that her burial place is not in Ramah [ref. to Jer. 31: 15] and not even near it, as the Ramah of Benjamin is a distance of four parasangs (*parsa*), and the Ramah in the mountain of Efraim is a distance of two days'—therefore Ramah is not a place[-name] but is used in a poetic way, meaning that her [Rachel's] voice carried far away. Jacob did not bury her in Bethlehem, which, he foresaw would belong in the future to the tribe of Judah, but he buried her on the border of the tribe of her son Benjamin 'and the road on which is the monument (*maṣevah*) is near Bethel on the border of Benjamin'. The last statement is not correct, as Bethel is quite a distance to the north of Jerusalem. The author of *Kaftor va-Peraḥ* confronted by the monument of the Tomb of Rachel (in its present location) and the contradictory literary sources ends by saying: 'and God knows the hidden truth' (p. 251). The Jewish exegesis which attempted to bring Efrat to the tribe of Benjamin was explained by Rachel being his mother. This is reflected in Eusebius, *Onomasticon*, who places Efrat in the tribe of Benjamin, whereas St Jerome insisted that the place is in the tribe in Judah.

Genizah fragments throw light on the history of the Jewish Near East, there is a considerable body of documents regarding pilgrims coming to Jerusalem from as far west as Spain and as far east as Russia. And there is no reason to see this as an innovation. The pilgrim is often called *ḥōgeg*, the celebrant, a Hebrew expression related to the Aramaic and akin to the Arabic *ḥajjī*, for one who goes on a *hajj* to the sanctuaries of Islam. Some of the testimonies reflect the difficulties of a pilgrimage not only in terms of danger but even simple communication. We know of a Jewish pilgrim from Russia or another Slavonic land who reaches Salonika and asks for a letter of introduction to the Jewish communities on his road to the Holy City, as 'he does not know the holy language [i.e. Hebrew], neither does he know Greek, or Arabic but only the language of Canaan'. The latter refers in medieval Hebrew to the Slavonic languages, as slaves, 'sclavi' were linked with the 'Canaanite slaves' of the Bible (Gen. 9: 26).

The main season of pilgrimages was the 'month of holidays', that is Tishri (September–October), with the concentration of New Year, Yom Kippur, and the Feast of Tabernacles. It is on this occasion that Jews from the Holy Land as well as from the Diaspora flocked to the Holy City. The name Jerusalem is often replaced by *beth ha-miqdash*, literally the Temple, which gave rise to the Arab name of Jerusalem as *al-Quds* or *al-Muqaddas*.[7] The celebrations are comprehensively described in a letter written from Jerusalem to Egypt in the middle of the eleventh century. 'There is no other consolation', the writer complains, 'but by making the round of the gates to bow and pray for mercy and forgiveness to return to Jerusalem in mercy and purify the Temple . . . and this is always our prayer in the synagogue [lit. little Temple], as well as on the Mount of Olives when our brethren, the children of Israel, come together in the month of Tishri to Jerusalem.' A special liturgy or ritual developed on this occasion. A piece of land was bought on the top of the mountain 'where the Divine Presence rested,

[7] So e.g. in a letter from the beginning of the 11th cent. Mann, ii. 91. Cf. *Sefer ha-Yishūv*, ii. 39 nn. 10, 17; 40 n. 22. Cf. S. D. Goitein, 'The Arabic Names of Jerusalem' (H), *Minḥah le-Yehuda: Festschrift for Y. L. Zlotnik* (Jerusalem 1950), 62–5.

(according to a midrash, after leaving the destroyed Temple),'[8] and prayers were performed here during the festival season 'facing the Temple of God on the seventh day of Tabernacles (*hoshana rabbah*) and all of Israel are blessed there, every city and city [or 'country and country'], its communities, its notables, its benefactors and all who remember Jerusalem'.[9]

Another contemporary letter mentions those pilgrims who came to the Holy City 'to take pleasure in her stones and favour the dust thereof [Ps. 102: 14] . . . and make the round of the gates of the temple and to pray there raising their voice in the blessing of God and to ascend the Mount of Olives chanting songs and to stay there in the days of feast facing the Temple of God'.[10]

There is little doubt that the prayer on the majestic summit of the Mount of Olives facing the Temple esplanade lifted the spirits of the congregation. Clearly there was some underlying feeling without any particular theological justification, as to the greater efficiency of these prayers. The view of the Holy City dominated by strangers and enemies was conducive to prayer for its liberation and restoration, and for the redemption of Israel. After the destruction of the Temple a particular ritual developed. The pilgrim beholding Jerusalem and the Temple Mount for the first time performed the mourners' rite, rending his garments and pronouncing particular prayers.[11] But in the strictly religious sense, as distinct from the profound spiritual impact of the experience, such pilgrimage did not have specially meritorious value.[12]

[8] The basic texts connected with the sanctity of the Mount of Olives, so important in all apocalyptic writings, are those of Zech. 14: 4: 'His feet shall stand in that day upon the Mount of Olives, which is before Jerusalem in the East' and Ezek. 11: 23: 'And the glory of the Lord went up from the midst of the city and stood upon the mountain which is on the east of the city.' Tractate *Rosh ha-Shanah* 31*a* (Engl. trans. M. Simon, London 1938); cf. *Lamentations Rabba*, poem 25) describes the 10 stages (journeys) by which the Divine Presence left the Holy of Holies after the destruction of the Temple. They end: 'and from the city [the Divine Presence moved] to the mountain [interpreted as the Mount of Olives] and from the mountain to the wilderness and from the wilderness it ascended and abode in its own place'.

[9] Mann, ii. 189.

[10] Ibid. ii. 186.

[11] Tractate *Mō'ed Qatan* 26*a*.

[12] The recurrent verses connected with pilgrimages are Ps. 102: 14–15: 'Thou shalt rise and have mercy upon Zion: for the time to favour her, yea, the set time, is come. For thy servants take pleasure in her stones and favour the dust thereof.' As late as the beginning of the 14th cent., when visiting of Holy Tombs had already become customary, an ardent supporter of such practices (*Kaftor va-Pheraḥ*, 298) could induce a

The strictly religious motivation found its expression in another set of values. The whole complex of religious precepts linked directly to the Holy Land and its particular holiness were not and could not be practised outside Israel. The Talmudic tractates dealing with them were ardently studied in the Diaspora, but their accomplishment was possible only in the Land of Israel. Those who sought for religious perfection thus had to move from the Diaspora and settled in the Holy Land. This obviously motivated only an élite of religious perfectionists.

It is thus quite difficult, and perhaps even impossible, to find a dominant, let alone a single motivation for pilgrims and pilgrimage to the Holy Land. What can be argued is that some motives seem to have been stronger than others. Chief among them is the consciousness of national and religious links and a sense of belonging coupled with a feeling of returning to the Homeland which seems to be present in all these pilgrimages and certainly in acts of migration and attempts at settlement. Though not always practised there was always the feeling that undertaking a pilgrimage to the Land of Israel, let alone yearning 'to go up to the mountain of the Lord' (Isa. 2: 3), was part of one's spiritual heritage. Thus the wandering minstrel of Jewish medieval poetry, the Spaniard al-Ḥarizi, wrote in a *maqāmah*:

> When I took up my theme, and said:
> When I to Zion from Spanish exile went
> My soul from depths to heaven made ascent
> Greatly rejoicing that day God's hill to see
> The day for which I longed since I had come to be.[13]

No Jew could ever feel a stranger in the Land of Israel, not only because of the knowledge that one had a claim,

rather moderate appreciation of the custom: 'It is therefore suitable (*raūi*) to frequent and visit these holy places *even* in our time, as it is doubtless that they guard forever something of their erstwhile sanctity and the same is true of the Tombs of the Just (*ṣiyūnei ha-ṣadīqīm*), as we were taught in the beginning of the Tractate *Ta'anith* 16*a* (trans. J. Rabinowitz): 'Why do they go to the cemetery [on Days of Fast]? With regard to this there is a difference of opinion between R. Levy b. Hama and R. Hanina. One says [to signify thereby]: "We are as the dead before Thee"; and the other says: "In order that the dead should intercede for mercy on our behalf".'

[13] Judah al-Ḥarizi, *The Taḥkemoni: The Twenty-Eighth Gate*, Engl. trans. V. E. Reichert, ii (Jerusalem 1973), 144.

so to speak, on Providence to make good its promise of old, but because the geo-historical vocabulary of the biblical and Talmudic period, was ever-present in the toponymy of the country—Arabic names hardly disguised their Hebrew origins.[14] But above all, the native or quasi-native Jewish population kept alive the ancient traditions. In theory the Jewish pilgrim had far more to visit than his Christian or Muslim contemporary. The former, who at least until the end of the fourth century was following sites and paths of the Old Testament far more numerous than those of the New, was later consciously nourished almost exclusively (but not entirely) on the New Testament. In addition to the numerous biblical sites, the Jewish pilgrim could also have visited places connected with Talmudic sages; the latter entered the ranks of sanctity not as a hierarchy of saints but as holy men, the Just Ones.[15]

This type of emotional reasoning, where biblical, Talmudic, and Midrashic teachings mingled with historical reality, is not particular to the Crusader period: in a sense, though with varying degrees of intensity it is a constant in the Jewish perception of the Holy Land. This is even more so when we deal with immigration and settlement as a particular aspect of pilgrimage.

Pilgrimages in the three monotheistic religions were ultimately founded on the Bible and on Jewish traditions,[16] but in Islam and to a lesser degree in Christendom we hear of scholars and men of piety who not only went on pilgrimages but also decided to settle in Jerusalem. In the tenth century the Arab Muqaddasi and in the eleventh century the Persian Nasir-i-

[14] The first Hebrew scholar of the historical geography of the Holy Land, the author of *Kaftor va-Pheraḥ*, 282, made the following remark 1322: 'May I let you know that the name of the townships and rivers which are in the Holy Scriptures, in the written and oral [i.e. the Talmud], their names did change very little among the Ismaelites.'

[15] Compare, however, the Introduction to ch. 7.

[16] On the Jewish practice and tradition, which was transmitted to Christianity, see S. Safrai, *Pilgrimage at the Time of the Second Temple* (H), (Tel-Aviv 1965). On Christian reluctance and opposition to pilgrimage see J. Prawer, 'Jerusalem in the Christian and Jewish Perspective in the Early Middle Ages', *Gli ebrei nell'alto medioevo* (Spoleto 1980), 761, 772 and *passim*. Cf. G. Constable, 'Monarchisme et pèlerinage au Moyen Âge', *Revue historique* 1971, 3–27. Id., 'Opposition to Pilgrimage in the Middle Ages', *Studia Gratiana* 19 (1976), 123–46. On the opposition within Islam, see M. J. Kister, ' "Thou Shall Only Set Out for Three Mosques": A Study of an Early Tradition', *Le Museon* 82 (1969), 173–96.

Khusrau commented upon the importance of those pious and scholarly men in Jerusalem's population.[17] This seems to have been common among the Karaite sect but less frequent in rabbinical Judaism. Unexpectedly, however, in the thirteenth century, the immigration and settlement of Jewish scholars in the Holy Land did begin to loom large in the history of Jewish immigration.

What characterized Jewish pilgrimage was certainly more linked to individual religious experiences or expectations than to the ritual of an institutionalized religion. Religiously motivated Muslims and Christians had by the fourteenth century a large number of shrines and places in many lands, and pilgrimage to these places was regarded as a meritorious act of piety. For the Jewish pilgrim, until the pietist movement of the eighteenth century there was no other place on earth: There was the Holy Land and Jerusalem only.[18]

Although not a precept—a *miṣvah*, or positive religious obligation—the act of pilgrimage remained a spiritual accomplishment to which one aspired. The collective historical memories eternalized in the Bible, the Talmud, and Midrashim—all permanent objects of synagogal recital or study—kept alive names, sites, and places of a long-gone past, idealized and glorified by countless generations. Sayings regarding the virtues of the Holy Land, accumulated during half a millennium, created images and perpetuated concepts which endured for centuries.[19] These virtues were not only its beauty and its glorified blessings of crops and fruits, but first and foremost its intrinsic sanctity bestowed on it by God, a sanctity inalienable and never abrogated. (There was, therefore, no greater sin than acts of misbehaviour in the Holy Land classified as infringements on that sanctity.)[20] Whatever was uttered and

[17] Mukaddasi, *Description of the Province of Syria*, trans. G. Le Strange, in *PPTS* iii. 35: 'in Jerusalem are all manner of learned men and doctors'; Nasir-i-Khusrau, *Diary of Journey through Syria and Palestine*, trans. G. Le Strange, in *PPTS* iv. 25: 'For this reason men from all parts of the world come hither to make their sojourn in the Holy City till death overtakes them.'

[18] See Judah Halevy's poem, below, pp. 143–4.

[19] Cf. J. Goldenbaum-Zahavi, *Midrashei Eretz Israel*, i (Jerusalem 1959). A more critical study is that by Yeḥiel M. Hacohen Guttman. *Eretz Israel ba-Midrash ve-Talmud* (Breslau 1929).

[20] Strongly phrased e.g. by Naḥmanides, *Commentary on Leviticus* xviii. 25; Engl. trans. and notes Ch. B. Chavel (New York 1974), 268–75. Cf. below nn. 83 ff.

recorded in the voluminous literary treasure of the nation acquired with time an absolute value. Migration from or abandoning of the Holy Land was regarded in Talmudic lore as sacrilege: he who leaves the Holy Land is likened to one who prays to pagan gods.[21] Those who leave the Holy Land will be punished by God:[22]

A man should always live in the Land of Israel, even in a city whose population is in its majority pagan, and let him not live abroad (*ḥūtz la-aretz*) even in a city whose majority of population is Jewish. Because whoever lives in the land of Israel is like the man who has a God, and whoever lives abroad is like a man who has no God, because it is written: 'to give you the land of Canaan and to be your God' [Lev. 25: 39]. Does this really mean that whoever lives abroad has no God [1 Sam. 26: 19]?[23]

Many of these utterances were recorded after the destruction of the Temple, when an important Diaspora already existed in Alexandria and in Babylon. Obviously medieval Jewry did not live according to these expressions of attachment to the Land of Israel, but neither did it forget them. The Holy Land as a source of inspiration, extolled and glorified yet never losing its earthly reality, helped to overcome the hardships, cruelty, and difficulties of living under the precarious protection of the Cross or the Crescent.

The great change which took place in the pattern of Jewish pilgrimage in the wake of the Crusades found its expression on different levels. It seems that the flood of Christian pilgrims in some way influenced the Jewish practice of pilgrimages. One should not exclude the possibility that Christian pilgrimages to holy shrines influenced the Jewish visits and prayers at the Holy Tombs of their own tradition. So also the Christian literary by-product of pilgrimages, the *itineraria*, probably influenced the emergence and propagation of similar Hebrew treatises.

[21] *The Fathers According to Rabbi Nathan* (*Avōth de-Rabbi Nathan*), Engl. trans. J. Goldin (New Haven 1955), ch. 26, 111. *Tosefta 'Abodah Zarah*, trans. J. Neusner (New York 1981), ch. 4: 3, par. D, 325. Tractate *Kethuboth* 110*b*, trans. I. Epstein (London 1936); ibid. 111*a*. R. El'azar argued that a man who lives in the Holy Land 'lives without sin', but he was contradicted by Rabina.

[22] *Midrash Tanḥuma*, ed. S. Buber (New York 1941), 107.

[23] Tractate *Kethubōth* 110*b*.

On the material level, the opening of the Mediterranean to European fleets and the continuing traffic with the Levant made Jewish pilgrimages more feasible and influenced their ethnic composition. Before the Crusades, pilgrimages emanated to a large extent from neighbouring Oriental Jewish communities: North Africa, but more frequently Egypt, Syria, Iraq, and Byzantium, were the largest sources of pilgrims. Pilgrims from Europe, although not unknown, were certainly a minority. With the Crusades, the picture changed; in addition to Jews from the Orient, we now witness Jewish pilgrims from Christian Europe travelling by sea to the Holy Land. In the thirteenth century, as we shall see, this movement changed from a movement of pilgrimage to that of settlement as it also changed the ethnic composition of the Jewish community in the Holy Land and its cultural outlook.

In the twelfth century, however, Jewish pilgrimages started out on different premisses. A group of people who settled in the Holy Land represented a particular trend in Jewish life in the Middle Ages, namely, asceticism. Long before the emergence in the twelfth century of the Ḥasīdei Ashkenaz, we hear about a movement called 'The Mourners of Zion'—(*Aveilei Ẓion*, Isa. 61: 3) for which asceticism was not only a way of life but had messianic connotations. The movement could claim a long history, or rather a long list of antecedents, because ascetic groups called *Perūshīm* (not to be confused with the homonymous Perūshīm or Pharisees of the Second Temple) who abstained from eating meat and drinking wine, came into being after the destruction of the Second Temple. Such groups existed in the early Middle Ages in Italy, Germany, Yemen, and the Holy Land. In all probability these spontaneous groups, though they lacked any formal organization, followed the same rules or patterns of behaviour, and they were found among Rabbanites and Karaites alike. The Karaite community of Jerusalem in the ninth century actually stated clearly that they had settled there to mourn the destruction of the Temple and to pray for the salvation of Israel.[24]

[24] Cf. H. H. Ben-Sasson, 'The Karaite Community of Jerusalem in the Tenth–Eleventh Centuries' (H), *Shalem* 2 (1976), 1–19.

Benjamin of Tudela described one of the four (Rabbanite) Jews whom he found in Jerusalem as belonging to *Aveilei Zion*.[25] If we go by the designation Benjamin bestowed upon them, the man belonged to a very closed circle of *Perūshīm*, which originated around the middle of the twelfth century in Southern France and represented an early trend in the development of the Kabbalah based on late Neoplatonic speculations but was not in any sense a heretic movement. They lived as recluses, devoting their time entirely and exclusively 'without interruption' to the study of the Torah, elucidating the inner meaning of the text as it transpired from an exegesis based on the conjunction of the letters of the Scriptures and their numerical values. This enabled the believer to address his prayers to the respective heavenly powers ruling the world, and ultimately hasten the descent of the Kingdom of Heaven.[26] This religious mood could move people to pilgrimage and eventually to settle in the Holy Land. Still, one has to bear in mind that in this basically spiritual attitude, the actual, physical place of prayer might have played only a minor role.

To this group belonged R. Abraham al-Constantīnī mentioned above, a member of a Spanish family from Constantine in North Africa, whom Benjamin of Tudela had met in Jerusalem *circa* 1170. R. Abraham had been in Jerusalem since at least 1146 as he told Benjamin the story of the miracle of Mount Zion which can probably be assigned to that year.[27] Petaḥyah of Ratisbon met him there some time later, *circa* 1170–80.[28] There are also other witnesses to his life in Jerusalem. A member of the same esoteric group, a relative of R. Abraham by the name of Joshiah,[29] went on a pilgrimage to the Holy Land and stayed with R. Abraham, who showed him

[25] *Benjamin of Tudela*, 39–40: 'R. Abraham ha-Ḥasīd al-Constantīnī ha-Parūsh, who was one of the Mourners of Jerusalem.' He is probably the same as R. Abraham the dyer, whom Petaḥyah of Ratisbon met in Jerusalem a few years later (*Voyages*, 53).

[26] G. Scholem, *The Beginning of the Kabbala* (H) (Jerusalem 1948), 86–7; G. Scholem, *Ursprung und Anfänge der Kabbala* (Berlin 1962), 201 ff., argued that there is no connection between these *perūshīm* or *ḥasīdim* and the *aveilei zion*, but both terms appear in the description of R. Abraham (n. 25). Perhaps it should be assumed that *aveilei zion* refers here to a way of life and not to a pietistic group.

[27] Benjamin relates the miraculous discovery of the royal Tombs ('Tomb of David') on Mount Zion, in all probability in 1146. Prawer, *The Jews*, 49; cf. below pp. 200–1.

[28] Cf. n. 25.

[29] Such esoteric teachings were often cultivated in family groups.

a Kabbalistic commentary on the *'Alenū* ('It is our duty to praise', a prayer which concludes all synagogue services), which was also in the possession of such a group in France.[30] Another member of the group, R. Jacob of Lunel, known as R. Jacob ha-Ḥasīd,[31] journeyed to Jerusalem and met yet another member of the group, R. Nahōrai the Jerusalemite.[32] The date is not clear but it seems plausible to assign it to the same period.[33] Such esoteric circles of ascetics were obviously very small and they kept in contact with each other through their writings and travellers.

This type of pilgrimage and settlement was confined, then, to a restricted group of ascetics. Other pilgrims with different motivations also settled in the Holy Land, together creating in the population a rich mosaic of origins. They will be discussed in the appropriate chronological sequence and historical setting; here we shall confine ourselves to an analysis of the acts of pilgrimage and their more salient characteristics and motivations.

In the twelfth century, in addition to those pilgrims who left famous itineraries, like Benjamin of Tudela and Petaḥya of Regensburg, or the authors of similar but less-known literary productions (like Jacob b. Nathanel and the anonymous authors of the *Tombs of the Ancestors*, to be discussed in the next chapter), we find some but not many famous names. Of special

[30] G. Scholem, *Beginning*, 86 n. 1; id., *Ursprung*, 203 n. 55.

[31] On R. Jacob of Lunel ha-Ḥasīd (the Pious), see G. Scholem, 'From Philosopher to Kabbalist: A Legend of the Kabbalists on Maimonides' (H), *Tarbiz* 6/3 (1935), 95–6.

[32] G. Scholem, *Catalogus Codicum hebraicorum I: Cabbala* (Jerusalem 1930), 202 n. 7. This is told by R. 'Azriel of Gerona; see *Commentarius in Aggadot auctore R. Azriel Geronensi*, ed. J. Tishbi (Jerusalem 1945), 46. He is called here *ish yerūshalaim*—the Jerusalemite—a term often applied not only to those who lived in Jerusalem but to those who had been on a pilgrimage there or lived in the Holy Land. Petaḥyah met one Nehōrai who followed ascetic customs in Tiberias: 'And R. Nehōrai is a physician and sells herbs in the market, and his son sits before him in the shop and they cover their heads so as not to look right or left. And he is a sage and a pious man.' This R. Nehōrai claimed descent from the great exilarch Judah ha-Nasi, the codifier of the Mishnah in the beginning of the 3rd cent.

[33] Scholem suggested that the pilgrimage took place after 1187 because of the Crusader prohibition which barred Jews from living in Jerusalem. But, as we have already seen, some families lived there by royal privilege, and in any case the prohibition did not prevent pilgrimages. Postponing the pilgrimage to the year of Maimonides' death (1204), which was the basis for a tendentious legend that at the end of his life Maimonides was interested in the Kabbalah, seems less plausible because the above R. Jacob of Lunel wrote a supplement to Rashi's commentary on Job as early as 1163. Cf. Bodl. 142 (Uri 112), Neubauer, no. 295, col. 59.

interest is the Spanish poet Abraham ibn 'Ezra, who spent a good part of his life travelling. He went on a pilgrimage to the Holy Land *circa* 1161 and devoted one of his poems to describing the dangers of the journey by sea.[34] He actually dedicated one of his poems to a friend who 'alighted from Jerusalem' and whose purpose was to visit the Holy City 'and the tombs of every prophet and of David, the meadows of Zion and Harel [the Temple Mount] and the foundation opposite the Gates of Heaven where God revealed himself to the seed of Ephraim'.[35]

Some pilgrims are no more than fleeting names; others can be identified and often connected with some Messianic expectations. Among the latter is R. Moses ha-Dar'i, who must have been a scholar of some standing as he is invoked by Maimonides regarding the rules of binding phylacteries (*tefillin*). He came to the Holy Land, probably from Dar'a in Morocco, some time after the middle of the twelfth century, and may possibly be identified as a self-proclaimed Messiah whose authenticity was almost accepted by Maimonides.[36]

The pilgrimage of Maimonides himself is of some interest. As this description comes from the pen of the greatest spiritual leader of medieval Judaism and at the same time allows us a glimpse of a Jewish pilgrim, as it were, in action, it is worth translating here *in extenso* the story of that pilgrimage:

On Saturday night on the fourth of the month of Iyar [18 April] I put to sea; and on Saturday the tenth of Iyar in the year 4925 of Creation [24 April 1165] there rose a wave to drown us and the sea was in great fury and I took the vow that these two days I would fast . . . I and my household and all our followers and I would order my

[34] *Diwān des Abraham Ibn Esra*, ed. by J. Egers (Berlin 1886), no. 185, p. 82, ll. 45–8. A later tradition, no doubt false, even indicated his burial place in the Holy Land as being with two other great poets, Ibn Gabirol and Judah Halevy; see *Tombs of the Ancestors*, 189.

[35] Published by S. Bernstein in 'Poems from an Unknown Diwan of R. Abraham ibn 'Ezra' (H), *Tarbiz* 5/1 (1934), 65–6.

[36] *Responsa of Maimonides* (to the scholars of Lunel), ed. J. Blau, ii. 543, no. 289 (ed. Freimann, no. 7), 543, and *The Epistle to Yemen*, ed. A. S. Halkin, Engl. trans. B. Cohen (New York 1952), pp. xix–xx.

children to do so to the end of time and that they should give charity according to their means. It was also part of my vow that I would stay alone on the tenth of Iyar, would not see anybody but would pray and study all day all by myself. And as I found no one on the sea [to save me] but [the Holy One] Blessed be He, so I would not meet with anybody unless forced to do so. And on Sunday night, three days in the month of Sīvan [16 May] I came out safe and sound from the sea and landed in Acre and I escaped apostasy and we came to Eretz Israel. On that day, I took a vow that it would be a day of gladness and joy, a day of feasting and giving charity to the poor—for me and all my household to eternity. And on Tuesday, the fourth of Marḥeshvan [14 October] in the Year [49]26 of Creation we left Acre to go to Jerusalem and this put me in danger. And I entered the Great and Holy House and I prayed in it on Thursday, the sixth day of Marḥeshvan [16 October]. And on Sunday the ninth of the month [19 October] I left Jerusalem for Hebron to kiss the Tombs of the Patriarchs in the [Double] Cave. And on that day I stayed in the Cave and prayed, glory be to Him for everything. And these two days, that is the sixth and the ninth of Marḥeshvan I vowed that they would be as Festive Days, days of prayer and rejoicing in God and in food and drink. Let God be my aid in all and [by his] favour may I fulfil my vow. Amen. And as I was privileged to pray in her [Jerusalem or the Temple] when she was ruined, so should I be allowed to see her, I and all of Israel, when she is consoled. Amen. On Thursday night and Tuesday [*sic*], on the twelfth of Sīvan [10 May 1166], God saw my misery and my brother arrived in peace and I made it a day of charity and fasting.[37]

Thus, Maimonides' voyage from Morocco to Acre lasted almost four weeks (18 April to 16 May). Maimonides stayed in Acre through the whole summer, almost six months until 14 October 1165. The only pilgrimage he mentions is that to Jerusalem and Hebron. The journey from Acre to Jerusalem took three days (14–16 October), and in Jerusalem he

[37] The text was found at the beginning of a Commentary on Tractate *Rosh ha-Shanah* wrongly assigned to Maimonides, but there is no reason to doubt the veracity and authenticity of the biographical note. It was copied by one R. Samuel b. Abraham Secal in Acre. The copyist is probably a man from a well-known wealthy family in Narbonne in the last quarter of the 13th cent. See J. Schatzmiller, 'Minor Epistle of Apology of Rabbi Kalonymos ben Kalonymos' (H), *Sefunot* 10 (1966), 27–8. The autobiographical note has been published several times; I have used the text published as *Jen Libanon* (= Yeīn Lebanon), *Trois manuscrits inédits*, ed. J. Brill (Paris 1866), 1.

remained for three days only,[38] whence he went to pray at the Tombs of the Patriarchs in Hebron. He then stayed on in the Holy Land for more than seven months (May 1166), when he was joined by his brother. All in all, Maimonides stayed in the Holy Land[39] for almost a year before leaving and finally settling in Egypt.

One should like to know more about his life in Acre (where, we assume, he returned after his pilgrimage to Jerusalem and Hebron), but the autobiographical note is mute on the subject. However, some glimpses can be gathered from other sources, like his later correspondence with the leaders of the community of Acre and especially of Tyre, with whom he continued to be in contact even after settling in Egypt.[40]

In the circle of these pilgrims there appeared a hitherto unknown genre of Hebrew literature, namely descriptions of voyages to the Holy Land which it would not be too far-fetched to assume were sparked off by a similar phenomenon among Christians, namely the appearance of the numerous *itineraria* of the Crusader period. There are ten Hebrew treatises of this genre extant from the Crusader period, and they represent all that has been preserved of a far larger literary output.[41]

The most famous pilgrimage of the twelfth century, and perhaps of all the Middle Ages, is that of Judah Halevy the greatest Hebrew poet. A very early legend embellished the

[38] His pilgrimage to Jerusalem raises many questions. Maimonides states clearly that he entered the precinct of the Temple esplanade and also the Dome of the Rock. The Hebrew text has explicitly 'Venikhnastī la-baīt ha-gadōl ve-haqadōsh ve-hitpalaltī bō'. Actually Maimonides ruled that in our times a Jew (because of impurity) is not allowed to enter the holy precinct. *Mishne Tora, Hilkhōt Beit ha-Beḥīra*, vi. 14–16. This was criticized and rejected by his contemporary R. Abraham ben David (ibid.) and the halakhic discussion continues to our own day. Maimonides' departure from the Holy Land and settling in Egypt was another thorny problem which is still discussed; see S. K. Mirsky, 'Maimonides in the Light of our Time' (H) *Perakim: Proc. of the American Hebrew Academy*, 1 (1956), 7–23; M. Havazelet, 'Maimonides' Attitude to the Land of Israel' (H), ibid. 2 (1959), 65–87.

[39] In several responsa he mentions religious observances followed in the Holy Land, like abstinence during the menstrual period and the binding of phylacteries (see above n. 36). *Responsa of Maimonides* ed. Blau, no. 320, ed. Freimann, no. 99.

[40] Actually Maimonides might have stayed in Tyre. On his correspondence with the scholars of Acre and Tyre, see above, pp. 54–5 and n. 33.

[41] See ch. 7.

story of this pilgrimage and has him dying facing the walls of Jerusalem, the ultimate and unattainable aim of his wandering.

Nobody has more beautifully and movingly expressed the Jewish yearning for Zion than this great poet of Spain. Verses from his poems would be recited over the ages throughout the Jewish Diaspora and would accompany the Jewish national revival of the nineteenth century:

> My heart is in the East, and I in the uttermost West
> How can I find favour in food? How shall it be sweet to me
> How shall I render my vows and my bonds, while yet
> Zion lieth beneath the fetter of Edom, and I in Arab chains.

Until our own times no Jew could read the following verses without sensing their permanent actuality in the darkness of endless Exile:

> Have we any heritage save the sanctuaries of God?
> Then how should we forget His Holy Mount?
> Have we either in the East or in the West
> A place of hope wherein we may trust,
> Except the land that is full of gates
> Towards which the gates of Heaven open.[42]

Since Jeremiah's Lamentations, written almost seventeen centuries earlier, no prophet or poet had expressed more movingly the Jewish feeling of homelessness and the nostalgia for a lost Zion.

Judah Halevy, philosopher and thinker as well as poet, strikes a different chord in his theological-political treatise *The Book of Kūzarī*. Here a distinct mood is created, perhaps even a different frame of perception. In the closing chapter of the treatise the hero, called *ḥaber* (Friend), tells the king of Khazaria of his decision to migrate to the Holy Land.[43] The king argues that a pure heart and strong desire can reach God from anywhere and warns of the perils of the journey; the hero

[42] From *Selected Poems of Jehuda Halevi*, trans. Nina Salaman (Philadelphia 1946), no. 1, and cf. *Ode to Zion*, no. 2.

[43] Critical edition (published posthumously) by D. H. Baneth, *Kitāb al-Radd wa'l-Dalīl fi'l-Din al-Dhalīl* (Jerusalem 1977), 227 ff. Engl. trans. H. Hirschfeld, *Book of Kuzari by Judah Halevi* (New York 1946), pt. 5, par. 22 ff., 258 ff.

answers with a set of responses some of which could also have been heard in the contemporary Christian camp.[44]

Directly relevant to our query as to the theological or philosophical explanation of Jewish pilgrimage and eventual settlement in the Holy Land is Halevy's statement of the unique standing of the Holy Land in the framework of Creation. The Holy Land is the Chosen Land, the Beloved of God, and only there can human deeds and actions be really God-willed and perfect. Nay, purity of heart and the sublimation of the soul in the highest degree can only be reached in the Holy Land.

The land awakens longings and desires of the purest quality not darkened by any thoughts of material gain; these are the most disinterested and therefore sublime of motives:

> This sacred place serves to remind men and to stimulate them to love God, being a reward and a promise, as it is written: 'Thou shall arise and have mercy upon Zion, for the time to favour her, the set time is come. For thy servants take pleasure in her stones and embrace the dust thereof' [Ps. 102: 14 ff.]. This means that Jerusalem can only be rebuilt when Israel yearns for it to such an extent that they embrace her stones and dust.

This brings religious fervour and theological reasoning within human grasp. The time of redemption, with the restoration of Jerusalem as its focal point depends on the human element: the strength and ardour of yearning, and the love of God. But these in their turn are in some measure linked with the Holy Land, which, in itself stimulates the holiest sentiments.

The dangers of the roads and the perils of pilgrimage put forward by the king of Khazaria as arguments against embarking on a voyage to the Holy Land are answered in a way that was actually voiced in the Christian camp by no less a figure than Bernard of Clairvaux. The *ḥaber* argues the spiritual importance of exile (*galuth*) almost in the sense of the original *peregrinatio*. It is the difficulties and sufferings on the road which

[44] Especially relevant is Guibert of Nogent's version of the speech of Urban II at Clermont, and even more so the ideas expressed by Halevy's contemporary, Bernard of Clairvaux, in his exhortations for the second Crusade and the *De Laude novae militiae*. Cf. J. Prawer: 'Croisade du salut des âmes', *Histoire*, i. 243–352.

bring about expiation in the religious sense of the expression. Here the exile comes near the notion of penance. Halevy strengthens his argument by quoting from the Tractate *Sanhedrin*: 'Exile atones for sin',[45] and in the case of the Holy Land the value of the 'exile' is enhanced by its end: 'if his exile brings him into the place of God's choice'.

The exile or pilgrimage in itself has meritorious value. 'In my opinion', says Halevy, 'it is better than seeking the danger of war in order to gain fame and spoil by courage and bravery. Nay, the reward is even greater than that of people who endanger their lives in Holy War [in Arabic in the original: *al-jihād*], though they believe to gain thereby a share in the next world (*'olam haba*).'

A contemporary of Urban II, or rather of Guibert of Nogent, would have been very much at home with an argument which contrasted the spiritual reward of those who braved the dangers of a holy pilgrimage motivated by 'the ardent desire to atone for sins' with the profits of a merchant who endangers his life for gain. Halevy's argument also closely resembles the reasoning of Bernard of Clairvaux. He who perishes on the road knows that he has atoned for his sins and obtained divine favour. But at this point the similarity with Bernard of Clairvaux ends. Halevy fought against the spirit of the Diaspora as being the negation of the natural order;[46] for him, the dominant and decisive factor is the Land of Israel. For him, pilgrimage is a new way of life; he 'is satisfied to spend the rest of his days in seeking the favour of the Lord' in the Holy Land. The Land of Israel is 'the sacred place which serves to remind men and to stimulate them to the love of God, being a reward and promise'.[47]

Though Judah Halevy's ardent desire to leave the Diaspora and emigrate to the Holy Land fired the imagination of future generations, it could hardly appeal in its reasoning to the masses. It was basically a religion of an élite group proclaimed by a great poet, not a call to be imitated by others.

[45] Tractate *Sanhedrin* 37*b* and Tractate *Berakhōt* 56*a*.

[46] Cf. J. N. Simhoni, 'R. Yehuda Halevy as a National Poet' (H), *Ha-'ivri he-Ḥadash* vii (Warsaw 1912), 56–80. Cf. below, n. 90.

[47] *Book of Kuzari* (above, n. 43), 261.

Different sentiments and voices were heard in other quarters of contemporary Jewry. It is in some of its most orthodox sections that we find hesitation and even opposition if not to pilgrimage as such then certainly to the idea of settling in the Holy Land. As early as the Mishnaic period, the voices which argued that living in the Holy Land was a supreme religious virtue were accompanied by others proclaiming more moderate views. With time such questions, though discussed in schools as a part of Talmudic studies were relegated to the realm of academic interests only. But by the twelfth century, and even more so in the thirteenth, things began to change.

The opinions of scholars were far from unanimous. On the one hand, a Tosafist of renown like R. Baruk b. Isaac of Worms (probably of French origin), the author of *Sefer ha-Terūmah* (The book of offering) written before 1202,[48] regarded not only pilgrims but actually settling in the Holy Land as a religious precept:

> It is true indeed that God loves the Land of Israel and happy is the man who lives therein, as even those who left it with the exile of Jehoiakim brought with them the stones and the dust of the Land of Israel [Ps. 102: 14] . . . *a fortiori* the man who lives in the Holy Land and fulfils the precepts which are obligatory therein, is privileged to live in the presence of the Holy One, be his name blessed.[49]

A section of his book deals, though in a rather cursory way, with religious precepts one is obliged to fulfil in the Holy Land only.[50] On the other hand, another Tosafist who lived some time earlier, R. Ḥayyim b. Ḥananel Hakkohen,[51] declared the actual abrogation or abeyance of the Talmudic law which compelled a wife to follow her husband if he decided to emigrate to the Land of Israel.[52] 'This is not used any more at our present time', he argues, 'because of the risks of travelling.

[48] Cf. Urbach, *Tosafists*, i. 346 ff. Later on, perhaps in 1208, he pilgrimaged to the Holy Land.

[49] This was to be even more strongly stressed by Naḥmanides. See below, pp. 157–60.

[50] *Sefer ha-Terūmah* (Warsaw 1897), 151–7.

[51] Urbach, *Tosafists*, i. 124 ff.

[52] Tractate *Kethuboth* 110*b*: 'If the husband desires to go up [to the Land of Israel or Jerusalem] and his wife refuses, she must be pressed to go up; and if she does not consent, she may be divorced without a *kethubah*. If she desires to go up and he refuses, he must be pressed to go up; and if he does not consent he must divorce her and pay her *kethubah*.'

The living in the Land of Israel is not an applicable precept now, because there are precepts obligatory in the Land of Israel and punishments [for trespassing against them] which we cannot carefully observe.'[53] In another comment he stated that the Talmudic ruling was valid, as long 'as there was peace on the roads, but now that the roads are infested, he [i.e. the husband] cannot compel his wife [to migrate to the Holy Land], because this is forcing her to be led to a place of wild beasts and robbers'.[54]

Thus he argues two interlinked issues. On the one hand the impossibility of a strict observance of precepts incumbent on those who live in the Holy Land; on the other the dangers of the roads and of the situation in the Holy Land under Crusader rule—and this in the face of clear evidence to the contrary. In either case, he clearly takes a negative attitude to the idea of settling in the Holy Land.

In the period of pilgrimage and emigration, the rulings of R. Ḥayyim Hakkohen on practical matters definitely carried weight. Such questions arose not only in France or Germany, the homeland of the Tosafists, but also in another corner of the Jewish Diaspora, namely in Egypt. The case in question even has a certain comic element. A man married a wealthy girl in Alexandria, and in an effort to secure part of her dowry (30 out of 100 dinars), he announced his intention of migrating to the Holy Land: if she failed to accompany him (which would mean leaving her home and parents) she would forfeit her dowry. The local court seems to have ruled that unless 'there was danger on the roads or there is any other impending difficulty' the wife would have to follow her husband to the Holy Land or lose her dowry. But they did not feel at ease with this decision, and the question was referred to Maimonides in Fusṭāṭ. From his *responsum* it transpires that this was a method of subterfuge or blackmail practised in North Africa, and that the Jewish courts there actually excommunicated or threatened to excommunicate anyone who tried this kind of ruse. Maimonides' ruling was that if the court was absolutely sure of the

[53] Urbach, *Tosafot*, loc. cit.

[54] *Haggahot Mordekhai*, par. 313. Cf. H. J. Zimmels. 'Erez Israel in der Responsenliteratur des Mittelalters', *Monaschrift für die Geschichte und Wissenschaft des Judentums* 74 (1930), 52 n. 2.

bona fides of the husband's declaration, then the wife should be compelled to follow him or be divorced and lose her *kethubah* (i.e. her rights as spelt out in the marriage contract); but should there be any doubt as to the real intentions of the husband, the court should protect the wife and not force her to leave her city.[55]

Apprehensions about living in the Land of Israel and fulfilling the required precepts, as associated with the particular view that accorded a positive value to the Diaspora, often resulted in reticence regarding the meritorious value of migrating to the Holy Land. Clearly there was no unanimity on the subject, and as we have already seen, both sides could find valid arguments for their opposing points of view in the vast corpus of the Talmud. In this context it is worth mentioning a rabbinical *responsum* which emanated from a particular group of pietists, the twelfth-century German Ḥasīdim.[56] Theirs was the most spiritual trend in the Franco-German communities. An anonymous author belonging to this group was definitely opposed even to pilgrimage, and his arguments are reminiscent of the opposition to the Crusades. Study and learning and the family, he argued, are far more important and should be preferred to voyages and pilgrimages.[57]

At the turn of the century, however, attitudes began to change; I shall try to prove that this change was ideologically connected with the defeat of the Crusaders by Saladin. As a matter of fact, the first wave of migration and settling in Jerusalem took place in the decade following the fall of Crusader Jerusalem in 1187; for almost a hundred years attempts at settlement would continue to change the character of the Jewish community in the Holy Land.

The first wave of migration on a substantial scale was described by al-Ḥarizi, who listed the different origins of the newly established community of Jerusalem: North Africa,

[55] *Responsa of Maimonides*, ed. Blau no. 363; ed. Freimann, no. 177.

[56] See G. Scholem, *Major Trends in Jewish Mysticism* (New York 1983³), ch. 3, pp. 80–118.

[57] I. Ta-Shema, 'Eretz Israel Studies' (H), *Shalem* 1 (1974), 81–97. A similar attitude but phrased in a different way was taken even by R. Meir of Rothenburg, who himself attempted to migrate to the Holy Land. See below pp. 162–3.

Egypt, France, in addition to Ascalonite and Palestinian Jews.[58] This first wave was followed by a great wave of migration from France which began *circa* 1209 and continued for several years. The salient characteristic of this movement in addition to its sheer size, was the presence of, and in all probability the leadership of, some of the outstanding scholarly and spiritual figures of the great school of the Tosafists from northern France and Germany, as well as scholars of standing from Provence and Languedoc.[59]

This major migratory movement was to continue throughout the thirteenth century. Among the most notable migrations was that of one of the greatest scholars from France, R. Yeḥiel of Paris, the head of the Parisian Academy, which took place *circa* 1259. This event was still remembered three generations later, when the author of the most remarkable Hebrew treatise about the Holy Land in the Middle Ages, *Kaftor va-Pheraḥ* (written *c.*1320),[60] quoted a contemporary Jerusalemite, one R. Baruk, as saying that: 'R. Yeḥiel of Paris of blessed memory intended to come to Jerusalem in the year of 5017 [1257] to offer sacrifices at that time.'[61] The complex theological problem of whether or not the practice of sacrifices could be renewed before the restoration of the Temple was never authoritatively resolved. The scholars of the Talmudic period were not unanimous. It was said that one of the three prophets (Haggai, Zechariah, and Malachi) who returned from the

[58] See pp. 69 ff.

[59] Ibid.

[60] The title of the book *Kaftor va-Pheraḥ* refers to the name of the author (ha-Parḥi) and is based on Num. 25: 23. The book has been published several times, but there is still something of a mystery surrounding the name of the author. Ishtorī, his first name (there is no basis for the transcription Eshtori), was interpreted as Ish-tori, i.e. the man who explores (there are Talmudic names Ashtor and 'Ishtor), a rather problematic suggestion. In Luncz's edition (ed. A. M. Luncz (Jerusalem 1897), ch. 6, p. 81), the author says that his family name is Parḥi (i.e. of the flowers or the flowering one) and refers to his birthplace as Floranza in Andalusia. Unfortunately, Floranza in Andalusia cannot be traced. This brings us back to a suggestion in Z. H. Edelmann's edition (Berlin 1871) by Niederhofheim (Introduction, 1) that the name is a pseudonym, and that the author's real name was Joseph, because the opening phrase of the treatise is: 'And thus said the Hebrew slave', which refers to the biblical Joseph (Gen. 39: 17). On the treatise see J. Prawer, 'R. Ishtori ha-Parḥi, the First Jewish Explorer of the Holy Land' (with bibl.; H.), *Eretz Shomron* 13 Archaeological Convention (Jerusalem 1973), 106–14.

[61] *Kaftor va-Pheraḥ*, 81. The text has R. Ḥananel but there is a general consensus that it should be corrected to R. Yeḥiel. On R. Yeḥiel, see Urbach, *Tosafists*, i. 448 ff.

Babylonian Exile argued 'that they could sacrifice even though there was no Temple',[62] because the Temple area was sanctified for eternity.[63] This was the view taken later by Maimonides, and while some opposed him (like his contemporary R. Abraham b. David of Posquière), this was the view generally accepted by the French Tosafists.[64] R. Yeḥiel—Sire Vives as he was called in French—played a major role in the life of French Jewry, being its most outstanding scholar in the middle of the thirteenth century. This brought him, in 1240, to the well-known disputation in Paris forced on him by the clergy, whose spokesman was the converted Jew Nicholas Donin. The tragic result of the disputation was the confiscation and infamous burning of the Talmud in the royal domain of France.[65] This tragic event, which as it later transpired undermined the existence of the great Jewish schools in France, was accompanied by growing attacks from the papacy, and Christian theologians against the Talmud as being allegedly the great obstacle in the way of Jewish conversion, quite apart from its blasphemies. In these circumstances, R. Yeḥiel decided to migrate to the Holy Land. Whether or not he actually thought of restoring the cult of sacrifices in Jerusalem is not known. Possibly, as there was no *halakhic* objection, he regarded it as a propitiative act to speed the coming of the Messiah. Among European Jewry he was remembered as 'R. Yeḥiel who went to Acre' or 'went to the Holy Land'. In 1258 he was still officiating in Paris, where he wrote an act of divorce, but the next we hear about him is from a *responsum* he gave which originated in Greece.[66] His later whereabouts were shrouded in uncertainty[67] until a fragment of a chronicle[68] was discovered

[62] Tractate *Zebaḥim* 62*a*.

[63] Tractate *'Eduyōth*, Engl. trans. H. Danby (London 1933), ch. 8 n. 6.

[64] *Talmudic Encyclopaedia* (H), ed. S. J. Zevin, iii (s.v. *beit ha-miqdash*), 233–54. The discussion was renewed in 1836.

[65] The confiscation followed the debate but the burning probably took place in 1242. There are many studies of the problem. See Urbach, *Tosafists*, 449–56.

[66] Preserved in the commentary of R. Asher ben Yeḥiel on Tractate *Yebamot*, ch. 4, par. 6, quoted by I. Ta-Shema in *Shalem* 1 (1974), 84.

[67] On the Talmudic Academy in Acre known as *Midrash Haggadol de Paris*, see ch. 8 n. 63.

[68] I. Ta-Shema, 'A New Chronography of the 13th-century Tosaphists' (H), *Shalem* 3 (1981), 324. An unfortunate lacuna deprives us of the date. A Jerusalemite tradition mentions the year 1257 but this should be corrected to 1259. See below, ch. 8.

recently which states explicitly:

R. Yeḥiel of Paris left together with his son R. Joseph[69] and R. Joseph of Sens. And our master R. Yeḥiel died on the ship and they wanted to throw him into the sea and bribes were given [lacuna] and he and his son remained in the city [lacuna] in the land of Morea.

We know of the pilgrimage of another famous figure some eight years later, in 1267, when the most renowned Spanish scholar of his age, Moses b. Naḥman, Naḥmanides (his Spanish name was Bonastruc de Porta), left Spain to settle in the Holy Land.[70] But we shall return to his story later.

At that time a new wave of migration, which by virtue of the similarities in composition and scale may be considered part of the former movement, started out from Europe. This time it originated in Germany in the summer of 1286 and was headed by R. Meir of Rothenburg. The movement must have been a large one and seems to be referred to in the Imperial decree of 6 December 1286 whereby the new ruler of Germany, Rudolph of Habsburg, ordered the confiscation of the property of Jews fleeing from Germany. The edict mentions by name the great centres of Jewish life: Speyer, Worms, Mainz, Oppenheim, and Wetterau, and the aim of those fleeing Germany is clearly stated as *ultra mare*, the customary name applied in Europe to the Crusader states in the East.[71] The story of that migration is preserved in the *Book of Customs of the Community of Worms*:

Our teacher and master R. Meir of Rothenburg of blessed memory, set out on a journey across the sea, he and his household, his daughters, son-in-law and all that he had. He came to a certain town amidst tall mountains, known in German as 'Lombardisches Gebirge' to wait there until all those who wished to journey with him arrived. Suddenly the wicked bishop of Basel rode from Rome through that same city accompanied by an apostate called Knipse—may his name and memory be blotted out—who recognized our teacher and reported the matter to the bishop and caused Count Mainhardt of Goertz [i.e. Gorizia on the Isonzo in the Veneto], the lord of that city,

[69] It is, however, possible that R. Joseph b. Yeḥiel (in his native French, Sire Délicieux), came later. See ch. 8 n. 66.

[70] See ch. 8 n. 71.

[71] *Monumenta Germaniae Historica, Constitutiones*, iii. 368–9.

to seize him on the 4 of Tammūz in the year of Creation 5046 and hand him over to King Rudolf.[72]

R. Meir remained incarcerated for seven years at Ensisheim and Wasserburg until his death in 1293 refusing to be ransomed by the community and thereby setting a precedent for royal extortion.[73]

As we have seen, the entire thirteenth century witnessed an extraordinary Jewish awakening, an awakening which was not limited to literary or liturgical creative activity but found expression in a recurrent stream of pilgrims and settlers to the Holy Land. These were not the Messianic upheavals of the second half of the eleventh and first half of the twelfth century; there was now a different climate and different sensitivities. Pilgrimage turned into a movement of migration with the avowed purpose of settlement, and those who participated in the movement were not anonymous individuals but some of the great Jewish scholars of the period.

Attempts to link this movement, which lasted for more than a century, from Saladin to the fall of the Crusader kingdom, with Jewish persecutions in Europe, seem doubtful. There were persecutions in the twelfth century which did not produce any recurrent migrations, and twelfth-century pilgrims, as far as we know, hardly belonged to the Jewish intellectual élite. And although the thirteenth century witnessed a deterioration in the general standing of Western Jewry, the strengthening of

[72] Quoted from the *Book of Customs* by A. Fuld commenting on Azulai, *Shem ha-Gedolim* (The names of the prominent) ii, ed. Ben Ya'akov (Vilna 1856), 284. On this source, see A. Epstein, 'Die Wurmser Minhagbücher', *Gedenkbuch zur Erinnerung an David Kaufmann* (Breslau 1900). Cf. I. A. Agus, *Rabbi Meir of Rothenburg*, i (Philadelphia 1947), 126. The text was published in a German translation by E. Carmoly, 'Gefangenschaft des R. Meir von Rothenburg', *Israelitische Annalen*, ed. J. M. Jost (1839), 348–9. He printed a MS colophon of a Venetian *Mishne Tora* (1524), which belonged to one Aaron Worms in Metz. The name of the apostate Jew is rendered here as Kampf. The funeral of R. Meir took place in Worms only under Emperor Albrecht in 1303. The tomb and the inscription still exist.

[73] The *Haggadah of the Birds*, a 14th-cent. illuminated Hebrew MS from Germany now in the possession of the Bezalel National Museum, Jerusalem has on the last page a picture of a bird with broken wings against the background of a city labelled 'Jerusalem'. This is interpreted as referring to the captive R. Meir of Rothenburg, who did not succeed in reaching the Holy City. See *The Bird's Head Haggada*, ed. M. Spitzer *et al.* (Jerusalem 1967).

the feudal monarchies guaranteed some security to the Jews. It was only in the last quarter of the century and in the beginning of the fourteenth century that the exploitation of the Jews was to reach its peak, accompanied by expulsion. It is this period and the following century which were to record some of the darkest pages of Jewish history. Yet the late thirteenth and the fourteenth centuries did not produce any recurrent let alone any great movements of migration, and among those who migrated very few, if any, belonged to the intellectual leadership of the Diaspora.

It is not the European West, the place of origin of the movement, but the Crusader East which holds the key to this new phenomenon. One of its major figures, Naḥmanides, provides a possible historical interpretation.

The victories of Saladin over the Crusaders were the catalyst of the movement, but it was what one may call the Jewish view of the Crusades which created a receptiveness and sharpened Jewish sensitivities in relation to the Holy Land and Jerusalem. The Jews, who for more than a millennium after the loss of their statehood neither lost their national and religious identity nor renounced the collective memory of their imagined greatness, now witnessed the gigantic confrontation between Christendom (Western Christendom which replaced Byzantium, the original *Edom* of the Jewish apocalypse, the great persecutor of the Just) and Islam. Both mobilized their resources, both clashed on a dozen battlefields; and although the military confrontation might be described as the war for world hegemony, in Jewish eyes both were actually fighting for the heritage of Israel, the Holy Land. The Christian Holy War and the Muslim Jihād was fought for the possession of the Land which originated the concept of a conquest ordained by God.

The Jewish Diaspora witnessed the changing vicissitudes of the wars waged in the Land of Israel, felt the tremor of Messianic upheavals amidst its Christian and Muslim neighbours, and developed its own specifically Jewish view of the events. The capture of Jerusalem by Saladin in 1187, which shook the Christian West, and the Third Crusade which came in its wake were preceded by Messianic visions common to the visionaries of all three religions.[74]

It is against this background that we have to understand the migration movements of the thirteenth century. What can be conjectured from circumstances is spelt out clearly by Naḥmanides.[75] This great scholar was forced to take part in a public disputation in Barcelona in July 1263 against the converted Jew Pablo Christiani assisted by the Dominicans Raymond de Peñaforte and Raymond Martini. The disputation, in the shadow of the confiscation and burning of the Talmud in France twenty years earlier, ended in the obvious victory of the Christians. Strangely enough Naḥmanides was presented with a royal gift with the royal remark: 'I have never seen a man defend a wrong cause so well.' At the request of the bishop of Gerona, Naḥmanides wrote down his arguments. The Dominicans, who were responsible for the disputation, now demanded (1265) his trial for having abused Christianity. Naḥmanides argued that before the disputation he had been promised royal immunity. The Dominicans appealed to Pope Clement IV, who urged James I of Aragon to proceed against Naḥmanides. Before any steps were taken Naḥmanides left Spain for the Holy Land, but Jews were henceforth compelled to attend Christian sermons in their synagogues and to submit their copies of the Talmud to censorship.

Naḥmanides' basic attitude to the Holy Land can be gathered from the works he wrote in his native Spain and from the sermons he gave on coming to Jerusalem (1267 or 1268), and in Acre on the eve of the Jewish New Year in 1269.[76] These

[74] On Messianic stirrings among Christians and Jews during the Third Crusade, see F. Baer, 'Eine jüdische Messiasprophetie auf das Jahr 1186 und der dritte Kreuzzug', *Monatschrift für die Geschichte und Wissenschaft des Judentums* 70 (1926), 113–22, 155–65. Some parts of the apocalypse 'The Prayer of R. Simeon b. Yoḥai' (*Tefillath Rashbī*) are assigned by the editor to the Third Crusade. *Midrashei Geūlah* (Chapters of Jewish Apocalypses), ed. J. Even Samuel (Tel-Aviv 1943), 276 ff., 282 ff.; but see B. Lewis, 'An Apocalyptic Vision of Islamic History', *Bulletin of the School of Oriental and African Studies* 13 (1951), 308–38; see also below, pp. 257–8.

[75] Cf. Y. Baer, *A History of the Jews in Christian Spain*, i (1966), 102 ff., 152–9. A detailed biography was written by C. B. Chavel, *Rabbi Moshe ben Nahman: His Life, Times, and Works* (H), (Jerusalem 1967). The author also edited Naḥmanides' major works and translated them into English (see next note).

[76] In one of the early editions (Lisbon 1489), the date of the sermon in Acre is indicated as 1268. This sermon was newly published in Chavel, *The Writings of Ramban* (H), i (Jerusalem 1963), 201–52; and in an English trans. by the same scholar in Ramban, *Writings and Discourses*, i (New York 1978), 235 ff. See below, n. 85.

sermons (of which more later), despite their academic character and rather tedious juxtaposition of biblical quotations, are examples of the newly awakened Jewish sensitivity to the Holy Land. His yearning for the Holy Land is strikingly expressed in his famous commentary on the Pentateuch. Begun in Spain, it was completed either in Jerusalem or in Acre where he settled and established a school which soon attracted students from neighbouring countries.[77] Whereas the traditional exegesis had confined itself mainly to studying the literal or figurative meaning of the texts with the primary objective of elucidating the halakhic content of the Scriptures, Naḥmanides' interpretations strike a new note, an emotional exegesis, redolent of the sights and the scents of the Homeland. Such voices had hardly been heard in biblical exegeses since Roman times and the Mishnaic sages.[78] Expounding Exodus 3: 8, where God promises to bring the children of Israel to the land of Canaan: 'a good land and a large, unto a land flowing with milk and honey', Naḥmanides elaborates: 'The air is good and wholesome for human beings, and all that is good is found here. . . . It has breadth: lowland, valley and plain are large and fair . . . a land for cattle with good pastures, and there is good water, and the milk increases in the cows . . . Its fruit is so fat and sweet that it is as if honey issues from the land.' Deuteronomy 8: 9 reads: 'A land whose stones are iron and out of whose hills thou mayest dig copper.' Naḥmanides elaborates: 'And one can find there a mine of copper and iron, which supply a great need of the inhabitants of the land indeed. Thou shalt not lack anything in it. There can also be found quarries of large stones, precious stones, hewn stones to build houses, city walls and towers.' There were new songs to be sung about Zion. No visions of Heavenly Jerusalem, no royal palace descending from heaven and no expectation of the Day of Judgement

[77] All his corrections and additions were sent from Acre. See K. Cahana, 'Ramban's Additions to his *Commentary on the Pentateuch*' (H), *Ha-Maʿayan* 9 (1969), 25–47. His foreign students are mentioned in his *Commentary on Genesis 11: 28.*

[78] Cf. J. Prawer, ' "Lovers of Zion" (*Ḥovevei Ẓion*) in the Middle Ages: Immigration to Palestine in the Crusader Period' (H), in *Western Galilee and the Coast of Galilee*, the 19th Archaeological Convention 1963 (Jerusalem 1965), 129–36 (shortened English trans.: 'Jewish Resettlement in Crusader Jerusalem', *Ariel* 19 (1967), 60–6. Cf. H. Rivlin, *The Virtues of the Holy Land in Ramban's Commentary on the Bible* (H) (*Maʿalot ha-Aretz*) (Jerusalem 1949).

when God will rebuild the Temple; instead, images of the land's fertility, its wholesomeness, farming, building, and security. These were new realities appearing, rather unexpectedly in biblical exegeses.

It was a new approach, very different from that of the great Maimonides, who had died two generations earlier. In Maimonides' classic and authoritative list of religious precepts or commandments which are obligatory on the Jews, that of settling or living in the Holy Land, was conspicuous by its absence. In his *Critique of the Book of Precepts*[79] of Maimonides, Naḥmanides stated with rather unexpected rigour:

> We were enjoined to possess the land given by God—may He be exalted—to our forefathers Abraham, Isaac and Jacob and we shall never leave it to any of the nations, neither shall we leave it in desolation, for as the Holy Scriptures says [Num. 33: 53]: 'And you must take possession of the land, and dwell therein: for I have given you the land to possess it',[80] and this means that we were ordered about the conquest in all generations. And I say that the commandment which is extolled by the sages namely the living in the Land of Israel as they said: 'Whoever lives abroad should be regarded as an idolator' [*Kethubōth* 110] because it is written [I Sam. 29: 19] 'for they have driven me out this day from my share in the inheritance of the Lord, saying: go serve other Gods', and some more extolling things—all this belongs to the positive precepts,[81] that is that we were ordered to possess the land and to live in it. And as this is a positive precept valid in all generations, it is incumbent on everyone and each one of us and even at the time of Exile.

Further on he continues:

> 'To take possession of the land'—and we shall never leave it to any of the nations or to desolation but to ourselves . . . and do not make any mistake by saying that this commandment was said in connection with the nations[82] . . . this is not so, because we were ordered to annihilate these nations when we were fighting against them. And if

[79] *Hasaggōt 'al Sefer Hamiṣvōth* (Jerusalem 1926) *Miṣvōth 'Aseh*, no. 4.

[80] From *The New English Bible* (Oxford 1970), 191, which in this phrase corresponds better to the original Hebrew than the Authorized Version.

[81] The religious precepts are divided into two main categories: positive precepts (*miṣvōth 'aseh*), that is, precepts which are accomplished by being done; and negative precepts (*miṣvōth lo ta'aseh*), prohibitions which are accomplished by refraining from given actions.

[82] The seven nations that lived in the land of Canaan before the Hebrew conquest.

they want to make peace—we will and we shall leave them on given conditions, but we shall not leave the land in their hands, nor shall we leave it to any of these nations for all generations.

His final conclusion is clear: the settling and living in the Holy Land is a religious commandment obligatory at all times. And he ends his exposition by quoting a well-known dictum from *Midrash Siphrei* (2nd cent. CE) on Deuteronomy 12: 29: ' "When the Lord your God exterminates, as you advance, the nations whose country you are entering to occupy, you shall take their place and settle in their land." . . . The living in the Land of Israel is a commandment which outweighs all other commandments.' This famous phrase became a politico-religious slogan. As we have seen, in leaving Spain and settling in the Holy Land, Naḥmanides practised what he preached.

It was the gigantic confrontation between Islam and Christianity which was the background to the new evaluation of the place of the Holy Land in contemporary Jewish thinking. On the one hand there was a revival of Messianic expectations and a resurgence of apocalyptic writings, on the other a more earthly approach clearly stated by Naḥmanides. Commenting on Leviticus 26: 32: 'I will destroy your land and the enemies who occupy it will be appalled',[83] he comes up with a startling and unexpected statement:

And these are good tidings proclaiming in all the lands of the Diaspora that our land does not accept our foes. And this is a decisive proof and a great promise, because you will hardly find in all the inhabited world a country which is so fair and spacious, settled from time immemorial, and which is as much ruined as this one. For ever since we departed from it, it has not accepted a single other nation or language. They all try to settle it, but it is beyond their power.

This is therefore not a particular expression of joy because of the Crusader disasters or of the victories of a Saladin or Baibars. It is the changing vicissitudes of the war and the

[83] Naḥmanides' *Commentary on the Pentateuch* is printed in almost all commentated editions of the Bible, like *Mikraōth Gedōlōth* (first edn. Venice, 1523 ff.). This famous commentary was surpassed only by that of Rashi (R. Solomon of Troyes), who wrote about 150 years earlier. In the following I use the edition of C. D. Chavel (above, n. 76).

undeniable fact of the desolation of the country, which point to the will of Providence. 'Great is the desolation of the land,' says Naḥmanides, 'a land so fair and spacious because they are not worthy of you and you are not right for them.'

As Providence had expressed its will unambiguously, so did history urge a solution for the fate of Israel. Commenting on Deuteronomy 12: 5: 'You shall ask for the place which the Lord, your God, will choose out of all your tribes to receive his Name and you will come thither', Naḥmanides says:

You should go to him from distant lands, and ask which is the way to the House of the Lord and you shall say unto each other: 'Come ye and let us go up the mountain of the Lord to the house of the God of Jacob'[Isa. 2: 3], as it is written: 'They shall ask the way to Zion with their faces towards her' [Jer. 50: 5]. And it is written in *Siphrei*: 'You shall ask'—you can ask from a prophet, from that you can infer that you can wait until a prophet will bid you to go. But the Scriptures say: 'His habitation shall ye seek and thither thou shall come' [Deut. 12: 15], that is to say: ask and you will find—and hereafter the prophet will bid you.[84]

For Naḥmanides, clearly the time had come to act. Not only prayers and yearnings but acts are needed in this generation which was chosen by Providence to witness the inability of the mighty Empires to capture and rule the Land of Israel. Naḥmanides, as we have seen, drew his own conclusions and had the courage of his convictions to leave Spain and settle in Jerusalem. Two of his sermons, one when he entered Jerusalem on 2 September 1267 (9 Elul 5027 of Creation), the other a sermon on the New Year, pronounced two years later in 1269 when in Acre, and a letter which he wrote to his son in Spain, bear witness to his mood and feelings.

The Jerusalem sermon, written in rhymed prose, is rather lengthy, and following the conventions of the period, full of biblical and midrashic quotations and clichés. Even so, the author succeeds in strongly communicating some basic ideas, over and above expressing his deep sadness on seeing the ruined

[84] *Sifre debé Rab: Der älteste halachische und hagadische Midrasch zu Numeri und Deuteronomium*, i, ed. M. Friedmann (M. Ish-Shalom), (Vienna 1864), par. 62. *Sifre* on Deuteronomy ed. H. S. Horovitz, and L. Finkelstein (Berlin 1939; repr. New York 1969), par. 62, 128.

city of Jerusalem.[85] Naḥmanides opens his sermon with a quotation from Ps. 122: 2–3: 'Our feet shall stand within thy gates O Jerusalem [Naḥmanides adds, 'House of God and gate to Heaven'], Jerusalem that is builded as a city that is compact together.' After describing her former glories he turns his eyes to the severely tested city:

And now my soul is in turmoil within me, and for these things do I weep, because in the city there is nothing but desolation and destruction. Our House of Holiness and Glory in which our forefathers praised God was burned down and all our delights were destroyed. And the ire of God increases against her for days innumerable, generation after generation . . . Our enemies are the judges; this one destroys and uproots the boundaries; and that one raises up and erects idols. Robbers entered it and profaned it and pray therein to a God who does not save. All the uncircumcised and unclean raise their voice in prayer in the Temple of God without a God they shout ho! ho! . . . And the fruit of the Land is a pride and adornment . . . and it is still a land which flows with milk and honey for those who dwell in her. I compare you, my mother, to the woman whose son died in her lap and painfully there is milk in her breasts and she suckles the pups of dogs. And despite all that, your lovers abandoned you, and your enemies desolated you, but far away they remember and glorify in the Holy City claiming 'The land is given to us for an inheritance' [Ezek. 33: 24]. But when they come to you and find in you all the delights of the eyes, they run away as if pursued by the sword, but nobody is pursuing them. The desolation in this fertile and spacious land in the midst of the land is great, because they do not deserve you and you are not fitting for them.

On coming to Jerusalem and beholding her he performs the mourning ritual for the dead and pronounces the dirges of Ps. 79: 'O God, the heathen are come into thine inheritance . . . We are become a reproach to our neighbours, a scorn and derision to them that are round us.' Naḥmanides does not mention explicitly either Muslims or Christians, but for the hint that the

[85] The sermon was printed at the end of Naḥmanides' Commentary on the Bible in the *incunabula* editions of Rome (1480) and Lisbon (1489). The text was published (following the Roman *editio princeps* and the Lisbon printing) in *Voyages*, 71–81. A heavily annotated edition is *Kithvey R. Moshe b. Naḥman*, i, ed. Chavel (Jerusalem 1963), 424–32. An English trans. is Ramban (Naḥmanides), *Writings and Discourses* by Ch. B. Chavel, ii (New York 1978): 'Prayer at the Ruins of Jerusalem', ibid. 697–725. I have partly used this important translation, but in some places it is too literal a rendering of the text.

former destroyed the land and the latter erected idols. In the Jewish perspective of the history of the Holy Land there is actually little difference between the former and the latter, as long as the Land of Israel is taken away from its rightful heir and possessor. But the time of reckoning is near, and one should expect divine intervention; yet it is human effort which will precede it. Thus it was Naḥmanides' basically activist view of the part to be played by the Jews in deciding their fate as linked to the Land of Israel which explained his own immigration to the Holy Land.

Naḥmanides' activism lingered on in certain circles. A generation after his death, an anonymous pupil of his who visited Crusader Acre[86] wrote: 'And now many are stirred and are willing to migrate to the Land of Israel. And many think that we are near the coming of the Messiah, as you see that the nations of the world are making everywhere the burden heavier on Israel; and other signs were revealed to the humble.' This is introduced by an extraordinary statement:

Let nobody think that the king Messiah will reveal himself in an unclean land; neither let him think that the Messiah will come to the Land of Israel amidst pagans. Whoever makes this mistake is simply not caring for the dignity of the king Messiah.[87] But the children of Israel who cultivate the Torah, men of piety and deeds from the four corners of the world, one of a city and two of a family, everybody

[86] Publ. by S. Assaf in a memorial volume for A. M. Luncz, *Koveṣ Yerūshalaim* (Jerusalem 1928), 51–61; repr. in *Voyages*, 98.

[87] This strange statement does not seem to derive from any known Talmudic or Midrashic source. But a 14th-cent. scholar, R. Meir Aldabari, grandson of Rosh (R. Asher), in his *Shvīlei ha-Emūnah* (The paths of faith), 10th path, says similar things, which he quotes from an unknown midrash: 'When many people from Israel, students of the Torah, men pious and active will come to live in Eretz Israel and settle in Jerusalem, each man according to the desire of his heart, and the spirit of purity and sanctity will move him, and they will come from the four corners of the world, one from a city and two from a family, and they will settle here so that he will have there a truthful field and heritage in the holy mountain and in Jerusalem, then the Creator, blessed be He, will hear their cries and will near the end of salvation.' The similarity was noted by S. H. Kuk, *Studies*, ii (Jerusalem 1963), 91. The text quoted above, however, is really the beginning of an eclectic Apocalypse and does not relate to our question. This statement coincides however, with an opinion voiced among Christians during the First Crusade. It is Guibert of Nogent who puts a similar idea into the speech of Urban II. The Antichrist has to fight Christians in the Holy Land. Consequently, Christians have to capture the Holy Land before his coming, which will usher in the appearance of the Messiah (*Guiberti abbatis Gesta Dei per Francos, RHC HOcc.* iv. 137–40).

whose heart is dictating it and he is moved by the purity of spirit and the love of holiness to come to the Land of Israel—to those the king Messiah will reveal himself, as it is written 'and I will take you one of a city and two of a family and I will bring you to Zion' [Jer. 3: 14].

And yet despite the ardour of Naḥmanides' faith and despite the fact that he himself migrated and settled in the Holy Land, his attitude to migration and settling was ambiguous. This was the result of his evaluation of the unique standing of the Holy Land in Creation: the Holy Land is directly ruled by Providence, whereas other lands are ruled by his heavenly appointees. The governance of the Holy Land is by the Divine Power called *Eretz* (Land), which is the tenth divine emanation called *Sheḥīna* (Divine Presence).[88] Consequently, the gist or the innermost meaning (*'iqar*) of the holy precepts is shared only by those who live in the Holy Land, and the exalted standing of the Holy Land places tremendous responsibility on those who live there. Commenting on Leviticus 18: 25 'And the land is defiled; therefore I do visit the iniquity thereof upon it, and the land itself vomiteth out her inhabitants'—though this related specifically to forbidden sexual relations—Naḥmanides stressed the particularity of holiness of the Holy Land ruled directly by God and not by angels or constellations.[89] It is therefore strictness of observation which is demanded from those who want to live in the Holy Land, and this obviously restricts the choice of potential settlers. This is perhaps the root of Naḥmanides' attributing a meritorious value to the Diaspora.[90]

Naḥmanides' rather ambivalent attitude to migration to the Holy Land precisely because of the spiritual virtues of the Holy

[88] A. Gottlieb, 'Naḥmanides as Kabbalist', *Studies in the Kabbalah Literature* (H), (Tel-Aviv 1976), 88–96.

[89] Naḥmanides, *Commentary on the Torah*, Engl. trans. Ch. B. Chavel (New York 1974), Lev. 18: 25, 268–75; cf. ibid. Deut. 4: 25.

[90] According to Naḥmanides, sufferings in Exile are rewarded by God. The accomplishment of religious precepts under a foreign ruler merits reward, whereas there is no special merit in their fulfilment under a king of Israel because they are a part of state law. This is stated in 'The Disputation of Barcelona' in Ramban (above, n. 76), ii. 672–4, and consequently could be construed as an argument *ad hoc* in the polemic. See, however, F. Y. Baer, 'The Land of Israel and the Diaspora in the Eyes of the Middle Ages' (H), *Meassef Ẓion* 6 (1934), 167–8. *Galuth* (Berlin 1936, Engl. trans. New York 1947), 52.

Land is repeated some fifteen years later by the most important figure in Ashkenazic Jewry, R. Meir b. Baruk of Rothenburg. He himself, as already noted, left Germany and attempted to migrate with his family to the Holy Land, but his pronouncements on the subject are somewhat muted by religious, halakhic considerations.

R. Meir stands firm on the fulfilment of the Talmudic precepts of vows taken to migrate to the Holy Land. A father cannot stop his son who has decided to migrate to the land, as in the realm of precepts such vows take precedence even over the respect due by children to their parents.[91] A succinct explanation is given to the phrase in Tractate *Kethubōth* that a man who lives outside the boundaries of the Land of Israel is like a man who has no God. This means, he writes, that the Divine Providence is essentially (*beʿiqar*) in Eretz Israel, ' "a throne facing a throne", as it is written [1 Kings 8: 48, 2 Chr. 6: 38].[92] The prayer is to Talpioth,[93] a hill (*tel*) to which all mouths turn.' However, when asked about the particular merits of the Holy Land in exonerating from the tortures after death (*ḥibūt ha-qever*), he nevertheless answers sharply: 'I do not know.'[94]

But when pressed to answer a query about the essence of the precept to migrate to the Holy Land, he answers that this is explained in Tractate *Kethubōth* 110*b*, where there is also an answer to the query about the forgiveness of sins (ibid. 111*b*). The gist of his answer, however, is a firm warning against those who would migrate to the Holy Land and not lead a life of ritual strictness and devotion. Maharam's *responsum* is reminiscent of similar utterances by Naḥmanides. The punishment for transgressions there is more severe because God's eyes are permanently on this land 'and the man who rebels inside the palace is not like the man who rebels outside it. The land will

[91] The enormous number of *Responsa* of R. Meir (known by the acronym *Maharam*) has not yet been critically edited. The *responsum* referred to in the text is quoted from R. Meir b. Baruk, *Responsa, Rulings and Customs*, ed. M. Bloch (Berlin 1891), par. 14, p. 5; ed. I. Z. Cahana, ii (Jerusalem 1960), no. 129.

[92] Jer. 3: 17: 'At that time they shall call Jerusalem the throne of the Lord.'

[93] The expression appears only once in the Bible, in S. of S. 4: 5, and probably means stronghold. Maharam, following the Talmud (*Berakhōt* 30*a*), makes a play on words: *Tel-Piyyoth*, the Hill of Mouths.

[94] *Tashbetz* (Collection of Responsa of Maharam by Samson b. Tzadōq) (Warsaw 1901), no. 560.

vomit the transgressors.' This is the reason, he writes, why the 'idolators' (i.e. Christians) fail in it 'and the land is ruined and the cities a shambles'. 'But whoever goes there for God's sake (*le-shem shamayim*) to live in sanctity and purity, there is no end to his reward; all this if he can make a living there.'[95]

R. Meir, like Naḥmanides, pursues perfectionism and religious rigorism as the basic condition which should guide and rule potential migrants. But the last *responsum* puts forward an additional limitation; asked why the *Amoraim*—that is, the (Babylonian) scholars of the third to sixth centuries—did not settle in the Holy Land, he answered that to do so they would have had to renounce their studies because they would have to earn their own living. Moreover 'one is allowed to leave Eretz Israel to follow one's teacher to study Torah'; *a fortiori* one should *not* leave one's master abroad and go to Eretz Israel, neglect one's studies, and roam around earning one's upkeep.[96]

Thus, given the alternative of living in Europe near the great centres of learning and easier sources of making a living and migrating to the Holy Land, R. Meir clearly chose the former. It is in the same vein that he answered a question regarding the whereabouts of the 'migration of the great' (apparently, the 'migration of rabbis' *c.*1209). He heard from their sons, he recalls, that the great men ordered their descendants to return (to Europe) because the land was not charitable, and they had to neglect their studies because they had to work hard for their maintenance. Moreover, there was no centre of learning and there were no experts fluent in the minutiae of precepts.[97]

And yet the hesitations of the great scholars, whether deriving from religious rigorism or from a perception of the value of the study of the Torah as compared to migration, was far from being shared by all. Some of those who hesitated nevertheless migrated themselves; and the state of the Holy Land, as well as the war between East and West for its domination stirred the imagination and catalysed migrations and attempts at settlement.

95 *Tashbetz* no. 559, and in *Teshūwoth Maharam*, ed. M. Bloch, 5, no. 14.

96 Ibid. no. 561; ed. Bloch, no. 15.

97 Ed. Bloch, no. 79, p. 187.

A new way of thinking emerged as the repercussions of the Crusades and of the Crusader domination of the Holy Land continued to be felt throughout the Jewish Diaspora. Writing at the turn of the century (*c.*1300), a Jew of Marseilles, R. Nissim b. Moses, commented on the situation of the Holy Land in a very similar way to Naḥmanides.[98] For him as for Naḥmanides, the great miracle of his time is the desolation of the Land of Israel, which yet remains the object of desire and jealousy of different powers, triggering off endless wars. Thus, a land which was once 'the joy of the whole earth' (Ps. 48: 3) is now utterly ruined. 'Our enemies who dwell therein have not succeeded in settling her since the day of the destruction of the Temple.' Neither Rome nor the Muslims held it for long, and even then they did not really strike roots in the country 'because there was always a sound of tremor and the threat of war'. Now there is a new factor adding to the insecurity and desolation, the Mongols (the Tartars). Hearing their approach, the population of the Holy Land hides in caves and behind rocks. Luckily, the Mongols cannot tarry 'because the water of the rivers and springs will not be sufficient for their horses and camels'. Obviously, then, it is only the Jews who can possess the Land of Israel and make it flourish again.

R. Nissim b. Moses of Marseilles probably knew Naḥmanides' commentaries, but whereas the latter referred mainly to the Crusaders, R. Nissim extended the argument to include Christians, Muslims, and Mongols. From the Jewish point of view, as we have said, there was no difference whatsoever.

In the beginning of the fourteenth century the same way of thinking—that is, urging activism towards settling in the Holy Land because migration and settlement were a necessary preliminary to the coming of the Messiah—was also expounded by a curious rationalist, Joseph of Argentière (Heb. Ibn Caspi) from southern France.[99] Again, it is a conclusion drawn from the final defeat of the Crusaders by the Muslims (1291). One of his treatises deals with the possibility of the

[98] R. Nissim b. R. Moshe of Marseilles, *Ma'aseh Nissim* (Story of a miracle), ed. J. H. Shor, in *Heḥalūtz* 7 (1865 repr. Jerusalem 1972), 89 ff. The quotations are from 102–3. There is a better reading by M. Hazani in *Zion* 47(1982), 373–6.

[99] Cf. S. Pines, 'The Probability of the Restoration of a Jewish State according to Ibn Caspi and Spinoza' (H), *'Iyun* 14 (1963), 289–318, repr. in *Studies in the History of Jewish Philosophy* (H), (Jerusalem 1977), 273–306.

restoration of the Third Temple.[100] In an aggressive bout of polemic he attacked exegetes whom he considered to be distorting the simple meaning of the Scriptures or questioning destiny (*ye'ūd*). There are even some, he said, 'who gave a hand to other nations who assign whatever they find [in the Scriptures], rightly or wrongly, to their Messiah. And the results included the horrible events in the wake of a disputation with the Christians.'[101] Resurrection in the hereafter, he argues, is more doubtful than the coming of the Messiah. Still, the exegetes are satisfied to find one mention of the Resurrection in the Scriptures, but as to the Messiah even twenty verses are not sufficient. The whole thing, however, should not be argued on the basis of exegesis, but on that of logic and reason, because logic convinces other nations, philosophers as well as simple people. It is in the realm of reason to observe the rise and fall of nations. This is taking place among Christians as well as among Muslims:

> In our own times the Muslims took Acre from the Christians, and before they took Galilee and Syria, whereas the Christians took from the Muslims the whole kingdom of Aragon and the island of Majorca. And is there any sense in it? Only God can answer this question. Therefore why should it be a miraculous event that the Land of Israel should be returned to us, if God wills it, from the Muslims?[102] The Land of Israel has changed hands in history and even now the king of France is preparing his 'passage'.[103] He may win [the war] or the land may remain with the Muslims. Consequently one can hardly answer the question, 'why are the Christians boasting against us and cursing us because we lost that land;[104] they will adduce that we revolted against their Messiah, as if God took counsel with them or revealed to them His secret.'

He turns to history for arguments—traditional history, and

[100] Joseph ibn Caspi, *Tam ha-Kesef*, ed. I. H. Last (London 1913): 8th treatise, 41 ff.

[101] This probably refers to the confiscation and burning of the Talmud after the disputation in Paris in 1240.

[102] Joseph ibn Caspi, *Tam ha-kesef*, 42.

[103] This is the exact translation of the Hebrew: 'la'avor sham'. *Passagium* was at that time the technical expression for a military expedition.

[104] He refers to the Christian theologians, who from the time of Antiquity saw in the destruction of the Temple and the Jewish state an irrefutable proof of the veracity of Christianity and the rejection of Judaism.

the sequence of the four kingdoms or four beasts.[105] Rome subjugated the Jews as she subjugated the whole world *before* the birth of Christ—but how does it prove their so-called historical argument? Precisely when the Romans finally accepted the Christian Messiah [Byzantium], it was the Muslims, who were infidels, who took the Land of Israel from them. Clearly Providence follows its own ways which are beyond human comprehension. Claiming to know God's reasons is pure madness.

Observing the continual changes,[106] one is forced to conclude the possibility, he argues, of the return of the Jews to the land of Israel.

> Is there no more clay in the potter's hand [Jer. 18: 6] to create a man like Moses or a smaller man who will argue before the king, and the king will hand over to him the Land of Israel. This happened under Pharaoh and Cyrus. Why should it not happen for the third time. God will send a man who will act like Moses, namely, he will go to the king of Egypt, or the king of Tartary. This may also happen otherwise. A king will rise and capture the Land of Israel from the hands of the sultan of Egypt. Like Cyrus he will call on the Jews to return to their land. This may be the Tartar king who is today the king of Babylon,[107] or it may be the king of France, [or] the emperor. Moreover, God may simply stir tomorrow or the day after the spirit of the present rulers to hand over the Land of Israel, and all the Jews in his kingdom and others from the four corners of the world will gather therein.[108] Man is unable to say or predict how God is going to act, but 'as a rule the thing is naturally [i.e. not miraculously] possible and no Christian who hears that can argue against me'.

Thus the circle was closing: nostalgia, pilgrimage, and eventual settlement, or attempts at settlement, resulted in a revival of Messianic ideologies nurtured on the permanent yearning for the ingathering of Exiles. Here and there a rationalistic spirit came up with a different solution: either that

[105] Babylon, Persia, Greece, and Rome, eventually Islam.

[106] At one point he adds humorously that the number of [apocalyptic] beasts is not limited or exhausted.

[107] The Mongol rulers of Baghdad and Iraq. Strangely enough, *c.*1300 Europe entertained the dream of having the Holy Land handed over to them by the Mongols. Cf. Sylvia Schein, '*Gesta Dei per Mongolos, 1300*: The Generis of a Non-event', *English Historical Review* 94 (1979), 805–19.

[108] Joseph ibn Caspi, *Tam ha-kesef*, 45.

the settlement of the Holy Land was a prerequisite of the coming of the Messiah, or that there was a political solution to the problem, a God-willed solution whereby a ruler from the West or the East in possession of the Holy Land would hand it over to the Jewish nation. Six hundred years were to pass before the partial fulfilment of either of these visionary dreams.

7

The Hebrew Itineraries of the Crusader Period

INTRODUCTION

TEN Hebrew descriptions of the Holy Land and its *memorabilia* have survived from the Crusader period.[1] One hesitates to call all of them 'itineraries', as some are no more than a rather dreary enumeration of 'Tombs of the Ancestors' or 'Tombs of the Just'.[2] And yet even the most jejune, once we get used to the particular interests of their writers, opens up an unexpected world of popular beliefs, where magic and enchantment mingle with reality, things seen with things experienced, and wishful thinking strives to bring the reader consolation through the intervention of the supernatural. Seen in this perspective, many a puzzling episode or description reveals its hidden code and explanation.

The itineraries were a new phenomenon in Jewish literature. Although a short Arabic fragment describing the gates of Jerusalem has survived from the late Fāṭimid period, perhaps from the eve of the Crusades, there can be little doubt that this was a newly emerging genre; it is hard to believe that among the thousands of Genizah documents no such itinerary would

[1] The earliest study of this literary genre was that of L. Zunz, 'Geographische Literatur der Juden von den ältesten Zeiten bis zum Jahre 1841', *Gesammelte Schriften*, i (Berlin 1878), 146–216, which appeared earlier in English as an appendix to the *Itinerary of R. Benjamin of Tudela*, ed. A. Asher, ii (London 1840–1), 230 ff. This was never continued on the same scale, although A. Ya'ari published important data regarding the itineraries in the bibliographies of *Voyages*. For an attempt to revise the chronology of itineraries of the Crusader period, see J. Prawer, 'The Jews in the Latin Kingdom of Jerusalem' (H), *Zion* 11 (1946), 43–50. This was accepted and used in the most extensive study of Jewish holy traditions by M. Ish-Shalom, *Tombs of the Ancestors* (H).

[2] *Qivrei avōth*, lit. 'Tombs of the Ancestors' may refer more particularly to the Patriarchs of the nation, but in this case it refers to the famous ancestors in general. Another appellation, *qivrei ṣadīqīm*, lit. 'Tombs of the Just' or 'Tombs of the Righteous', is very often used to describe the tombs of the Sages of the Talmudic and later periods.

have survived if it had ever been written. The rise of Hebrew itineraries in the twelfth century is the result of the growth in the scope of Jewish pilgrimage coming from Europe (and hence the use of Hebrew rather than the Arabic current in the Near East), and the effect of a similar development in the Christian world.

Obviously, the information that can be gleaned from the different Hebrew itineraries includes valuable *realia* of the Holy Land under Crusader rule. Thus, for example, information on the network of roads used by our pilgrims shows that they differed from those used either by contemporary Christian or Muslim pilgrims or by the Crusader or Muslim armies. In addition to the main highways—like the coastal road, or that which began near Hebron in the south, moved over the mountainous part, Judaea and Samaria, then through Galilee and Banyās on the frontier of the kingdom to the emirate of Damascus in the north—the itineraries indicate a large number of small roads, obviously part of the regular secondary communication network although often no more than village paths, which criss-crossed Lower and Upper Galilee and served to link the places of Jewish pilgrimage. The places in which tombs were venerated are, incidentally, an important addition to Palestinian toponymy, as almost all had a venerable past going back to biblical times, and even the more recent ones at least to the Roman or Byzantine periods. Moreover, even where reference is made to a tomb but no village is explicitly mentioned, the existence of a village can be inferred; there must have been a Jewish community in the immediate neighbourhood to be the physical carriers of the real or legendary traditions which, transmitted from generation to generation, became hallowed in Jewish lore, many of them surviving to our own times.

As we have seen, in the Crusader period the location of the tombs would frequently be marked by some kind of distinctive feature, often a small dome (Heb. *kipah*), sometimes a tree or a grove (almost always imbued with some miraculous properties).

On the religious level, these Hebrew itineraries preserve the memory of a large number of places venerated by the adherents of two or even all three monotheistic religions. Some enjoyed this privileged position because their monuments commemorated personalities common to all the Holy Scriptures. Such was the case with the tombs of the Patriarchs in Hebron, or the Cave of Elijah on Mount Carmel. In other places, monuments were venerated by Jews and Muslims. Some of them, we suspect, had different traditions attached to them by the different religions. The Crusader sarcophagus (brought from Acre) venerated as the tomb of Mohammed's companion Abū Ḥureira in Yabneh (Crusader Ibelin) was venerated by the Jews as the tomb of Rabban Gamaliel of Yabneh. As the veneration of the different tombs was part and parcel of a popular level of religion, it was all the more easily accepted by different religious faiths.

The pilgrimage to the Holy Land was regarded by some as an end in itself; for others the pilgrimage to the Holy Land was part of a longer voyage. Only two of the authors of the extant itineraries belong to this latter category: Benjamin of Tudela and Petaḥyah of Regensburg. All the others regarded the Holy Land as the sole aim of their pilgrimage. They also have a great deal in common in motivation and practice.

After the destruction of the Second Temple, pilgrimages were never again institutionalized, whether on the lines of the Muslim *ḥajj* or even the less formal Christian *peregrinatio ad Terram Sanctam*. When the thrice-yearly pilgrimages to Jerusalem to appear before the Lord at His Sanctuary ceased as obligatory precepts, there actually arose a very strong current in Judaism opposed if not to pilgrimages as such then at least to one of their new aims and features: the veneration of tombs. The biblical episode of the death of Moses which stated that he was buried in the Land of Moab 'and nobody knows the place of his burial until today' (Deut. 34: 6), was interpreted by the Sages: 'so that the children of Israel should not come thither and construct a Temple and bring sacrifices and incense. Moreover to prevent the Gentiles from polluting his tomb by their idolatry.'[3] The practice was thus regarded as idolatry or necromancy (Deut. 18: 11). Nevertheless, the visiting of tombs and offering some kind of prayers was both practised and condemned; thus in the New Testament, where the Scribes and

[3] *Pesiqta Zutarta*, ed. S. Buber (Vienna 1874), on Deut. 33; p. 68.

Pharisees are accused of the veneration of the tombs of prophets and the righteous (Matt. 23: 29, Luke 11: 47–8). There was, however, nothing specifically Christian about such condemnation; the censuring followed rabbinical ideas. Nearer our own period, in the tenth century, a famous Karaite scholar, Sahl b. Maşliaḥ, condemns the practice in the strongest way:

> And how should I let these goings-on pass in silence when several of the practices of idolatry are to be found among some of Israel? They sit at the tombs, they sleep in the clefts of the rocks and they supplicate the dead saying: 'Rabbi Yose the Galilean, pray, heal me, or give me a belly [i.e. make me pregnant]', and they light candles on the tombs of the *ṣadīqīm*, and burn before them incense and they bind clumps[?] on the palm tree of the *ṣadīq* against various diseases and they celebrate on the tombs of the dead *ṣadīqīm*, and make there their vows and they appeal to them and ask them to give them what they desire.[4]

It is even possible that formal prayers were offered as a part of the rite of visiting the tombs of the holy men.[5]

Although the visiting of the Tombs of the Just played such a preponderant role in the pilgrimage, it was obviously the visit to Jerusalem which was the central aim and event. No doubt this was in commemoration of the thrice-yearly pilgrimages of olden times, which justified the hardships and dangers of the voyage. It was not only an act of mourning for the time of passed glory, but an act of prayer to hasten the rebuilding of the Temple and the Holy City. The majority of pilgrims probably also attributed a particular efficacy to prayers offered in the hallowed ground around the Temple or facing it on the Mount of Olives.

Once the pilgrim reached Jerusalem, a number of religious practices would be followed. Foremost was the rite of the mourners—particularly, rending one's garments—and the pronouncing of the appropriate prayer on beholding Jerusalem for the first time. The city, though flourishing, was always regarded as 'ruined' because of the destruction of the Temple and its Holy of Holies. The magnificent Dome of the Rock on the Temple esplanade further accentuated the foreign rule in

[4] Publ. by S. Pinsker, *Lickute Kadmoniot* (Vienna 1860), app. 31–2.
[5] Mann, ii. 357. More examples in *Tombs of the Ancestors*, 17–19.

the Holy Place. A similar ritual was again performed on seeing the Temple for the first time. It was then only natural that the Jewish pilgrim should visit in turn the gates of Jerusalem, a circuit which became a kind of liturgical procession.[6]

After Jerusalem the most popular and important site of pilgrimage seems to have been to the Tombs of the Patriarchs in Hebron. This is one of the very few places, perhaps the only one, which had a tradition of veneration, although tombs of other biblical personalities were indicated in the Bible and in Talmudic literature (for example, the tombs of Rachel, Joseph, Joshua, Samuel, and the very problematic tombs of David and other kings of Judah).

Curiously enough, but for very rare exceptions, our itineraries do not mention the offering of prayers at the tombs. The chief exception was the Tombs of the Patriarchs in Hebron, which probably contained an invocation for the intercession of the fathers of the nation on behalf of the person praying or the nation. It is worth noting that such prayers are rarely even mentioned at the Tomb of Rachel, the mother of the nation, who, according to tradition, weeps over the fate of the Children of Israel; this popular custom, although practised today, is not noted in our itineraries.

Among the particular features of our itineraries is that biblical reminiscences proper do not play a dominant role in the descriptions. Except for the construction of the First Temple, no other event connected with the biblical period comes to the fore: no famous battles, no great events, no place of miracles of the period of the nation's glory. If such events are to be somehow guessed or understood, it is only through the mention of the tombs of their dramatis personae.

If biblical history is conspicuously absent, it is the later period of Jewish history—the end of the Second Temple and the following centuries—which is salient. But here again, it is not the great events of Jewish history under Roman and Byzantine rule that fill the pages of our itineraries, but the silent tombs of the Sages of the Talmudic period. This strange fact can hardly be explained by assuming that the mentioning

[6] Additionally, prayers were recited on visiting the different gates. See Mann, *Texts*, i. 459; the full text, *Ṣalawāt al-Abūāb fī'l-Quds* (The prayers at the gates of Jerusalem), was publ. by L. N. Goldfeld in *Haaretz* (daily) of 19 May 1972.

of a tomb is a kind of a *pars pro toto*. Thus, it was not history as such, not the great events, which our pilgrims had at heart.

The particular focus on the tombs of the Talmudic Sages can be partially explained by the preponderance of Talmudic studies in the great Jewish centres of learning, but possibly we have to look in a different direction for an explanation. The existence of the tombs, the possibility of listing them and visiting them represents a kind of historical reality which carries with it the notion of a divine promise of the resurrection of the nation in its own Homeland. For a people that clings to memories, the Holy Tombs are a guarantee of the fulfilment of that promise. The question of whether the Promised Land was real or heavenly, which created tensions in Christian thought at the time of the Crusades, was never a subject of controversy in Judaism. For the Jews, the Promised Land to which they would return was a real and earthly land: only whether the means by which the Ingathering of the Exiles would take place was to be real or miraculous was open to discussion. Until then the tombs of the great ancestors and sages were there in the Land of Israel to remind one, and as it were, to keep alive the Jewish claim to the Holy Land, ruled as it was by God's will alternately by different powers. By enumerating the tombs of their ancestors buried in the soil of the Holy Land, the Jews stake a claim to their Land. Theirs is an older and more fundamental claim than that of the others. Those who drew up the lists of the tombs and those who read them had a tangible proof of Jewish presence in the Holy Land.

This claim to the Holy Land, the belief in its inalienability, is strengthened by permanent divine intervention and the miraculous events which happen there every day. God's providence guards the tombs of the holy men from the sacrilege of being touched by the gentiles (Muslims and Christians alike). Only Jews can approach them. This leads clearly to an antagonistic attitude to the powers prevailing in the land—in the twelfth century, anti-Christian, in the thirteenth anti-Muslim—but the object of the antagonism was in fact of no matter as long as the prerogatives of Israel were guarded.

If such was the role of the tombs, this obviously raised a question of their authenticity. It is in the forged itinerary of R. Menaḥem of Hebron that we find an echo of such queries and doubts as early as the first half of the thirteenth century.[7] He writes:

> And whoever sees this treatise about the *ṣadīqīm* whose names were written down, let them not be suspicious and they should not say in their hearts that I wrote to please them and that I wrote to extract money from them. It is clear and known before the Creator of the World, that this I received from the Westerners.[8] And if the observer questions and asks how it is that the Westerners know about the *ṣadīqīm* who have been buried there for 3,000 years? I, the writer, will answer him: they know it from the mouth of the Westerners and not from the writer, because those who live today in Eretz Israel have never been exiled. When the wicked Titus, son of the Emperor Vespasian, exiled some of them he [also] left some, and the people who live today in Eretz Israel are their descendants and they received [the tradition] from each other beginning with the destruction [of the Temple] and they know the whole thing. And they were under the rule of Ishmael, as well as the king of Babylon, king of Egypt, king of Assyria, and king of Jerusalem.

Thus, medieval Jewry is assured of the authenticity of the tombs of its great men, all of them Sages, a few men of action and heroes of battles. The former had the force of appeal to the hearts of the believers, the latter are bypassed in silence.

As the itineraries are written by Jews and for Jews, they feature another strong characteristic: they are written in a kind of spatial and historical vacuum. Were it not for anti-Christian or anti-Muslim remarks, we should be at pains to know to what period they relate. They are unabashedly Judaeocentric; if Christians or Muslims are reported as appearing at the same Holy Tombs, it is solely to emphasize their Jewishness. The Jewish pilgrim walks through his Holy Land without any regard to others. He does not share the Tombs of the Patriarchs in Hebron with other religions, nor the Cave of Elijah on Mount Carmel. Kfar Kana (Cana Galilaeae) was the burial place of the prophet Jonah or the sons of Jacob—there was no mention of a famous marriage there. It meant nothing to Jew or Muslim and was never mentioned. On this point the Jewish itineraries do not differ from their Christian counterparts; the

[7] *Hameamer* 3 (1919), 42 ff. See below, Itinerary F.

[8] 'Westerners'—*bnei ma'aravah*—was a current expression for the inhabitants of the Holy Land (as seen from Babylon). The expression was still in use in the 13th cent.

latter utterly ignored the non-Christian traditions. Neither held edifying elements with regard to other religions.

The analysis of the Hebrew itineraries that follows is not a study in historical geography, nor even in the 'holy geography' of the Holy Land. An excellent study regarding the Jewish perspective of the subject exists[9] and there is no reason to follow a well-trodden path. The purpose here is to characterize each itinerary, paying attention to its author, known or anonymous, the date of the treatise, and its contents. In some cases, this will bring us to conclusions as to the manner in which the itinerary was written, and how it was transmitted. Finally, we shall try to envisage the roads followed by our pilgrims.

A. SEFER QABBALATH ṢADĪQEI ERETZ ISRAEL (QIVREI AVŌTH)

The earliest treatise of this new Hebrew literary genre was called by its publisher *Qivrei Avōth* (Tombs of the ancestors) and assigned to the period of Muslim domination. The dating is definitely erroneous; as we shall prove below, the text clearly belongs to the Crusader period.[10]

The author is not entirely anonymous as he indicates his name in an acrostic: 'I am the man Yinaḥesh ben ha-Ḥaber Yiṣḥaq who did it.' 'Yinaḥesh' (lit. will guess, will prophesy) is not known as a name, and it has been suggested that it refers to Joseph (based on Gen. 44: 15). In this case the name of the author would have been Joseph b. Isaac. Additionally, we learn that the father carried the title *Ḥaber*, that is, Associate or Fellow of the Yeshiva or Academy. Although we do not know to which Academy he refers, it certainly puts his father in the framework of the Orient and links him either with the Academy of the Holy Land (in Damascus) or with one of the ancient Academies of Babylon. This in itself would point to the eleventh or twelfth centuries.

The text, however, permits more accurate identification.

[9] See above, end n. 1.

[10] This Genizah fragment, no. 2699 in the E. Adler collection, was published by A. Marmorstein in *Meassef Ẓion* 2 (1926), 31–9. The same codex contains, in addition to liturgical poetry, a large number of magic prescriptions in Hebrew and in Arabic.

Speaking of Mount Zion in Jerusalem, the author indicates: 'An idol stands on the cave wherein are the tombs of the kings and it [the cave] is sealed.' Obviously no Muslim would allow a statue in a sanctuary.[11] And again, in the description of the Temple of Solomon he refers to priests and their chants, and perhaps even to the statue of the Virgin and her child. The end of the treatise, though mutilated, leaves no doubt as to its general meaning. The author, who calls his treatise *iggereth*, that is, Epistle (p. 34, ll. 4–5), here invokes God's vengeance on the wickedness of Edom, the traditional name given first to Byzantium and then to Christendom at large. This is not the only clue to the date of the pilgrimage. Our pilgrim reports seeing the tombs of the Patriarchs in Hebron, but says that he had to view them from the outside—as he puts it, 'I saw them clandestinely through a window' (p. 34, l. 11) in his own expression. This must have happened after the 'discovery' of the tombs in 1120, when a Christian sanctuary was established inside the Herodian building.[12] The timing can be further narrowed down as the 'discovery' of the Royal Tombs on Mount Zion can be dated to 1146 or 1153.[13] The *terminus ad quem* cannot be later than 1187. It is true that it might have been in the short period of Christian domination of Jerusalem between 1229 and 1244, but during that period, following the truce of Frederick II with al-Malik al-Kāmil, the Temple esplanade was in Muslim hands and obviously no Christian statuary would have remained there. There is only one item in the treatise which does not fit into the general chronological picture. Speaking about Tiberias and its many Holy Tombs, our author mentions the tomb of Maimonides (p. 37, l. 15), who died in 1205 and, according to some traditions, was brought from Egypt and buried in Tiberias.[14] This would assign our treatise to the thirteenth century, but as this is against overwhelming proof to the contrary, it can be regarded as an interpolation of a later copyist, who also (see below)

[11] Marmorstein, *Meassef Zion* 2. 35, ll. 39–44 and pp. 38–9.

[12] 'Canonici Hebronensis de Inventione Sanctorum Patriarcharum', ed. P. Riant, in *AOL* ii A, 411.

[13] See n. 51.

[14] *Sefer Yuḥasīn ha-Shalem* [*Liber Juchassin*] (The complete book of genealogies), ed. H. Philipovsky, 220.

interpolated the Cave of Elijah into Mount Carmel near Tiberias. The author, then, is an Oriental Jew who went on a pilgrimage to the Holy Land under Crusader rule in the twelfth century. He is one of the few who explicitly state, at the end of his introduction that the purpose of his writing was to record the places that his feet had trodden.[15]

The poem, written in rhymed prose, has 128 lines (though a few lines could be missing). In the introduction (ll. 1–16), the author explains that he wanted to sing the virtues and riches of the Holy Land, but under existing conditions, 'his heart which yearned to speak about her virtues' had yielded instead tears and a tale of woe.

The main body of the poem is the description of his journey, which begins in the south with a visit to Hebron. This makes it plausible to assume that he came to the Holy Land by land, almost certainly with a caravan making its way from Egypt to the Crusader kingdom. It is to be noted that he never descended from the mountainous part of the country to the coastal plain or to the coast itself, but, as we shall see, this is rather common in the Hebrew itineraries. None of the Crusader ports was ever visited![16] The itinerary goes from Hebron in the south to Lebanon in the north, at which point the pilgrim ends his description. The only apparent deviation from this straight route is the rather unexpected appearance of a Mount Carmel between Nablus and Zippori (Sepphoris) (p. 36, l. 21), but this deviation, as we shall see, was more apparent than real.

Having started in Hebron, he clandestinely visited the Tomb of the Patriarchs. From here he continued to Ḥalḥul, Teqoʿa, and the Tomb of Rachel near Bethlehem. Singularly, neither he nor any other Jewish traveller seems to have entered Bethlehem. From the Tomb of Rachel he continued straight to Jerusalem. Here his description begins with the Royal Tombs

[15] Different dates have been advanced. A. Marmorstein assigned it to the foregoing Muslim period. I. Ben Zvi assigned it to the Crusader period (*Meassef Zion* 4 (1930), 148), but later relegated it to the 13th cent. S. Krauss (*Haolam* 21 (1935), 342) assigned it to the Christian rule of the Holy City, 1229–40. This is clearly impossible, as the Temple Mount then belonged to the Muslims. The dating *c.*1146–87 was proposed by me in *Zion* 11 (1946), 43–5. Whereas the *terminus ad quem* 1187 is clear, the *terminus a quo* (*c.*1146) is conjectural. See also below, Itinerary of Benjamin of Tudela, p. 201.

[16] The exceptions were European pilgrimages like that of Benjamin of Tudela or the anonymous pupil of Naḥmanides.

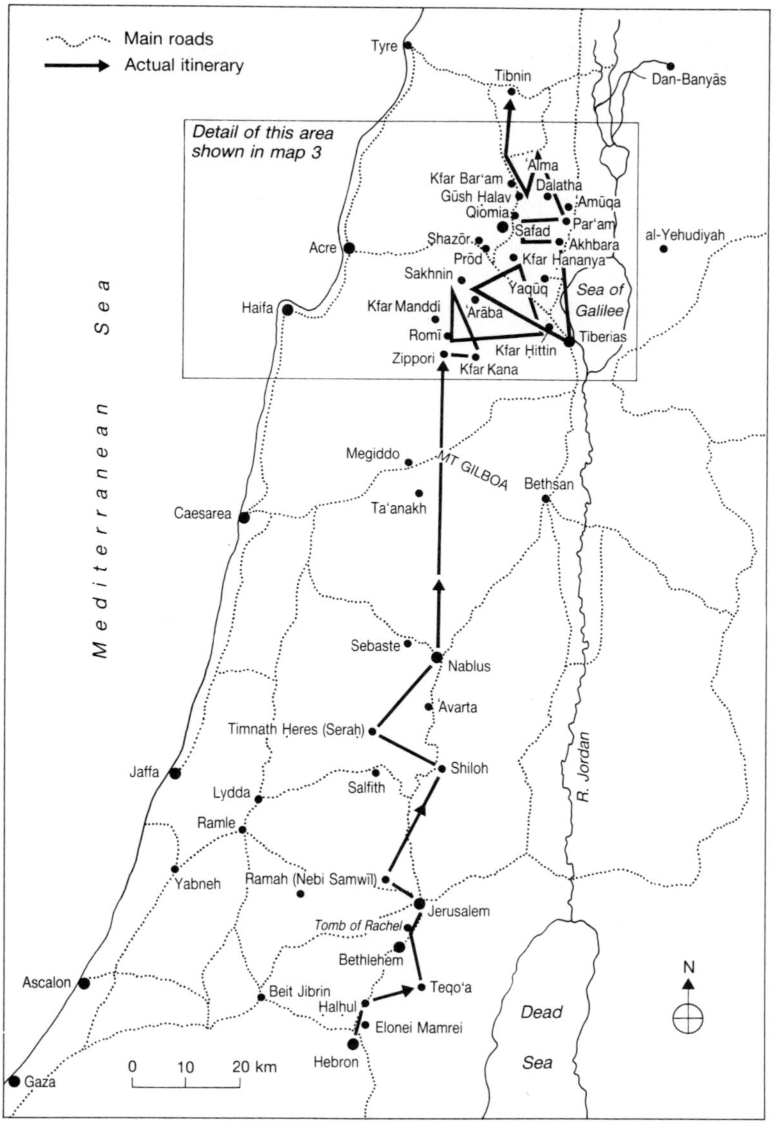

Map 2. The itinerary of the author of *Sefer Qabbalath Ṣadīqei Eretz Israel (Qivrei Avōth)*

on Mount Zion, where the sacrilegious statuary breaks his heart. The tombs themselves are in a cave which apparently he did not visit. But from Mount Zion he looked at the Temple of Solomon (probably in the general sense of the Temple esplanade and not necessarily the Dome of the Rock or the Mosque of al-Aqṣā), which, he says, is now served 'by enemies and heretics' (p. 35, l. 12) and an idol holding a child stands where the Holy of Holies had been. He then visits the 'Double Gates', that is, the 'Gates of Mercy' (*sha'arei raḥmīm*), or the 'Golden Gates' of Christian lore, that is, the eastern side of the Temple esplanade. Descending the Valley of Josaphat he sees the tombs of Absalom and Zechariah and ends up by climbing to the top of the Mount of Olives.

From Jerusalem his itinerary led to Ramah (that is, Nebi Samwīl), to Shiloh,[17] and hence to Timnath Seraḥ (Kfar Ḥeres), the traditional tomb of Joshua b. Nun.[18] Hence he continued to Nablus, where after mentioning Mount Gerizim and Mount Ebal he mentions the tomb of Joseph b. Jacob. Here, unexpectedly, he introduces Mount Carmel and the Cave of Elijah the Tishbite, followed by places in Galilee, beginning with Zippori.

The location of Mount Carmel in the itinerary, indicated here (p. 36, l. 21) as being between Nablus and Zippori, is obviously problematic. Not only is it a geographical impossibility but it also interrupts the otherwise very realistic description of the roads taken by the pilgrim. This, however, is not the only itinerary where we face this difficulty. In the forged itinerary of Menaḥem of Hebron written in 1215 (see Itineray F below), a Mount Carmel is mentioned as being to the west of Tiberias (*Hameamer* 3 (1919), 40), and another—this time the real one—is mentioned in the Bay of Haifa (ibid., p. 41). In view of the general reliability of the geographical indications, clearly some kind of confusion was introduced on this point. It seems that the problem can be solved by paying attention to other points

[17] *Meassef Zion* 1 (1926), 36, l. 5. This is not very clear. He mentions the sons of 'Ali, but as in the previous line he speaks of the prophet Samuel. This might have been a continuation based on the biblical tradition (1 Sam. 4). Shiloh might have also been introduced as a simple biblical reminiscence.

[18] Josh. 24: 30; Judg. 2: 9: 'Timnath Seraḥ [or T. Ḥeres], which is in Efraim on the north of the Hill (*har*) of Ga'ash.'

they furnish. The itinerary of Menaḥem of Hebron indicates Mount Carmel as being the location of the tombs of Jochebet mother of Moses and his wife Zippora. These tombs are usually described as near Tiberias, more particularly on a mountain nearby called Rās Amās.[19] The place is quite clearly designated by Menaḥem as Mount Carmel opposite Tiberias (pp. 40 ff.). This strange identification (which did not, as we have seen, replace the real Mount Carmel above the Bay of Haifa) can probably be explained by popular etymology. The famous rich man of the Bible, Nabal 'was a man of Maon whose possessions were in Carmel' (1 Sam. 25: 2). The biblical stories centre on events in the vicinity of Hebron, and consequently the names wreak havoc with medieval geography. Benjamin of Tudela went from the River Kishon [Qishon] between Acre and Haifa and reached 'Kfar Naum and this Kfar of Naḥum, that is Ma'ōn the place of Nabal the Carmelite', and thus created a Capernaum on the coast of the Mediterranean.[20] In our case it is the existence of a Maon (Ma'ōn) near Tiberias which transferred the name of Carmel to the ridge to the west of Tiberias. Once Carmel was mentioned, it was natural to follow it with the Cave of Elijah.

In Galilee our pilgrim arrived at Zippori (Sepphoris) and then made several excursions before reaching Tiberias: from Zippori east to Kfar Kana, north to Sakhnin, south to Romi and east again to Hattim (Kfar Ḥittin), north to Arbel, and again to the west to 'Araba and Yaqūq (Ḥaquq), and finally south-east to Tiberias. This is a rather erratic itinerary which points to the pilgrim's staying in the area for some time and making his excursions from a central point.

From Tiberias his journey took him to 'Arāba, through

[19] *Tombs of the Ancestors*, 76, 101.

[20] *Benjamin of Tudela*, 32. Cf. Rappaport in the notes of Asher's edition of *Benjamin of Tudela*, ii. 79–80. As to the Crusader's toponymy, they obviously knew perfectly well that Capharnaum was near the lake of Tiberias, but nevertheless 'added' this Capharnaum to the south of Acre. See, for example, 'Les Pelerinaiges por aler en Iherusalem' in *Itin. à Jérusalem et descriptions de la Terre Sainte*, ed. H. Michelant and G. Raynaud (Geneva 1882), ch. 2, p. 90. 'Les Chemins et les pèlerinages de la Terre Sainte', ibid. 180. The same in Burchard of Mount Zion, *PPTS* xii. 6 and Marino Sanudo *PPTS* xii. 2, where A. Stewart identifies the place with Kfar Lam and not the generally accepted Tel Keniseh. The latter, a small Crusader fortress was photographed and described by E. von Mülinen; 'Beiträge zur Kenntnis des Karmels', *Zeitschrift des Deutschen Palästina-Vereins* 3 (1908), 52–4.

Arbel and Yaquq and back to the hot springs of Tiberias.[21] From Tiberias he moves to ʿAkhbara and Kfar ʿAnan (i.e. Ḥananya), Shazōr, and Miron. From Miron and its Holy Tombs he goes east to Kfar Parʿam, and through Nabartein to ʿAmūqa, and hence to Dalatha and to nearby ʿAlma. From here he goes unexpectedly south to Gūsh Ḥalav (Giscala) and the Kfar Barʿam. From there he proceeded to Tibnin (known in Hebrew sources also as Timnen and hence Timnath as used by our own author). From Tibnin he goes south to Kadesh Naftali on the road to Banyās, and finally to Lebanon and the tomb of the prophet Zephaniah. All in all this itinerary includes thirty-four places in the Holy Land.

This rhymed treatise is no doubt a testimony to an authentic pilgrimage in the Holy Land, and not a text created far from the scene in the author's study. We can also assume that it was not written during the pilgrimage but composed, based on notes, after its completion. The language is very artificial and the elaborate use of biblical, sometimes recherché expressions, does not tally well with the dreariness of the description. What is particularly striking is the comprehensive listing of tombs, which has seldom been surpassed in its scope. As this is one of the earliest compositions of this genre, or perhaps the earliest, this is rather unexpected. It is surprising that there were no earlier attempts to provide a basis for later elaboration. This difficulty has now partially been resolved by the discovery of a fragment of an earlier itinerary (the preserved fragment relating to Jerusalem) written in Arabic, which the editor has ascribed to the first half of the tenth century.[22] Moreover, a Hebrew text dating from the eleventh century—the so-called *Scroll of Ebyatar* describing the funeral of the *gaon* Elija b. Solomon (1083), whose body was carried from Tyre to Daltōn (Dalatha)—mentions the tombs of Yosei ha-Galīli, Jonathan b. ʿUziel, Hillel and Shammai, Elʿazar b. ʿArakh, and Elʿazar b. ʿAzaryah in Daltōn. Some of these tombs were later mentioned as being in Daltōn or neighbouring places. This, with

[21] In Tiberias he mentions the tomb of Maimonides. As the latter died in 1205 this is clearly a later interpolation.

[22] 'A Jerusalem Guide from the Cairo Genizah', ed. by J. Barslavy, *Eretz Israel* 7 (1964), 69–80. On the *Scroll of Ebyatar* see above, ch. 3 n. 49.

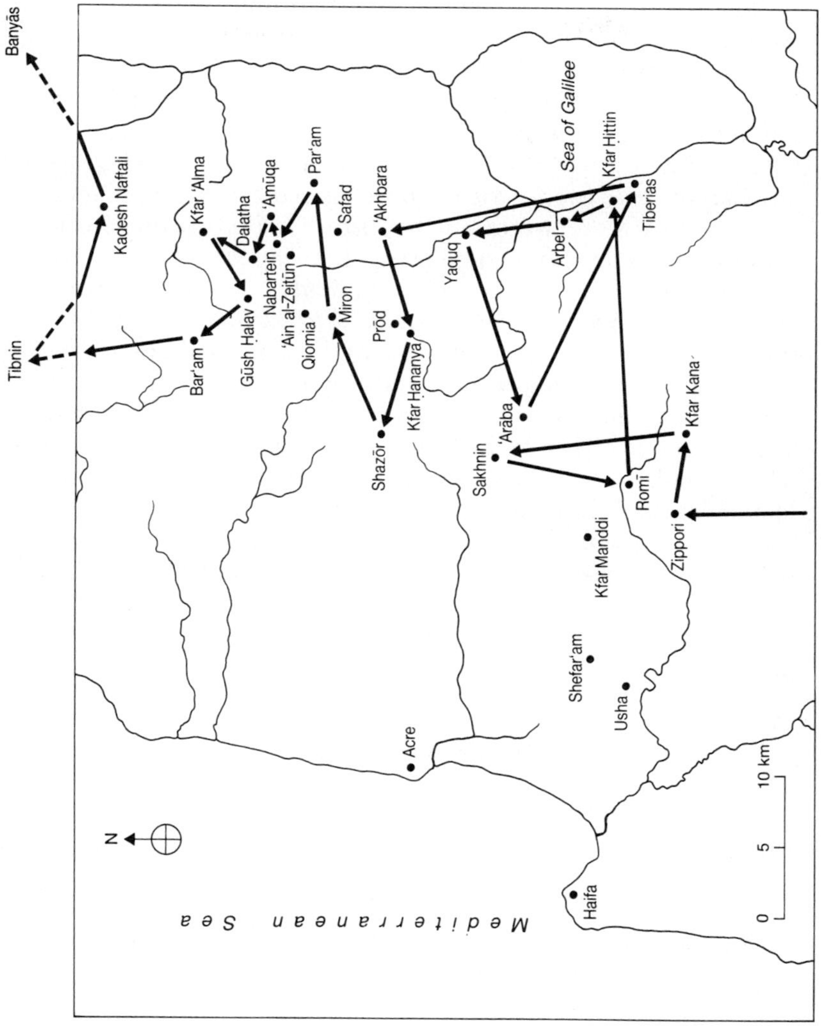

Map 3. The itinerary of the author of *Sefer Qabbalath Ṣadīqei Eretz Israel* (*Qivrei Avōth*): the north (detail)

the foregoing occurrence, proves the existence of the tradition of Holy Tombs at least a century earlier.

And yet this only partially solves our problems, because the Arabic text is more of a guide than an itinerary, and consequently its interest and perspective are different. Its existence, however, proves that our treatise had forerunners which have not yet come to light.[23]

Our itinerary had a strange destiny. A treatise called *Qabbalath Ṣadīqei Eretz Israel*, written in the fifteenth century, plagiarized our treatise in a shortened version.[24] Whereas our author always speaks in the first person: 'I voyaged', 'I went', the author of the later treatise says explicitly: 'I found it in one version of the *Sefer Qabbalath Ṣadīqei Eretz Israel*' (The book of the tradition of the Just of Eretz Israel). This explains why all the Christian elements of the twelfth century itinerary were not copied—they had simply ceased to be relevant.[25] Instead we find entries referring to Muslims. Thus, speaking of R. Meir, whose tomb was in Tiberias, the later treatise adds 'and the Ismaelites call him R. Meir al-Ḥanq, that is to say the Strangler', or again, whereas the earlier itinerary has: 'Iddo [the Seer] is buried in Dan', the later one adds: 'Dan is Leshem [Josh. 19: 47], Pamias in the language of the (Mishnaic) Sages and in Arabic Banyās and here is [the tomb of] 'Iddo the prophet.'

B. THE ITINERARY OF JACOB B. NATHANEL (1153–1187)

Another interesting itinerary[26] belonging to the twelfth cen-

[23] One can also mention the list of Gates of Jerusalem assigned to the eleventh cent. See Preface, n. 6.

[24] The contrary has been argued, e.g. by M. Ish-Shalom, *Zion* (H) 4 (1938), 161, but he later accepted the view expressed here (*Sinai* (H) 7 (1940), 152). The shortened treatise was printed in the *Sefer Yuḥasin ha-Shalem*, 228*b*, and rep. in *Hameamer* (H) 3 (1919), 83.

[25] This can also be proved by stylistic comparisons. Whereas the original was written in rhymed prose and often forced into particular phrasings for the sake of the rhyme, the later treatise is written in simple prose but because it tries to stay close to the original, it often includes things which simply do not make sense.

[26] Published by L. Grünhut from MS Camb. Add. 539 as an appendix to *Die Rundreise des R. Petachjah aus Regensburg* (Frankfurt 1905) under the title *Sipur Massa'ōth* (The story of voyages), 4–17. Engl. trans. E. N. Adler, *Jewish Travellers*, 92–100.

tury[27] was written by one Jacob Nathanel. From the introductory phrase—'and places of Eretz Israel and the Tombs of the *ṣadīqīm* which are there, which was composed by R. Jacob b. Nathanel Hakkohen of blessed memory, when he entered the Holy Land'—we know that the text that has survived is only a copy. The copyist took considerable liberties with his text, and sometimes one even has the impression that pages were copied in the wrong order.

The first part (pp. 4–6) deals with Jerusalem and the southern part of the country: Hebron, Bethlehem, Jerusalem, Beit Nūba, Lydda, Dodanīm, Yabneh, Ashdod, Ascalon, Gaza, ʿAzata, Madon, and ʿAzeiqa. The description of Gaza is followed by a paragraph on Egypt (pp. 6–7); this might seem a logical continuation of the pilgrimage, except that there is then a sudden transition to Galilee (p. 7). The itinerary continues southwards to northern Ephraim and then back to Tiberias, Miron, ʿAmūqa, Kfar Ḥananya, Har Gaʿash, Timnath Seraḥ, Zippori, Kfar Kana, and Nablus. After a description of the tombs in Galilee (pp. 7–10), we travel to the coast, to Acre, and then southwards to Caesarea (pp. 10–11).

At this point we return to Hebron, the Tomb of Rachel, Jerusalem; and again to the hot springs of Tiberias (p. 13). It is possible that this last part (Hebron, the Tomb of Rachel, Jerusalem, and Tiberias), bringing us back to the places already described in the first part, was composed as a kind of explanatory supplement as it has a clear polemical bias. The treatise then ends unexpectedly: 'On Mount Sinai there is a synagogue (*knesseth*) of Ishmaelites and there is a city at the foot of the mountain and its name is Tūr Sin. Having been privileged to write this, may I also merit to go there and die there. Here is the end of the things seen by Jacob Hakkohen which I [*sic*] saw in Eretz Israel.' The wish seems to be that of the copyist and not that of the original author; further, the last

[27] Strangely, M. Steinschneider suggested 13th–15th cent. (*Yerūshalaim*, ed. M. Luncz, 3 (1889), 48); L. Grünhut (p. 5) suggested the 13th cent., on the basis of the Christian elements; Ish-Shalom, 'The Tradition of Holy Tombs' (H), *Sinai* 7(1940), proposed late 13th cent. I. Ben-Zvi, *Collected Papers*, ii. 197 and iii. 242, vacillated between the 12th and the 13th. A. Yaʿari, *Voyages*, accepted Grünhut's reasoning and dating. Prawer, *The Jews*, argued 1153–87 and this was later accepted by Ish-Shalom, *Tombs of the Ancestors*, 10.

phrase makes little sense and can be explained only by the copyist's ignorance or negligence.

Our pilgrim visited some twenty places in the Holy Land, though not in the order indicated in the copyist's edited itinerary. Some of these indications are partially wrong and must be the result of bad copying. So for example: 'The burial place of Hannah [mother of the prophet Samuel], and the burial place of Rachel near Jerusalem one and a half parasangs (*parsa*) on the road to Jericho [*sic*]. Efrat and Bethlehem are two villages' (p. 4).

Some parts of the itinerary list places known from biblical times, but without mentioning any tombs in them. Thus our pilgrim mentions Nob (Beit Nūba), the city of the priests, whence he goes to Lydda and nearby (one parasang), Dodanīm (location unknown), then Yabneh (Ibelin) and a place rarely mentioned in the Crusader period—Ashdod (p. 5). From there he continues along the *via maris* to Ascalon and Gaza. The next three places to which he alludes—Madōn (Jos. 11: 1), 'Azatah (the name, meaning 'towards Gaza', appears in Judges 15: 1 and 16: 21 in this form, but is otherwise unknown) and 'Azeiqa (in Judaea; Josh. 10: 10)—is curious indeed as these places seem not to have been mentioned since biblical times, and their location here is quite inconsistent with the rest of the itinerary: thus, 'Azeiqa is well inland and not on the road indicated, and the biblical Madōn was in Galilee.

As we have seen having interrupted his itinerary in the south with a paragraph on Egypt—the Land of Goshen and the pyramids—the itinerary suddenly turns to Galilee, to the tombs of Hillel and Shammai, traditionally located at Miron, and the tomb of Jonathan b. 'Uziel, traditionally located at Kfar 'Amūqa (in the latter cases the place names are not indicated), and to Kfar Ḥananya. The indication of the distance from here to Har Ga'ash in northern Ephraim as 'three parasangs' is wrong, for the distance is far greater.

Despite the state in which this itinerary has come down to us, it contains some interesting and curious elements which should not be overlooked. Some refer to the Muslims, others to the Crusaders. Thus, 'The priests', he says 'once washed [dishes] in the Pool of Siloam; a plate fell from the hands of one of them, and they found it in the Well of Ascalon [described earlier as the 'Well of Abraham'], and it had been brought by the water from the Pool of Siloam, and the priests [here *galaḥim*—lit. the tonsured ones—usually used in a pejorative sense] who went there recognized it' (p. 5). As we shall see, the question of water supply touched on here interested all pilgrims. Thus, Jacob b. Nathanel appears to have thought that an underground tunnel connected the Pool of Siloam in Jerusalem with the Well of Abraham in Ascalon.

The pilgrim was fascinated by the innumerable tombs he encountered. Miron in Galilee is dominated by the tombs of the heads of the two great scholars of the Talmudic period, Hillel and Shammai.

There are two great caves inside the mountain and they have small entrances ... And I asked the local people how they had ever cut those caves because the mountain is all stone. So they showed us a book in which we saw it was written that in the year in which they neither sowed nor ploughed as it is written: 'and it shall bring forth fruit for three years' [Lev. 25: 21; to compensate for the Sabbatical seventh year], and during these three years they built the caves. And behind them there are around a hundred caves and nobody knows whose they are. And in all these burial places, they are like a box [i.e. ossuary] inside a house, and each is in stone and has a cover of stone. (pp. 6–7)

In Tiberias in the burial place of R. Kahana he found ossuaries preserved in a large cave 'and people of all nations light candles on them, and sick people and barren women come here and are cured' (p. 9).

In a large cave in Tiberias, he says 'there are caves like houses, because this is the way of burial, four on four, like four hundred on four hundred, and they are cemented by lime and the gentiles take out [the bodies of the dead] because they look for the gold threads with which the shrouds were sewn, and on each bed [ossuary] it is written so and so, the son of so and so' (p. 9).[28] Obviously such sacrilege met its divine punishment.

A knight from Provence saw that [the uncircumcised] are lighting many candles. He said to them: who is he [that is buried here]? They told him: a Jew, a *ṣadīq* and he heals the sick and helps barren women.

[28] The sacrilegious treatment of Jewish tombs is also noted in the vicinity of Jerusalem by *Benjamin of Tudela*, 37.

He answered: you are fools to venerate a Jew so highly. He took a stone and threw it to the earth and then he raised his hand to throw another, and as he was riding a horse he immediately fell and died. And immediately the clergy and bishops (or prelates: *hegemōnīm*) gathered [and said:] this happened not because he [the *ṣadīq*] is a Jew, but because he injured the teacher of Jesus. This angered him [Jesus] and it is he who killed him (p. 8).

The sacrilege was thus immediately punished, but the Christian clergy who allowed this syncretistic cult of prayers on a tomb hallowed as a holy place by Jews had to explain the mysterious death. The explanation given is very much in tune with the polemical attitude of the pilgrim: the Jew in question was the teacher of Jesus, and it was for this reason that the Christian God killed the knight. Obviously the Jews knew better.

The itinerary is full of edifying miracles. Thus, at the burial place of Joseph son of Jacob in Nablus, 'A Samaritan entered with the uncircumcised [Crusaders] and said: who is he? They told him: Joseph son of Jacob. He had in his hand an axe with which he struck the tomb—you can still see the dent. Without even a convulsion he died, and they took him out dead' (p. 10).

At an unspecified place (but near Tiberias, if to go by other traditions) was the tomb of Zipporah, wife of Moses, guarded by a lion inside a forest where nobody was allowed to cut the trees. A man trespassed and the lion followed him to his home and killed him (p. 10). In Acre, we learn, 'inside the gate is the tomb of Eleazar the Hasmonean.[29] And the great abomination [*to'eva*, i.e. the cathedral] which is in Acre—it is said that this was his [Eleazar's] Academy' (p. 10). More wonderful things happened in Caesarea. Here was the tomb of the Ten Martyrs.[30] A gentile who was buried at the entrance appeared in a dream to the inhabitants of the city screaming that he was being severely punished for this sacrilege. Twelve angels, all in

[29] The tombs of the Hasmoneans were in Modi'in, but medieval tradition mentions a Hasmonean tomb and in our case also a gate in Acre. This is based on 1 Macc. 12: 48, which tells how Tryphon killed Jonathan, the son of Mattathias the Hasmonean, who was treacherously induced to enter Ptolomais. Eleazar fell at the battle of Beth Zechariah, crushed by an elephant that he had killed. Cf. Ish Shalom, *Tombs of the Ancestors*, 190.

[30] *'Asarah harugei malkūth*, the Ten Martyrs—ten scholars, victims of Hadrian's persecutions, a famous object of Jewish legend.

prayer shawls, are permanently present in the tomb. Obviously grass never grows in the place of martyrdom (p. 11).

In the episode relating to Hebron, polemical elements are mixed with authentic data.

In Hebron, I, Jacob entered disguised as a Christian pilgrim[31] into the Cave which was built by the Christians, a fabrication to cheat the world. Half of it was built by Joseph [son of Jacob] the *ṣadīq*, but others say that it was built by King Solomon. At the side of the half of the building the priests erected an abomination,[32] that is the city (*medīna*) that is the Double Cave [*sic*], and the part which was built in the time of David was destroyed. And here is a place from which Adam was created and therefore they take earth from here and they build houses from it and there is always an abundance of earth and at every hour it is full.[33] And the treasures are built in it and the priests say: 'these are the treasures (*oṣrōth*) of the Mothers' (i.e. the wives of the Patriarchs). And when the pilgrims (*tōʿim*) want to enter they cannot; only a single man with a candle [can enter] because it is very deep. And there are six tombs, three on one side, three on the other, and they [the guardians] say to the pilgrims: these are Abraham, Isaac, Jacob, Sarah, Rebecca, and Leah. But this is a lie, because there is a large and strong wall of lime and shards between the new graves and the entrance to the Double Cave and they have no right to destroy it. Because once the priests made a small window and a wind came out and killed all of them, and they closed the window. And the stone which is near the entrance, it was King Solomon who built it (pp. 11–12).[34]

There follows a vivid description of the lighthouse in Alexandria ('in Arabic *manāra*', he adds): 'Here they put a light above at night so that the ships do not get lost. The light is seen in Africa, Provence and Acre'. Another wondrous place in Alexandria is the Academy (*beit-midrash* = library) where Alex-

[31] The term used is from the Heb. *tōʿehu*—one who takes the wrong road, wanders, or makes a mistake. In the Hebrew chronicles of the time of the Crusades, *tōʿeh* (pl. *tōʿīm*) was the usual term for Crusaders, either in the sense of 'misguided one' or from *peregrinus*, more exactly, wanderer, pilgrim. This also explains the contemporary Hebrew use of that expression for pilgrims to Mecca, the *ḥajjī*. Cf. *Benjamin of Tudela*, 55.

[32] Heb. *toʿeva*—here meaning church or monastery.

[33] The miraculous properties of the soil in Hebron for medical purposes are also noted by Christian pilgrims of the period.

[34] The *pia fraus* of the Christian priests and the miracles of the Tombs are mentioned in all Hebrew itineraries. Cf. e.g. *Petaḥyah of Regensburg*, ed. L. Grünhut (Frankfurt 1905), 34 (above, n. 26).

ander studied under Aristotle. Here he notes a strange decoration: 'the face of a man, a face of an eagle, a face of a lion, a face of an ox'—the most important elements of Western iconography, based on Ezekiel 1: 10.

Returning now to the Valley of Josaphat 'where stones are being thrown',[35] we learn:

And every day at least a hundred people die and they are brought down from the Gate of Benjamin;[36] and they go around between Zion and the Pool of Siloam a steep descent [and then they climb] until they come to the top of the Mount of Olives. And there are three large pits. And I ask how come that the pits are not full? They answered: there is here boiling water and we do not know where they are flowing to. And I, Jacob, said before the rabbis[37] (*ha-rabbanim*) that is what was said by our lord Isaiah [31: 9]: 'Saith the Lord, whose fire blazes in Zion and whose furnace is set up in Jerusalem' (p. 13).

The itinerary refers to Jerusalem several times, but near the end our pilgrim comes back to it: 'I stood on the tomb of [intentional lacuna], four cubits deep in the stoning-place.'[38] Clearly he is referring to the Holy Sepulchre without spelling out its name. Another reference to Jerusalem is so mangled as to be extremely unclear (pp. 4–5), although the following interpretation may be suggested:

In Jerusalem there is the Tower of David and the Temple and the courtyard and they are new. But the Western Wall and the substructure are buildings of King Solomon; the Gates of Mercy and the Ablution Pool of the priest and the monument of Absalom, and beneath the Mount of Olives, opposite the [Temple] courtyard, which was made in his [Solomon's or Absalom's], time there is a tower above a tower and there is no through way.'

Despite its obvious mutilations, the itinerary of Jacob Nathanel still has some merit, mainly in giving us a glimpse of things

[35] From later sources we know about stones being thrown at the Tomb of Absalom as punishment for his disobedience; similarly, stones were placed on tombs as a way of securing a place at the Last Judgement, which will take place in the Valley of Josaphat.

[36] John of Würzburg notes 50 dead brought out of the Hospital of St John. Cf. Johannes Wirzburgensis, *Descriptio Terrae Sanctae*, ed. T. Tobler (Leipzig 1874), 159.

[37] This is rather an unusual expression. Moreover, it is not clear where he expounded its exegesis to the rabbis. The expression was used as a mark of distinction from the Karaites. In the thirteenth cent. as we have seen, it denoted scholars of European origin.

[38] The place used for execution in Mishnaic times. Cf. Tractate *Sanhedrin* 6: 1.

seen and emotions felt by a Jewish pilgrim in the Christian-dominated Holy Land. The list of tombs is shorter than elsewhere, and many a place is mentioned without them. Clearly the pilgrimage took place in the Crusader period; witness the many references to Christian priests, and the anti-Christian remarks. In fact its date can be narrowed to a shorter period because Ascalon is in Crusader hands, which means that its author went on his pilgrimage after 1153 when the city was captured from the Muslims. The *terminus ad quem* must be 1187.

Little more can be learned. Our pilgrim probably came from Egypt, or at least Egypt was included in his itinerary. The language is obscure on this point, but it is not clear whether this should be attributed to the copyist or the author. The latter seems to have been a man of some knowledge, explaining a strange phenomenon by quotations from Leviticus and Isaiah. We may perhaps assume that he came from southern France as he mentions Provence twice, but the itinerary concentrates more on Jewish holy places than on geographical details. Whatever the case, the text is so mutilated that there is no chance of rational reconstruction.

C. THE ITINERARY OF BENJAMIN OF TUDELA (1169–1171)

The most famous traveller and the best known of all medieval voyages was that of the Spanish Jew, Benjamin of Tudela. His itinerary, as edited by M. N. Adler in 1907 based on all known manuscripts (one seemingly from the thirteenth century), as well as in the earlier edition by A. Asher based on manuscripts but also on the two earliest printings, which had an English translation (there were earlier translations in other languages), has become easily accessible to modern research.[39]

[39] *Editio princeps* Constantinople 1543 and Ferrara 1556. Full bibliographical details are to be found in the introduction of M. N. Adler to his edition of *The Itinerary of Benjamin of Tudela: Critical Text, Translation and Commentary* (London 1907; phot. repr. New York, s.d.). The quotations below indicate the pages of the BM MS printed in the Adler edition. Cf. also *The Itinerary of Rabbi Benjamin of Tudela*, ed. A. Asher, 2 vols. (London and Berlin 1840–1). The first volume comprises text and an English translation; the second contains studies and commentaries by Asher and scholars such as L. Zunz and S. J. Rapoport that retain their value.

Benjamin started out from Tudela, Spain *circa* 1166 and was on the return journey some six years later, that is in 1171, returning to Spain in 1173. He visited the Holy Land and its neighbouring countries between 1169 and 1171. The reasons for undertaking such a long and in some places perilous journey have never been satisfactorily explained. Considering this journey in comparison with other itineraries of the period that have survived in Hebrew, it is clear that his was not a simple pilgrimage to the Holy Land. In fact, the visit and the pilgrimages in the Holy Land are not given such prominence in the itinerary as to assign them particular value or for them to be conceived as a meritorious act of piety. On the other hand, though Benjamin was certainly acquainted with commerce this was not a business voyage either, at least not in the sense of closing business deals during the voyage. Curiosity, no doubt, and lust for travel played their role in the motivation, but from the frequency with which the subject is mentioned, the idea of visiting the Jewish communities to learn about their size, structure, eminent leaders, and scholars must have loomed large in planning and embarking on the voyage. It is plausible and tempting to accept M. N. Adler's view: 'Like Joseph, the traveller would be dispatched with the injunction: "I pray thee see whether it be well with thy brethren . . . and bring me word again [Gen. 37: 14]".'[40]

From Spain, Benjamin travelled by land and sea to Marseilles; his route then passed through Rome, southern Italy, the island of Corfu, Greece, and Constantinople. He visited some of the Aegean islands, then Rhodes and Cyprus and from there he crossed the sea to the Kingdom of Lesser Armenia and hence to Antioch. From here, in the lands under Crusader rule, he travelled south from the Principality of Antioch to the County of Tripoli and to the Latin Kingdom of Jerusalem. After quite a thorough tour of the Holy Land he went to Damascus, then ruled by Nūr al-Dīn, and to Baghdad, the resplendent capital of the caliphate. He then visited Persia and the Persian Gulf at Baṣra, Aden, and finally crossed to Assuan and Egypt. From Egypt he travelled via Sicily, Italy, and

[40] Adler, p. xii. His argument that Benjamin was looking for an asylum in the East for his brethren suffering persecution in Christian Europe and even in Muslim Spain is less convincing.

Germany, returning finally to his native Spain.[41] His visit to the Holy Land was thus only part of a more extensive voyage to the Levant and definitely not its only goal. Moreover, holy places take up a very small part of the narrative; this makes it unique in comparison with other itineraries, at least in the form in which they have come down to us. Our interest here, however, will be with the Holy Land only.

The main chronological indications of the itinerary were outlined by H. Graetz and narrowed down by others, especially L. Grünhut. Benjamin crossed Cilicia before the death of King Thoros, who died in 1167. He was in Nūr al-Dīn's Damascus in 1170, and in Egypt before September 1171. The wars in Iran in which the Turks defeated the Persians were in 1168–9 (so Grünhut). It is thus argued that Benjamin visited Palestine and Syria *circa* 1167–9, and nearer the first date (so B. Dinur).[42] I would suggest revising the chronology in the light of an additional event mentioned by Benjamin. According to a manuscript in the British Museum, in describing Tripoli in Lebanon he wrote, 'and in the years long gone by there was an earthquake when many Gentiles and Jews perished because houses and walls fell upon them and there was great destruction at that time there and in the whole Land of Israel and more than 20,000 people perished' (p. 27). But two other versions (Epstein MS and the *editio princeps*) printed by Asher read differently: 'and in those days there was an earthquake . . .' This phraseology clearly implies that it occurred at the time of Benjamin's visit.[43] If this is the case, then the text refers to the famous earthquake of 29 June 1170 in Tripoli. The description of that event as given by William of Tyre (xx. 18) tallies well with that of Benjamin: 'The entire city of Tripoli was reduced to a heap of stones and became the burial place

[41] There is a large scholarly consensus for the view that some parts of Benjamin's descriptions, e.g. those of Persia and the Land of the Mongols (the land of Prester John), relate to places not actually visited by the traveller, and that these descriptions depend on oral witnesses. See, in this context, the map itinerary indicating the routes mentioned by Benjamin in M. N. Adler's edition (above, n. 39).

[42] H. Graetz, *Geschichte der Juden* (Leipzig 1902) vi, n. 10; M. N. Adler, 61–2; L. Grünhut, *Die Reisebeschreibungen des R. Benjamin von Tudela* (Jerusalem 1903), German part, introduction, 5–11 and ibid. 22–3 n. 4; B. Dinaburg (Dinur) in *Meassef Zion* 2 (1924), 7 n. 1.

[43] In Hebrew (BM MS): 'Uvayamīm ha-rishonīm ra'asha ha-aretz.' The other version begins 'uvayamīm hahem hir'īsha ha-aretz' etc.

and common sepulchre of the citizens who perished with it.' The whole chapter then continues with the story of the horrible results of the earthquake in Muslim and Christian Syria and Phoenicia. If Benjamin actually refers to that event (and not, as argued by Grünhut, to the earthquake of 1159), then Benjamin was in Lebanon and later in the Holy Land in the summer of 1170. This was actually argued by Joseph Schwarz in 1852 but refuted on the grounds that it did not tally with the time Benjamin spent travelling in the different countries, but the argument is not decisive.[44]

The chronological differences are minimal, however, relative to the far more thorny problem of the compilation of the itinerary. A detailed analysis of the description of the Holy Land brings us to the conclusion that though some parts of the itinerary may actually reflect a diary, there were also notes taken *en route*, and later an attempt was made to integrate them more or less successfully into a general narrative. I suggest that the description of the Holy Land comprises several distinct parts; despite efforts to join them neatly, the creation still shows the 'seams' in the tailoring.

Having visited Armenia, Benjamin entered the realm of Crusader domination at Antioch (p. 26). He continued along the coast to Laodicea, Jabalah, Tripoli, and Gebal [Byblos, Jubail]. His description of the Latin Kingdom begins with Beirut, whence he travels along the coast to Sidon, Sarepta, Tyre and Acre. Here he notes: 'this is the beginning of Eretz Israel' (p. 31), probably a reference to the boundary of sanctity delimiting the Holy Land which was marked between Acre and Haifa.[45] Having visited Haifa and Mount Carmel he passes through 'Capharnaum'[46] and reaches Caesarea. Thus far we can follow our itinerary without any geographical difficulty. At Caesarea he turned inland through Qaqūn to Lydda (p. 22). At this point the itinerary shows inconsistencies which can

[44] *Das Heilige Land* (Frankfurt 1852), 38. On this important study, originally written in Hebrew, see R. Röhricht, *Bibl. geographica Palaestinae*, 373, no. 1777. Grünhut's argument that Benjamin speaks about an earthquake which shook not only Tripoli but Palestine as well actually tallies (against his argument) with the events as told by William of Tyre.

[45] On Acre as the 'beginning of the Holy Land' but outside its boundaries, see ch. 8 n. 3.

[46] On this 'Capharnaum' on the coast, see n. 20.

hardly be explained by lines of communication known to exist at that time. Benjamin's aim was clearly to reach Jerusalem, and whether the journey started from Acre or Jaffa, Lydda would normally have been the starting point for the ascent to the Holy City. But from Lydda the itinerary takes an unexpected direction, proceeding not east to Jerusalem but to the north, to Sebaste. Taking into account the road network known to us from the period, this means that he had to retrace his steps to Qaqūn, from where he could reach Sebaste, as in practical terms there was no other direct link between Lydda and northern Samaria. From Sebaste he continued to Nablus, and then moved far to the north to Mount Gilboa, bordering the Valley of Jezreel (p. 34).

A lacuna just large enough to accommodate a place-name (Bethsan?) or an indication of distance prevents us from knowing his immediate next step. But clearly we are now moving southward, and the next stop of which we have record is at a place he calls 'Val de Luna' and in Hebrew 'Valley of Ayalon'. It has already been convincingly proved that here he was following a popular etymology. The historical Valley of Ayalon[47] is between Latrun and Ramle, a location preserved in the place name Yālū. This is clearly away from his route; instead he is certainly referring to Luban, (Crusader Lubanum), which was on the road he was taking, which he linked with the Hebrew *Lebana* (moon). From here he passed through al-Bira, which he calls by its Crusader name Mahomerie-la-Grande (the Great Mosque), and finally reached Jerusalem.

Reviewing this early part of the itinerary seems to point to the fact that two separate journeys have been welded into one. It is improbable that a pilgrim on his way to Jerusalem should suddenly turn off at Lydda and journey through the whole of Samaria and north to the Valley of Jezreel and Mount Gilboa before continuing to Jerusalem. It seems more likely that having reached Lydda he would have continued directly to

[47] In the Valley of Ayalon Joshua b. Nun won the famous battle against the Amorites (Josh. 10: 12). In answer to his prayer the sun stopped at Gibeon and the moon in the Valley of Ayalon until he accomplished his victory. This was probably the origin of the Crusader name Val de Luna, although I have been unable to find the name Val de Luna, though clearly of Frankish origin, in Crusader sources.

Jerusalem, and that the excursion from Sebaste, Nablus, and Mount Gilboa to Jerusalem really belongs to a different segment of the itinerary.

Leaving Jerusalem, the itinerary continues south through Bethlehem to Hebron and then west to Beit-Jibrin. At this point our itinerary turns suddenly north to Latrun (*Toron de los Caballeros*; *Toronum militum* in the Crusader toponymy) and then Nebi Samwīl, which would normally have been visited coming from al-Bira to Jerusalem. Even stranger is the route from Nebi Samwīl through Mahomerie-la-Petite (Qubeība), Bethnoble, and Ramle to Jaffa, because the traveller must already have passed Qubeība on the road from Latrun to Nebi Samwīl. Looking at this segment of the itinerary, the disturbing part seems to be that which included Beit Jibrīn, Nebi Samwīl, and the two Mahomeriae: Mahomerie-la-Grande, that is al-Bira, and Mahomerie-la-Petite, that is al-Qubeība. My feeling, as I have said, is that this was inserted, not without leaving traces, into a different route. In any case the traveller certainly did not follow the order given in the itinerary. From Jaffa he then moves south to Ibelin (Yabneh) and ends at Ascalon. He did not continue to Gaza and Darum.

From Ascalon in the south the itinerary moves back to Lydda (p. 44), and then through Zar'in to Zippori and Tiberias. This is not impossible, but is certainly circuitous. The last part is taken up by visits to several places in Galilee, seemingly as excursions from Miron: to Taimin (or Timnah), 'Alma, and then north to Kadesh Naftali and Banyās (p. 56), where he leaves the Crusader kingdom for Damascus.

The total number of places recalled in the itinerary is thirty-six. Before analysing the itinerary on the level of geographical, historical, and religious traditions, however, a few remarks should be made about the measurement of distances.

The measurements of distances used by Benjamin of Tudela are rather disappointing if the intention is to use them in deciphering the obscurity of our traveller's movements. Basically, he uses two space measures: a day's journey, and a measure of Persian origin, the *parasang*, which entered Talmudic literature (and also the Greek and Roman systems of measurement) in its Aramaic form as *parsa* or *parsā*, which is equivalent to 4.5 kilometres. This corresponds to the reckoning in the Crusader itineraries, which also count days of voyage and miles of road. The Crusader mile as used, for example, by William of Tyre, seems to correspond to 1.5 or 2 kilometres. (In fact, Benjamin also uses, though in two places only, the measure 'mil', or mile.)

There are about thirty instances, all inside the Crusader kingdom, where Benjamin of Tudela uses the parsa. Where the existing road network goes back to the Roman or Byzantine period, such that it can be stated with great certainty that Benjamin travelled on the same or almost the same routes, we can therefore try to evaluate the accuracy of the itinerary. For this purpose we shall look at a few of the clearer examples.

The distance from Acre to Haifa is indicated as 3 parsa. The actual distance is about 22 kilometres, that is to say that the parsa is roughly equivalent to 7 kilometres. We may compare this with Sebaste–Nablus, a 10-kilometre distance, which is given as 3 parsa (so here 1 parsa = 6 km approx.) Other examples: Jerusalem–Bethlehem, 2 parsa (actually 8 km, so 1 parsa = 4 km), Bethlehem–Hebron, 6 parsa (actually 36 km, so 1 parsa = 6 km), Jaffa–Ibelin, 5 parsa (actually 29 km, so 1 parsa = 6 km), and Miron–'Alma, 2 parsa (actually 12 km, so 1 parsa = 6 km). In these examples the parsa ranges between 4 and 7 kilometres, but alas this cannot be used as a standard measure. From Nablus to Mount Gilboa, over 40 kilometres, the distance is indicated as 4 parsa; from Luban to al-Bira, a distance of around 20 kilometres, only 1 parsa. Some distances are simply absurd, as when the 40 kilometres between Beit Jibrīn and Nebī Samwīl, where there is no direct road, is given as 3 parsa; or at the other extreme, Ramle–Jaffe, roughly 17 kilometres, is given as 5 parsa, which works out at a little over 3 kilometres per parsa. All we can conclude is that though there is some basic notion of a parsa corresponding to some 5–7 kilometres, this is not applied with any rigour. True, we must make allowances for copyists' errors, but their extent remains beyond our conjecture; how Benjamin actually calculated the distances thus also remains a mystery.

J. C. M. Laurent (1864), the editor of Burchard of Mount Sion (1280) evaluated the *leuca*, that is, the 'league' used by the pilgrim to indicate distances, as an hour's march on foot. Obviously there were no other means for the traveller of calculating distances except by the time it took to walk (and even time units were rather imprecise). The same could be assumed for Benjamin's parsa, though it is my feeling that he refers to riding and not to walking. This would also explain the different lengths of the parsa because the travelling time from point to point would depend so much on the conditions of the terrain. However, even this would not explain some of the more extravagant indications.

Using Benjamin's measures of distance we can evaluate roughly how long he spent in the Holy Land. By adding up the distances counted in days from Beirut southward we get fourteen days. To this we have to add the more problematic parasangs. The total number is about 90, and taking 1 parsa as about 7 kilometres, we arrive at about 630 kilometres. Taking 25 kilometres as a daily ride gives us some 25 days. This would mean that Benjamin spent around one and a half or two months in the Holy Land. This is longer than the time spent in the Holy Land by another pilgrim, Samuel b. Samson (four weeks), but his visit was less extensive as he did not visit the cities on the coast.

Let us now turn to other aspects of the itinerary, aspects which reveal some of the techniques of travelling and, even more, the attitude to places or monuments seen by our traveller. Unlike other Hebrew itineraries, Benjamin's description is filled with details of cities and castles, mountains and rivers. He is conscious of the importance of the different ethnic and religious groups, their spiritual heads and political sovereigns. No doubt his knowledge of Spanish facilitated contacts with the European Frankish population, and many a name reflects this French–European influence.

Antioch was ruled by Bohemond le Baube, and the strange sect of the Ḥashīshtīn, living near the city of Sidon, which, he reports, 'fights with the Edomites, that is the Francos and with Tripoli that is Tarablus al-Shām' (p. 27). Travelling along the coast he passes from Laodicea to Jabalah. Benjamin's toponymy is characteristic as he valiantly attempts to identify the Arab and Crusader French place names with their biblical antecedents. 'Gebel is . . . on the coast of the Land of Israel' (p. 28), where he notes the ruling Genoese dynasty of the Embriaci. He then passed through 'Beirut that is Beeroth', and came to 'Ṣaida which is Sidon'. To the east, in the mountainous region of the city, on the confines of the Latin Kingdom, he found the Druzes. Benjamin of Tudela is in fact the first European to describe the sect and its beliefs (p. 29). He correctly notes the position of Sarepta (Ṣarafand) of Sidon whence he arrives in Tyre. The city and its southern port, which he found flooded, and the famous port of the Phoenician capital merit detailed descriptions (p. 30). From Tyre he goes 'to Acre that is Acco in the tribe of Asher and she is the beginning of the Holy Land and she is on the coast of the great sea and here is the great port which serves the Crusaders (*tōʿim*) who come by ship to Jerusalem' (p. 30). He continues south to Cayphas, which he wrongly identifies with Ḥefer (possibly a misreading of Haifa?), and notes the Jewish cemetery at the foot of Mount Carmel, and the Cave of Elijah. 'Here', he says 'the Edomites [= Christians] built an altar [he uses *bamah*, indicating a pagan altar] which they call St Elias' (p. 31). Continuing along the coast he passes a place which he identifies wrongly, as did his Crusader contemporaries, with 'Caparnaum' as discussed above. He continued to 'Cesarea' (Crusader Cesaire), which he identified (wrongly) with Gath of the Philistines, but knew its Graeco-Roman name, Caesarea (p. 31). At this point he abandoned the coastal road and went inland through Qaqūn (Crusader Caco) which he wrongly identified with Keʿīlah (Josh. 15: 44), which is actually near Hebron. Here to 'St George that is Lydda'. In Sebaste, he records, despite its fertility, 'there are no Jews' (p. 32). He notes, however, the ruins of the palace of King Ahab the son of Omri. Nablus, that is Shechem, inhabited by Samaritans merits a detailed description (pp. 33–4) before he continues on his way, following the mountainous ridge of Samaria until its descent to the eastern part of the valley (of Jezreel but the name is not mentioned) and Mount Gilboa.

The Valley of Ayalon, discussed above, is 'called by the Edomites Val de Luna' (p. 34). He mentions al-Bira by its Crusader name Mahomerie-la-Grande, which he wrongly identifies with Gibeon.

The most detailed description, however, is that of Jerusalem, giving us considerable insight into the thoughts and interests of a Jew on visiting Christian-dominated Jerusalem.

The beginning, to say the least, is surprising: 'Jerusalem, which is a small city, fortified by three walls' (p. 34). Even in Benjamin's experience, a city with walls 4 kilometres long could hardly be called small. Even more surprising are the 'three walls' of Jerusalem: the only time the city could boast three walls was a generation or so before its destruction by Titus! I strongly suspect that this strange piece of information somehow drew its inspiration from Josephus.[48] Crusader Jerusalem certainly never had more than one line of walls. Benjamin is struck by the mixture of nationalities and religions. 'Jacobites and Syrians (or Armenians), Greeks and Georgians, Franks and people of all tongues' he notes in great amazement (p. 34). Then he is impressed by the strong city fortifications. The Tower of David, with its ancient foundations 'built by our ancestors and the rest by the Ismaelites', the headquarters of the Hospitallers and Templars, their hospital and contingents are successively described. 'The Hospital ride out, four hundred knights, and there rest the sick who come there and they receive all their needs in life and death.' The headquarters of the Templars is the 'Templum Salomon', that is the palace built by King Solomon: '300 knights ride out every day to war not counting those who come from the Land of the Francos and from Edom and who take a vow to stay there days or years until the fulfilment of their oath' (p. 35).

It is only now that Benjamin mentions 'the great *bamah*, [altar of idolatry] called Sepulchre, where was buried the man to whom all the pilgrims go'. In the 'Templum Domini' he says, 'was the place of the Temple and Omar ben al-Khatab built over it a great and beautiful dome'. It is on this occasion, actually for the first time since entering the Holy Land, that Benjamin's description assumes a 'pro-Jewish' note. 'The gentiles [Christians] do not bring in any image or effigy, but they come there to pray' (p. 36). This statement did not correspond to reality, but perhaps contained a kind of vindication of the Jewish Holy of Holies.

A number of other places also drew his attention: 'the Western Wall which was one of the walls in the Holy of Holies

[48] Josephus, *Wars*, v. 4, 71 ff. The Hebrew version (not translation) was composed around the middle of the 11th cent. The reference to a third wall is in *Josippon Gerionides*, ed. D. Flusser (Jerusalem 1978), 353.

and it is called the Gate of Mercy (*Sha'ar ha-Raḥamīm*) and all the Jews come thither to pray before the wall in the courtyard' (p. 36).[49] He mentions the Stables of Solomon built from very huge stones by that king, as well as 'the pool where the priests slaughtered the sacrifices and all the Jews coming here write their names on the wall'. We cannot identify the place referred to, but the fascination of the Jewish pilgrims with the water installations on the Temple Mount has already been noted. He may possibly be referring to the Birket Banī Isrāīl, between the Temple enclosure and the Gate of Josaphat, which he mentions next as leading to the Valley of Josaphat; some Hebrew medieval inscriptions, certainly by pilgrims, have actually been found at the entrance to the courtyard.[50] Through the Gate of Josaphat (a name Benjamin adopted from the Crusader toponymy), he went to the valley of the same name, though he also mentions its ancient Hebrew name, the Brook of Kidron. This brought him to the Pool of Siloam, which has little water 'and the inhabitants of Jerusalem for the most part drink rainwater, which they have in the cisterns of their houses' (p. 37).

On Mount Zion, he reports, where there is a church (*bamah*) of the uncircumcised, there is also the Tomb of the House of David and the kings who ruled after him. At the time of his visit the entrance was not known because of a miraculous event which had happened fifteen years earlier. A part of the church wall had collapsed, and the Patriarch of Jerusalem ordered it to be reconstructed using stones from an ancient building, 'from the fundament of Mount Zion'. During the excavation the opening of a cave was discovered. The diggers entered it in search of treasure. And behold, 'they came to a great palace built on marble columns overlaid by silver and gold. In front was a table of gold, a sceptre and a crown and this was the

[49] The meaning of the phrase is not clear. The Gate(s) of Mercy are in the Eastern Wall of the Temple, whereas the Western Wall (or Wailing Wall) has no gate—unless the expression is to be understood figuratively? Cf. the material collected by I. J. Jahuda, 'The Wailing Wall' (H), *Meassef Zion* 5 (1929), 95–163.

[50] There is a remarkable concentration of buildings connected with the Jews in this area (Madhnat Banī Isrāīl, Birket Banī Isrāīl, Bāb Asbāt, Zawiyat al-Lawī), and a number of Hebrew inscriptions have been discovered in the northern part of that wall. Cf. S. Klein, *History* (H), 75–7. M. Ben-Dov, 'Hebrew Inscriptions Carved on Stone from the Temple Mount and its Surroundings', *Cathedra* 40 (1986), 3–30. M. A. Friedman, 'The Hebrew Inscriptions on the Temple Mount' (H), *Cathedra* 43 (1987), 193–4.

tomb of King David and to the left the tomb of King Solomon as well as the tombs of all the kings buried there from among the kings of Judah' (p. 39). Alas, at that moment, a storm wind arose from the mouth of the cave and smote the diggers, and a voice ordered them to leave immediately. The story was related to the Patriarch who turned to R. Abraham al-Constantini for an explanation. The latter identified the place as the royal tombs, and though R. Abraham was ready to enter and invited the Patriarch to join him, the diggers refused to lead them there. It was clear that God did not want to show the tombs. Benjamin of Tudela heard this story directly from R. Abraham in Jerusalem. 'The Patriarch then ordered that the place should be closed up and hidden from the people until this day' (pp. 39–40). As Benjamin visited the Holy Land probably between 1169 and 1171, the events related probably occurred *circa* 1154–6. I have not found any reference for these dates to any extraordinary events on Mount Zion. A few years earlier, however, in January 1146, lightning struck the Church of Mount Zion (and also the Holy Sepulchre). The church was in great danger of collapsing, and the omen terrified the whole city. It is not impossible that the damage done to the Church of Mount Zion on this occasion was the reason for repairs and the basis of the miraculous tale related by Benjamin.[51]

Not far from the city, about three miles distant, was an ancient Jewish cemetery: caves in which were Jewish tombs sealed by tombstones with dated inscriptions. The latter had now been destroyed by the Crusaders, who were taking the stones to build their houses. Such plunder we know not to have been an isolated instance; another Jewish traveller likewise remarked on the excavation of cadavers in Galilee to recover golden threads from the shrouds.[52]

Having visited Jerusalem the traveller went south to Bethlehem (called *Beth-Leon*), bypassing the tomb of Rachel with its eleven stones crowned by a dome supported on four columns.

[51] Cf. W.T. xvi, ch. 17. As to R. Abraham, see above ch. 6, and n. 27. We must nevertheless bear in mind that Benjamin's story might have been influenced by Josephus, *Jewish Antiquities*, xvi. 179–82. Herod's attempt to reach the royal tombs failed and his two bodyguards died because of a flame which came out from the cave. The place was immediately sealed by a white monument.

[52] See above, Itinerary of Jacob b. Nathanel, text and n. 28.

Here he notes: 'And all the Jews who pass here write their names on the stones of the monument' (p. 40). Further to the south he reached *Saint Abram d'Ebron*, that is Hebron.

The famous Machpelah ('Double Cave') was duly visited. The 'Jewish claim' comes to the fore here in his account of the Gentiles having constructed six graves there 'and they say to the pilgrims that these are the tombs of the Patriarchs . . . but if a Jew comes thither and gives money to the guardian, he will open an iron entrance, which is a part of the structure of our Forefathers and there he will go down, passing two empty caves until he reaches the third with the real tombs which also have inscriptions stating the names of the buried (p. 41). Benjamin notes in Hebron a Jewish custom, obviously still current in his day, of bringing the bones of the deceased, even from far away, in special caskets and burying them there.[53]

Hebron was the most southerly point to be visited by Benjamin in the mountainous part of the country. From here he turned north-west to Crusader Beit Jibrīn: 'Bet Gobrin that is Maresha', a remarkably good identification, and the further north to Nebi Samwīl, which he calls '*Saint Samuel de Shiloh* which is Shiloh' (p. 42).

On that place Benjamin has a remarkable story: 'When the sons of Edom [the Crusaders] took Ramle which is Ramah, from the hands of the Ismaelites they found the tomb of Samuel of Ramah (ha-Ramati) in the synagogue of the Jews. The Edomites took him out and brought him to Shiloh and they built over it a large church (*bamah*) and called it Saint Samuel of Shiloh until this day (p. 42). This story, as many others, rests on etymology.[54] In this case the name of Ramle, a relatively new name, because the city was only erected in the eighth century, became Rames in Crusader toponymy, or Ramah and their derivatives. As the prophet Samuel lived and was buried in the biblical Ramah (1 Sam. 25: 1), and at the same time his tomb was considered to be in Nebi Samwīl, to the

[53] On bringing bones to Hebron in the 12th cent., see *Sefer ha-Yishuv*, ii. 8. A recent photograph inside the cave shows the name 'Abraham' in Crusader characters on a large stone. Z. Yeivin, 'Additional notes on the Machpela' (H), *Annual of the ha-Aretz Museum* (1985–6), 53–62, phot. 61.

[54] The vicissitudes of the site may represent two divergent traditions, a basically Jewish one which was accepted by the Church Fathers and a later Byzantine tradition. Cf. J. Jeremias, *Heiligengräber in Jesu Umwelt* (Göttingen 1958), 44–6.

north of Jerusalem, the place from which the Crusaders saw Jerusalem for the first time in June 1099 (hence its Crusader name Montjoye), a 'translation' in the best medieval tradition was constructed and the body moved to Nebi Samwīl, that is 'Saint Samuel', which our traveller connected with the name Shiloh as the prophet was in the service of the temple of that place from childhood.[55] It seems, however, that the Crusaders identified Montjoye not with Shiloh; but usually with Ramah and Mizpah.

The next journey brought Benjamin west to Qubeiba, which he calls by its Crusader name Mahomerie-la-Petite, or in Latin Parva Mahomeria (Mahomerie-la-Grande, that is al-Bira, had already been mentioned on the road south from Nablus to Jerusalem), which he identified (wrongly) with Gibeah of Saul and Gibeah of Benjamin (p. 42). He continued westward on the road to Ramle bypassing Beit Nubā (Crusader Bethnoble) identified with Nob of the priests, reached Ramle, which he calls by its French name Rames, a strongly fortified city. Because of the confusion with the biblical Ramah, he writes: 'And there are walls from the time of our ancestors as they found so written on the stones' (p. 43). In this great city he mentions a Jewish cemetery, very probably that of the Jewish community which had existed here more than three hundred years before the Crusader conquest. Finally he reached the end of the western road at the port of Jaffa.

From Jaffa he explored the coastal road southward to Ibelin, which he correctly identified with Yabneh, the place of the ancient Academy (*Midrash*), then a 'Palmis' which doubtless represents a Crusader 'Palmaria' or 'Paumier', which he identified with 'the ruined Ashdod of the Philistines'. Actually, Ashdod disappeared at the time of the Crusaders; only a small castle, a *Castellum Beroardi*, remained on the coast as a pale souvenir of the once flourishing city. Finally he reached 'Escalona that is Ascalon' (p. 43).

What Benjamin has to say about Ascalon is rather strange. He distinguished between the city he saw and ancient Ascalon

[55] As early as the beginning of the 14th cent., the real identity of Shiloh was already known to Ishtori ha-Parḥi who correctly identified it with the village Sailun.

which he found in ruins 4 parasangs distant. The former he says, was built by Ezra the priest, and its name was once Bnei Braq. 'It is a great and beautiful city and merchants come to her from everywhere because she is situated at the utmost frontier of Egypt . . . and in its midst is the well which was dug by Abraham at the time of the Philistines' (pp. 44–5). The references to Ezra and Bnei Braq are confusing; they can partly be explained—at least the place name—by a local tradition which places Bnei Braq (Josh. 19: 45), actually to the east of Jaffa, in this vicinity. This tradition was known to Eusebius who in his *Onomasticon* (54. 3) identified 'Barak' with a village 'Barkai' near Ashdod. This corresponds with today's Barqa, north east of Ashdod. I do not see, however, how Ezra the priest got involved in the story.

Leaving the south he moved north and reached Lydda, and from there he went to 'Garin which is Jezreel', that is Jenin (Grand Gerin of the Crusaders) or Zarʿīn (Petit Gerin), and hence through 'Saffuriah which is Zippori' to Tiberias. In Zippori, correctly identified, he mentions, rather exceptionally, the tombs of the great exilarch, Rabbi Judah ha-Nassi, and his son Gamaliel, some other sages, and the tomb of the prophet Jonah. He then moved east to Tiberias, which is curiously described as being 'located on the River Jordan, which is called the Lake Kinnereth' (p. 44).[56] *En passant* he notes that the Jordan enters the Dead Sea. Tiberias merits the mention of its hot springs and several tombs. One of the versions here refers to the tomb of Judah Halevy (p. 45)—if not a misreading, then no doubt a later interpolation.

The road from Tiberias leads the traveller north to 'Teimin which is Timnath' (p. 45), that is Tibnin (Crusader Toron), a distance which he covers in two days, and then back south to Miron. This is rather strange as one would assume that he passed through Miron on his way from Tiberias to Tibnin. From Miron he goes to 'Alma and finally 'Kades that is Kadesh Naphtali' (p. 46) on the road to 'Banyās that is Dan and there is a cave from which flows out the Jordan which after 3 miles is

[56] Here the text must be faulty as all the different versions are confused at this point.

joined by the [river Arnon] which comes from Moab'.[57] And in the front of the cave is the altar of the 'graven image of Micah where the children of Dan sacrificed in ancient times [Judg. 17 ff.] and there is the altar of Jeroboam where was the golden calf. Until here is the frontier of Eretz Israel towards the uttermost sea [Deut. 11: 24].' This is the last place mentioned in the Holy Land; and the next place cited is Damascus, ruled by Nūr al-Dīn the king of the *Turcos* (p. 46).

D. THE 'CIRCUIT' (SIBŪV) OF R. PETAḤYAH OF REGENSBURG (1174–1187)

Few itineraries fared worse than that of Petaḥyah of Regensburg. It was edited at least twice, more probably three times, until it ended up in the mutilated form known to us today.[58] And yet this was one of the most important geohistorical treatises of its age, describing a voyage which began in Prague in Bohemia, continued through Poland, southern Russia, and the Crimea, then east to Tartary, the land of Khazaria, Armenia, and Kurdistan, south through Iraq and Syria to Palestine, and back to Europe. More than several hundred years were to elapse before any journey of similar scope would be narrated in Europe, though descriptions and travel writing of that kind were already current in the Muslim Orient. Obviously, then only a small part of the narrative was concerned with the Holy Land; the parts dealing with Babylon, that is Iraq, and with Syria, where Petaḥyah admired the great flourishing centres of Judaism, were far more extensive.

[57] This identification is obviously wrong. The Arnon served as the boundary between the tribe of Reuben and the southern Moab, whereas here it is apparently applied to one of the Jordan tributaries.

[58] No MS of any value is extant. The best one was used for the *editio princeps* of Prague 1595. A MS in the Leipzig municipality library was used by J. C. Wagenseil, who published the text with a Latin translation in Exercitationes (Strasburg 1687), 168–200. The text has since been published many times with translations into European languages. Cf. R. Röhricht, *Bibl. geographica Palaestinae* (Berlin 1890; repr. with additions by David H. K. Amiran, Jerusalem 1963), 40. The best recent edition (from which I quote) is that of L. Grünhut with a German translation: *Die Rundreise des R. Petachjah aus Regensburg* (Jerusalem and Frankfurt 1905). Cf. the edition with a French translation by E. Carmoly, *Tour du monde ou voyages du rabbin Pétachia de Ratisbonne*, extrait du *Nouveau journal asiatique* (Paris 1831), text and Engl. trans. A. Benish (London 1856).

We are lucky to have in the preserved itinerary enough indications to reconstruct, at least partially, the way in which the text was written. Clearly, the final text was composed only after the traveller's return from the Orient, in Ratisbon. In several places there are indications of how the existing text was composed. 'And the Head of the Academy [of Baghdad, Samuel b. ʿAli Hakkohen] wrote down for him [Petaḥyah] who are the Amoraim [Talmudic Sages, third to sixth century CE] who are buried there, but he [Petaḥyah] forgot the writing in Bohemia. And from Bohemia he came here [apparently Ratisbon] and he told all his journey from Bohemia to the eastern parts of the world' (p. 19, ll. 9–12). Then again in the description of the road from Mosul (Nineveh) to Syria: 'And all the cities which R. Petaḥyah passed, he told us their names and how many days he went from one to another, but there is no need to write that down' (p. 28, ll. 7–8).

The impression we get, then, is that several methods were used by R. Petaḥyah to record his experiences. There is little doubt that parts of his journey were described when still on the road. Possibly he also kept a kind of log-book of places and distances, noting also his immediate impressions in describing places and meetings or events. Additionally he collected material supplied by local people in the different countries. And yet it is doubtful if he actually wrote down the story of the whole voyage. It seems far more likely that having arranged or ordered his notes, he told his marvellous tale to an audience, perhaps to one person who put the story in writing. The first to have made an early record of the story, but in doing so unfortunately editing it, was R. Judah ha-Ḥasid in Ratisbon. But this version was then edited again by a man who speaks of himself as being in the audience, or having had R. Judah ha-Ḥasid's version in front of him. This second 'editor' noted that the astrologer R. Solomon in Mosul told R. Petaḥyah what he saw in the stars as to the date of the coming of the Messiah: 'but R. Judah ha-Ḥasid did not want to write it down, in case he might be accused of believing R. Solomon' (p. 7, ll. 7–8). The text, as it has come down to us, appears to have had one more, final 'editor'. The man who wrote the introduction of the itinerary as it has survived (p. 1):

These are the discoveries [or novelties] of R. Petaḥyah . . . and all the discoveries, the miracles and wonders done by the Blessed One, which he saw and heard and he wrote them to be remembered, to be told to his nation, the Children of Israel, about the virtues and might of the Blessed One, who performs miracles and wonders day after day. And God, blessed be He, will take pity on us and will gather us from all the four corners of the earth. Amen.

Seeing that the stress on the miraculous and wonderful in the introduction fits so well with the preserved text, I would venture that the writer not only wrote the introduction but also took a hand in 'editing' the itinerary according to his own lights. It is thus impossible to say how much the surviving text reflects the original tale. Moreover, the condensed text preserves only those parts which interested the 'editors', but does not necessarily reflect the interests, at least not clearly, of Petaḥyah himself.

In contrary to the paucity of our knowledge of all the other pilgrims, we know rather more about Petaḥyah because the colophon of the text states 'Here endeth the story of R. Petaḥyah, the brother of R. Isaac ha-Lavan of the Tosafists and of R. Naḥman of Regensburg of blessed memory' (p. 36). This information on R. Petaḥyah's family, which happens to have had some scholarly standing, permits us to place our traveller in a certain context. The family hailed from Prague and had connections with Ratisbon. Its gifted young men went to study in the great centre of learning in France under Rabbenu Tam (i.e. Jacob b. Meir), the grandson of Rashi (R. Solomon of Troyes) in Ramerupt or Troyes. R. Isaac b. Jacob 'the white-haired' (this is the meaning of *ha-Lavan*) who studied in France, lived in Prague and later in Ratisbon, where he took office as a *dayyan*. He wrote *Tosafot* to several Talmudic tractates. This explains R. Petaḥyah's connections with Prague and Ratisbon, and also why he would have undertaken a journey to Russia, because its scholars were in contact with Prague.[59] But there must have been a vast difference between R. Isaac ha-Lavan, the sober and meticulous expounder of the Talmudic law, and his travelling brother. The latter, to judge by the itinerary, was of a completely different character.

[59] See Urbach, *Tosafists*, ii. 215–21.

Coming after the pilgrimage of an Oriental Jew and then probably of a Provençal and a Spanish one, the itinerary of R. Petaḥyah is the first by an Ashkenazi traveller. The journey took place in the last quarter of the twelfth century. He mentions Damascus as being ruled by Egypt (p. 28, ll. 11–12), which clearly fixes a *terminus a quo*, namely October 1174, when the great capital of Syria fell into the hands of Saladin, ruler of Egypt. And as Bethlehem and Jerusalem are in Christian hands, the description cannot be later than 1187. In Bethlehem, Christian priests (*kōmarīm*) tried to move stones from Rachel's tomb to a church and obviously failed (p. 32, ll. 4–7); in Jerusalem, clearly under Christian rule, the Gentiles tried in vain to erect statues in the Temple (Dome of the Rock). In Jerusalem, he also notes, 'the pit [i.e. Holy Sepulchre] on one side and the Hospital of the Poor on the other. And the earth is rent and called "Valley of the son Hinnom" [Josh. 15: 8; 18: 16] and there is their cemetery' (p. 33, ll. 4–8).

In the existing itinerary ('Excerpt' as it was called by H. Graetz), there are two elements which draw our special attention: the traveller's uncommon interest in the Jewish communities in the great Eastern Diaspora of the nation, and in the marvellous and stunning, whether natural or miraculous. The descriptions of the riches and might of Baghdad and the power of the Head of the Academy—both reminiscent of resplendent royal courts, but only weakly based on reality—were doubtless intended to bring a ray of hope to the Western Diaspora.

Paradoxically enough, or rather, unexpectedly, it was mainly the lands of the Levant outside the Holy Land which harboured the miraculous. The miraculous, however, does not exist for its own sake. It always has an apologetic or polemic message. Written for a Jewish European audience tales of the miraculous carried the message of God's providence never abandoning its chosen nation wherever they may be. The saints, prophets, *ṣadīqīm*, although respected by Muslims and Jews alike, retain their 'Jewishness'. The hallowed tomb of the prophet Ezekiel as well as the tomb of the prophet's pupil, Baruk b. Neriah, are not to be profaned, on penalty of death; Muslims who tried to open the tomb were immediately struck dead (p. 11). The tomb of Ezekiel, a focal point of Jewish Oriental pilgrimage, is venerated by Jews and Muslims alike

(p. 13) and proves its miraculous powers even to the mighty (p. 14). Again, Jews and Muslims venerate the tomb of R. Meir 'the Strangler', whose appearance to the Sultan in a dream sufficed to prevent the robbing of his tomb (p. 18). Such stories and many more must have strengthened the spirit of the Jews. They were not just abandoned to the mercies of their surroundings, because in the Orient miracles were seen and experienced as everyday events. The climax is reached, according to R. Petaḥyah just a generation before his visit, in the time of Solomon, the father of the present Exilarch, Daniel. The ruling sultan came back from the Ḥajj 'to Mecca where is the tomb of Muhammed and there it is trodden on and a decomposed cadaver, rotting and such a bad smell comes out from the tomb, that a man cannot stand it. And he [the sultan] said to his people that there is no truth neither in the [Saracen] nor in his religion.' The later religion he contrasted with that of Baruk b. Neriah; not only was he preserved, but even his prayer-shawl was preserved in his tomb. Alas, he (the sultan) did not have long enough 'to convert himself and all his nation before his death' (p. 27).

The miracles do not stop at the border of the Holy Land but strangely enough are definitely fewer, either because less were actually recorded or because the 'editors' took more liberties with their text. I prefer to assume that fewer miracles were actually recorded.

Petaḥyah entered the Holy Land from the north, through Banyās from Syria. However, from here we are at a loss to describe his pilgrimage in an orderly manner. What the itinerary has preserved is scattered information without any geographical continuity. Thus, between descriptions of Upper and Lower Galilee the narrator introduces Yabneh and its miracles, and after Kfar Kana (the name is not specifically mentioned, but the tomb of Prophet Jonah, which is mentioned, was traditionally here), he jumps to the Tomb of Rachel and then to Jerusalem. Stories of Jerusalem then mingle with those of Hebron and then lead us back to Babylon.

It is thus impossible to retrace Petaḥyah's stay in the Holy Land with any accuracy. Twice (pp. 31, 33) he remarks that the length of the Holy Land is that of a three-day journey, but he would clearly have stayed longer if he indeed visited all the places he indicated (p. 16) all over the country.

Miracles abound throughout. There is the wonderful fragrance emanating from the tomb of Rabbi Judah ha-Nasi (the editor of the Mishna, second century CE) in Zippori (p. 29). In Yabneh there is a wondrous spring which gushes forth six days a week but yields not a drop on the Sabbath (p. 30). In Miron a huge stone receptacle fills itself miraculously (there is no spring beneath it, we are assured) in the presence of decent people, but becomes completely dry when untrustworthy people enter (p. 30). Har Ga'ash of the Bible, the traditional site of the tomb of Joshua b. Nun and Caleb b. Jephunneh, is explained 'etymologically': the land trembled after the death of Joshua (p. 31).

In Kfar Kana is the traditional tomb of the prophet Jonah. A temple (*heikhal*) marks the tomb, in the midst of an orchard full of every variety of fruit. Despite the fact that the guardian of his tomb is a gentile he warmly welcomes Jewish visitors and offers them fruits, saying: 'Jonah the son of Amittai was a Jew and consequently it is by right that you should partake of what is his.' Obviously no fruits were offered to non-Jewish visitors.

Petaḥyah visited the Tomb of Rachel, but neither he nor any of the other pilgrims of the Crusader period mentions particular prayers at the tomb, such as was the practice later, to invoke Rachel's intercession on behalf of her dispersed children. Of the tomb itself: 'there are eleven stones each for each tribe of Israel excepting Benjamin' (Rachel died in giving birth to him). All the stones are of marble, topped by that of Jacob; it was this stone 'that the Christian priests (*kōmarīm*) took away a distance of a mile and built it into a church [lit. 'building of idolatry'], but next day they found it on the tomb [of Rachel] as before' (p. 32).

In the midst of all these wonders we unexpectedly find a more realistic note. Describing the Dead Sea, where he saw Sodom and Gomorrah, he remarks 'there is no grass there', but 'the pillar of salt', states the text, 'he did not see and it does not exist'. Neither did he see the stones erected by Joshua in Gilgal (p. 33). One wonders if this remark, so strongly contrasting with the general tone of the description, is not perhaps part of the original treatise of a rather critical pilgrim, which somehow escaped the scissors of the 'editors'.

In Hebron, where Petaḥyah succeeded in entering the Double Cave despite evading the watchful guardian, his description is a remarkable mixture of information and marvels:

Behold in the Cave there is a huge temple built by Abraham. And there are huge stones, 27 or 28 in each corner [probably layers], and each is 70 cubits. And he gave gold to the man in whose hands were the keys of the Cave to bring him to the Tombs of the Patriarchs. He opened and at the entrance there was an idol and inside three crypts (*kūkhīn*), and the Jews in Acre told him: 'beware because they put three corpses at the entrance of the Cave. They say these are the Patriarchs, but they are not' (pp. 33–4).

After taking an additional payment and an assurance that he never allowed any gentile to enter, the guardian of the tombs

brought candles and let him inside. He descended some steps [he had already descended fifteen] and he entered the Cave which is very large. And in the middle of the Cave there is an opening in the floor, and the floor is all rock and all the caves are in the cavity of the rock. And above this opening there were slabs of iron, so thick that a man cannot have made them and they must be of heavenly make. And a storm wind was blowing through the openings between the slabs of iron. And he could not enter with [lighted] candles and so he understood that this is the place of the Patriarchs and prayed there. And when he stood at the opening of the Cave there was a storm wind blowing which threw him back time and again (pp. 33–4).

Near Hebron was the Biblical Plain of Mamrei (Heb. Oaks or Terebinths of Mamrei) where a dying man asked his son to show our pilgrim the tree on which the angels had leant. 'And he showed him a beautiful olive-tree [*sic*], split into three parts and there is a marble stone in the middle. And it is their tradition that when the angels sat here the tree split into three parts.' Nearby he was shown Sarah's well and her tent, 'and near Mamrei is a plain and not far away clear and sweet water of that well of Abraham and the stone on which the Patriarch circumcised himself'. The dying man also confessed to have seen here on Yom Kippur an angel of fire who prayed at the well of Sarah (pp. 35–6).

Just one line is given to the great Crusader centre of commerce in Acre, just enough to say that there is a Jewish community and that the Jews there warned him against a deception practised by the Christian guardians of the Tombs of the Patriarchs in Hebron.

The itinerary continues, Har Gaʿash, the traditional place of the Tomb of Joshua son of Nun, follows Arbel. Yabneh is mentioned and then the Tomb of Rachel, the Dead Sea with Sodom and Gomorrah, Hebron, and Jerusalem. In the latter he visited the Mount of Olives. From here he saw the Temple Mount, 'its esplanade 23 cubits high':[60]

> [it] is very spacious and beautiful and there is the Temple, which was built by the Ishmaelites in ancient times. When Jerusalem was in the hands of the Ishmaelites sacrilegious men came and informed the king of the Ishmaelites that there was an old man among them who knew the plan of the Temple and the courtyard. And the king pressed him so much until he forced him to disclose its position to him. And the king who favoured the Jews said: 'I want to build a Temple there and only Jews will be allowed to pray there.' And he built the building of marble stones, a splendid building, from red and green marble and of many designs. And the gentiles [i.e. Christians] came and erected statues in it but they fell down and so they built a statue in the thickness of the wall, but in the Holy of Holies it could not stay (pp. 32–3).

What a wonderful story to lift the spirit of the Jews in the Diaspora! Strange as the whole story sounds, one wonders if Petaḥyah had picked up, somewhere, the Jewish Jerusalemite tradition of how some Jews accompanied the conquering Muslim army to Jerusalem in the seventh century and showed the Muslim conquerors the Temple esplanade which under Byzantine rule became the dunghill of the city.[61] Additionally he was obviously campaigning against the Crusader prohibition which barred the Jews from Jerusalem: no cross or statue could ever be erected in the Holy of Holies of the Jewish Temple.[62] No less marvellous and edifying is the story of the

[60] The text here is spoiled. It could also mean 'Between the roof and the floor there are 23 cubits.'

[61] This tradition is preserved in a Genizah fragment published by S. Assaf in *BJES* 7 (1939), 22–8, repr. in *Sefer ha-Yishūv*, ii (Jerusalem 1947), 17–18 n. 13. A part of this tradition is repeated by Qalqashandi, ibid. 17 n. 10.

[62] This continues the Jewish anti-Christian polemic against erecting crosses on the Mount of Olives facing the Temple esplanade. See e.g. Theophanes, *Chronographia*, i. ed. de Boor (Leipzig 1883), 342.

'Golden Gates', or the 'Gates of Mercy' as they are called in the Hebrew sources (*sha'arei raḥamīm*), the eastern gates of the Temple esplanade:

And this gate is filled with stones and lime and no Jew is allowed to enter it, *a fortiori* any gentile. Once the gentiles wanted to clean and open it, but an earthquake made Eretz Israel tremble and there was chaos in the city and so they desisted. And there is a tradition among the Jews that Divine Providence was exiled through this gate,[63] and is destined [through this gate] to return. And the gate is facing the Mount of Olives and the Mount of Olives is lower [*sic*] and whoever stands on the Mount of Olives can see it. (pp. 34–5)

After describing Hebron and its miracles, Petaḥyah mentions the oppression of the Jews in the lands of the Greeks (probably Byzantium), and ends up again with Babylon and its brick buildings.

An enumeration of the places in the order mentioned by Petaḥyah of Regensburg makes it entirely clear that nobody could ever have written an itinerary in that order, let alone tried to travel following these geographical indications. As indicated by R. Petaḥyah, the Holy Land (the land across the Jordan in the west) is to the west of Banyas. From here the order given is Tiberias, Zippori, Usha, Shefar'am, Acre, Yabneh, and then upper Galilee, where he mentions Arbel. Then Har Ga'ash in Samaria, back again to Galilee to Kfar Kana, then to the Tomb of Rachel. Here, out of any context, Ḥaran (in Transjordan). Then Jerusalem, the Dead Sea, Sodom and Gomorrah, Hebron, again Jerusalem. A reference to Damascus is followed by the Plain of Mamrei. Here we abruptly leave for Greece or Byzantium and Babylon. All in all, only sixteen places are mentioned in the Holy Land in the greatest disarray, though some north/south differentiations can be discerned. This probably reflects the original structure of the text. Most baffling, though we know that R. Petaḥyah entered the Holy Land from the north, we do not know how he returned to Europe. Whatever the case, there is no mention of Egypt.

Such phrases as: 'And in Eretz Israel there are communities, but they have no more than a hundred, two hundred or three

[63] Petaḥyah refers to the tradition that after the destruction of the Temple divine Providence exiled itself from the Temple esplanade. There are 10 stations in that exile. Tractate *Rosh ha-Shanah* 31*a*.

hundred [inhabitants]' (29), have hardly any value. Actually the phrase was meant to point out that Palestine communities are smaller than those of Babylon. There is also an apologetic phrase: speaking about Greece at the end of his itinerary he remarks, 'And there are here many communities, that Eretz Israel would not be able to sustain if they existed there' (p. 36).

Not much more can be said about this 'circuit' unless a lucky find brings to light a different version of the itinerary, but even as it is, it is a valuable testimony to the perception of the Holy Land, to the image Jews kept alive in the Diaspora, and particularly its emphasis on miracles that would serve as a constant reminder of the concern of Providence for the Children of Israel.

E. THE ITINERARY OF R. SAMUEL B. SAMSON (1210)

This itinerary is one of the very rare descriptions of the Holy Land where we know the author, his companions, and the date of the events.[64] Though truncated at the beginning and at the end, as the copyist or 'editor' evidently had his own idea of what should be transmitted to posterity, it contains important information about the method of travel, the experience of the voyage, descriptions of places seen, and the attitudes of a Jewish pilgrim in the first decade of the thirteenth century.

The major elements to be described are given in the copyist's opening phrases:

These are the things which are worthy of being recorded, understood, and known, [namely] the places of the tombs of our Ancestors, due to whose merits the world exists.[65] And this [the position of tombs] will be clear as I write it down according to a man who was in Eretz Israel

[64] The text was published by A. Berliner in the Hebrew part of the *Magazin für die Wissenschaft des Judentums*, called *Ozar Tov*, ed. A. Berliner and D. Hoffman (Berlin 1876), 35–8. Important explanations by A. Berliner were printed in *Magazin* 3 (1876), 157–160 and by M. Steinschneider, ibid. 218. French trans. A. Carmoly, *Itinéraires*, 123–69, English trans. E. N. Adler, *Jewish Travellers*, 103–11. Partial reprint by Luncz in *Hameamer*, iii. 26–35. The quotations are from the best critical edition publ. by F. Schulcz, *A Letter from Samuel b. Samson* (Weitzen 1929), based on the unique Parma MS 563, no. 18. Cf. De Rossi, MSS *Codices Hebraici*, ii (Parma 1803), 87.

[65] On this Talmudic tradition see E. E. Urbach, *The Sages* (Jerusalem 1979^2), 487.

with the Rav R. Jonathan Hakkohen of Lunel, and his name was R. Samuel b. R. Samson, who journeyed with him in the Land of Goshen and crossed the desert with him and came with him to Jerusalem. And from here on I shall speak as he spoke in his writing and this was in the year [4]970 [of Creation].[66]

The parts mutilated obviously described the beginning of the pilgrimage, beginning at least from Alexandria, which the copyist or 'editor' did not regard as worth preserving and the end is Ninveh (probably Mosul)[67] The itinerary in the Holy Land probably began after crossing the desert in Gaza, and its high point was the pilgrimage to Jerusalem, whence our preserved text actually begins.

The description of the roads is detailed and on the whole reliable. As the author indicated the halts dictated by the Sabbath, we can estimate the time of the pilgrimage in the Holy Land (that is, without Egypt and the later voyage to Mosul) as having lasted around four weeks.

The general direction of the voyage was from south to north, from Egypt through the Holy Land to Syria and Iraq. It is to be noted that our pilgrims never descended from the mountainous inland; in political terms, the whole pilgrimage was thus in the Ayyūbid-held territory of the interior without any excursion to the Crusader coast to the west.

Among the group of fellow travellers, five people are mentioned by name: R. Jonathan of Lunel, an exilarch (*rosh ha-gōlah*) probably from Mosul, two companions—Saʿadya and Tobias—and Samuel b. Samson, the author of the itinerary. But the group numbered more people; we hear during the visit to Hebron that the exilarch was accompanied by a group of people (*siʿah*) (p. 7). The itinerary thus describes a group of Jews hailing from different countries who went on a pilgrimage, at least part of the way together. This is a unique testimony, but, we can assume that other pilgrims also travelled the same way. In all probability they were also accompanied by hired guards; travelling in guarded groups was advisable

[66] The quotation is from p. 5.

[67] Ninveh was here wrongly identified with Neveh in Transjordan. Cf. ibid. 13 n. 12. In medieval usage, as already noted by Carmoly and Luncz, it usually referred to Mosul. Cf. Mann. *Texts*, i. 479 n. 9, and also Riccoldo de Monte Croce, *AOL* ii. 260 n. 16.

as much for social and religious reasons as it was for the sake of security. The outstanding personality of the group was obviously R. Jonathan Hakkohen of Lunel, scholar, philosopher, and staunch supporter of Maimonides on matters[68] of *halakha.*

Twice we hear about the rulers of the country. The exilarch, we read, brought with him 'a seal [i.e. a sealed letter] from the king and from the fraudulent Muhammad who is the caliph' (ibid). This probably refers to an Ayyūbid ruler of Damascus and to Nāṣir al-Dīn, the caliph of Baghdad. Then again at the end we read in a kind of colophon: 'Samuel b. Samson who came from Jerusalem and Galilee in the year 970 and he has a seal [sealed letter] from the king of Jerusalem to witness [the veracity of] this letter [or treatise]' (p. 13). It is plausible to assume that he is referring to an Ayyūbid commander of the city of Jerusalem and not to Jean de Brienne, the king of the Latin Kingdom of Jerusalem, whose favour would have been of little help to pilgrims travelling through Muslim territory.

The visit to Jerusalem begins from the west, that is, through the Jaffa Gate (name not specified); passing the Tower of David, the pilgrims reached the Temple Mount. The description here is not very precise in its vocabulary and can be interpreted in different ways. My own suggestion though not very satisfactory, is the following:

> and we came to prostrate ourselves at the edge of the courtyard ['*azarah*]. And we fell on our faces opposite the gate which led outside in the direction of 'Ein 'Etam, which was the House of Ablution of the priests. And there at that opposite gate in the western wall, rising from the foundation of the wall there was a kind of large hall and from here the priests came down through a tunnel to 'Ein 'Etam. And this was the Place of Ablutions (p. 3).

This seems to mean that after prayer in the western part of the esplanade, near the 'Porta Speciosa' of the Crusaders (the 'Gate of the Chains' of the Muslim and Jewish tradition), the pilgrims went out of the city to the 'Gates of Mercy' (Golden Gates) which are called here the Western Wall, as they were also called by Benjamin of Tudela.[69] The 'pilgrim's great hall'

[68] See ch. 8.
[69] See above, 'The Itinerary of Benjamin of Tudela', n. 49.

may refer to the two naves of the richly decorated chapel built by Justinian.

The biblical ʿEin ʿEtam (1 Chr. 4: 32, 2 Chr. 11: 6) was near Solomon's Pools not far from Bethlehem. At the time of the Second Temple the waters of the pools supplied water to the Water Gate near the Temple through an aqueduct (Tractate *Yoma* 31, *Zevaḥīm* 54*b*). Knowing the Talmudic description our pilgrim imagined that the pool was near the Temple and the aqueduct became a tunnel. This is probably the basis of our pilgrim's assertion. However, it is difficult to identify the place to which he refers. One is tempted to suggest the Pool of Siloam, though he later mentions the place by name after visiting the Mount of Olives on the road to Hebron.

On the first Sabbath the company prayed twice (probably morning and evening), on the Mount of Olives and in the presence of a *minyan*, that is, ten adults. From Jerusalem they went to Hebron, stopping at the Tomb of Rachel (no mention of a prayer), then possibly at the site of the Tomb of the prophet Nathan[70] in Ḥalḥul, and finally at Hebron. Here the exilarch and his company, who had letters from the sultan (of Damascus?) and 'from the fraudulent Muhammed, that is the caliph', were allowed to enter the Double Cave, but the rest of the company had to wait a whole day until at midnight they were smuggled into the place through the intervention of a (Jewish?) dyer who lived in Hebron and the connivance of the Muslim guardian. The Patriarchs' Tombs are one of the very few places in which prayer is indicated as the aim of the visit. As the pilgrims explained to the guardian: 'we said to him we came from a far away land to pray in this place and to prostrate ourselves at the place where our ancestors trod' (p. 7). Twenty-four steps led to the six tombs where the pilgrims prayed 'and asked for mercy'. The building (the mosque) had been built, he says, six hundred years previously, that is after the Muslim conquest of the seventh century. The pilgrimage to Hebron and back seems to have lasted three to four days.

The next stage of the pilgrimage led from Jerusalem northward to Nebi Samwīl, called Ramathaim, and then to al-Bira, which he calls by its biblical name Beeroth, where they saw the

[70] Cf. *Tombs of the Ancestors*, 58.

tomb of the prophet Samuel, 'and here we slept and the place is very much ruined'—an interesting remark bearing witness to the destruction of the Crusader settlement of Mahomeria.

There is some uncertainty as to the next stop. One of the possible readings is: 'And we woke up in the morning and went between Bethel and Hai [Gen. 13: 3] and we saw the place where Abraham erected the altar' (p. 7). From here they travelled through Shiloh on the northern road to Nablus and the tomb of Joseph son of Jacob. Here the company celebrated the Sabbath (the second since arrival in the Holy Land), before continuing to Bethsan and to Tiberias and its Holy Tombs.

Tiberias served as the base for a number of excursions which brought them to different Galilean villages. The first was to Arbel (passing a place our author calls Kfar Ḥiṭṭīm, but which is not the famous Hattin correctly mentioned later on). Following the road, our pilgrims must then have returned to Tiberias. They then travelled to the real Hattin with the tomb of Jethro, a day's journey, which brought them back by night to Tiberias (pp. 8–9).

The next excursion from Tiberias led them through Yaquq (traditional tomb of the prophet Habakkuk), Kfar 'Anan (Ḥananya), and an unidentifiable place called Lydda,[71] where they spent the night (p. 9), and then Safad, where they spent the next night. Here the group split up and our Samuel went with the exilarch to Kfar Par'am, 'Amūqa, Nabartā, and back to Safad where they spent the Sabbath (the third of the pilgrimage). In all these places, he records, there were Jewish communities of more than five *minyanīm* (i.e. fifty adults).

The fourth week of the pilgrimage began with a visit to Giscala (Gūsh Ḥalav) and by-passing Qisma, to Miron and the famous tomb of R. Simeon bar Yoḥai. In Giscala, we hear, the feast of Purim was celebrated (p. 12). This dates our pilgrimage to the spring of 1210, more exactly to March, which corresponds to the month of Adar II in which Purim was celebrated in the year in question (4970 of Creation). From here the pilgrims went to 'Alma, Dalatha, and Bar'am,[72] where they found ruins of a *beit-midrash* with inscriptions: 'This was

[71] The text is not very clear and consequently the interpretation is difficult. See text of F. Schulcz (above, n. 64), 9 nn. 49–50. Cf. Barslavi, *Studies*, 122.

[72] Here I have followed the text as corrected by L. Sukenik in *Zion* 2, 111.

done by Shalom b. Levy',[73] and some remains of other buildings (p. 11). It is of interest to note 'that everywhere that we came more than two *minyanīm*[74] welcome us, and this to honour the exilarch' (p. 12).

The last part of the journey took them from Bar'am to Banyās with the cave and the sources of the Jordan, and then to Damascus and finally Mosul (p. 13).

Our narrator, like almost all his contemporaries, is accompanied on his journey by miraculous phenomena. It goes without saying that they are edifying in the senses of showing Providence's hand in favour of the Jews. Even syncretic cults develop at tombs hallowed by the Jews. He has a recollection of Christians trying to build a chapel on the Mount of Olives (p. 6), but whatever they built tumbled down—a story we have already heard from another pilgrim. Near Nablus and the tomb of Dinah there is a charmed orchard, from which no one is allowed to take as much as one leaf (p. 8). In 'Alma too a grove near a tomb is charmed, and 'nobody is allowed to take a leaf from it and it is venerated by the Muslims' (p. 12). The holy tomb in Safad (of R. Ḥanīnā b. Horkenos) is also venerated by Muslims, who keep an oil-lamp burning there permanently (p. 9), and the same happens at the tomb of Jonathan b. 'Uziel in 'Amūqa, which is also a place 'at which the Muslims take solemn oaths' (p. 10).

A great miracle happens at the tombs of the founders of the two great schools of Jewish *halakha*, Hillel and Shammai (first century BCE), and of their pupils as well as the great mystic Simeon b. Yoḥai at Miron. Here our pilgrim saw five wondrous wells, two are always full and one dry, he says, and on the other hand one half-full and the other entirely full. The exilarch ordered candles to be lit in order to find the inexhaustible sources of water but could not find them (pp. 10–11).

Perhaps more than any other pilgrim, he mentions buildings which he considers to have been ancient synagogues. In Ḥalḥul

[73] On these inscriptions see S. Klein, 'Inscriptions from Ancient Synagogues', *Proc. of the Institute of Jewish Studies* 2 (Jerusalem 1925), 27 ff.

[74] It is difficult to know where the writer is referring to. Even earlier, after mentioning Par'am, 'Amūqah, Nabartā, and Safad, he says 'and in all these places there are more than five *minyanīm*', that is, 50 adults; then, as we have seen, he mentions 20 adults. This latter figure seems to relate to Giscala, Qismā, Miron, 'Alma, Dalātah, and Bar'am.

(?) on the tomb of the prophet Nathan, there is a mosque, a 'House of Disgust' in his vocabulary (p. 6). In the midst of Arbel he saw the ruins of a synagogue built by Nathai of Arbel (p. 8); in Bar'am he found a synagogue, one of the twenty-four synagogues built by R. Simeon b. Yoḥai. He tells us that of the twenty-four synagogues, 'some are still standing, others are destroyed' (p. 10).

This, as we have said, is rather a sober itinerary, one of the few providing information on a group of pilgrims. As to R. Jonathan of Lunel, we know that he probably did not go to Damascus and Mosul but in any case we find him in the Holy Land where he was later joined by the great wave of scholars who came from France. It may have been that he was one of the first to arrive, and after a month's pilgrimage established himself more permanently.

F. THE FORGED ITINERARY OF R. MENAḤEM OF HEBRON (1215)

An itinerary signed by one Menaḥem of Hebron has given rise to many misgivings among scholars. Beginning with A. Neubauer who first published it, from MS Bodl. Or. 135, until more recent times, it has been regarded as a wholesale or partial forgery.[75] This was in no small degree based on the fantasies of the second part of the itinerary, but also on a number of strange expressions in the first part of the itinerary. In many quarters there has nevertheless been some hesitation to condemn it out of hand as a forgery. Some scholars were inclined to assume that it was not entirely a fabrication, in that some parts of the text are drawn from an actual itinerary. The fact that an excellent paleographer like I. Sonne thought we were dealing with an ancient manuscript (he assigned it to the beginning of the fourteenth century), and a more recent and very detailed examination of the Oxford manuscript by

[75] Published by A. Neubauer in *Ha-Levanon* 5 (1868), no. 40, 626–9; repr. by A. M. Luncz in *Hameamer* 3 (1919), 36–46. Quote from the more accessible *Hameamer* 3 reprint. On the controversy as to authenticity, see I. Ben-Zvi, *Remnants of Ancient Jewish Communities in the Land of Israel* (H) (Jerusalem 1965²), 512–17. The strongest antagonist was S. Klein, who regarded it as a 19th-cent. forgery; see 'The Letter of R. Menaḥem of Hebron', *BJES* 6 (1939), 19–29 and his *History*, 291–2.

M. Beit-Arié, another eminent paleographer, concluded that the itinerary, as well as the whole codex, were written at the beginning of the thirteenth century, could have weighed in favour of its authenticity.[76]

As already indicated, the itinerary is composed of two parts, and it is in the second that the name of the writer appears: R. Menaḥem b. Perez ha-Ḥebroni. This has been one of the causes of the doubt surrounding the manuscript. In the introduction he bears the title 'Cantor (*shalīaḥ ṣibūr*) who officiated for eight years in Hebron' (p. 36). The date is clearly indicated as Tammuz (4)975 of Creation (p. 38), that is, the summer of 1215. However, neither the name nor the function nor the profession described above appear together in the treatise. The first part is signed: Menaḥam ha-Ḥebroni (p. 42); in the second we find Menaḥem b. Perez ha-Ḥebroni (p. 43). This does not make the itinerary more credible but at least helps to reduce the uncertainties surrounding it.

The name Menaḥem b. Perez has obvious Messianic connotations. A Jewish apocalypse from among the earliest (before the sixth century) mentions Menaḥem b. Ḥezekiah and Menaḥem b. 'Amīel as names of Messiahs, the first to be born near Bethlehem, the latter in Jerusalem. This found its counterpart in a later apocalypse (*Sefer Zerubbabel*) where the Messiah b. Joseph, Neḥemiah b. Ḥushiel, was born in Galilee and the Messiah b. David, Menaḥem b. 'Amiel, appears in Jerusalem.[77] One should also remember that both Menaḥem and Neḥemiah mean 'consoler'. The name of the father of the alleged author of our itinerary is no less allusive: Perez. Perez, the first-born son of Judah, was the founder of the most important family of that tribe and the ancestors of the royal house of David (Ruth 4: 12–18; cf. Matt. 1: 13). Obviously it is impossible to say with certainty that this in itself is proof of fabrication, because both names were, as they still are, in current usage; but taken in conjunction with other elements I am inclined to think that the name was meant to project the feeling of a mysterious message

[76] See I. Sonne in Ben-Zvi (above, n. 75), 512 n. 16; and cf. M. Beit-Arié, *The Only Dated Medieval Hebrew Manuscript Written in England 1189 CE* (Oxford 1985), 16–17; and see below, n. 86.

[77] *Midrashei Geūlah* (Chapters of Jewish apocalypse), ed. J. Even Shmuel (Tel-Aviv 1943), introduction, 54, 106, 289–90. Cf. M. Ish-Shalom in *BJES* 10 (1943), 85–6.

from the Holy Land. Even the fact that the author is ostensibly a cantor, *shalīaḥ ṣibūr*, the man who speaks for the community, and from Hebron, the site of the Tombs of the Patriarchs, would have bestowed upon his work a kind of halo of sanctity.

The itinerary is actually recorded as beginning in Hebron. After an uneventful visit to the Tombs of the Patriarchs, the author moves—to the tomb of the prophet Jonah (probably Ḥalḥul), then he visits the Tomb of Rachel in 'Efrat, that is Bethlehem near Jerusalem, 2 parasangs to the east' [*sic*]. He then stayed in Jerusalem, and prayed, he tells us, with an important community whose members were versed in the study of Talmud, Mishna, and the Bible. On Mount Zion he saw the tombs of the kings and was also able to see the site of the Temple and the Western Wall 'which still exists'. From the text it is not clear to what he refers: to the Wailing Wall or to the Golden Gates, as they were called by Benjamin of Tudela (among others). From the Mount of Olives he saw the altar built by Ezra (Ezra 3: 2–3), and in the Valley of Josaphat the tombs of Zechariah and of Absalom. As to the former, it is quite interesting that he indicates 'Zechariah who was a priest and prophet', that is, Zechariah son of Jehoiada (2 Chr. 24: 20–22). At this point the geography of the itinerary begins to be confused. For some reason our pilgrim goes first to Nablus, then mentions Nebi Samwīl (Ramah) with the tomb of the prophet Samuel and then goes back north to Galilee. Alas, the list is very confused and it is doubtful whether the order in which places are listed corresponds to any actual order of visits. The itinerary brings us far north to Giscala (tombs of Shemaiah and Avtalion), in the centre of the area of the Holy Tombs, then to Miron (written 'Meidor') and further to the north to Kadesh Naftali, Timnatha (probably Tibnin). Here he mentions the tomb of the biblical Barak b. Avinoam, which is usually indicated as being in Kadesh Naftali, whereas Tibnin usually appears as the location of Shamgar b. 'Anath's tomb.[78] The traveller then goes to Safad (spelt 'Sipht'), where he spends some time; we have his description of the heat of the summer of 1215.

It becomes even more difficult to follow the itinerary now, as different tombs are mentioned but not their position. Assum-

[78] See *Tombs of the Ancestors*, s.v. Timnah.

ing, however, that in mentioning the tombs he refers to their traditional locations, he visited, consecutively, ʿAmūqa (the tomb of Jonathan b. ʿUziel, which he says is near the Jordan!), Qiyomia (tomb of R. Jose demin Yōqrat), Kfar Barʿam (tomb of R. Naḥman Ḥatūfā), and ʿAlma (tomb of R. Elazar b. ʿAzariah). Like some other pilgrims, he records visiting the 'Land of ʿArab', (a name which was probably confused with the village of ʿArraba), then Shazōr and Kfar ʿAnan (Kfar Ḥananya). Rather strangely, our author indicates that this is the site of the famous tomb of R. Simeon b. Yoḥai, though this is traditionally placed at Miron. His synagogue, he says, is in the city and 'the inhabitants of the city still pray therein' (p. 39). In Tiberias he mentions the hot springs of the city, Ḥammeī Tveryah, in which he bathed, and adds 'there is a paved road between the sea [of Galilee] and the hot springs of Tiberias, when the people (*ʿammei ha-aretz*) want to go from Tiberias to Bethsan and hence to Damascus' (p. 39). 'Tiberias', he remarks, 'is Raqat; there is the wall of the city on one side and on the other Mount Carmel.' Raqat is known to have existed before Herod Antipas founded Tiberias, and to give the new city a venerable 'genealogy' it was claimed that it was built on the site of ancient Raqat. This well-known Talmudic tradition[79] is repeated here (as to 'Mount Carmel', see below). He also mentions the tomb of R. Meir,[80] and recalls that 'the prayer house of R. Yoḥanan [b. Zakkai] is inside the city and all the inhabitants of the city pray there'. Our pilgrim notes that he prayed there 'because I was asked', that is to say, he led the prayer as cantor. In a strange order, or rather, in complete disorder, he then mentions Kfar Tanḥūm, which is Kfar Naḥum or Capernaum, where he found 'a great cemetery near the city and there are many great tombs, great hollowed rocks about 500 and in each rock were buried the Just and they did not name them to me' (p. 40).

The description of Galilee ends with Arbel. Here the visit to Galilee is interrupted for some reason, and our pilgrim says that he went to Har Gaʿash (near Nablus) and the traditional

[79] Tractate *Megillah* 5a.

[80] The attempt (*BJES* 8 (1940), 11–14) to identify him with the French Tosafist whom al-Ḥarizi met in Jerusalem is clearly wrong in the light of new evidence. Cf. above, ch. 4 n. 49.

tombs of Joshua son of Nun and Caleb son of Jephunneh which are also venerated by the Muslims. The Tomb of Dinah, which all other pilgrims put at Arbel, is here near Nablus, the place where she was raped. There are miraculous trees on her tomb, we are told, and whoever takes one leaf from them dies (p. 40). But as the next tomb is that of Sheth b. Enosh, whose traditional burial place was in Arbel, it is not impossible that these two tombs actually belong to Arbel and the order was interrupted by the tombs of Joshua and Caleb at Har Ga'ash.

Here the description becomes even more erratic until mention of Mount Carmel with the tombs of Jochabed mother of Moses, and Zipporah his wife (p. 40). We have already discussed this 'Mount Carmel' near Tiberias in connection with another pilgrim, and the reader is referred to the earlier explanation.[81] However, almost all traditions place the tombs of these biblical ladies between Arbel and Tiberias.

From here the itinerary continues to the northernmost city of Dan 'and there is a large community and very important people therein and I remained there for four days and walked to the east of the city with the city's inhabitants and they showed me the Cave of Paneas [written Aspamia instead of the usual Pamias, i.e. Banyās] and the spring of the Jordan coming out and flowing out from beneath the cave' (pp. 40–1). Then we find a further mention of 'the Land of 'Arab', which is obviously in this case Kfar Bar'am, with the traditional tomb of Queen Esther, Pinhas b. Yair, and the prophet Obadiah. Having turned from Banyās to the south, to 'the Land of 'Arab', he continues clearly to Yaquq and the tomb of the prophet Habakuk (although the name of the place is not mentioned explicitly). He then journeys to Nablus, unexpectedly mentions spending two days and nights at the Sea of Jaffa (p. 41), then apparently continues to 'Nob of the Priests, which is Beit Nubā', but returns to Jaffa before continuing

[81] See section A, text and n. 19. M. Ish-Shalom has suggested that tradition placed the tombs of Jochabed and Zipporah on this imaginary 'Mount Carmel' because of a misinterpreted passage in Tractate *Shabbat* 35*a* which states that the 'Well of Miryam' (sister of Moses) wandered with the Hebrews in the desert until the death of Miryam (Tractate *Ta'anīth* 9*a*). It reappeared in the Holy Land, was in the sea of Tiberias, 'and whoever wants to see it let him climb to the top of Mount Carmel and see a kind of a sieve in the sea and this is the well of Miryam'. This is also mentioned in other Talmudic sources; see S. Klein, n. 75 above, at the end.

north to Caesarea and Haifa. Here he visits the places connected with the traditions of Elijah and Elisha and then comes to Acre, which merits no more than a mention. This part ends with an enigmatic statement: 'And hence [from Acre] I went to Bethsan, Tyre, Sidon, and Beirut' and finally to Cyprus and Nicosia. Here he stayed for a long time, presumably before going home.

The description of the journey is followed (pp. 42–6) by a collection of fables. Each story begins 'And R. Menaḥem b. Perez told us also'. In one place it is stated clearly that Menaḥem, though he called himself ha-Ḥebroni, that is, of Hebron, was not an inhabitant of Palestine. This is indicated by the phrase: 'And he also told us now when he returned and came back to his homeland and the voyage was made by sea' (p. 44).

Despite the valiant defence of the authenticity of this itinerary by I. Ben-Zvi,[82] and more cautiously by others, I am now convinced that the text of the itinerary is a forgery, though not always for the reasons put forward by S. Klein, the strongest antagonist of the itinerary.[83] Even disregarding the second part of the treatise, which is just a collection of strange *fabliaux* (they may well fit with the other parts of the codex), the text is not a description of any real voyage, let alone a guide for a prospective pilgrim: it is not only distorted but also an inadequate and false guide to the location of the Holy Tombs. Should we regard it as a text of Palestinian origin designed for 'export'? There seems little justification for this. Moreover the polemical references, to Muslims and Christians, always present in other itineraries, are missing here. And though it is known that Jerusalem had a Jewish community at that time, there is no proof whatsoever of the existence of a Jewish community in Banyās. It would be superfluous to summarize again all the inadequacies of his descriptions here, including the 'change' in the position of the traditional tombs.

To strengthen the 'veracity' of his story, the forger quotes 'the Sons of the West' (*bnei maʿaravā*) who never abandoned the Holy Land and testify to the authenticity of the Holy Tombs (p. 42). The miracle at the Tomb of Dinah daughter of Jacob

[82] See above, n. 75.
[83] Ibid. Klein's *History*, pp. iii–iv, gives a short English summary.

is thus also ascribed to the Sons of the West' (p. 40). But the use of the expression 'Sons of the West', which would indicate that he came from the Orient, was very archaic in the thirteenth century, and moreover he inadvertently wrote that he went to his homeland by sea (p. 44). A similar interesting lapse is when he reports that a ship's captain once told him that they had gone far from their kingdom, a distance of six months (!) and then they encountered 'human beings, small—very, very small—called in the vernacular (*be-la'az*) *marmoziesh*: small, like little four-year-old children'. The vernacular expression is clearly derived from the French *marmotter* and the noun *marmouset*, that is 'small boy' (e.g. Villon).[84] This brings us from the Orient to France and fits in well with other parts of the codex.

This itinerary is therefore a forgery, but not, as has been suggested, by a writer of the nineteenth century.[85] This is a thirteenth-century forgery, and a rather clumsy one, composed by using bits and pieces of other Hebrew itineraries (S. Klein has already pointed out R. Samuel b. Samson's itinerary as one of his major sources) already in circulation in the Diaspora of the West. The time can be even more accurately determined: a thorough codicological study has fixed the date of the composition of the codex of which our treatise is a part as before 1260.[86] Moreover, M. Banitt's linguistic examination of the codex, which was entirely written by one hand (the name indicated is Samuel), has fixed the origin of the manuscript in northern Champagne in France, between 1215 and 1260. There is no reason to suppose that our itinerary was an exception in terms of time or space.

G. THE IMPRESSIONS OF A JOURNEY TO THE HOLY LAND BY JUDAH AL-ḤARIZI (1216–1217)

One may legitimately ask if the fragments of poems and

[84] I should like to express my thanks to a scholar of Romance languages, my colleague M. Bannit, who confirmed my suggestion.

[85] Argued thus by S. Klein. Students of itineraries always remember the very famous and clever forgery of a mid-19th-cent. scholar of repute, E. Carmoly, who invented the itinerary of one Isaac Chelo. This itinerary is unfortunately still being quoted by unwary scholars, even though the forgery was proved almost 50 years ago.

[86] M. Beit-Arié, 'MS Oxford, Bodl. Or. 135', *Tarbiz* 54 (1985), 631–4.

rhymed prose left behind by al-Ḥarizi, a wandering Jewish minstrel, should be included in this chapter. The information he conveyed about Jewish communities in the Latin Kingdom has already been discussed earlier and rather extensively, but nevertheless I think there is some value in reconstructing here his voyage and stay in the Holy Land. As I have said, this is hardly an itinerary in the usual sense of the word; but the reputation of the writer as well as the glimpses he gives of the experience of travelling by sea or crossing the desert in a caravan vindicate its place in this chapter.

In the twenty-eighth *maqāmah*, al-Ḥarizi gives the date of his coming to Jerusalem as 1148 since the destruction of the Second Temple. As medieval Jewry fixed the date of destruction in 68 or 69 (instead of 70), al-Ḥarizi is referring to 1216 or 1217.

It so happens that his journey to the Holy Land and his pilgrimages there are described in two different Hebrew versions of his *Taḥkemoni* and additionally in his own Arabic version of his poems. One of the Hebrew versions has an excellent English translation by V. E. Reichert and it is to this translation that I shall refer here. The other Hebrew version, with a rather longer description of the voyage, was published by S. M. Stern, who has also provided us with a detailed account of the Arabic version.[87]

It is in the beautiful introduction to the twenty-eighth *maqāmah*, the 'Jerusalem Maqāmah' that al-Ḥarizi describes his motivation and feelings in leaving Spain and going on pilgrimage to Jerusalem.[88] Hardly has the yearning for Zion ever been expressed in more elegant language; its sheer beauty tends to persuade the reader of its sincerity.

The different versions of the pilgrimage differ in the amount of detail, but as there is no reason to suspect one or the other of false information, they can be used concurrently. The Arabic version states briefly that al-Ḥarizi started out from Bilbais, the easternmost city of Egypt, and came to Jerusalem. A chapter in the fiftieth *maqāmah* of one of the Hebrew versions is more

[87] *The Taḥkemoni of Judah al-Ḥarizi*, trans. E. V. Reichert, 2 vols. (Jerusalem 1973). S. M. Stern, 'An Unpublished *Maqama* by Al-Ḥarizi'. See details above, ch. 4 nn. 8, 14.

[88] Reichert, *Taḥkemoni* 143–6. In the Arabic version he mentions the Fifth Crusade (1218–21) and its failure. Stern, 'An Unpublished *Maqama*', 194.

elaborate, but we shall be using a fuller version more suitable to our purpose.[89]

On this journey he meets a permanent interlocutor, his *alter ego*, whom he calls Ḥaber the Kenite. The latter tells him how he reached Alexandria (Nō Ammōn), and this probably reflects al-Ḥarizi's own experience in coming to Egypt. 'I rented me a daughter of the seas, a Negress and not from among the daughters of Eve, black and beautiful, quick like lightning moving and speeding on the wings of the wind, travelling without feet and flying without wings.'[90] This sea voyage took him to Egypt and the seemingly predestined meeting with al-Ḥarizi. Their road led from Egypt through the 'huge and terrible' desert, where they suffered from the intolerable heat. After this difficult passage they finally reached Gaza, where they celebrated their happy escape.[91]

This short account can be supplemented with a longer account by the same author which as far as I know is the only description of a Jew crossing the Sinai desert from Egypt to the Holy Land. He made this journey with an Arab caravan and can hardly find words enough to praise their behaviour.

And I lodged with the tents of Kedar [i.e. Arabs, S. of S. 1: 5], and I joined the company of the most venerable Arabs, descendants of people of opulence . . . they accommodated me in their shade and my tent was amidst their tents. I was with them in the shadow of strength and courage, and they were my haven and citadel . . . and never did I feel any worry as long as I was with them.[92]

It seems that on the journey from Gaza they travelled at night, finally reaching Jerusalem where al-Ḥarizi was to stay for a full month.[93] We know already about how he met the leaders of the new Jewish community here,[94] but in another *maqāmah* we find him as a pilgrim in the Holy City. 'These were days as if carved from rubies, as if cut from the trees of life, as

[89] Reichert, *Taḥkemoni* 190. This second Hebrew version publ. S. M. Stern is based on an Oxford MS. See ibid. 186.

[90] Stern, 'An unpublished *Maqama*', 203, ll. 20–3.

[91] Ibid. 205, l. 20.

[92] Ibid. 202, ll. 20–3.

[93] Ibid. l. 24.

[94] See above, ch. 4. In the Arabic version they are introduced as 'the greatest scholars of the lands of the Franks (*bilād al-Ifranj*)' (Stern, 188).

if stolen from the stars in heaven. We went out every day to weep for Zion, which is mourning for her children ... we grieved for her destroyed palaces and the remains of her buildings. We journeyed to the monuments (ṣiyūn) of the Just which are all around her.'[95] Some days they went up the Mount of Olives to pray, looking with sadness at the Temple Esplanade which had become a place of idolatry ... From the buildings of old nothing was left but only 'remains to sadden the hearts of those who remember'.[96] Here, he says, he ends the story of his pilgrimage in the Holy Land before going to Damascus; but actually we know that his way led from Jerusalem to Safad and it was from there that he reached Damascus.[97]

H. THE ITINERARY OF R. JACOB, THE MESSENGER OF THE YESHIVA OF ACRE (*CIRCA* 1258–1270)

This is the shortest and dreariest of the Hebrew itineraries—actually no more than a list of places and the tombs to be found there.[98] As to the date of its composition, we can assume some time after about 1258, when the French scholars, originally led by R. Yeḥiel of Paris after passing through Greece, arrived in Acre (R. Yeḥiel died on board during the crossing) and before about 1270, as the list does not mention the tomb of Naḥmanides. It seems that we also now have some data about the R. Jacob: according to a recent study he was a kind of professional fund-raiser on behalf of the Academy in Acre, and we can

95 Stern, 'An Unpublished *Maqama*', 205, 24–8; cf. Reichert, 420.

96 Ibid. 207, l. 5.

97 On his alleged visit to Acre see below ch. 8, p. 268 and n. 52; On the end of his pilgrimage see the Hebrew version, *maqāmah* 46 (Reichert, *Taḥkemoni* 305).

98 There are two MSS extant. One, from the 15th cent., belonged in the mid-19th cent. to a well-known scholar, E. Carmoly, who published it with some other itineraries. *Eileh ha-Massa'oth* (These are the voyages) (Brussels 1841), 4–8. The *incipit* of the heading is *Eileh sīmanei*. The same small codex also has an itinerary from Paris to Acre, via Marseilles, Sardinia, and Tunis, but this itinerary has been published only in its French translation. Another MS is indicated as Fond Sorbonne, no. 222. There are no significant differences between the two MSS. I quote from *Hameamer* 3 (1919), 51–3. Cf. Carmoly's French translation in his *Itinéraires*, 174.

actually follow him and his son Donin from France to Venice in 1278, where he boarded a ship bound for Acre.[99]

The heading of the manuscript reads as follows: 'These are the monuments of the tombs in Eretz Israel which were brought by R. Jacob, the truthful messenger of R. Yeḥiel of Paris, who has in his Yeshiva 300 students, may God protect them. And the afore-mentioned R. Jacob went and came back from all the districts of Eretz Israel and [he was] in Acre and in other places to bring great charitable donations to the Midrash ha-Gaddol of Paris.'[100] This rubric was obviously added but has more historical interest than the inventory of tombs which follows. It is also this heading which has generated heated debate about information included in it and its contribution to the history of the Jewish community in Acre in the middle of the thirteenth century.[101] The 'monuments' at the beginning of the quotations are indicated by the Hebrew expression *sīmanīm*, which literally means signs or marks, so there can be little doubt that the author wanted to indicate the visible signs on the tombs, domes, and the like.

The first impression is that of a rather confused list, but with the exception of the first place he mentions, Pamias (Paneas, i.e. Banyās in the north)[102] and Teqoʿa, at the southern end of the country (also mentioned in the first opening phrase), the list in fact comprises an itemization of tombs. It begins with Mount Carmel, which is consistent with a pilgrimage beginning in Acre, where the Yeshiva was located. After Mount Carmel and the altar of Elijah he adds 'and on the slope [of Carmel] the cemetery of Acre, at a distance of 4 miles [he uses the measure *mil*] from Acre'.[103] From the Crusader capital he continues directly east to Galilee, where the majority of the tombs were located. He journeyed to Shazōr, Kfar Ḥanan, and Prōd and then to the famous tombs of R. Simeon bar Yoḥai and the students of Hillel and Shammai in Miron. Moving north he reaches Kfar Barʿam, Giscala (Gūsh Ḥalav), and the

[99] About R. Jacob the messenger, see below, ch. 8 n. 68.

[100] *Hameamer* 3 (1919), 51.

[101] On this controversy, see ch. 8 n. 67.

[102] This phrase is struck out in the Parisian MS.

[103] On this cemetery, see ch. 8 n. 3.

northernmost point on his itinerary—ʿAlma. Then, in the direction of Tiberias he visits Nabarteīn, ʿAmūqa, and ʿAin Zeitūn, very near Safad. We know that in ʿAin Zeitūn a Jewish community existed,[104] but for some reason it is not mentioned in the itineraries. Safad is not mentioned but would have been passed on the way south to ʿAkhbara, Yaquq,[105] Hattin, Arbel, and Tiberias. In addition to the tombs traditionally located here he notes R. Meir *qaṣin*[106] and the Tomb of Maimonides.[107] From here the list continues to the south, through Zippori, Romi or Romā, to Nablus, Avarta, Kfar Ḥeres, Shiloh, and Jerusalem. Strangely, the only line dedicated to the Holy City reads: 'Jerusalem, the Holy City, may she be rebuilt and reconstructed speedily in our time. In Zion there is the burial place of the Kings of Israel' (p. 53). The itinerary then mentions Ramah, that is Nebi Samwīl, the Tomb of Rachel near Bethlehem, and Hebron. Here, unexpectedly, the treatise ends with a mention of Safad. We shall certainly not be wrong if we regard the last item as an interpolation or some kind of afterthought by the author as it is clearly not mentioned in the proper order.

This inventory of tombs contributes very little new to the geography of the Holy Tombs. But we must remember that the text was in the hands of someone other than the author: the person who wrote the introduction. The relevance of this will be discussed in the next chapter. In the present context, the importance of the text lies in that it was written for a fund-raiser for a Palestinian yeshiva to carry as a means of collecting money in the Diaspora. Probably there were more texts and more messengers of this kind. This would also explain the appearance, almost in the same period, of forgeries like the letter of R. Menaḥem of Hebron.

[104] On the community of ʿAin Zeitūn, see above.

[105] The majority of pilgrims spell it Ḥaqūq, thus relating it to the prophet Ḥabaqūq (corr. Hebrew spelling), whose tomb is shown there. The real name of the place is Yaquq. There is a strange spelling in *BJES* 8 (1940–1), 11–14.

[106] The identification by M. Ish-Shalom can no longer be upheld in the light of al-Ḥarizi's *maqāmah*; see below, ch. 8 n. 44.

[107] On the very controversial Tomb of Maimonides in Tiberias, see *Tombs of the Ancestors*, 192–4.

I. THE ITINERARY OF THE ANONYMOUS PUPIL OF NAḤMANIDES: *TOṢŌTH ERETZ ISRAEL* (1270–1291) AND *EILEH HA-MASSA'ŌTH*

The last itinerary[108] which can be assigned to the Crusader period has a baffling title, *Tōṣōth Eretz Israel*, which probably meant 'Comings and Goings in the Land of Israel'.[109] S. Assaf, who published the whole text, assigned it to 1270–1320, and in this has been followed by others (like A. Ya'ari). Yet, there can be little doubt that the treatise should be assigned entirely to the Crusader period.[110] This can be conclusively deduced from the description of the road from Acre to Tyre, Sidon, and Beirut. 'All these cities on the coast', he says, 'are fortified and one goes to them by land or by sea' (p. 1)—a situation which clearly points to a period before the loss of the Latin Kingdom. Additionally Acre is the starting point of at least eight (or nine) pilgrimages, and this would have hardly been possible after 1291. Moreover, the date is also clear from the interest and knowledge of the tombs of the great European scholars who migrated to the Holy Land in the thirteenth century.[111] Consequently, I suggest that the treatise was written between 1270, the year of the death of Naḥmanides, whose tomb our pilgrim mentions as that of 'my master Moses b. Naḥman of Gerona' at the foot of Mount Carmel (p. 1, l. 16) and the fall of Acre, the last Crusader bastion on the Palestinian coast.

[108] The unique MS of the itinerary is in the Firkovich Collection, no. 764, in Leningrad. Short excerpts were published by A. T. Neubauer in *REJ* 10 (1885), 105–7 and reprinted by A. Luncz in *Hameamer* 3 (1919), 67–8. The text was copied by Harkavi in St Petersburg in 1886 but not published until 1928 by S. Assaf in *Yerūshalaīm: Memorial Volume Dedicated to A. M. Luncz* (H) (repr. in his *Sources* (Jerusalem 1946), 74–90). In quoting from this edition I refer to MS pages and lines indicated by the editor.

[109] The noun is to be found in the Bible in the sense of 'goings out' or 'outlets'; cf. Josh. 15: 4; Ezek. 48: 30.

[110] Prawer, *The Jews*, 25 n. 111; S. H. Kuk, *Studies*, ii. 308–14; cf. id., in *Sinai* 7 (1940) 80; and id., 'Unknown Cemetery at the Foot of Mt. Carmel' (H), *BJES* 11 (1944–5), 65–6.

[111] That is to say that there must have been a Jewish community in Acre which could furnish our pilgrim with the necessary information about the tombs in the cemetery; but the Jewish community of Acre was exterminated when the city fell in 1291.

We may also assume that the pilgrim was the great scholar's student not in the Holy Land but in the West. An expression like: 'The copy of the Mishna which I bought in Eretz Israel' (p. 3, l. 16) indicates clearly enough that the author came from abroad and thus probably studied under Naḥmanides in Spain. Another expression: 'Blessed be the Lord, God of Israel who rewarded me and showed me Upper Galilee and Lower Galilee and the Tombs of the Ṣadīqīm there' (p. 6), would hardly have been written by a native or inhabitant of the Holy Land.

The itinerary itself is interesting and important in showing the main roads of communications and pilgrimage of that period, as well as detailing the attractions of particular places to the Jewish pilgrim. The anti-Christian tone which was so prominent in the twelfth-century itineraries gives way here, as one could expect from one travelling mainly through Judaea, Samaria, and Galilee, all Muslim-dominated areas, to comments on Muslims. At the same time the pilgrim diligently noted places where a tomb hallowed to the Jews is also venerated by Muslims—this, no doubt, to enhance the Jewish tradition. Thus, on the altar of Elijah 'the Ishmaelites burn candles for the sanctity of the place' (p. 1, l. 25). In Miron at the burial place of Shammai and Hillel and their pupils (Simeon b. Yoḥai is mentioned after the story of the miracle) he remarks: 'Here gather all of Israel and the Ishmaelites on Second Passover.[112] They pray here and read psalms. And when they see water coming out from inside the cave all rejoice, because this is a sign that the year will be fertile.' Very often, actually, there was no water but during the prayers it miraculously appeared (p. 6, l. 22 *et. seq.*). A good observer, he makes an interesting comment on Hattin. Here the Muslims built a prayer-house (he uses the non-pejorative expression *beit tefillah*) over the tomb of Jethro, Moses' father-in-law (that is, Nebī Shuʿīb of Muslim and Druze tradition). The pilgrim adds: 'And we saw there a window in the cave, because the Ishmaelites are usually building prayer houses near the *ṣadīqīm*' (p. 8, ll. 27–30). A small contribution to the thesis of continuity of the Holy Places.

[112] Today the great celebration in Miron is on *Lag ba-ʿOmer*, 33 days after the first day of Passover.

Contrary to the majority of Hebrew itineraries, our pilgrim begins his pilgrimage in the Holy Land from Acre. There is no doubt that he came to the great Crusader commercial centre from Europe by ship. Nine of his seventeen or so excursions begin in Acre, from whence he journeys north, south and south-east, and later on due east. This is reminiscent of the pilgrimage of Burchard of Mount Sion, his Christian contemporary (1280). At the end of his pilgrimage he left Acre again on his way to Damascus.

Another particular feature is that in addition to the overland roads to Jerusalem through Samaria, he also mentions the sea road from Acre to Jaffa and thence an inland road to Jerusalem.

The total number of places mentioned, namely fifty-five, makes this the largest of all our itineraries. However, it is doubtful if he really visited Tyre, Sidon, and Beirut, or only jotted down their names on the road north of Acre; the places are mentioned but almost nothing is said about them.

First to be indicated is the road to the north, to Tyre, Sidon, and Beirut (wrongly called by a biblical name, Beeroth), 'which can be reached by land and by sea'. The distances are measured in parasangs[113]—7 to Tyre, 7 from Tyre to Sidon, 10 from Sidon to Beirut and are obviously far from being exact. But the pilgrimage clearly starts from Acre, where he mentions a 'Hasmonean Gate' and a boundary of the Holy Land linked to the return of the Babylonian exiles.[114] From Acre his road leads along the beach of the Bay of Acre to Haifa. The location of Crusader Haifa roughly corresponded to today's Bat Galim, a suburb on the shore to the south. It is not far from there, at the foot of Mount Carmel, that he visits the second cemetery used by the Jewish community of Acre.[115] Here were buried the European scholars and sages who immigrated to the kingdom in the thirteenth century. Among them he mentions: 'my master and teacher R. Moses b. Naḥman (Naḥmanides) of Gerona' (p. 1, l. 17). On the slope of the mountain he visits the Cave of Elijah; it is not clear if he descends from there or

[113] On the parasang see section C: The Itinerary of Benjamin of Tudela, where it is shown to be equivalent to 5–7 km (above, p. 196).

[114] Cf. above section B: The Itinerary of Jacob b. Nathanel, n. 29.

[115] See ch. 8 n. 3.

continues to the top of the mountain until he reaches Elijah's altar, also venerated by the Muslims who, he says, light candles here (p. 1, l. 25). This is no doubt the place venerated for centuries on the highest point of the mountain, known by its Arab name Muḥrakah. From here he could see the brook of Qishon (called by the Crusaders 'Rivière de Cayphas') and the place of the slaying of the priests of Baal (1 Kgs. 18). Next he mentions a place called Jezreel, which he reports as being only a *parsa* from Elijah's altar. The place is therefore to be sought not far from Muḥrakah, on the top of the mountain. Here he ends his first excursion and returns to Acre.[116]

His second excursion, proceeding from Acre in a southeasterly direction, reached two places not mentioned by any other traveller, namely, Usha and Shefar'am (Crusader: Le Saffran). The first became famous in Jewish history as the place where far-reaching legislation was enacted after the destruction of the Second Temple. Characteristically, our pilgrim simply mentions the distance from Acre and makes no mention of memorable events or Holy Tombs. From Shefar'am he returns to Acre.

He then leaves Acre again for Zippori, to visit the tomb of Rabbi (Judah ha-Nasi) the great exilarch who codified the Mishnah in the second century CE. A Christian pilgrim would have continued a few miles further south to Nazareth, but obviously our pilgrim had no such interests. From Acre again, he indicates the road to Kfar 'Anan (Ḥananya) which he evaluates as a day's journey.

After these pilgrimages in Galilee he moves on to his fourth pilgrimage, from Acre to Jerusalem. According to his account, one climbs and marches along (the ridge of) Mount Carmel, bypasses Jezreel on the left, from where one sees Mount Tabor on the left in the far distance; continuing east through the

[116] Our author says it is half a parasang from Elijah's altar to this place. This should mean that it is on Mount Carmel. The author says, however, that Jezreel 'is the place where Ahab went because of the rain', thus referring to 1 Kgs. 18: 44–6 when 'Elijah ran before Ahab [who was in a chariot escaping the rain which was approaching following Elijah's prayer] to the entrance of Jezreel.' The miraculous prowess of Elijah must have been misinterpreted by our pilgrim, who therefore understood the distance as being small. Actually Jezreel (Crusader Zarin) is in the Valley of Jezreel near Mount Gilboa. Our pilgrim mentions Jezreel again (p. 2, l. 3, bottom) as half a parasang from (the top?) of Mount Carmel.

Valley of Jezreel (which is not mentioned by name) one came to Meggido, Ta'anakh (Crusader Tannoch—both places never before mentioned in the itineraries), and finally Nablus. He then adds, 'and there is another road, the road of Samaria, and the mountains of Samaria are exquisite in their beauty' (p. 2, l. 8)—probably the road often used by the Crusaders leading from Nazareth through Jenin to Nablus.

These last roads are mentioned only as leading to Jerusalem; no holy places are mentioned along them except the tomb of Joseph. He adds: 'And there is another route from Acre to Jerusalem, namely, by sea to Jaffa and from Jaffa to Jerusalem by land through Ramah (Nebi Samwīl) a distance of eight parasangs' (p. 2, ll. 8–9). In reality the distance is about 70 kilometres. Our pilgrim also indicates a fourth route, from Acre by land to Jaffa and then inland to Jerusalem. Having described the different routes leading from Acre to Jerusalem, our pilgrim goes back to describe Nablus. He halts there for a Sabbath and engages in discussion, probably with the Great Priest of the Samaritans whom he calls *Rav* (p. 2, l. 16). He mentions the Passover sacrifices of the Samaritans and the fulfilment of the biblical curse on Mount Ebal and the blessing on Mount Gerizim. It seems that he is the only one of our pilgrims to call the former 'the Blessed Mountain' and the latter 'the Cursed Mountain', commenting, 'It is possible that because of the blessings and curses they are so called' (ibid., l. 15; cf. Deut. 11: 29).

On leaving Nablus his road led south through 'Avarta to a place he calls Gibeah of Benjamin, which is either Ramallah or al-Bira, and then to Ṣofīm, from which he beholds Jerusalem for the first time. It is tempting to identify Ṣofīm as Ramathaim Zophim, the residence of the prophet Samuel, that is Nebi Samwīl or the Crusader Montjoye, though he later mentions the place as Ramah.[117] Here he performs the obligatory rite of mourning on beholding Jerusalem in its ruin, a rite to be repeated in Jerusalem itself on beholding the Temple in ruin (p. 2, ll. 25–7). Jerusalem takes up a special section in the description (printed text, pp. 78–80), far more detailed than in

[117] The identification can be argued not only because this is the first place from which one sees Jerusalem, but also because Ramathaim Zophim is identical with Ramah.

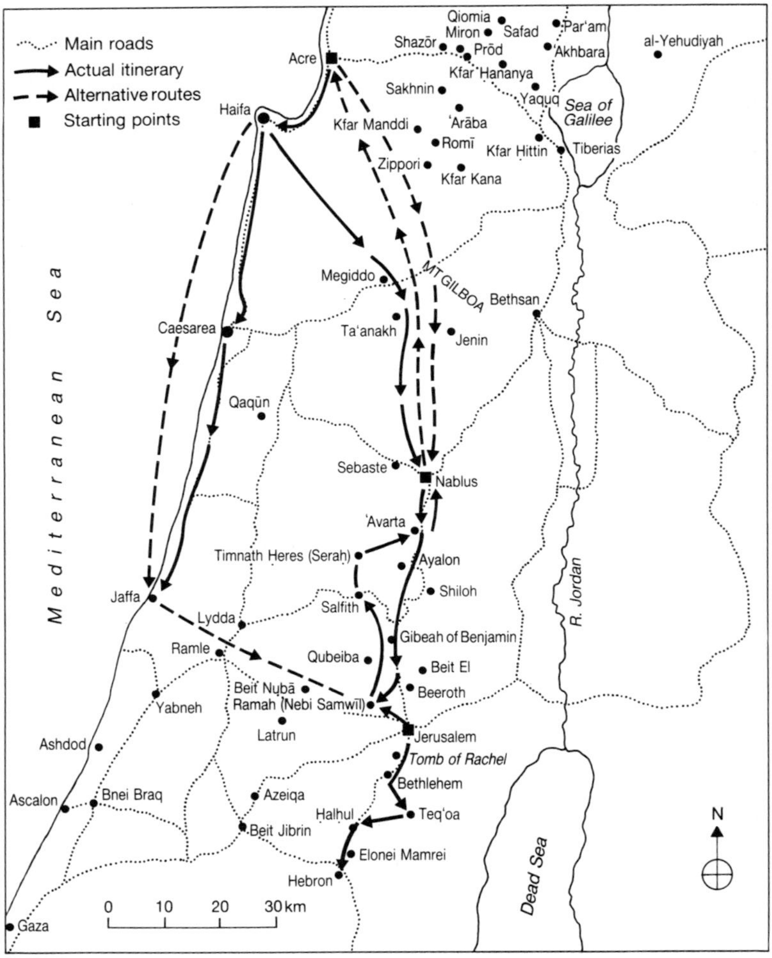

Map 4. The itinerary of the anonymous pupil of Naḥmanides

other Hebrew itineraries. He ascends one of her ruins, probably on the Mount of Olives, from which he sees: 'The Temple Mount and the wall of the courtyard (*'azarah*), the courtyard of the women, the courtyard of the priests and the courtyard of Israel, the place of the altar and of the Temple and the Holy of Holies' (p. 2, ll. 27–9). Here again, on seeing the ruins of the Temple, as the religious precept obliged, he rends his garments for the second time. In Jerusalem he goes down to the Pool of Siloam; like the other pilgrims, he finds it fascinating. He notes: 'Its waters come out from the Temple Mount, from beneath the mountain until they come here. Hence they flow to the gardens of the city to irrigate them and people immerse themselves here. It is said that the waters have healing properties and therefore the Ishmaelites wash here.'[118] He then goes through the Valley of Josaphat, which he says is bounded by the Temple Mount in the east and south, and finds a Jewish cemetery. The cemetery is in the southern part of the valley, near the cleft of the Valley of Hinnom, between two mountains. From here he ascends the Mount of Olives where he reaches a kind of protruding platform or ledge (*īṣtabā*) opposite the entrance of the Temple, and 'this is the reason why prayers were offered here'. In the Valley of Josaphat he describes the Monument of Absalom, 'a quadrangular building, very high with columns round it, and all is made from one stone [a monolith], a very beautiful building' (p. 3. ll. 13–14). Nearer to the Pool of Siloam he finds 'a quadrangular building. It is said that this was a pagan temple of the Greeks' (p. 3, l. 15).

Our pilgrim then ascends Mount Zion from the Valley of Hinnom. Here he mentions the royal tombs 'and there is an old building called the Temple (*heikhal*) of David facing the Temple and candles are burning here because of the sanctity of the place'. The meaning is not clear, but he probably refers to a building enclosing the Tomb of David, 'Some say that the Ark of the Covenant which was brought by David rested here until he built the Temple. Not far away is the Tower of David, built of huge stones. You can see that this is an ancient building and

[118] The healing properties of the Pool go back to the traditions of the Second Temple as described in the New Testament miracle of healing the blind (John 9: 7). This belief continued in the Crusader period and was transmitted to the Muslims. Cf. G. Le Strange, *Palestine under the Moslems* (London 1890), 221.

it is now in Jerusalem [*sic*].' After describing the immense Temple esplanade of 360 *ammōth*, he remarks that on the Sacred Rock (*even shtīyah*) the kings of Ishmael built a magnificent building and made it a prayer place, covered by a very beautiful dome above the Holy of Holies. A keen observer, he describes a structure in front of the Dome of the Rock 'to the East, standing on columns and a dome above them. It is possibly the "outside altar" which was in the Courtyard of Israel'. He saw Ishmaelites gathering there 'on the day of their festivity, around three thousand, and going around in a procession, as if in dance, as the Jews—be sure to make a distinction between unclean and pure—used to go around the altar'[119] (p. 4, ll. 9–13). On the south side there is a slope down which you can walk, like a kind of ramp, which was on the south side [of the Temple]. 'And here are caves open to the outside of the walls of the outside courtyard and they enter beneath the Temple Mount and one enters them until you almost reach the Sacred Rock; and perhaps these are the tunnels (*meḥīllōth*) under the Temple' (p. 4, ll. 14–17).[120]

After mentioning the tombs of Simeon the Just and the prophet Haggai, he mentions 'The Cave of the Lion' on the other side of Jerusalem (p. 4, ll. 24–30):

Here are the bones of the Just who suffered martyrdom to 'sanctify the [divine] name' (*yīḥūd ha-shem*) at the hand of the king of Greece [or Byzantium]. He decided to burn the bones the next day, but when the night came a lion carried them from the lower pool which was full

[119] The 'ledge' mentioned earlier is probably the huge stone at the top of the Mount of Olives described in a Jewish 'Guide to Jerusalem' written in Arabic as 'the Jewish prayer place at the top of the mountain'. It was '10 *ammōth* long, 2 *ammōth* wide and 2 *ammōth* thick'. (An *ammah* is about 70 cm.) It was called 'Kūrsi Rāis', the Chair of the Head. According to tradition this was the place where Providence stood for $3\frac{1}{2}$ years after leaving the Temple and the city and before going up to heaven (J. Barslavi, 'A Guide to Jerusalem from the Geniza' (H), *Eretz Israel* 7 (1964), 74). As to the solemnities practised in the Temple, he is referring to the custom practised on the last day of the Feast of Tabernacles. The words between the dashes repeated in *Eileh ha-Massa'ōth,* are indicated there by vowels only, certainly from fear of the Muslims. The structure referred to is the elegant dome known in Muslim times as *Kubbat al-Silsilah* or Dome of the Chain, and under the Crusaders as the Chapel of James the Less. Cf. G. Le Strange, *Palestine under the Moslems*, 151–3.

[120] He is probably referring to the openings near the Templars' compound at the mosque of al-Aqṣā. The *meḥillōth* under the Temple are mentioned in the Talmud several times, e.g. Tractate *Pesaḥīm* 86. Over the centuries there were stories of people entering the Dome of the Rock through hidden entrances.

of them and brought them to this cave. And when the morning came the lion was found at the entrance of the cave with the dead. Thus it became known to the king and all his people that they were holy and so they remained there until today.

This marvellous story in praise of the Jews and their religion goes back a long way, to the Persian invasion and the sack of Jerusalem in 614 CE. It was also assigned to that period by the Crusaders: the latter venerated the *Carnarium leonis* or *Carnier del Lyon* near the Pool of Mamillah. The most detailed description is that of John of Würzburg (*c.*1165): 'Before the [Jaffa] gate of Jerusalem near a lake which is facing south, you can see that Cave to which by the order of God Almighty, a certain lion brought during the night almost 12,000 martyrs killed under Chosroes. Hence it was called *Carnarium leonis*.'[121] A memory of the massacre of the Christians lingered on for ages, and was adopted by the Crusaders who even built a chapel and instituted prayers there. Obviously the Jewish pilgrim could not leave the miracle entirely to the Christians: when it came to martyrs there was strong Jewish competition, so the miracle was recast so as to favour the Jews.

After the visit to Jerusalem our pilgrim continues south to Hebron, passing the Tomb of Rachel. Here again, the description is more detailed and clear than in other itineraries. Two stones at the length of the tomb and two at its width are at the base of the monument. There are five layers of these stones. This brings their number up to ten. They are topped by a huge stone which covers the pile of stones on all sides. The number of stones corresponds to the ten tribes. The top stone was added by the Patriarch Jacob. The infant Benjamin could not bring his stone, neither did Joseph because he was only eight years old or because he was too sad at the death of his mother (p. 5, ll. 4–11). In comparison, Benjamin of Tudela says of the monument: 'made up of eleven stones, corresponding with the number of the sons of Jacob. Upon it is a dome resting on four

[121] Johannis Wirzburgensis, *Descriptio Terrae Sanctae*, ed. T. Tobler, *Descriptiones Terrae Sanctae*, ch. 17 (Leipzig 1874), 166. Cf. *Citez de Jerusalem*, ch. 18, ibid. 214. The latter does not mention Chosroes, but cites the existence of a chapel where mass was celebrated every day. 'Carnarium' means collective grave. In its Christian garb the story is told for the first time by Strategius *c.*760, that is, 150 years after the event. Cf. J. Wilkinson, *Jerusalem Pilgrims Before the Crusades* (Harminster 1977), 162, 215.

columns' (p. 40). With the passage of approximately a hundred years between two pilgrimages (*c.*1170–*c.*1270), only the foundation block apparently remained *in situ*, whereas the columns and the dome disappeared.

From the Tomb of Rachel, bypassing Bethlehem, he continues to Teqoʿa and Ḥalḥul (he calls the place Ḥarḥūr) near Hebron itself. Here he mentions the Tombs of the Patriarchs (no description), and adds an interesting remark: 'New Hebron is near the Cave, but ancient Hebron was higher up on the mountain' (p. 5, ll. 13–14).

Returning to his base in Jerusalem he journeys to the north. He mentions 'Ramah, which is Nebi Samwīl', and Sarfith (Salfith near Nablus), which he wrongly identifies with Zarephath (Sarepta) or Sarafand of Elijah (1 Kgs. 17: 8–24). Here, in the mountains of Samaria, he visits Timnath Ḥeres and then returns through ʿAvarta and Nablus to Acre (p. 5, ll. 5–11). This ends the pilgrimages in Samaria and Judaea, and the pilgrim returns to his base in Acre.

Acre now becomes the starting-point for very extensive pilgrimages in Galilee. (Later Tiberias will fulfil the same function for another section of Galilee.) From Acre he goes due east to Shazōr, Kfar Ḥanan (Ḥananya), and then north to Miron. From Miron and its celebrated tombs of Shammai and Hillel and R. Simeon b. Yoḥai he goes to Prōd (Faradiyah). Starting out again from Miron he visits Giscala (Gūsh Ḥalav). Another excursion, again from Miron, leads him to Kfar Barʿam where he admires the synagogue of R. Simeon b. Yoḥai: 'a magnificent structure, large and stone-clad, the columns very large; I never saw so magnificent a building' (p. 7, ll. 19–20). From here he returns to Giscala, continuing to ʿAlma and then south to Dalātha, Nabarteīn, Qiomia, ʿAmūqa, Parʿam, ʿAin al-Zeitūn, and Safad (which he spells Shfīṭ).

From here he journeys south through ʿAkhbara and Yaquq to Tiberias, the starting-point for his return to Acre. From Tiberias he goes to Arbel and the village of Hattin, where he admires the local spring: 'Nearby there is a spring where the water comes down from the top of the mountain through a hidden crevice in a great rock. You cannot see it, but you hear the noise of the water as if it were running through bronze

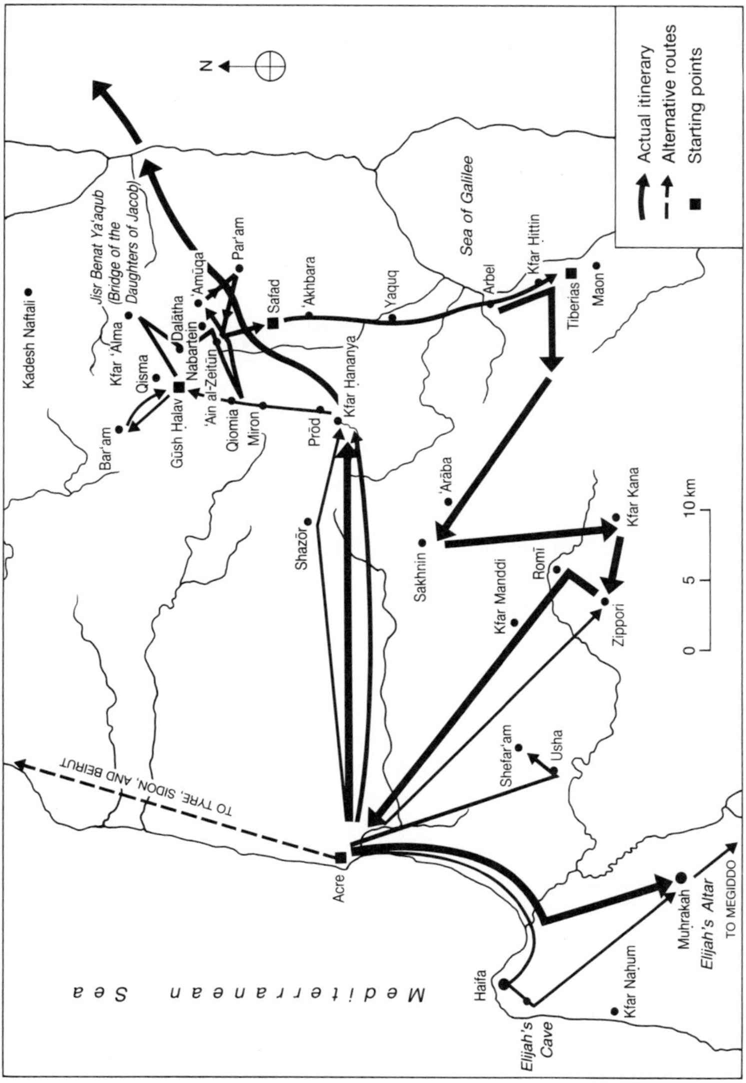

Map 5. The itinerary of the anonymous pupil of Naḥmanides: the north (detail)

vessels. It is said this is the bucket of Miriam [sister of Moses]' (p. 9, ll. 3–5).[122] From here he goes to ʿAraba and Sakhnin, Kfar Kana, Zippori and Ramah (Romī), where he notes a tradition that this is where the Messiah will come from (p. 9, ll. 20–1).[123] From Romī and Kfar Manddi he returns to Acre.

The last journey leads from Acre due east to Kfar Ḥananya and then north-east to a bridge over the Jordan, probably the Bridge of the Daughters of Jacob (*Jisr Benāt Yaʿaqūb*), and the road to Damascus.

The last part of our treatise (printed text, pp. 86–90) is taken up with an extremely extensive compilation of *laudes* regarding the Holy Land compiled from the Bible, the Talmud, and the Midrashic exegesis,[124] not only elucidating the holiness of the Land but also its particular relation with God and the Jews, its true heirs: the Children of Israel are the elected nation, Eretz Israel is the elected land enjoying divine grace. Whereas each land has its own responsible angel, the Holy Land is the realm of God himself. Consequently, living in the Holy Land is a particularly meritorious act, *a fortiori* the adoration of God therein. 'And you cannot even compare a man who serves the king in his own palace and one who serves him under foreign rule' (p. 11, l. 10). Time and again he comes back to a dictum in *Siphré* (in a midrash on Deut.): 'Living in Eretz Israel equals [the performance of] all the precepts of the Torah.' Rather unexpectedly the treatise ends with an epilogue which, despite the author's declaration, relates only slightly to what has gone before. Because of its historical and ideological importance, I translate it *in extenso*:[125]

And so we saw[126] what was said by our ancient Sages, who spoke about the coming of the Messiah. Let it be His will that he should come speedily in our own time. And that is what they say: Let nobody

[122] On the Well of Miriam in the Lake of Galilee see n. 81.

[123] This is based on a Midrashic exegesis claiming that the place extended to the city of Tyre, which in Hebrew is Ṣor, can be understood as 'Ṣar' meaning 'the oppressor'; thus a connection was made between the wicked oppressors Rome and Tyre and this Galilean village.

[124] This part was not copied as S. Klein stated (*History of the Jews*, 290) from Naḥmanides' *Sermon on the New Year*, but some of the ideas are common to both. See the *Sermon*, Engl. trans. Chavel i. 347–53.

[125] Ibid. 13, ll. 12–26.

[126] Actually he refers not to the foregoing but to his subsequent exposition.

ever think that the Messiah will appear on an unclean Land, and neither should one err in thinking that he will also come to Eretz Israel among Gentiles. Whoever makes such a mistake is not sensitive to the honour of the king Messiah.[127] But Children of Israel who study the Torah, men of piety who excel in good deeds [*anshey ma'asé*; the expression can also mean 'practical men'], hailing from the four corners of the earth one of a city and two of a family [Jer. 3: 14], every man whose heart was lifted and he volunteered because of the purity and the love of the holy to come to Eretz Israel—it is to those that the Messiah will reveal himself, as it is written: 'and I will take you one of a city and two of a family, and I will bring you to Zion' [Jer. 3: 45]. And how lucky you are, you in whom it will be fulfilled what was prophesied: 'The spirit will be poured upon us from on high' [Isa. 32: 15], and there[128] they explain at length the question of the coming of the Salvation through the two Messiahs, the Messiah son of Ephraim (or Joseph) and the Messiah the son of David.[129] Let it be his will that this should happen in our time. And many are already inspired and are willing to migrate to Eretz Israel. And many think that we are near to the coming of the Messiah, seeing that the nations of the world make heavier the burden on Israel in so many places, and many other well-known signs[130] have already been revealed to the humble.

This rather unexpected epilogue, which points to some Messianic stirrings in the last quarter of the thirteenth century ends the itinerary. Its novelty lies in the continuation of the *laudes* of the Holy Land in the Jewish religious perspective with

[127] This idea that the Messiah will not come to the Holy Land as long as it is inhabited or ruled by gentiles seems not to be traceable in Jewish sources. The only parallel so far indicated comes from a rather late rabbinical source, namely Meir Aldaby the grandson of R. Asher b. Yeḥiel (Rosh) in *Shvīlei ha-Emūnah* (14th cent.). Cf. S. H. Kuk, *Studies*, ii. 91. Meir Aldaby, however, summarized in his treatise (many editions), ch. 10, par. 1 ff, an ancient Jewish apocalypse which begins like our text but has little or nothing to do with it. The statement of our pilgrim, however, of the conditional appearance of the Messiah is to be found in the speech of Urban II at Clermont, as invented by Guibert of Nogent, *Gesta Dei par Francos, RHC HOcc.* iv. 140.

[128] Our author is referring to a Midrashic, probably eschatological text, which he is copying or commenting on.

[129] According to the pattern of the Jewish apocalypse before the coming of the Messiah from the House of David a forerunner of the tribe of Ephraim will reveal himself (not a false Messiah!); he will be killed and his death will usher in the coming of the Saviour, the Messiah of the House of David.

[130] In the Jewish as well as the Christian apocalyptical traditions, persecutions and tribulations of every kind are among the signs that will announce the approach of the Day of the Last Judgement.

the expectation of the Messiah and an exhortation to migrate to the Holy Land.

At an unknown time the treatise *Tōṣōth Eretz Israel* underwent a significant change. An anonymous writer copied it, changed its character, and made a rather remarkable addition. This text is referred to from its opening phrase as *Eileh ha-Massaʿōth*[131] (These are the voyages). The changes and additions followed a clear pattern to justify the new title, and the purpose is clearly stated in the prologue: 'These are the voyages of the Children of Israel who want to prostrate themselves on the Tombs of the Ancestors and the Righteous which are in Eretz Israel and to bow and to pray in the House of the Holy of Holies and that of our Glory, the place in which our Forefathers praised God. Let it be rebuilt speedily in our own time.'[132] As the text of *Eileh ha-Massaʿōth* was published a hundred years before *Tōṣōth* there was some reluctance to redefine the relation between the two *opuscula.*[133] There can be little doubt, however, as to which is the original and which the copy: the writer of the *Eileh ha-Massaʿōth* is, without doubt, the plagiarizer of *Tōṣōth.* This clearly transpires from the suppression of all personal elements to be found in *Tōṣōth.* Thus, referring to his voyage to Nablus, the author of *Tōṣōth* states: 'And one Shabbath I entered into a discussion with their [Samaritan] Rav'[134]—whereas in *Massaʿōth* this is suppressed. The difficulty relating to the Pool of Siloam, which the author of *Tōṣōth* solves to his own satisfaction with the help of a copy of the Mishna he bought in the Holy Land,[135] is again suppressed in *Massaʿōth.* The author of *Tōṣōth* learns in Damas-

[131] *Eileh ha-Massaʿōth* is in the Casanatense MS collection in Rome, bound together with the Travels of Benjamin of Tudela. It was copied by A. Berliner and published by L. Grünhut as an appendix to his edition of *Benjamin of Tudela* (Jerusalem 1903), 145–64. The text was also published (a rather rare edition) from a different MS (whose end is missing) by E. Carmoly, (Brussels 1841), and was then reprinted several times including in *Agudath Agadōth*, ed. A. M. Luncz (Jerusalem 1885). In what follows I have used the text as published by L. Grünhut with variants by E. Carmoly.

[132] Ed. L. Grünhut, (above n. 131), 145, ll. 1–5.

[133] S. Assaf who published the *Tōṣōth* (see above, n. 1) argued that *Eileh ha-Massaʿōth* were written a generation before the *Tōṣōth.* Consequently he also regarded the *Tōṣōth* as a plagiarism of the other. The authenticity of *Tōṣōth* was argued by J. Prawer, *The Jews*, 25 n. 111 and S. H. Kuk, *Sinai* 7 (1941), 80 and accepted by M. Ish-Shalom, *The Tombs of the Ancestors*, 14.

[134] *Tōṣōth*, 2, l. 16.

[135] Ibid. 3, ll. 15 ff.

cus about the levelling of the Mount of the Temple by a Muslim ruler, which, in his opinion, explains what is to him a problematic aspect of Jerusalem's topography;[136] he thanks God for having found him worthy to go on a pilgrimage to Upper and Lower Galilee;[137] in Safod he is prevented from visiting a given tomb 'and we did not go there because they would not allow us to enter the cave';[138] the exegesis about the Galilean village of Romī quoted above—all such and similar episodes are systematically omitted from *Eileh ha-Massaʿōth*.

I have not found any conclusive clues as to the identity of the plagiarist. It can be argued, however, that he composed his treatise not very long after *Tōṣōth* was edited. Thus he indicated the coastal cities between Acre and Tripoli in Lebanon as being fortified, which fits the Crusader domination of the area far better than a later period, but this is not a decisive proof as it can be rightly argued that he simply copied what he found in his model.[139] But even if the date remains a mystery, we may venture to make a suggestion as to the origin of the author. Whereas the author of *Tōṣōth* was clearly a Westerner coming from Europe, the author of *Eileh ha-Massaʿōth* may have been an Oriental. The fact that he did not list the tombs of the great luminaries of France who migrated in the thirteenth century and were buried in the cemetery of Acre seems significant in this context. Possibly he did not regard them on a par with the ancient Righteous or the more recent Maimonides, whose tomb he mentions in Tiberias (p. 156, l. 4). Not even Naḥmanides, the revered teacher of the author of *Tōṣōth*, buried with other scholars in the cemetery at Acre, is mentioned. This would fit an Oriental Jew better than a European one. Moreover, summarizing the list of these European scholars, he uses a particular generalization 'some great pious men (*ḥasidim*) who came from overseas (*meʿever la-yam*)' (145). To call French scholars 'men from Overseas' is understandable from the

[136] *Toṣōth*, 4, ll. 20–1.

[137] Ibid. 6, ll. 11–14.

[138] Ibid. 8, ll. 6–7.

[139] None the less, the fortified cities of the *Tōṣōth* go from Acre to Beirut. In *Eileh ha-Massaʿōth* the list includes a synagogue in Tyre, and to the north: Jubail (Gibelet) and Tripoli and some places in Transjordan. There are also some other additions. It is therefore possible that there was also another, earlier text, perhaps even used by both writers. *Tōṣōth*, however, is a true copy of an authentic pilgrimage.

geographical point of view of an Oriental Jew, but not from a European viewpoint. From Europe, *Outremer* is clearly the Holy Land. One can corroborate this conclusion from the fact that when using a strongly pejorative expression against Islam ('to distinguish the unclean from purity', (see above on Jerusalem, p. 239) he does not spell out the offending expression but only notes the vowels without the consonants. This can be explained as a device to avoid the wrath of Muslims—something which would not concern a writer from Christian Europe.

As I have said, these indications are suggestive rather than conclusive evidence of the writer's place of origin. His purpose was not to tell a story or account of a pilgrimage but to write a kind of manual or inventory of the Holy Tombs. These he divided geographically into those inside the 'religious' boundaries of the Holy Land and those 'abroad' that is, outside these boundaries.[140] Accordingly, he begins with Acre and its cemetery near Haifa, which were 'inside the boundaries' of those who returned from the Babylonian Exile, and leaves out the beginning of *Tōṣōth* which indicates here the road from Acre to Beirut. Having succinctly copied from the latter the whole bulk of material which listed and described the Holy Tombs (with the omissions already indicated), the author of *Eileh ha-Massaʿōth* now adds a substantial addition, which he introduced as follows: 'These are the voyages one travels from Eretz Israel abroad, whoever wants to pray in the sanctified synagogues built in the early ages and prostrate himself on the Tombs of the Righteous who are buried abroad.'

From the geographical point of view the description falls into three parts which have no territorial connection. It begins with a short paragraph dealing with the southern part of the country, returns north to Acre and thence includes Lebanon, parts of Syria and Transjordan; and then, starting back from Damascus, extends to Syria, the north and south of Iraq, and finally Persia. As we have seen, the geographical scope is vast comparable to the extensive journeys of Petaḥyah of Regensburg or Benjamin of Tudela. Here we shall content ourselves with considering those places in the Holy Land which are not mentioned in *Tōṣōth* and which the plagiarist must have taken from another source or sources.

[140] On this distinction see ch. 8 n. 3.

The author, then begins his description with the south. Between Gath (possibly Ashdod) and Gaza is Yabneh (Ibelin) and the tomb of Rabban Gamaliel topped by a beautiful dome 'and this is a prayer-place of the Ishmaelites and the Ishmaelites call it Abū Ḥureira [written Hudreira]'.[141] The account then jumps to the north following the first part of *Tōṣōth* from Acre to Beirut but adding to the original the tomb of the prophet Zephaniah in Mount Lebanon (near Sidon). From here he starts on a very extensive journey to the north and east. From Beirut (Beerōth) to Jubail (Gevul, corr. Gebal) where he finds a synagogue dedicated to the prophet Elijah. The next place noted is 'Sinai', that is Sin, which was identified with Tripoli in Lebanon, then Latakia (Laodicea) with its two synagogues. From there he moves to Syria and Iraq. He re-enters Syria and moves from Ḥamath and to Ḥoms, Baalbek (Baʿaloth), and Qadaq(?). From Baalbek he continued south to Transjordan; where he mentions places never noted by Jewish pilgrims, who did not venture into this area:[142] Naveh (Nebo) and Zaruʿa (Zoreʿa), Darʿa (Edreʿaa), Ajlun (Eglōn), al-Salt, al-Yehudiyah (Kfar Yehūda, east of the Lake of Galilee) where he reaches Jisr Banāt Yaʿaqūb (Gesher Yaʿakov). He then makes a surprisingly large jump south to Jericho (only one parsa away!), Sodom, and Gomorrah again to al-Salt, and to Jebel Aharūn (Hor ha-Har) with the tomb of Aharon in Transjordan. Then he returns to Syria, Iraq, and far east to Persia.

Here ends this remarkable *opusculum*, which has taken us on a long trip among the biblical, Talmudic, and Midrashic memorabilia in the Near East. Its purpose was clear—a mapping of the ancient synagogues or tombs to which local Jewish tradition assigned origins in antiquity. This was a particular map, the Jewish map of the Near East, where

[141] Ed. L. Grünhut (above n. 24) 158, ll. 5–8. This paragraph is missing in the Carmoly edition. The tomb venerated today is actually a Crusader sarcophagus (which can be stylistically dated to the last quarter of the 13th cent.), brought to its present location probably from Acre after the fall of the city. It is venerated by Muslims as the tomb of Abū Ḥureīra, a companion of Muhammad, and by Jews as the tomb of Rabban Gamaliel of Yabneh, head of the Sanhedrin (2nd cent. CE). Cf. L. A. Mayer and J. Pinkerfeld, *Some Principal Muslim Religious Buildings in Israel* (Jerusalem 1980), 23 ff.

[142] The names in parentheses are the Hebrew names of the Itinerary.

neither political powers nor boundaries played any role whatsoever. Made in an ahistorical framework of religious expectation, the voyage ends with the hope of witnessing the resurrection of 'all the Righteous and the Just'.

8

The Thirteenth Century

THE salient feature of Jewish life in the Second Kingdom created in the wake of the Third Crusade is the shifting of Jewish centres from the Muslim-dominated interior to the Crusader-ruled coast. This development finds its explanation in the economic and political situation of the country. The interior of the country, some three-quarters of the former Crusader territory, witnessed a steep decline in its economic life. Closed in between the desert in the east and the Christian-dominated coast in the west, it remained an almost purely agricultural area. Moreover, the frequent changes of political sovereignty among the descendants of the Ayyūbid dynasty as well as the permanent threat of a Crusader *reconquista* led to the destruction of fortresses and fortifications which might provide the Crusaders with a foothold in the interior. In these conditions, the Jewish communities abandoned the interior and concentrated in the great urban conglomerations of the coast. However, these developments had no effect on the existence of Jewish rural agglomerations in Galilee.

The community most affected was that of Jerusalem. Reconstructed after Saladin's conquest, it was to enjoy a period of growth in the wake of the waves of migration at the end of the twelfth and more particularly at the beginning of the thirteenth century. Yet neither fervour nor zeal could overcome material difficulties. Jerusalem was hardly a centre of commercial activity, nor did it enjoy the status of a capital under the Muslims as it had done under Crusader rule. To these objective difficulties, which became a permanent feature of the city's history lasting until our own times, were added the military ravages, the dismantling of its walls, and finally the renewed Crusader occupation of the city (1229–44). When this was over, following Muslim and Khwārizmian attacks, the city lay in ruins. A generation later, in 1268, Naḥmanides described the situation of the city and its Jewish community in a letter to his son Naḥman, who remained in Spain, as follows:

And what shall I tell you about the land? Great are the ravages and great the desolation. As a rule whatever is more holy is more ruined. Jerusalem is more ruined than anything else, and the land of Judaea more than Galilee. And yet despite the ruin she [Jerusalem] is goodly indeed and her population is near two thousand, and among them about three hundred Christians, refugees from the sword of the Sultan. And there are no children of Israel therein, because since the coming of the Tartars they ran away and some were killed by the sword, except for two brothers, dyers, who buy the [monopoly of] dyeing from the governor. On a Saturday up to a *minyan* [i.e. the quorum of ten males necessary for public prayer] will gather in their house. We exhorted them and we found a ruined house built with marble columns and a handsome dome and we took it for a prayer house, because the city is a shambles and whoever wants to appropriate ruins does so. And we volunteered to repair the house and they already began its renovation. They [also] sent to Schechem [Nablus] to bring therefrom the Torah Scrolls which were in Jerusalem and they smuggled them out when the Tartars came. They will be deposited in the prayer house and there they will pray because many come to Jerusalem from Damascus, Ṣōbā [Aleppo] and the land of Egypt and all the districts of the Land [of Israel] to see the Temple and weep for it.[1]

Whatever the difficulties of interpretation, there is little doubt as to the general accuracy of the description of the state of Jerusalem around 1268. From a population of some 20,000 under Crusader rule, the city came down to less than 2,000 Muslims and 300 Christians, no doubt Oriental Christians.

[1] The letter, written in 1268, was published for the first time in an appendix to Naḥmanides' *Commentary on the Pentateuch* printed in Lisbon in 1489. The letter was newly edited from two 15th- and 16th-cent. MSS in Munich (Cod. heb. 357, f. 52; Cod. heb. 56, f. 405) by B. Z. Kedar, 'A Contribution to the History of the Jewish Community in Jerusalem in the Thirteenth Century' (H), *Tarbiz* 41 (1972), 82–94, repr. with a slightly enlarged commentary in *Jerusalem in the Middle Ages: Selected Papers* (H), ed. B. Z. Kedar and Z. Baras (Jerusalem 1979), 134–6. The authenticity of this letter was somewhat suspect; some of the historical details contained in it and similarities with Naḥmanides' other writings induced some scholars to suspect a forgery. It was customary to interpret the Tartars as the Khwarīzmians who captured Jerusalem in 1244, and Naḥmanides would have hardly referred to them a generation later. Again, the smuggling of the Torah Scrolls from Jerusalem to Nablus was unexpected. But a strong case for the capture of Jerusalem by the Mongols in 1260 was argued by B. Z. Kedar, ibid. 122–30. Cf. Prawer, *Histoire*, ii. 411. As to Nablus, the presence of a Muslim garrison there meant that it could offer safe refuge for the Torah Scrolls from Jerusalem. For additional Arabic and Armenian sources see J. Prawer, 'Notes on the History of the Jews in the Latin Kingdom of Jerusalem' (H), *Shalem* 2 (1976), 103–12; Engl. trans. *Immanuel* 9 (1979), 81–7.

The Jewish community, which between 1190 and 1229 had made an attempt at reconstruction, had disappeared. As already explained the Jews were barred from residing in Jerusalem during the renewed but short-lived Crusader domination between 1222 and 1244. It seems that some attempts to create a community were made between 1244 and 1260, and such efforts were more vigorously pursued with the coming of Naḥmanides in 1267. Yet despite his efforts, which may have culminated in the establishment of a school, and despite the Jews who came on pilgrimages to Jerusalem, no substantial community was established. Since the 'migration of the rabbis' discussed above and the repeated attempts during the next two generations to settle in Jerusalem, Jewish life had clung to the coast, mainly to Acre, which became a flourishing centre of Jewish life. Nothing is more indicative of this than the personal seal of Naḥmanides recently discovered near Tel-Keisān to the south of Acre.[2] Not far from the place in which the seal was found but on the coast—actually at the foot of Mount Carmel, near Crusader Haifa, was a large Jewish cemetery which served Acre.[3] It was here that an anonymous pupil of

[2] Discovered in 1972. I. Shachar 'The Personal Seal of Naḥmanides' (H), published by the Israel Museum (Jerusalem 1973), repr. in *Jerusalem in the Middle Ages* (above, n. 1), 137–47. The inscription reads: 'Moses son of R. Naḥman of blessed memory of Gerona. Be strong (*ḥazaq*)'.

[3] Crusader Haifa was on the coast on the site of modern Bat-Galim. According to Talmudic traditions Acre was outside the boundaries of the Land of Israel, whereas Haifa was inside. The boundaries referred to are of the areas actually settled by those who returned from the Babylonian Exile. Cf. S. Klein, 'Das tannaitische Grenzverzeichnis Palaestinas', *Hebrew Union College Annual* 5 (Cincinnati 1928), 197–259; I. Press, *A Topographical Historical Encyclopedia of Palestine* (H), i (Jerusalem 1951[2]), pt. 5, 40–55. In all relevant sources 'The walls of Acco', remain outside these boundaries. The boundaries were important in the context of precepts obligatory in the Holy Land but not outside, such as some types of tithes and offerings (*trūmōth, ma'asserōth*) and the laws of *shevī'it*, all linked to agriculture. The boundary was sometimes regarded as differentiating the degree of sanctity.

The Jewish community of Acre used two cemeteries: one to the east of Acre but considered to be inside the boundaries of the Holy Land; and one at the foot of Mount Carmel beneath the Cave of Elijah, probably used by the more notable families. Cf. J. Braslavsky 'Acre and the Cemeteries of Eretz Israel', *Studies*, 123–8 (includes bibliog.). It is a remarkable fact that the notions of the ritual boundaries of the Holy Land somehow spilled over into the Christian usage. A French text of the middle of the 13th cent. reads: 'Et sachéz ke Acre n'est pas de Terre de promission ausi cum est Caïphas, car un flum devise la Tere Seynte entre Acre et Caïphas, k'est apelé le Flum de Caïphas.' The *Flum de Caïphas* is the biblical Kishon. *Les Chemins et les pèlerinages de la Terre Sainte* in *Itinéraires à Jerusalem et descriptions de la Terre Sainte aux XIe–XIIIe siècles*, ed. H. Michelant and G. Raynaud (Paris 1882), 190.

Naḥmanides listed the tombs of some of the most prominent scholars: R. Samson b. Abraham the Tosafist, his son R. Jacob, R. Joseph of Burgundy, the son of R. Yeḥiel of Paris, called Sire Délicieux, R. Joseph of Sens, R. Jacob of Segura and 'my teacher and master Rabbi Moses b. Naḥman of Gerona, be blessed the memory of the just and the saint'.[4]

Many a name mentioned here belongs to the migrations of the beginning and the middle of the thirteenth century; some even indicate a second generation of the new settlers. Many of those buried in the cemetery at Acre had tried to strike roots in Jerusalem but finally settled in Acre, others in Tyre.[5] Obviously economic opportunities in the two main centres of Crusader commerce made living conditions easier; moreover, these two great ports were also the main gateways for European and Jewish immigration. Cosmopolitan as all major Crusader cities, Acre and Tyre offered adequate means of existence to craftsmen and bankers, to men of free professions like physicians, but also to merchants and middlemen; and the Jews would for the most part have belonged to those social and economic categories.

In Tyre as well as in Acre we can assume a certain continuity in the life of the Jewish communities. In Tyre there was no Muslim occupation or Crusader *reconquista* because Tyre was the only city not captured by Saladin or his commanders after the disaster of Hattin. Led by Conrad of Montferrat, who by an almost miraculous coincidence appeared in the Phoenician port when it was on the point of surrender to Muslim troops, it remained Christian, and there was therefore no interruption in the history of its Jewish community.

The earliest evidence of the existence of a Jewish community in Tyre after the Third Crusade is to be found in the papal correspondence with Joscius, archbishop of the city, in December 1198, dealing with Jews who want to be baptized without renouncing a matrimonial alliance concluded before baptism. Innocent III answered a question raised in this

[4] The text is known from its incipit as *Tōṣōth Eretz Israel* see critical edition by S. Assaf in *Yerūshalaīm: Memorial Volume Dedicated to A. M. Luncz* (H), ed. I. Press and E. L. Sukenik (Jerusalem 1928), 51–66 and repr. Assaf, *Sources* 74–90; see also above ch. 7, Itinerary I.

[5] For more details see below, pp. 264 ff.

connection in the affirmative.[6] Yet in fact we have clear proof of their continuous existence in the city perhaps even some years earlier, *circa* 1193. The community of Tyre reached a level of standing and learning praised by Maimonides, who as we have seen corresponded from his residence in Fusṭāṭ with some of its prominent scholars and later with their disciples. The fate of his community by the close of the Third Crusade is revealed in the famous inventory of the *baiulo*, that is the consul general of Venice in Syria, Marsiglio Zorzi. Writing in 1243 he notes that the Jews who lived in the autonomous Venetian 'third of the city'[7] had been unjustly 'commandeered' by the king for over fifty years; they no longer paid taxes to the Venetians nor were they judged in Venetian courts.[8] He is referring, it seems, to a situation created *circa* 1193, that is, a short time after the end of the Third Crusade, a time when the ruling powers of the kingdom paid very little attention to political treaties and obligations concluded three generations earlier, and Venetian property, as well as some sovereign rights of the commune, fell into oblivion or were disregarded.[9] The Jewish community, which lived in the Venetian Quarter, that is in the eastern part of the northern port of the city (the southern, or 'Egyptian port', was not in use in the Crusader period), became directly subject to the king of Jerusalem. During the struggle between Frederick II Hohenstaufen against the local baronage, the Venetians joined the latter and successfully reclaimed their privileges in the kingdom. One of these was the right of jurisdiction over the Jews in the Venetian

[6] *Innocentii III Epistolae I, ep. 514, PL*, ccxiv. col. 475. The text has been analysed by B. Z. Kedar in *Tarbiz* (H) 53 (1984), 400–1.

[7] Following the agreement between the kingdom and the Venetians, the famous *Pactum Warmundi* of 1123, the latter received a third of all conquests in which they participated. The major prize of this agreement was the third of the city and of the lordship of Tyre. Cf. J. Prawer, 'The Italians in the Latin Kingdom', *Crusader Institutions*, 229 ff.

[8] Tafel-Thomas, *Urkunden zur älteren Handels- und Staatsgeschichte der Republik Venedig* ii (Vienna 1856), 358–9: 'Judei, qui manent in nostro tercierio—iam bene per L annos—per dominum Regni qui contra Deum et iusticiam nobis detinebantur, ita quod non iustificabantur in nostra curia, nec aliquem reditum faciebant; nunc autem per Dei gratiam in nostra curia iustificantur, et in omnibus dominantur, sicut Rex dominantur [*sic*] illos, qui manent in suis partibus.'

[9] Marsiglio Zorzi later refers to the usurpation of Venetian rights by King John of Brienne (1210–12, then regent for his daughter 1212–25).

Quarter, which also included the payment of the poll-tax, *capitatio*, a descendant of the Muslim *jizya*, paid to the authorities by the non-Latin population, as it was paid by non-Muslims under Muslim rule. The sum of 1 besant was to be paid yearly by every male above the age of fifteen. A small payment, it was probably more a token in recognition of sovereignty than a contribution of real economic value.[10] The inventory goes on to list seven names, obviously heads of families, and an additional two sons, probably living with their parents but above the age of fifteen. The Venetian officials had no difficulty in spelling the names David, Daniel, Moyse, and Symon, whereas such Oriental names as Simol, Hebe, Mahamar, Mahafa, Harham and Brahi were misspelled.

Some Jews also lived in other quarters of the city. The Venetian inventory mentions them in the royal part of the city,[11] and an almost contemporary Genoese inventory of Genoese possessions in Tyre, written seven years later, in 1250, by the commune's consuls in Syria, Simone Malocello and Ogerio Ricci,[12] mentions them in their own quarter. Let us recall that Benjamin of Tudela, who visited Tyre around 1170, reckoned its Jewish population as 500 souls.

The Jewish community in the Venetian part of Tyre lived in a cluster of houses near the churches of St James and St Nicholas.[13] The inventory speaks of a 'domus Judaeorum', which could be interpreted as a 'house' or as 'houses of the Jews' near a 'fondaco' which belonged to the bishop of Caurole but was destroyed during an earthquake (possibly that of 1202). The area is described as bounded in the east and north by the house of Peter of Scandalion (i.e. Iskanderūne north of Acre), on the west by the house of the son of one Peter Ruffus and the 'house of our Jews', and in the south by the public road which led to the churches of St James and St Nicholas.

The Jews in the Genoese Quarter of the city, which was to

[10] On the legal position of the Jews, see above, ch. 5. The same royal encroachment upon Venetian rights also applied to Oriental Christians, weavers by profession, in the Venetian Quarter (ibid. 359).

[11] See end of text quoted in n. 8.

[12] G. Desimoni, 'Quatre titres des propriétés des Génois', *AOL* ii*b*. 223.

[13] The church of St Nicholas gave its name to a street, *ruga*, near the Greek Orthodox church of Sancta Maria Graecorum (Tafel-Thomas (above, n. 8), 386, and cf. 364).

the west of that of the Venetians, also lived in a 'domus Judeorum', 'house' or 'houses of the Jews', bounded in the south by the house of one Peter Pennesinpa, now taken over by the commune, and on the other sides by the house of the archbishop and the houses of Raymond Sultan and the Templars, on the west by the house of one Symon, and on the north by a public road.

It seems from the above description that the Jews did not all live in one quarter, as one would expect, but in three different centres. Despite this division we tend to assume that this was not the case, and that the Jewish agglomeration was somehow partitioned between the different autonomous powers. But this is a conjecture only, and we have to keep in mind, as attested by the documentation from Venetian Acre, that the communes could force 'their Jews' to live in their respective quarters.[14]

Not much more can be learned about the Jewish Tyrian community. The last we hear of it was in 1283, when Hugh of Lusignan, king of Cyprus and Jerusalem, entered the city. As usual on such occasions, a procession of the local population went out to receive him. The Jewish community was led by Samuel the physician, bearing the Holy Scrolls. Somehow he stumbled, falling on to a priest walking in front of him carrying a tall cross; the cross fell and smashed the physician's head.[15]

Thereafter the community disappears from our documentation.[16] We know that Tyre was abandoned by the Crusaders without a fight a short time after the fall of Acre on 18 May 1291 (the last Crusader stronghold, Pilgrim's Castle, was abandoned at the end of May or beginning of August 1291). What happened to the Jewish community after the Crusaders

[14] On the Jews in the Venetian Quarter in Acre see below, p. 262.

[15] *Le Templier de Tyre* in *Les Gestes des chiprois*, ed. G. Raynaud (Geneva 1887), par. 419, p. 214. R. Röhricht, *Gesch. des Königreichs Jerusalem* (Innsbruck 1898), 986, inadvertently understood 'la tore des Juis' as the 'Jewish Tower'. Obviously it means here 'the Torah of the Jews'. The error is repeated in L. Lucas, *Geschichte der Stadt Tyrus zur Zeit der Kreuzzüge* (Berlin 1896), 56.

[16] The Hebrew itinerary *Eileh ha-Massa'oth*, ed. L. Grünhut (Jerusalem 1903), 158, appended to Grünhut's edition and German translation of Benjamin of Tudela indicates an important synagogue of the greatest beauty in Tyre. The source, however, depends on another description of the Holy Land the *Tōṣōth Eretz Israel* written between 1270 and 1291 which does not mention the synagogue. On these sources, see above ch. 7.

left the city is unknown, but there is no reason to assume any drastic changes at that time, and any future change would have been connected with the general shift in the country's demography in the Mameluke period—the abandoning of the coast and concentration inland.

It was Acre, now the unofficial capital of the Crusader kingdom, which became the undisputed centre of Jewish life in the thirteenth century. The existence of the community in Acre was probably not interrupted by the city's destinies during the Third Crusade. The city changed hands, surrendering first to Saladin on 10 July 1187 and after the famous three years' siege to Richard the Lionheart on 12 July 1191, but in neither case was the city taken by force. The local population was not massacred following the capitulation, but there was an exodus of the Muslims from the city once the Crusader domination was restored.[17] We do not know what happened to the Jewish community, which Benjamin of Tudela had numbered at two hundred souls,[18] during these difficult and tumultuous times, although we may perhaps gain some impression from the following excerpt from an ancient Jewish apocalypse which possibly refers to some actual events connected with the Third Crusade:

> And the king of the West will reinforce his hosts in the land and from the land of Joktan [Gen. 10: 25] a king will come forth and his hosts will be strengthened in the land ... And Gog and Magog will attack each other and they will kindle fear in the hearts of the gentiles and Israel will be cleansed from all its sins and will not be expelled any more from its place of prayer [the Temple] ... And the kings from the Land of Edom [Christendom] will come to an end and the inhabitants of Antioch will revolt and will be pacified [?], and Ma'ozyah [Tiberias] and Samaria will be consoled and Acre and Galilee will be saved; and the Edomites and Ishmaelites will fight each other in the Valley of Acre until their horses will sink in blood and will neigh; Gaza and her daughters [neighbouring townships] will be stoned; Ascalon and Ashdod will be overawed and Israel will go out from the great city (*qiryah*) and will go to the East [a distance of] 45 days ... and their Messiah will appear and they will be

[17] On Saladin's conquest of Acre, see Prawer, *Histoire*, i. 658–9; on the Crusader conquest and the fate of its local population, ibid. ii. 67–8.

[18] *Benjamin of Tudela*, 31.

consoled and they will please in learning [?] their king, and will praise in song their king, and all the evil-doers will be condemned in the [last] Judgement.[19]

As always in apocalyptic prophecies, names, places, and events can only be partly identified with specific events. The biblical Joktan, related to the tribes of Arabia, denotes here a ruler from the Orient, which might possibly refer to Saladin. The Hebrew expression for 'gentiles', *goyim*, may denote all non-Jews but is usually understood to refer to Christians. The central message refers to the fact that the Jews would no longer be barred from the Temple, and this may point to the abolition of the Crusader law barring the Jews from Jerusalem, unless it refers in a larger sense to the re-establishment of the Jewish cult in the Temple. The 'Valley of Acre' or 'Plain of Acre' as the battleground of Islam and Christendom, as well as the horses sinking in blood, are *topoi* recurrent in all Jewish apocalypses. The image of the horses is found earlier in the Apocalypse of St John 14: 19–20.[20] As to the different places mentioned concerning the Vision of the End—all are biblical names, but one would hesitate to assign them any particular role (not even to Tiberias, which was the prelude to the disaster of Hattin), but for the dramatic note that 'the kings from the Land of Edom will come to an end', which might reflect the defeat of the Crusaders by Saladin; but at that time even this was only a pious wish.

We are brought nearer the reality of events in Acre following its conquest by a Crusader proclamation, an edict we can assume to have been promulgated almost immediately after the capitulation of the city to the hosts of the Third Crusade. Though conceived in general terms, it was clearly also intended to cover the Jews of Acre. The assize preserved in the legal

[19] This fragment was assigned by L. Ginzberg to the siege of Acre in 1104, L. Ginzberg, 'The Vision of the Last War', in *Genizah Studies in Memory of S. Schechter*, i. *Midrash and Haggadah* (New York 1928), par. 32, 310–12. It seems more probable that it actually relates to the Crusader siege of Acre of 1189–91. Another apocalypse 'updated' to suit the new circumstances was publ. by E. E. Urbach, 'An Apocalypse of the late Crusade' (H), *Eretz Israel* 10 (1971), 58–63. The text contains a new fragment of a Midrash, which is based on the 'Prayer of R. Simeon b. Yoḥai'. A new study of the 'Prayer' remains a *desideratum*.

[20] The famous story told by the chronicles of the First Crusaders was probably inspired by the same source.

treatise known as the *Livre des assises des bourgeois* was enacted to regulate problems of property, and the more stringent problem of lodgings in the newly conquered city.[21] The Crusaders who took part in the siege, overwhelmingly from Europe, settled immediately in the old part of the city, which was bounded in the south by the great port. This caused difficulties, as the former Frankish inhabitants of the city, who had left their houses five years earlier when capitulating to Saladin, demanded the return of their legitimate property. Quarrels and fights broke out between the Franks and the European newcomers, reaching a point that the intervention of the French and English kings, Philip II Augustus and Richard the Lionheart, the leaders of the Crusade, became necessary in order to establish peace in the city. The ancient claims were officially and legally recognized and accepted, and the former Frankish inhabitants recovered their property.[22] We assume that it was in this connection that a law was promulgated relegating the city's non-Frankish inhabitants—that is Oriental Christians, Muslims, and Jews—to the new, and consequently less aristocratic suburb of the city. This part of the city, the so-called Mont Musard, was not yet fortified.[23]

The text of the assize regarding the non-Frankish minorities

[21] *Livre des assises des bourgeois*, ch. 243, *Lois*, ii (Paris 1843), ed. Beugnot, 178; ed. E. H. Kausler, ch. 238.

[22] On the events in Acre, see J. Prawer, 'L'Établissement des coutumes du marché à Saint-Jean d'Acre', *Revue historique du droit français et étranger* 28 (1951), 338. On the intervention of the kings of France and England: *Eracle* xx, ch. 1; *RHC HOcc.*, ii. 175–6 and Benedict of Peterborough, *Gesta Regis Henrici II*, ed. W. Stubbs (London 1867): 'Pisani et nummularii et caeteri mercatores receperunt infra civitatem Acrae, per distributionem servientium regis Angliae et regis Franciae, mansiones suas in foro rerum venalium reddituri inde singulis annis solitos redditus' (16–18 July 1191). The fact is still remembered in a Pisan charter of 1227: 'recognovit . . . quod Francigene occupaverunt post recuperationem terre suprascripti hospitalis . . . et domus et rex Anglie recuperavit hospitali suprascripto [Sti Spiritus] et domos restituit, dedit et concessit communi Pisano ut commune haberet predictum hospitale iure patronatus (G. Muller, *Documenti sulle relazioni delle città Toscane coll'Oriente Cristiano e coi Turchi* (Florence 1879), no. 63, 94–5).

[23] On the development of Mount Musard see D. Jacoby, 'Montmusard, suburb of Crusader Acre: The First Stage of its Development', *Outremer*, 205–18. According to this study the walls of Mont Musard were built between 1198 and 1212 (ibid. 213). This contradicts the description of Wilbrand of Oldenburg (1212), who stated (bk I, 1, 2) that the city is quadrangular in shape, which hardly fits with the triangular shape of Mont Musard. I have suggested a slightly later date. Cf. 'L'Établissement' (above, n. 22), 335–7.

seems clear. The heading reads: 'Here you will hear what was established and ordered by the common assent of the kings and knights and burgesses and the [Italian] communes, where should be and reside (*ou devent estre et maner*) in the city the Greeks and the Syrians and the Jacobites and the Nestorians and the people of Mosul [*Mosserans*; perhaps Maronites] and the Armenians and all the other Syrian languages.'[24] The text continues 'Let it be known that the kings (or king) and all other people so established in common, that no Syrian, nor any man or woman is obliged to payments in the market (*fonde*), such as Syrians, and Greeks, and Nestorians and Jacobites and Samaritans and Jews and people of Mosul (or Maronites), all these people should lodge from the market up; and down from the market of Acre no one should be, by law and assize, because (otherwise) the lord will never have his right from what was established to be taken from them, as you will hear in the following.

This edict relegates the non-Frankish 'minorities' living in the city of Acre to an 'upper market' (*la fonde en amont*), which is certainly to be identified with Mount Musard, as opposed to the 'lower market' (*la fond en aval*) in the old city. There is some controversy as to the scope of the *assise*.[25] Literally interpreted, which seems to be the only possible interpretation of a legal document, it created a particular quarter for the minorities, an element which existed *de facto* one way or another in all Crusader cities, if not by any official orders then by the natural inclination of minority populations to live together.[26] Another explanation suggested is that the decree, basically a fiscal one, was intended to assure the royal revenues due from the

[24] *Livre des assises des bourgeois*, ed. Beugnot, ch. 243. Observe the interesting generic name for the Oriental languages: 'toutes autres lengles suriennes'.

[25] J. Richard, 'Colonies marchandes privilégiées et marché seigneurial', *Moyen âge* 59 (1953), 325–40; Id., 'La Confrérie des Mosserins d'Acre et les marchands de Mossoul au XIIIe siècle'. *L'Orient syrien* 11 (1966), 451–60, argued that the Mosserins mentioned here are not Maronites, as is usually understood, but merchants from Mosul. The absence of Muslims in the decree can be explained as reflecting the situation immediately following the capitulation of the city. Cf. Prawer, *Histoire*, ii. 67–8. C. Cahen, 'A propos des coutumes du marché d'Acre', *Rev. historique du droit français et étranger* 41 (1963), 287–90, opposes the expression 'ghetto' I used there but not the substance of the matter.

[26] Cf. J. Prawer, 'Crusader Cities', in *The Medieval City in Honor of R. S. Lopez*, ed. H. Miskimin *et al.* (Yale 1977), 193 ff.

commercial activities of the minorities, which possibly differed from the customs paid by the Franks.[27]

These two interpretations are clearly neither contradictory nor mutually exclusive. It was in the logic of things that once the non-Franks were relegated to a particular quarter, the Crown assumed its rights to assure its revenues by forcing them to use the royal market in Mount Musard and barring them from the autonomous markets of the communes or even Military Orders in central Acre.[28] We have already met with a similar case of a minority group living together and being taxed in a particular way in the royal city of Tyre.[29] Another case, which we will discuss later is precisely that of Acre, where, in 1271, the Venetian authorities ordered the Jews, as subjects of Venice, to live in a Venetian Quarter.[30]

This Crusader decree, which seems to have been the result of a situation created immediately after the re-establishment of Frankish rule in the city, is also the earliest affecting the Jewish community after the restoration of the kingdom. A few years later, in 1206, a charter of the Teutonic order mentions the buying of a property near the 'domus Judaeorum' and a 'rua Judaeorum' in Acre.[31] The area in which the houses or street (eventually quarter) was situated is not indicated, but the circumstantial evidence is significant. The Teutonic order bought a house which was part of a fief or burgess tenure of a knight, one John Tort, held by Lady Hauhis (or Haulis). The house was bounded on the east by the houses of the monastery of Mount Tabor and the houses of one Beloais and a main (royal) thoroughfare and the houses of one Peter Bordin; in the west the house of Bonefrage son of Sahit (i.e. Ibn Faraj son of

[27] Cf. J. Richard (above, n. 25).

[28] On the possibility of autonomous markets of the Military Orders, see Prawer (above, n. 26), 190, and J. Riley-Smith, *The Feudal Nobility and the Kingdom of Jerusalem 1174–1277* (London 1973), 71.

[29] See the case of Syrian weavers in Tyre (above, n. 10).

[30] *Deliberazione del maggior consiglio di Venezia*, ii, ed. R. Cessi (Bologne 1931), *Septima rubrica*, i. 15–16. On the geopolitical division of Acre see J. Prawer, *Crusader Institutions*, map on p. 231. Cf. D. Jacoby, 'Crusader Acre in the Thirteenth Century: Urban Layout and topography', *Studi medievali* 3/20 (1979), 1–45.

[31] E. Strehlke, *Tabulae Ordinis Theutonici* (Berlin 1869), no. 41, 33.

Sa'id), the house of the Jews and the Street of the Jews and the stable of the 'scriptor' Renerius. The names of the proprietors or inhabitants of the houses without doubt point to an area inhabited by Orientals, people like Ibn Faraj, Ibn Sa'id, and a married priest of the church of Mary Magdalene, which was obviously a church of the Jacobites.[32] This fits well with the Jews relegated with other non-Latins to Mount Musard. The fact that what seems to be an Oriental name, but is not necessarily so (Joannes Daht)—is to be found later (in 1207) in central Acre is hardly conclusive, as such ethnic divisions were certainly blurred with the passing of time.[33] Moreover, charters of the Teutonic Order which have recently been published clearly point to the concentration of a non-Frankish population in Mount Musard. The area is described in 1271 as *rabbat*, the Arabic equivalent of *faubourg*. In Acre this could only mean Mount Musard. The landmark buildings in this area are the Church of St George of the Greeks, the Greek convent of St John, and a church of St Sergius—all indications that it was an Oriental quarter. One property-owner is named as Set Lahoue, which is Arabic for Lady Lahoue, and her son is Faeb, that is, Fahid.[34] All this corroborates the assumption of the concentration of the non-Frankish population, and among them the Jews, in Mount Musard.

The Jewish community of the first two decades of the thirteenth century probably fitted in well in Mount Musard. As its ethnic composition was largely the same as in the twelfth century, it must still have been mainly composed of Oriental Jews, whether natives of the Holy Land or of the neighbouring countries. Obviously there was a sprinkling of European immigrants. Very soon, however, the European immigrations, by virtue of the quality and in some measure their

[32] The married priest was obviously non-Latin. The main Jacobite sanctuary in Jerusalem was the Church of Mary Magdalene. Cf. J. Prawer, *Latin Kingdom*, 228. For Acre see R. Röhricht, *Regesta*, s.v. S. Mariae Magdalenae ecclesia.

[33] D. Jacoby, 'Venetian Jews in Crusader Acre 13th century' (H), *Cathedra* 20 (1981), 51–6. There is no substantial argument against the Mount Musard location.

[34] M.-L. Favreau-Lilie, 'The Teutonic Knights in Acre after the Fall of Montfort (1271): Some Reflections', *Outremer*, 273–4 and n. 9; 282–3.

number, were to play a major role in the history of the community.

Other pieces of information, although sporadic, illustrate the continuous existence of the Jewish community. In 1210 the Jews participated with the rest of the population in the procession which welcomed King John of Brienne into the city,[35] and a year later the Roman Imperial envoy from Germany, Wilbrand of Oldenburg, mentioned the Jews among the inhabitants there.[36]

Whatever the size of the Jewish community in the beginning of the thirteenth century, there is little doubt that it began to grow in importance in the second quarter of the century. The major reason for this growth might have been the aftermath of the wave of immigration between 1209 and 1211, and the fact that the interior of the country was impoverished and certainly poorer than the coast. Moreover, after the middle of the thirteenth century and for the next four decades, the progressive conquest of the Crusader coast by the rising Mameluk power, accompanied by a systematic policy of destruction of the maritime cities to prevent the landing of the much-feared European Crusade, wrought a major demographic change which resulted in the forced concentration of the European population in Acre. There is little doubt that the Jewish communities on the coast also moved to the well-fortified centre of Crusader commerce.

As the main gate to the Holy Land, Acre witnessed the entry of a long list of Jewish pilgrims and potential settlers. Some of the pilgrims were well-known personalities who had made a name for themselves in scholarly activity so the memory of their pilgrimage was preserved. Thus in 1211 an Italian scholar R. Isaiah the Elder of Trani, author of 'Decisions' (*Psaqīm*) on the Talmud and Tosafot on some Talmudic tractates came to Acre; a *responsum* preserved by chance contains a short geographical note on the geography of the Holy

[35] *La Continuation de Guillaume de Tyr*, publ. M. R. Morgan (Paris 1982), i. 48, pp. 60–61.

[36] *Wilbrandi de Oldenborg Peregrinatio*, ch. 1, in J. C. M. Laurent, *Peregrinatores Medii Aevi Quatuor* (Leipzig 1864), 163.

Land.[37] But the names of countless others probably remain unknown.

The remarkable pilgrimage of R. Shem Tov b. Isaac of Tortosa from Spain took place a few years later. As an old man he recalled his visit to Acre as a turning-point of his life. Unable to remember a particular religious precept he asked a rabbi who studied mathematics about it. The latter rebuked him and then persuaded him to give up his occupation as a merchant and devote himself to the study of the Torah. Later on we find him teaching medicine to Christians in Marseilles.[38] It has recently been suggested that this R. Shem Tov b. Isaac is identical with the R. Isaac b. Shem Tov who unwittingly played a role in the first great and tragic dispute over Maimonides' philosophical treatises.[39] The man in question, R. Isaac b. Shem Tov, came to Acre in 1235 and from there sent a letter to the leader of the Egyptian Jewish community, the *nagid* Rabbi Abraham son of Maimonides, informing him of the

[37] The *responsum* was published by S. Schechter in the *Jewish Quarterly Review* 4 (1897), 97: 'The sea is the western border of Eretz Israel and Acco is on the sea-board in the north, and Ascalon on the sea-board in the south. Between Ascalon and Acco there is a journey of about two days. And I travelled from Acco and I went from west to east and I went through the whole land of Galilee which is in the north of Eretz Israel and I moved through the east of Eretz Israel on the bank of the Jordan and I went also to the south and I came and stayed overnight in Ascalon. And I journeyed from Ascalon to Acco on the sea-board.' Cf. S. Krauss in *Meassef Zion* 1 (1926), 124. S. Schechter suggested that R. Isaiah travelled with the '300 rabbis'. Cf. recently S. Abramson, 'On *Sefer ha-Leqet* of R. Isaiah of Trani' (H), *Sinai* 65 (1969), 103–8.

[38] He prefaced his translation of the 11th-cent. Muslim physician Zahrawī with the following note: 'Before I was busy trafficking by sea and by land. It so happened that once overseas in the city of Acre I asked a colleague of mine a most important question of *halakha*. He rebuked me, as he himself was studying mathematics. I was ashamed and made a vow to return to the study of the Torah and by then I was thirty. I returned from overseas to the city of Barcelona, got rid of all my business and studied under my master R. Isaac b. Meshullam. The study became my permanent occupation and business an occasional one . . .' In one place he says: 'I taught [probably medicine] to the Christians here in Marseilles.' M. Steinschneider, *Die hebräischen Übersetzungen des Mittelalters und die Juden als Dolmetscher* (Berlin 1893), 148, 741, par. 476. Cf. H. Graetz, *Geschichte der Juden* vii (Leipzig 1902[4]), 103–4 and n. 2.

[39] S. H. Kuk, 'R. Isaac b. R. Shem Tov from Acre' (H), *Studies* ii. 262–5. The argument, based on similarity of names and proximity of dates does not seem to be decisive. To correspond with Abraham Maimuni in 1235 Shem Tov would have had to be sufficiently learned, but by his own admission he was 30 when he visited Acre, and began studying seriously only after his return to Europe. This hardly fits with the praises heaped on him by Abraham Maimuni. See next note.

outbreak of the Maimonides dispute in Montpellier, the interdict imposed on the study of his philosophical works, and the intervention of the Christian authorities which resulted in the burning of the philosophical treatises.[40]

Pilgrimages from Spain found their counterpart in pilgrimages from central Europe, for example, that of the Rabbi of Regensburg, Moses b. Ḥisdai, known as R. Moses from Tachau (in Bohemia) and called by Naḥmanides 'R. Moses of Poland'.[41] He himself recalls: 'when we were privileged to come to the Land [of Israel] and fulfilled there the commandments regarding offerings and tithes'.[42]

With time, the growing immigration, mainly, as far as we can see, from Europe, created a substantial community in Acre. As early as the 1220s a number of scholars lived in the city, and in the thirties it became an important centre for men of learning, strong enough to raise its voice in protest against attempts at the usurpation of power by the claims of traditional authorities.

One can assume that almost immediately after the destruction of the walls of Jerusalem by al-Malik al-Muʿaẓẓam in 1219, those who attempted to strike roots in the Holy City moved to the coast, more particularly to Acre. At some time between 1211 and 1214, Samson of Sens settled in Acre, and his

[40] The events are related by Abraham Maimuni twice: once in the treatise to the communities of Provence and Spain (*The Wars of the Lord*, written in 1235), and again in a letter to R. Solomon b. Asher. Both were published several times but are usually quoted from the Appendix to the *Collection of Responsa of Maimonides (Qoveṣ Tshūvōth ha-Rambam)*, ed. A. L. Lichtenberg (Leipzig 1859), pt. 3, 17*a*. A more recent and critical edition (using a Vatican MS Neophyti. Cod. XI, 82–92) was published by R. Margolioth, *Rabbenū Abraham b. ha-Rambam: Milḥamōth ha-Shem* (Jerusalem 1953), 47–75, and the letter ibid. 76–8. The Vatican MS was written on 17 Adar I (4)995 (that is, Feb. 1235), a short time after the writer arrived in Acre in Shevat (4)995, i.e. Dec. 1234 or Jan. 1235. The text of the *Wars of the Lord* does not mention the name of the correspondent 'And we did not know clearly until we received a missive from Acre . . . which told us what happened', but in the letter to R. Solomon b. Asher he adds: 'And we did not know the events clearly how they happened until this year came to Acre the venerable sage, the physician R. Isaac b. R. Shem Tov . . . of blessed memory . . . sent to us a long missive, which told us the events in detail.' (p. 77.)

[41] He was buried in Neustadt near Tachau. R. Moses is mentioned in the *Novellae* (*Ḥidūshim*) of Naḥmanides to Tractate *Gittin* 81, pt. 3. Cf. E. E. Urbach 'The Participation of German and French Scholars in the Controversy about Maimonides and his Works' (H), *Ẓion* 12 (1947/8), 152–3. Cf. Urbach, *Tosafists*, ii. 420–5.

[42] *Responsa of R. Bezalel Ashkenazi*, par. 2 quoted by E. E. Urbach, *Tosafists*, i. 420. Cf. S. H. Kuk, 'R. Moshe b. R. Ḥisdai Tachau' (H), *Studies*, ii. 294–7.

tomb as well as that of some of the members of his family was later shown in the cemetery of the community.[43] We would also assume that the two brothers R. Meir and R. Joseph of Clisson (Brittany), who died in 1220 and 1221 respectively,[44] moved to Acre after the destruction of the walls of Jerusalem before leaving, perhaps for business purposes, for Damascus.

It is plausible to assume that the presence of the great Talmudic authority of his age, R. Samson b. Abraham of Sens,[45] in Acre contributed to the spiritual life of the Jewish community. His presence, moreover, transplanted not only the particular system of the French school to the Holy Land, it also transferred attitudes which erupted into the acrimonious first dispute over the philosophical works of Maimonides. R. Samson of Sens, though admiring the *halakhic* sides of the great philosopher, was deeply committed in the debate regarding the resurrection of the dead. Maimonides' rather ambivalent view came under a heavy attack from R. Abraham b. David of Posquière, and in an acidulous way by Meir b. Todros Halevy Abulafia, who also attacked some of Maimonides' *halakha* statements in the same vein.

[43] *Tōṣōth Eretz Israel*, ed. S. Assaf, *Sources*, 76. The date 1214 (4974) is indicated in the recently published 'New Chronography', *Shalem* 3 (1981), 323 (see below, n. 44). This would explain Urbach's argument (*Tosafists*, i. 217, 273, n. 35) why al-Ḥarizi, who visited the country in 1216–17, did not mention him in Acre. Generally speaking, however, not much reliance should be placed on an argument *ex silentio* based on al-Ḥarizi (see above ch. 7, Itinerary C, and cf. below, n. 51–2). Moreover, there still remains the difficulty that Samson is described as a very old man at his death (based on the *Responsa* of Maharshal 29, ibid.) but at that time he was about 64 years old, which hardly fits the epithet. H. Gross (see below, n. 45, p. 139) suggested *c.*1230–5 as the year of death at the age of about 85. There is a vague passage in Abraham Maimuni's *Wars of the Lord*, ed. R. Margolioth (Jerusalem 1953), 54, where after mentioning the migration of R. Samson of Sens and that one of his pupils opposed to Maimonides, he says: 'And it happened after three years that news came from the city of Montpellier that a division broke out among the scholars and this caused a split among the people.' Theoretically one could interpret this passage as three years after 1211, i.e. 1214. There was no dispute in 1214, however, but Maimuni learned about the new one in 1235, which would refer us back to 1232.

[44] The dates of their deaths are indicated in the short chronographical fragment published by I. Ta-Shema, 'A New Chronography on the 13th-century Tosafists' (H), *Shalem* 3 (1981), 319–25 and are corroborated in the Arabic version of a *maqāmah* by al-Ḥarizi. The latter indicates that R. Meir died several months before his brother R. Baruk in Damascus (S. M. Stern, 'An Unpublished Maqama by Alharizi', *Papers of the Institute of Jewish Studies* i (Jerusalem 1964), 200–1; cf. Y. Ratzaby, 'An Arabic *Maqama* by Alharizi' (H), *Criticism and Interpretation* xv (Ramat Gan 1980), 19).

[45] Cf. H. Gross, 'Étude sur Simon b. Abraham de Sens', *REJ* 6 (1883), 166–86; 7 (1883), 40–77.

Generally speaking, Abulafia found many supporters among those who tended to a literal explanation even of Talmudic lore (the *Aggadah*). R. Samson did not follow suit. Though he gave his support to Abulafia's criticism of the foregoing question, he took exception to the criticism of the *halakha*; R. Samson then joined in excommunicating Maimonides' philosophical book.[46] All this happened before R. Samson's migration to the Holy Land. This might have been why he chose not to pass through Cairo and visit Abraham Maimuni (that is, the son of Moses Maimonides) on his way to the Holy Land.

Thus, in the wake of the immigration from France, Acre became a centre of anti-Maimonidean feelings. There is even a curious (but perhaps not reliable) note about the continuation of the anti-Maimonides dispute by R. Samson of Sens after he settled in the Holy Land.[47] It was even rumoured that Abraham Maimuni excommunicated R. Samson, but the rumour was unfounded. Maimuni himself states that he learned about R. Samson's criticism only after the latter's death.[48]

The settling of R. Samson of Sens and some time later of other French scholars created or strengthened the current trends and attitudes of the French Tosafists. This would have added to the variety of Acre but not created tensions had it not been for their attitude to the philosophical works of Maimonides. Oriental Jewry as a whole opposed any attack on their great leader. The adherence was almost intuitive without any particular attempt to enter into a philosophical debate. Abraham Maimuni was able to state in his *Wars of the Lord* without any qualification: 'And those who hold to false beliefs in these matters in the land of Babylon [Shin'ar] and the Orient, in

[46] H. Gross, 'Étude sur Simon b. Abraham de Sens', *REJ* 6 (1883), 178.

[47] There is an enigmatic fragment in *Sefer Yūḥasin*, ed. H. Filipowski (London 1857), 218, which has an episode about R. Samson entering into a discussion against an otherwise unknown R. Kaleb, a pupil of Maimonides: 'He entered into a discussion about Maimonides in Galilee [Heb. *galīl*, which can also mean 'district'] after he wrote the *Yad* [his major compendium on the *halakha*, the *Mishneh Torah*] and R. Kaleb, a pupil of Maimonides won the argument.' The name of Acre is not explicitly mentioned.

[48] *Wars of the Lord* (above n. 43), 55: 'And the rumour spread by another liar, that I excommunicated R. Samson of blessed memory to protect the name of my father and master of blessed memory, is a lie he invented from his heart. God forbid that we, ignorants, should excommunicate him to protect our name.'

Syria and in the Holy Land, in the land of Egypt and in the Magreb are a negligible minority.'[49] Maimuni's statement is corroborated at the time of the writing of the *Wars of the Lord* in 1235, when one of his correspondents hesitated to mention by name the opponents of Maimonides in Acre.[50] All that time the bulk of the community must have been composed of local or Oriental Jews, all adherents of Maimonides.

These new stirrings in the intellectual life of the city make al-Ḥarizi's remark about the community of Acre rather enigmatic. 'Never in my life', he wrote, 'did I ever see anything like that. All of them are ignorant and there is none who would enter into the breach.'[51] These are extremely harsh words about a community of the size of Acre, and could hardly apply to a city in which a significant number of Tosafists were living. It has been argued that al-Ḥarizi visited Acre around 1216, that is, before the spiritual centre of Jerusalem had to be abandoned for the safety of Acre. Such a possibility exists. Another explanation could be that al-Ḥarizi denigrated faces and places which were not generous or piqued his vanity. I myself have grave doubts that al-Ḥarizi ever visited Acre. His itinerary is not clear about this and the poem he wrote about the great Crusader capital does not prove any familiarity with the place: 'Then Acre spoke and said: I am the topstone and my soil is holy soil. Indeed I am the rose of Sharon. Round about me are Carmel and Lebanon, and Tabor and Mt. Hermon.'[52] Clearly these are biblical paraphrases taken out of their context and applied to Acre (cf. Isa. 29: 17, Ps. 89: 13). I think that his voyage from Egypt to Syria went through the Ayyūbid-dominated parts of the Holy Land, and the fine-sounding phrases cover up his ignorance. There is therefore nothing to be learned from him as to the Jewish community in Acre.

The growing strength and importance of the community became evident in the 1230s. At this time authority over the community was suddenly claimed by the *nasi* Hodaya b. Jesse,

[49] *War of the Lord*, 54.

[50] See above, n. 40.

[51] That is to say, able to mend their ways and guide them in the right way. *Taḥkemoni*, ch. 46.

[52] *Maqāmah* l, trans. Reichert, i. 334.

a descendant of the Babylonian exilarchs who traced their origin to the royal house of King David.[53] He threatened and actually excommunicated individuals and even whole communities who refused to obey his orders.

A similar situation had already occurred in Alexandria where the community had taken upon itself a solemn obligation under oath (*ḥerem*). As they could not fulfil the obligation (details of which are unknown to us), the community asked the visiting exilarch to absolve them from it. The exilarch decided to use this as a pretext for pecuniary demands. The community consented to a smaller sum, but the exilarch refused to give absolution from the ban.

When similar conflict between the community and the *nasi* erupted in Acre, the man who organized the opposition was a scholar of French origin, R. Joseph b. R. Gershon, who had lived for some time in Alexandria and was a *dayyan* and member of Abraham Maimuni's court there but later settled in Acre.[54] Opposing Hodaya's high-handed behaviour, he wrote a number of formal questions (*sheelōth*) to the *nagid* Abraham Maimuni who answered in quite a conciliatory way but in principle supported Joseph b. Gerson. On the basis of this *responsum* the leaders of the community of Acre promulgated a set of 'Statutes [*Taqqanōth*] of the Sons of Acco' establishing the ruling custom in the community.[55]

It is important to follow the leading questions of Joseph b.

[53] *Nesiim* (exilarchs) existed outside Babylon as early as the end of the 10th cent. in Fusṭāṭ, Jerusalem, and Damascus. Hodaya b. Jesse was probably the son of a Damascen *nasi*, Joshiah b. Jesse, whom Ḥarizi met. He stayed for some time in Egypt, and Abraham Maimuni, despite later conflicts, speaks of him with reverence. This was due more to his office and genealogy than his personal merit: 'But the above mentioned exilarch, let God construct his abode, he hails from a great family. By genealogy, he is a descendant of kings and from the progenies of prophets and he is an old man who was brought up in his country among scholars.' Mann, i (1920), 175–6 (includes earlier bibliog.) and in more detail id., *Texts and Studies*, i (1931), 398–400.

[54] On R. Joseph b. Gershon see Mann, ii. 370–1. R. Joseph b. Gershon later left Acre and died on his way to Babylon. A eulogy of R. Joseph b. Gershon written by El'azar b. Jacob ha-Babbli mentions his death 'when on a journey to Babylon'. His scholarship and learning are described here in most glowing terms. See G. Poznanski, *Babylonische Geonim im nachgaonäischen Zeitalter* (Berlin 1914), 64, poem 9.

[55] Published by A. H. Freimann, 'Taqqanōth Ḥakhmei Acco' (H), *Aluma*, ed. B. M. Levin (1936), 30–2 and again in *Abraham Maimunis Responsa*, ed. A. H. Freimann and S. D. Goitein (Jerusalem 1937), 25–6. Here too are the questions sent to Abraham Maimuni and his responsa (ibid., p. 4, 13–19).

Gershon. The *nasi*, as it transpires, claimed that those excommunicated by a *nasi* are *eo ipso* excommunicated everywhere in Israel. Such a claim, it was rejoined, was not practised or operative any more, as such competences belonged to a king or *gaon* (head) of the Academy of Eretz Israel only. But since ordination (*semīkha*) in the Talmudic sense of the expression had been interrupted and there was no *semīkha* outside the boundaries of the land of Israel, nobody could rightly raise claims on that basis. 'Moreover even if we had a *nasi* according to law and precept, still the scholars of our time have the power to depose him if he does not follow the way of righteousness.' At this point the pride and self-consciousness of the learned intellectuals come to the fore. 'The *nasi*', he says, 'is not more learned or versed than I in the study of religion. And though he claims that he is a *nasi* and son of a *nasi* I am for my part a scholar (*ḥakham*) son of a scholar and grandson of a scholar and this goes back several generations'.[56]

Based on Abraham Maimuni's *responsum*, the 'Sons of the Community of Acco inside the Boundaries of the Tribe of Asher' proclaimed: no man, neither *nasi* nor *ḥakham* should be allowed to excommunicate any man in Israel unless with the agreement of three notables of the community in each city (*'al pī shlōsha ḥashūvei ha'edah shebkhol 'īr*). And if the three agreed to excommunicate him on the basis of what they considered a transgression (*'aveirah*), and this based on clear and well-founded testimony, the excommunicated person can proceed to the residence of a *ḥakham*, confess repentance, and make reparation, and then they must reinstate him. If he deserved to be punished by a fine, the monies were to profit neither those who excommunicated him nor the man who was the primary cause of excommunication, but would go to the poor or to the synagogues. Any other procedure is declared null and void. This Statute of the Sons of Acco is signed by eleven scholars, among them the descendants of the 'three hundred rabbis' who had migrated to the Holy Land a generation earlier and obviously R. Joseph (he signed himself Jehoseph) b. Gershon.

[56] Freimann and Goitein, *Abraham Maimunis Responsa*, 15.

As Abraham Maimuni wrote his *responsum* at the beginning of 1234 (13 Adar 4994) and died in 1238, that *Taqqanoth* of Acre must have been promulgated near that time.

Acre appears, then, as a fully fledged community organized on traditional lines. It is led by lay notables of the city, a group of wealthy and influential people whose voice is decisive in communal affairs; yet at the same time it is the scholars who decide on penance, reparations, and reconciliation. Those who signed the Statutes do not appear as members of a court, but rather as members of an Academy or perhaps even different schools which taught in the city.

It was at the time at which the Statutes were drawn up that the disturbing news of the burning of the philosophical books of Maimonides in Montpellier reached Acre. This was followed by the excommunication in Saragossa (1232) of R. Solomon of Montpellier and his adherents who had caused the dispute and tragedy. The news created tension in the city. Isaac b. Shem Tov, who wrote from Acre to Abraham Maimuni, was very careful not to mention names. Abraham Maimuni, who received the news in Cairo in the winter of 1235, states that the letter also contained 'the signatures of confused people, men of wisdom, piety and orthodoxy . . . and their names should not be mentioned, as this may cause them damage or they may be in danger because of delators'.[57] Traditionally the Jewish communities in the Orient venerated Maimonides as the great Sage of all ages, but Acre—no monolithic community—was actually a hotbed of dissent.

The impression left by these events is recorded in a curious letter with an apocryphal bias written by R. Hillel of Verona to R. Isaac b. Mordecai, physician to Pope Nicholas IV. This, he says, he heard from R. Jonah of Gerona himself (the leader of the campaign against Maimonides) under whom he studied (apparently 1259–62) in Barcelona. When the news of the burning of the Talmud just forty days after the burning of the philosophical works of Maimonides reached R. Jonah and his followers, they were so heart-broken that they took an oath of

[57] See above, n. 40.

contrition 'to go and pray on the tomb of our Rabbi [Maimonides] in public (*beminyan ʿasara*) and to weep on his tomb for seven days asking forgiveness.' They also swore to confess: ' "I undertake to prostrate myself on Maimonides' grave and to confess that I spoke out against his books" '. R. Jonah repeated this confession in Paris, Montpellier, and Barcelona. In the end he did not fulfil his vow or go on a pilgrimage to Maimonides' tomb, although he intended to do so, but at the request of the community stayed on in Toledo. He died an unnatural death, which was interpreted as heavenly punishment: 'but those who fulfilled their oath were forgiven, those who did not were cut off without leaving any progeny'.[58]

In the second quarter of the thirteenth century the Jewish community of Acre settled down; one has the impression that it became 'westernized', in that the leading men of the community were now of European origin. Some of them still belonged to the generation of the 'three hundred rabbis' of the wave of immigration between 1209 and 1211; others were their descendants, and others were more recent immigrants. The names of the eleven signatories of the Statues of the Sons of Acre are mainly of French origin: R. Jacob the son of the famous Rabbi Samson of Sens, R. Joseph b. R. Gershon, Rabbi Joseph of Burgundy,[59] R. Joseph of Saintes or Soissons,[60] R. Jacob of Zagora.[61] Some other signatories, like R. Joseph b. Rabbi Matatyah, R. Juda, and R. Samuel

[58] The letter was written almost 50 years after the events, during the second attack on Maimonides' philosophical works in 1284–90. The letter was printed in *Taʿam Zekenīm*, ed. A. Ashkenazi (Frankfurt 1854), 70–2. In this connection we hear of the tomb of Maimonides, although the place is not specified. A tradition attested to since the end of the thirteenth cent. locates the tomb in Tiberias. On the whole question, see I. Ben Zvi, 'The Tomb of Maimonides' (H), in *Remnants of Ancient Jewish Communities in Eretz Israel* (Jerusalem 1965), 509–12.

[59] R. Joseph of Bourgogne (Burgundy) is probably the Tosafist R. Joseph from Saulieu. See H. Gross, *Gallia Judaica* (Paris 1892, repr. Amsterdam 1969), 646.

[60] The Hebrew spelling can read 'Seinos' but also 'Santais'. Ad. Neubauer in *REJ* 10 (1885), 105–7, and H. Gross, *Gallia Judaica*, p. 662, identified the place with Sens and the man as a nephew of R. Samson of Sens. S. Kraus ('L'Émigration de 300 rabbins en Palestine en l'an 1211', ibid. 82 (1926), 345 n. 2) regarded the name as a copyist's mistake. Harkavy suggested 'Soissons' but this does not seem very plausible.

[61] The Hebrew spelling can be read Zigura or Zigora. Ad. Neubauer (n. 60) suggested Zogara in Macedonia, whereas Harkavy suggested Segura.

are also known from a short fragment from the Geniza.[62] There is nothing to indicate the place of origin of other people mentioned.[63] As these signatures occur on an official proclamation, we can assume with some certainty the predominance of Europeans, more particularly of the French element, in the major Jewish community under Crusader rule.

This trend became even more pronounced in the next generation. Soon after 1258 the community was strengthened by the arrival of a group of immigrants from France who had started out with Rabbi Yeḥiel, the head of the Academy of Paris. A later Jerusalemite tradition fixed the date of pilgrimage as 1256 or 1257, but this is probably a copyist's mistake, as we have evidence that on 29 Marḥeshvan (50)18, that is, 7 November 1258, Rabbi Yeḥiel signed a divorce and was therefore still in Paris.[64] It seems very doubtful that Rabbi Yeḥiel would have started out late in the same year, that is in the winter; I would rather suggest that he went in the spring *passagium* of 1259 (which still corresponds to the Hebrew year 5018).[65] Rabbi Yeḥiel himself died on the journey and was buried in the unknown port of Morea, but the rest of the group reached the Holy Land and settled in Acre. There is some uncertainty as to the fate of Rabbi Yeḥiel's son R. Joseph. One source can be interpreted as indicating he joined the group

[62] Where they are listed as following a particular custom of praying. Mann, ii. 370–1.

[63] They are: Isaac b. Isaac, Ebyatar b. Joseph, Petaḥyah b. Samuel, Neḥemiah b. Nathanyah, Abraham b. Yeḥiel, and Eliezer son of the benefactor (*nadiv*) Jacob.

[64] *Sefer Miṣvōth Gadōl* (Venice 1547, rpr. Jerusalem, 1961), *Hilkhōt Gittin* (end), 133. On the Jerusalem tradition the author of *Kaftor va-Pheraḥ* i. 81, learned from one R. Baruk whom he met in Jerusalem.

[65] The *passagium paschae* left the Christian ports in Apr.–May; the *passagium aestiuale* left later in the summer, in Aug. or Sept. For some time in the beginning of the 13th-cent., the Venetians organized a winter *passagium*, but this seems to have been exceptional. Cf. W. Heyd, *Histoire du commerce du Levant* (Leipzig 1885), 180–1. This new attempt to date R. Yeḥiel's departure from Paris can be corroborated by a fragment relating to R. Tobias b. Elijah which mentions R. Yeḥiel's visit to his school in Vienne in the Dauphiné. According to this interesting fragment, Vienne was on the main road from Paris to Marseilles and hence to Acre. E. Carmoly, *Itinéraires de la Terre Sainte* (Brussels 1847), 187–8. H. Gross's suggestion (*Gallia Judaica*, 528), would make it even more plausible that the departure took place in the spring from Paris to Marseilles and hence by ship to Acre. H. Gross has already suggested 1259, and more probably 1260, as the date of departure.

some time later after release from imprisonment, but a chronographical fragment published recently states explicitly that he began the voyage with his father R. Yeḥiel. R. Yeḥiel's son Joseph, known by his French surname Sire Délicieux,[66] and his companions settled in Acre and established 'The Great Academy of Paris' (*Hamidrash Haggadōl de Parīsi*).[67]

It has recently been suggested that the Academy, in financial difficulties, sent a professional money collector to the Jewish communities in Europe to ask for financial help.[68] The envoy carried with him a kind of exhortatory treatise, known from

[66] The son, R. Yeḥiel, is known as Sire Délicieux from the *responsa* of R. Solomon of London; Cf. H. Gross (*Gallia Judaica*, 527) who read in MS Bodl. no. 781, 2° Cat., 152; Sire Deu-le-Saut, or Die-le-saut, ibid. 91. Dieu-le-saut can hardly be attached to the son's name Joseph (Gross, ibid. 92), but Sire Délicieux can be meaningfully attached to Ben-Porat Joseph in the Heb. (Gen. 49: 22); cf. S. H. Kuk, *Studies* ii. 137. The *responsum* of R. Solomon of London refers to an imprisonment of R. Yeḥiel's son (in all probability in the wake of some persecution): 'and he made a public vow to go to Eretz Israel when he is liberated from the imprisonment. And his father released him from the obligation because of the respect due to his still living father.' The last phrase has obviously been corrupted by the copyist. S. H. Kuk (*Studies*, ii. 138) tried to explain it by assuming that he was released from his oath by his grandfather. In any case the vow was taken before 1258, when R. Yeḥiel was still alive. R. Joseph migrated later, and his tomb is mentioned as being near Acre by the anonymous pupil of Naḥmanides in *Tōṣōth Eretz Israel*.

[67] 'The Great Midrash [Academy] of Paris' is mentioned in the opening lines of the itinerary and exhortatory text 'These are the Monuments of the Tombs' (*Eileh simanei*), printed as an appendix to *Die Reisebeschreibungen des Rabbi Benjamin von Tudela*, ed. L. Grünhut (Frankfurt am Main 1904), 140 ff. On this treatise see ch. 7. The title 'Great Midrash' (*Midrash gadōl*) belongs to a vocabulary used in France, cf. M. Güdemann, *Geschichte des Erziehungswesens und der Cultur der abendländischen Juden* i (Vienna 1880), 268 and *passim*. The controversy as to the site of the Academy has never been definitively solved. Some scholars have assumed that the Academy was in Paris, others have argued that it was in Acre; the latter was advocated by S. H. Kuk (*Studies* ii. 137–41). This seems more plausible as it would explain the 'Monuments' treatise, carried by R. Jacob, the messenger to Europe; one could hardly imagine a messenger from Paris collecting money for a French Academy in Acre (see next note). It was only natural that the Academy should commemorate its spiritual founder R. Yeḥiel of Paris. The name could also imply, as is customary today, that the studies pursued there were in the tradition of the Academy of Paris, i.e. the Tosafists of Northern France. A different view was taken by H. Graetz (*Geschichte der Juden* vii. 109), by L. Zunz (in his commentary on *The Travels of Benjamin of Tudela*, ed. and trans. A. Asher (London 1840), no. 47, p. 258) and by I. Ben Zvi in *Mizrah Oumaarav* [*Mizraḥ u-Ma'arav*] (H), iii, pt. 203, all of whom argued that the Academy was in Paris.

[68] It has recently been suggested that the messenger R. Jacob can be identified with the owner of a MS of *Sever Miṣvōth gadōl* copied in Ferrara. This R. Jacob and his son Dōnīn, who came from France took a ship in Venice and sailed for Acre in 1278, were kind of professional fund-raisers or charity collectors I. S. J. Wolfsohn, 'The Parma Colophon of Abraham b. Ephraim's Book of Precepts', *JJS* 21 (1970), 39–49.

its *incipit* as 'These are the Monuments of the Tombs', that is, a list of Holy Tombs (of venerated biblical personalities and Talmudic Sages) in the Holy Land. The letter of exhortation mentions that there were at that time 300 students in the Great Academy of Paris in Acre. The number seems very high but one has to bear in mind that in the thirteenth century Acre was the gateway to the Holy Land and consequently all Jewish pilgrims or immigrants who came by sea passed through the city. Moreover, the expression 'students', *talmīdīm*, does not necessarily refer only to regular students; following Jewish customs throughout the ages, a large section of the congregation in all walks of life would daily devote some time for study and they would also be considered *talmīdīm*. An Academy or *beit midrash* of this type without fixed income revenues from property would depend for its maintenance on outside help. In a large community like Acre, often composed of pious but not necessarily practical immigrants, not to mention people who went to the Holy Land to end their lives there, there was always a large group of needy people. The poor were often vulnerable to conversion; in 1264, for example, Pope Urban IV ordered the patriarch, the churches, and monasteries of Acre to provide food and lodgings for 'the poor Saracens and Jews' and induce them to conversion.[69] The fate of the Academy which, in the nature of things must have perpetuated the system of teaching of the French Tosafists, is unknown. However, it seems that a Rabbi Baruk,[70] whom Ishtori ha-Parḥi encountered in Jerusalem around 1320, might still have been one of its students.

The variety of people and scholars in Acre was enriched by the arrival of one of the greatest scholars of that age, the Spaniard Moshe b. Naḥman, known as Naḥmanides who left Jerusalem in 1268 or 1269; we find him preaching his famous 'Sermon on Rosh ha-Shanah' (New Year) in Acre.[71] Very little is known of his stay in the city. He certainly either joined one of the schools there or established his own, perhaps bringing with

[69] See the text published by B. Z. Kedar, 'Notes on the History of the Jews of Palestine in the Middle Ages' (H), *Tarbiz* 42 (1973), 416.

[70] On R. Baruk see n. 64.

[71] The Hebrew date is 5029 or 5030 of Creation. This 'Discourse' (*drasha*) is a monument to learning and the method used in the great Schools of *Halakha*. Eng. trans. C. B. Chavel in *Ramban (Naḥmanides): Writings and Discourses* i (New York 1978), 239–353.

him his Jerusalemite pupils. In one of his writings he mentions the 'long Tosafoth' of Rabbi Elḥanan (of Dampierre), a twelfth-century scholar, which he found in Acre.[72] A fleeting notice mentions a Kabbalist who went to meet Naḥmanides in Acre,[73] and there is a short passage by Naḥmanides about the discovery of a *shekel* of the Second Temple period in the city.[74] It can be assumed that Naḥmanides contributed to the life of the community and its schools during the two or three years before his death, adding to the variety of spiritual currents which made Acre a centre of communal tensions.

In addition to his accomplishments as a scholar—one of the greatest in the third quarter of the thirteenth century—Naḥmanides represented a particular type of piety and mysticism. Although a pupil of the school of Gerona mystics, who brought over their teachings from Provence, in the first half of the thirteenth century, Naḥmanides became an independent and towering figure. His teachings became the object of exclusive commentaries by such scholars and Kabbalists as R. Isaac Todros and R. Solomon b. Adret. His main contribution to Kabbalistic literature was a commentary to *Sefer Yeṣīra* (Book of Creation), a classic in early Kabbalah literature. But a great mass of kabbalistic interpretations is to be found in his other writings, among them in his Commentary on the Pentateuch. The main exponent of his teachings was soon to be R. Isaac of Acre in his *Meīrat 'Einayim* (Enlightening).

The content and intrinsic value of Naḥmanides' contribution to the study of the Halakhah and Kabbalah are outside the scope of this study. Suffice it to mention here his particular interest in the kabbalistic system of *ṣimṣūm* (God's self restriction), which was to become prominent three hundred years later in the Kabbalah of R. Isaac Luria (abbr. Ari) in Ṣafed.

[72] The commentaries of R. Elḥanan did not enter the canon of the printed Tosafoth. The above 'Discourse' has 'In this city [Acre] I have seen the long Tosafoth of R. Elḥanan' (ibid. 268).

[73] G. Scholem, 'Contribution to the Study of the Kabbala in the 13th Century' (H), *Tarbiz* 16 (1944), 140. The Kabbalist's name was R. Sheshet of the Catalonian Des Mercavell family. He is mentioned by R. Isaac of Acre in *Sefer Meīrat 'Einayim* (MS Munich 17, p. 226), saying that R. Sheshet went to Naḥmanides in Acre near the end of his life asking for advice on Kabbalistic matters ('The Mystery of Incarnation', *Sōd ha-gilgūl*).

[74] For Engl. trans. see above in n. 71, end of vol. ii (New York 1978).

However, a particular trait of Naḥmanides in the teaching of the Kabbalah is his insistence that these were teachings destined for an élite group only, and his consequent objection to their diffusion. The teachings, he says, 'should not be made known by any type of reasoning but from the lips of a Kabbalistic scholar'.[75]

Naḥmanides, scholar and Kabbalist, was also an admirer of Maimonides—even though he had reservations about some of the latter's teachings he nevertheless regarded him as the greatest scholarly authority—and may have had a restraining influence on Maimonides' opponents. Even so, and even though he equally exerted a restraint on the dissemination of Kabbalistic teachings, he certainly added to the variety of currents swirling at the surface and beneath the surface of the greatest centre of Judaism in the Holy Land at that time. Moreover, Naḥmanides' principle of limiting the teaching of Kabbalah to the elect was not necessarily followed by his students.

Thus in addition to the two or three main groups representing the traditions of Oriental Jewry and the scholarship of southern France and Spain on the one hand and that of northern France and Germany on the other, a new group emerged, probably after the second quarter of the century, namely that of the Kabbalists. It seems Kabbalists migrated to the Holy Land on an individual basis as early as the twelfth century: such was probably R. Jacob ha Nazīr (the Hermit) of Lunel,[76] and possibly R. Nehōrai, an alleged descendant of the great exilarch of the second century,[77] R. Judah Hanasi. Whatever the case, the appearance of Naḥmanides in the Holy Land and eventually in Acre strengthened the nucleus of Kabbalistic circles, even though they belonged to different trends in the new mystery schools. One of Naḥmanides' pupils, R. Solomon b. Samuel Petit, was destined to play a role in the

[75] E. Gottlieb, 'Ramban as a Kabbalist' (H), *Studies in the Kabbala Literature* (Tel-Aviv 1976), 88–96.

[76] G. Scholem, 'From Scholar to Kabbalist' (H), *Tarbiz* 6 (1935), 96–7.

[77] *Die Rundreise des R. Petachjah aus Regensburg*, ed. L Grünhut (Frankfurt 1905), 29. One wonders if a fundamentalist trend as represented by R. Moses b. Ḥisday of Tachau (see above, nn. 41–2) did not continue to exist in Acre. R. Moses opposed any type of philosophical or mystical study or interpretation.

dispute which divided Acre and in its wake the communities of the Near East and Europe. It seems that a fleeting visit by another Spanish adherent of the Kabbalah, Abraham Abulafia, may have left more permanent traces than has hitherto been assumed. The latter, visiting the Holy Land in search of the legendary river Sambation, arrived in Acre in 1261 after the decisive battle against the Mongols at ʿAin-Jalūd (he refers to a war between Crusaders and Muslims which prevented him from setting out on his quest for the legendary river). Resigning himself to not finding this fabled river he returned to Europe. Still a young man of twenty, on returning to Europe he became an adherent of Kabbalism. His was a particular trend, that of prophetic Kabbalah based on the hermeneutics of divine letters. In Sicily some time after 1287, he wrote the Book of Precepts, an exegesis on the ritual of the blessing of the priests, at the request of Solomon Hakkohen b. Moses Hakkohen, whom he describes as 'the Galilean from the Holy Land'.[78] Solomon Hakkohen, whom Abulafia mentions as his pupil, apparently studied under him in Europe. Abulafia's influence also shows in the treatises of R. Isaac of Acre (*Yitzhak demin ʿAcco*), especially in his Treasure of Life (*Ọsar ha-Ḥayim*).[79] R. Isaac escaped from Acre at its fall and found refuge in Spain. One of the versions of this book mentions the Kabbalist R. Joseph b. Solomon 'the Galilean from the city of Safad'. To this group of Kabbalists one can also add R. Shem Tov the Spaniard from Léon who wrote 'The Gates of Justice' (*Shaʿarei Ṣedeq*) in 1290 or 1295 either in Safad or in Hebron.[80] This

[78] See extract from Abulafia's *Oṣar Eden Ganūz* (The hidden treasure of Eden): 'And God's spirit moved one, and I left [Aragon], and I came straight to Eretz Israel by land and sea, and I intended to go to the River Sambation, but I could not go out from Acco, because of the war between the Ismaelites and Christians, so I abandoned the plan and returned to the Empire of Greece [i.e. Byzantium].' *Beth ha-Midrash Sammlung*, ed. A. Jellineck, iii (Jerusalem 1938), p. xl.

[79] The work preserved in Paris (BN Heb. MS 853, 38–79) was the subject of a Hebrew University doctoral thesis by M. Idel. I summarize here his conclusions as well as his study 'Eretz Israel and the Kabbalah in the Thirteenth Century' (H) *Shalem* 3 (1981), 119–28 (Engl. summary, ibid. ix). Cf. A. Gottlieb, 'Illumination, Contemplation, and Prophecy in *Sefer Oṣar ha-Ḥayim* of R. Isaac of Acre' (H), *Studies in the Kabbalah Literature* (Tel-Aviv 1976), 231–42.

[80] G. Scholem, '*Shaʿarei Ṣedeq*: A Kabbalistic Pamphlet by a Pupil of R. Abraham Abulafia, Ascribed to R. Shemtov (ibn Gaon?)' (H), *Kirjath Sepher* 1 (1924), 127–39. The name and the origin of the man are not clear.

treatise, like the previous one, belongs to the same trend of Kabbalism as that of Abraham Abulafia.[81]

The remarkable common denominator of these Palestinian Kabbalah treatises was their spiritual propinquity to the Muslim Ṣūfi teachings (excepting the Kabbalah system of Abulafia), which a great scholar, Y. Baer, thought to be somehow linked to the Franciscan Joachimists. This has brought the most recent student of the problem (S. D. Goitein) to the conclusion that such a Ṣūfi trend existed among Oriental Jews, especially in Egypt, and in our case in Safad in Galilee and in Acre, before the appearance of Abulafia. He points out that Abraham Maimuni, the son of Maimonides, and his colleague Abraham ibn Abū Rabiʿah had already joined such a pietist circle,[82] and that Abraham Maimuni spent some years in Acre. It is thus quite possible that the teachings of Abulafia were absorbed by such a pietist circle, and it was here that the elements of both systems were integrated. This possibly happened in the circle of Rabbi Nathan, a student of Abulafia and teacher of R. Isaac of Acre.[83]

The existence of pietist circles and Kabbalist scholars should not overshadow the importance of the *halakha* scholars in the city, especially as there was no clear division between these two currents of Jewish intellectual life. It was the inclination towards a rational Aristotelian philosophy which united oppositions and broke down barriers in the community. The scholars of Acre began to find a place on the intellectual map of the Jewish world; they certainly did in the Near East. One reason why almost none of their works has come down to us is the destruction of the community. Thus the *responsa* of the great Spanish scholar R. Solomon b. Adret preserve an interesting episode.[84] A question from a scholar who almost certainly lived

[81] It is perhaps not irrelevant to remark that these Kabbalists were even at this time linked to the city of Safad, which in the 16th and 17th cents. was to become the great world centre of the new 'practical' type of Kabbalah.

[82] S. D. Goitein, 'Abraham Maimonides and his Pietist Circle', in *Jewish Medieval and Renaissance Studies*, ed. A. Altmann (Cambridge Mass. 1967), 145–65. Id., 'The Soteriology of R. Abraham Maimuni', *Proceedings of the American Academy for Jewish Research* 35 (1967), 75–98; 36 (1968), 35–58.

[83] M. Idel (above n. 79), 124, argues that this synthesis was transferred to Spain by R. Isaac of Acre in the last decade of the 13th cent.

[84] *Responsa of Rashba*, vi (publ. several times since 1490; Warsaw 1868, repr. New York 1958), no. 69.

in Acre but somehow did not belong to the establishment was put to the scholars of Jubail (perhaps Jabala but not Byblos, otherwise the author would probably have used the biblical name Gebal), regarding a levirate marriage (*yibūm*). They decided on the matter, but 'there is a custom among all the scholars of Eretz Israel and of Babylon, that when a question is asked nobody signs it [i.e. no decision is taken] and so they say: "Let the scholars of Acre teach us what to do in this case." And when the question came before the community (*qahal*) I kept silent and did not say a word until I heard that some of the scholars of Acre did not agree [*meṣafṣfīm*, lit. are whistling, but following Is. 10: 14, it means to dissent, to query].' The scholar who wrote to Rashba did not agree with the decision of the scholars of Acre. 'In the meantime'; he says, 'the people of Jubail do nothing and remain undecided whether to follow the decision of some of the scholars of Acre or to follow the advice of a humble man like myself.' In the event, Rashba decided against the scholars of Acre.

Rashba was in direct correspondence with the scholars of Acre. This correspondence can be dated as later than 1270.[85] His correspondents were an otherwise unknown R. Elijah of Acre, and Joseph (perhaps Joseph of Sens),[86] whom he addresses in one place in a rather extravagant manner: 'I know you are as wise as God's angel, and no mystery of scholarship is hidden from you to explain the *halakha* and to understand the meaning.'[87] Answering a question regarding levirate marriage he writes at the end: 'And this brings out the truthfulness of the teachings of our French scholars of blessed memory ... Although there is another way pursued by some of my teachers, this seems to me to be the right one, and I will not go into details at length. I know they are your people.'[88]

Two decades later, R. Meir of Rothenburg, the great

[85] *Responsa of Rashba*, i (new repr. Bnei Brak 1958), nos. 30, 53: precepts regarding unleavened bread (*ḥameṣ*) before Passover; no. 587 commenting on Tractate *Kiddūshīn* 84. Here Rashba mentions (at the end): 'Moses b. Naḥman of blessed memory'. Naḥmanides died in 1270.

[86] See above, n. 60. He can probably be identified with R. Joseph of Sens buried near Acre. *Responsa of Rashba*, par. 346, contains answers to a collection of 15 questions from this scholar.

[87] Ibid. no. 355.

[88] Ibid. no. 348.

luminary of German Jewry, was in correspondence with the scholars from Acre almost until the fall of the city.[89]

The Jewish community at Acre in the last quarter of the thirteenth century was thus more heterogeneous than any other community in the Jewish world. Native Palestinian Jewry, or at least those living there for generations, were intermingled with immigrants from northern France and Provence, Germany, Spain, Italy,[90] and North Africa. Different traditions and different tempers in the close confines of the Jewish Quarter of the city easily led to tensions and confrontations. Spanish and Languedoc Jewry had already been split by the dispute regarding the philosophical writings of Maimonides two generations earlier. We saw that its reverberations were also felt in Acre, but the major scene of events was in Europe. However, the last phase of the dispute took a different turn. The discussion had died out in the West following the shock of the burning of Maimonides' philosophical works, followed in turn, though not causally connected, with the burning of the Talmud in 1244, but it erupted again in the eighties and now its centre was in Acre. This should be attributed less to the particular structure of the society than to the existence of different cultural backgrounds and scholarly traditions which clashed and became decisive in moulding the confrontation.[91] The events in Acre probably took such a course because the community lacked any recognized leadership accepted by all. Even the appearance of Maimonides' grandson David around the middle of 1285 (when he was temporarily deprived of the office of *nagid* by the Egyptian authorities) did not alleviate the situation, and the memory of his illustrious ancestor did not assure him any particular position. The ethnic and more particularly

[89] *Rabbi Meir's von Rothenburg bisher unedirte Responsen, Teschuwot Maharam* (*Sha'arei tshūvōth*), ed. M. A. Bloch (Berlin 1891), no. 108, regarding a divorce (*geṭ*). This *responsum* was written after R. Meir's incarceration and can be dated. R. Meir writes at the end: 'I have no Tōsafōth on the Tractate *Gittīn* at my disposal, neither books of Decisions . . . and if it is shown that the Tōsafōth or Decisions, *psaqīm*, take a different view in any of these cases, my opinion should be disregarded, because what does a wretched man know, sitting in darkness, in the shadow of death and chaos by now for more than three and a half years.' As R. Meir was captured in Lombardy in 1286, the *responsum* was written in 1289 or 1290.

[90] In the second letter of Rabbi Hillel of Verona (see below, n. 106) he mentions Shalom b. Joseph of Ferrara living in Acre.

[91] It was the other way round in Spain. Cf. Y. Baer, *A History of the Jews in Christian Spain*, i (Philadelphia 1966), 236 ff.

cultural structure polarized the community: most Jews of the Orient wholeheartedly espoused the defence of Maimonides who was highly regarded and admired as the unchallenged authority in all fields of life and thought. European Jewry took a different attitude.

The dispute broke out at the instigation of R. Solomon b. Samuel ha-Ṣarfati, that is, the Frenchman, known in the spoken vernacular as R. Solomon Petit, who headed one of the schools in the city. It is difficult to see why the debate broke out precisely at that time, but it was possibly because the presence of David Maimuni reignited the old controversy. R. Solomon Petit, an adept in the Kabbalah apparently followed the school of Gerona and saw in the study of the rationalizing philosophical works of Maimonides a threat to Judaism and orthodoxy.[92] He came out with a strong condemnation of the philosophical works of the master and even attacked the memory of Maimonides himself.[93]

The immediate reaction in Acre is not known, but it evidently split the community. R. Solomon b. Adret was to refer later on to the two opposing camps as 'R. David son of Abraham Maimuni and his followers' and 'the opposing sect'.[94] Clearly R. Solomon Petit did not feel strong enough in Acre. A battle of words based on letters, treatises, and missives ensued. The correspondence spread far and wide, from Baghdad and Mosul in the East, to Italy, Germany, France, Provence, and Spain in the West. Some is still extant and the polemics can thus be partially reconstructed.[95]

[92] His pupil Isaac of Acre later wrote in his lost *History (Divrei ha-Yamīm)*: 'And I call upon heaven and earth as my witness . . . that one day we, the students, sat and studied in Acre, let her be rebuilt and reconstructed, before our teacher and master R. Solomon ha-Ṣarfati ha-Qatan [Petit] of blessed memory.' He continues how his master Solomon ridiculed and disparaged Aristotle, who tried to seduce the wife of his pupil Alexander the Great. The fragment is preserved in *Sefer Meīrat 'Einayim*, quoted by H. Graetz, *Geschichte der Juden*, vii. 415.

[93] The teachings of Gerona are to be found in R. Isaac b. Samuel of Acre. Cf. G. Scholem, 'A New Document Regarding the Beginning of the Kabbala' (H), in *Sefer Bialik*, ed. I. Fichman (Tel-Aviv 1934), 142.

[94] See below nn. 115 ff.

[95] Several reconstructions have been attempted: H. Graetz, *Geshichte der Juden* vii. 415–19, app. 8: 'Salomon Petit und das Datum des Bannes über die Antimaimuniden in Akko'. Mann, *Texts* i. 419; J. L. Fishman, *The Negidūt in Israel* (H), 40 ff. A more exhaustive study is E. Strauss, *The Jews in Egypt and Syria* (H), i (Jerusalem 1947), 130–49. Cf. B. Dinur, *A Documentary History of the Jewish People*, 2nd ser.: *Israel in the Diaspora*, ii, bk. 4 (Tel-Aviv/Jerusalem 1969), 225–37.

Both sides wrote to scholars abroad soliciting moral support. Those who felt strongly either way on the philosophical works of Maimonides responded, seemingly by signing a form of declaration. Rather unexpectedly, a large number of scholars in Northern France and Germany came out in support of Maimonides. This probably urged the anti-Maimonides group to engage in direct and more vigorous action. A letter sent from France in the second half of 1286 to R. David Maimuni in Acre describes the events, some corroborated by other sources, in detail.[96] 'Let me make it known my lord through this letter which speaks the truth [or: which I truthfully quote from a writing] about the enemy, and his followers, who harboured evil designs but failed. They were brought to their knees and fell and we stood up and were encouraged.' On 5 Tammūz (29 June seemingly 1286 but more probably a year earlier, 29 June 1285) God 'moved the spirit of the great bishop (*hegemōn*), father of all the bishops (*abī kol ha-hegemōnīm*)', to announce in all places of prayer: 'So spake the great bishop: "God in heaven gave me the power and strength, the force and the might. And he ordered me to be bishop over all the nations to proclaim prohibitions and to restrain the lusts of all mortals." Consequently, having read the books of sciences (or wisdom) I became fluent in them. My wisdom brought me to read the books of Rabbi Moses and to study the *Guide of the Perplexed*.' He found the book most constructive especially as it attacked the theory of the eternity of the Universe. 'And although there are very serious remarks in his works to deny the veracity of our religion, we should not worry too much as he declares [openly] that he is a Jew.' This sounds like some *arenga* of a papal bull and is followed by: 'And now hear you all the nations a declaration from the pope and all the bishops: he who contra-

[96] 'A Letter to R. David the Grandson of Maimonides', publ. A. E. Harkavy in *Hakedem: Vierteljahrschrift für die Kunde des alten Orients und die Wissenschaft des Judentums* 3 (1912), 111–14. Cf. Mann, *Texts*, i. 422. All following quotations are from this letter. As to the alleged quotation from a papal bull, cf. the encyclical of Honorius IV, 25 May 1285, announcing his election after the death of Martin V: 'Sicut fuerit voluntas in coelo, sic fiat; exemplari doctrina vocatum ad regendum Ecclesiam, dirigendam et protegendam tanquam Salvatoris vicarium in summi Pontificatus apice, populi christiani salutem instruens et informans, ut instar ipsius pericula regendi gregis abhorreat, in occurrendo illis sua non metuat.' Baronius, *Annales Ecclesiastici* xxii (1880), 555.

dicts our saying and does not follow our command . . . will pay a fine of a hundred silver coins to the court of the bishop. Because he who criticizes the *Guide of the Perplexed* or prevents its study openly or by hidden means will be punished by the above fine.'

Although the dating is conjectural because only the day and month are indicated, this seems to fit the chronology of events. The papal intervention probably corresponds to the time of Martin V (1281–85) who at that time actually resided in Rome. The letter goes on to say that Solomon and his followers tried to revive the ecclesiastical prohibitions of some fifty years earlier (1232) but failed. The papal intervention, we are told, was instigated by two Jewish notables from Rome, both supporters of Maimonides, R. Isaiah and R. Meir, who paid 100 gold coins from their own pocket. R. Isaiah seems to have been a friend of the Kabbalist Abraham Abulafia and like him an admirer of Maimonides.[97] It is impossible to say how much confidence should be placed in this information which was contained in a letter to the Nagid R. David Maimuni recommending one Abraham ibn Tayyeb to him, although the writer protests the absolute veracity of his information. The fact that during this attack on Maimonides we do not hear of any church intervention could have been as much the result of a timely Jewish intervention or new intellectual currents in the Christian world.[98]

The question of chronology is a very complicated one. In the later correspondence we find the date 5050 (that is, 1290) as the date of the outbreak of the debate and following it the excommunication of the exilarch of Damascus,[99] but the text

[97] He is mentioned by Abraham Abulafia in an autobiographical fragment in *Oṣar Eden* (Treasure of Eden), publ. A. Jellineck, *Beth ha-Midrash*, iii (Jerusalem 1938), p. lxi. Having reached Acre he went and studied in Capua, where he had a small number of pupils, and 'taught in Rome to two city notables R. Isaiah and R. Zadaqia my allies of blessed memory'. The identification and dating were proposed by B. Dinur (above, n. 95), 271.

[98] So in the first letter of Hillel of Verona to Maestro Gajo, he indicates that he wanted to bring Solomon le Petit 'before the scholars of Israel and the scholars of the Gentiles to let him prove what kind of heresy he found in the writings of Maimon'. On the letter, see p. 18 in source cited below, n. 106.

[99] See the defence of Maimonides by Shem Tov b. Joseph Falaquera, publ. in the appendix to *Minehạt Kanaōth* (Pressburg 1838), 182–5. As to the author, see I. B. De Rossi, *Codices hebraici* (Parma 1803), cod. 142, 92–3.

of the exilarch's excommunication bears the date Tammūz 5046, or summer of 1286.[100] The excommunication by the exilarch of Mosul in Iyyar 1599 of the Seleucid era, corresponds to spring 1288,[101] and finally we have the excommunication of R. Samuel Hakkohen, the Head of the Academy of Baghdad, as Tishrei 1600 of the Seleucid era, that is, 1289.[102] Clearly, the great debate raged in the period between 1286 and 1289, although I would suggest a slightly earlier date for the beginning of the events, say 1284,[103] when R. Solomon Petit came out openly against Maimonides (though we do not know if he also attacked the halakhic works of the great teacher), and came to an end in 1291.

At the time of the dispute, Jewish Acre was split by internal strife; because of the heterogeneous ethnic origins of the population news spread rapidly far and wide, reaching first the communities of the East. The exilarch of Damascus, Jesse b. Hezekiah, whose family boasted a prodigious genealogy,[104] issued a series of public letters warning against any doings which might attack Maimonides. The warning was not restricted to Acre or to the Holy Land, but was sent to other communities—neighbouring ones like Babylon and Egypt and also, clearly, to Europe. The exilarch's letters must have had a great impact and a number of European scholars including some in Northern France and Germany 'gave their signatures', meaning that they gave their consent to the warning.[105]

As the situation in Acre was apparently none too favourable to the anti-Maimonides faction, R. Solomon decided on a propaganda tour to Europe. He went to the 'far-away islands of the sea' (meaning, he crossed the sea to far-away lands) and brought 'signatures' of scholars supporting the anti-Maimonides position. The exilarch did not actually see the letters

[100] The excommunication by Jesse b. Hezekiah, exilarch of Damascus, was followed by that of the community of Safad publ. in *Kerem Chemed* 3, ed. S. H. Goldenberg (Prague 1838), 169–73.

[101] Publ. S. Z. H. Halberstam in *Jeschurun* vii (Bamberg 1871), ed. J. Kobak, 69–76 and again in *Ginse* [*Ginzei*] *Nistaroth*, iii, ed. J. Kobak, (1872), 113–23.

[102] Halbestam, *Jeschurun* vii. 76–7.

[103] Dinur (above, n. 95), 45, 271, suggested 1284–85 as the date of the outbreak of the dispute.

[104] See Poznanski (above, n. 54, 123–4 and n. 1). Cf. also Mann, ii. 359 and n. 4.

[105] All the details are known from the letter of the exilarch (above, n. 100).

brought from Europe—he says that R. Solomon had 'writings with the signatures of rabbis therein according to him'—but their contents were clear. 'They promulgated a decision to prohibit the reading of the *Guide of the Perplexed* and to conceal it for eternity.' The exilarch's anger rose on seeing that some of the signatories were the same as those who had earlier agreed with him when he sent his own circular letter of warning and 'they signed their names in the letters purporting to excommunicate and anathematize whoever may attack the *gaon* Rabbenu Moses of blessed memory or any of his books and we have [their letters] with us'.

It must have been during this propaganda tour that R. Solomon travelled through Italy. A scholar of standing, R. Hillel b. Samuel of Forli, known as Hillel of Verona (actually his grandfather Eleazar lived in Verona), author of a philosophical treatise *Tagmulei ha-Nefesh* (The rewards of the soul), heard that R. Solomon had come from Germany to Ferrara and hence to Acre.[106] Only later did Hillel learn that Solomon 'made the scholars of Ashkenaz sign letters which disparaged the teachings of Rabbenu Moses and especially the *Guide of the Perplexed* and to condemn them to destruction'. Had he known the truth, he said, he would have followed Solomon even to Ancona to bring him before Jewish and Christian scholars and destroy the letters of condemnation; he was now anxious to be assured that Solomon found neither followers nor support in Rome.

It must have been on the return journey from Germany through Italy that the events of the papal court described above took place. It would therefore seem that the date can be established as the summer of 1284 or the summer of 1285, that is during the pontificate of Martin V. Though unsuccessful in obtaining ecclesiastical intervention in Rome, R. Solomon came back to Acre with substantial backing from Ashkenazi scholars and issued a prohibition on the philosophical writings of Maimonides.[107] Jesse b. Hezekiah the exilarch of Damascus, retaliated in the summer of 1286 by excommunicating all those

[106] See two letters of R. Hillel of Verona to his friend R. Isaac b. Mordecai, physician to Pope Nicholas IV, known as Maestro Gajo, in Rome, publ. by Z. H. Edelman, *Chemda Genuza* (Königsberg 1856), 18–21, 21–2. Printed also by A. Ashkenazi in *Ta'am Zekenim* (Frankfurt 1865). Cf. I. Elbogen, 'Hillel da Verona e la lutta par Mose Maimonide', *Annuario di studi ebraici*, 1935–7 (Roma 1938), 99–105.

[107] Edelman, *Chemda Gnuza*, 18.

opposing the study of Maimonides' books. He also excommunicated all those who had possessed texts of the anti-Maimonides prohibition, unless they handed them over to R. David Maimuni, or to the 'ten notables of the city' to be burned. The situation must have been critical—or was it in retaliation for Solomon's appeals to the Roman curia that the exilarch went so far as to invoke 'the authorities of the gentiles of the world'?[108] Although the exilarchs of that period enjoyed little influence or power, the name still bore the prestige of centuries.[109] It was soon after, in the summer or autumn of 1286, that the proclamation of the exilarch of Damascus reached the Holy Land and even Italy.[110] We do not know the scale of the reaction; what has survived is the very solemn excommunication by the community of Safed. This was done 'with some of the scholars of Acre'—some but not all—on the traditional tomb of Maimonides, presumably in Tiberias,[111] and decided by the rabbinical court of the community.

The dispute did not abate. In Iyyar 1289 the exilarch of Mosul, David b. Daniel entered the fray by excommunicating the opponents of Maimonides. The text of the excommunication[112] begins with a rather pompous *intitulatio* listing his genealogy through the last seven generations. 'We have heard', he writes, 'that a man by the name of R. Solomon b. Samuel has arisen in Acre and attacked and ridiculed the teachings of the great light, our teacher and master Moses b. Maimon, let him rest in peace, in the *Guide of the Perplexed*, because he understands nothing of it'. Solomon b. Rabbi Samuel seeks

[108] Text of excommunication (above, n. 100).

[109] The exilarch ends his letter of excommunication with an exegesis on 1 Chr. 28: 1: '"Hear me brethren and my people"—if you obey me—you are my brethren and my blessing be upon you; if not you are my people, and I will rule you by the rod.' Cf. Abraham Maimuni about the exilarchs, above n. 53.

[110] The heads of the community of Safad say that they received the text of the excommunication of the Exilarch (*Kerem Chemed* (above, n. 100) 3. 172). In the second letter of Hillel of Verona (above, n. 106), 21, the excommunications from Damascus and Mosul are mentioned as contained in the letter of Maestro Gajo from Rome.

[111] See the text of the excommunication in *Kerem Chemed* (above, n. 100) 3, 172 ff. It is signed by: 'Moses Hakkohen the son of the great Rav our R. Judah Hakkohen of blessed memory, ʿObadya b. Samuel who agreed with the consenters; and I Elʿazar b. R. Tamīm did likewise; Isaac b. R. Solomon the Proselyte (*ha-ger*).' One of the MS Bodl. 2218 has 'city' instead of 'Acre' and Edelman has argued that this may refer rather to Tiberias. Cf. Strauss (above, n. 95), 132 n. 31.

[112] Published by S. Z. Halberstam in *Jeschurun* vii, 69–76.

power, he says, and consequently 'let [him] be cursed by the God of Israel and let him be the anathema of the God of the hosts'. In the strongest possible language, Solomon and his followers are cast out from the community. The memory of the events of Montpellier two generations earlier, or the more recent attempts of R. Solomon in Rome, seem to have prompted an anathema 'on all those who are delators or complain before the gentiles of the world to hide for posterity any of the treatises written by . . . Maimonides or to prohibit their study'. Nobody is allowed to absolve a man from this anathema except for the exilarch himself and David Maimuni, on whom he bestowed this privilege. In the latter case the penitent had to make a pilgrimage to the tomb of Maimonides, and in the presence of ten people, remove his shawl (*miṣnefeth*) from his neck and confess his sin saying: 'I sinned and I acted distortedly against the God of Israel and the memory of Moses b. Maimon of blessed memory'; and the ten will say 'you are absolved'. This act of confession and absolution was to be recorded in writing and sent to David Maimuni who would grant the final absolution.

On 30 Tishrei 1288 R. Samuel Hakkohen b. David, the head of the Academy of the Diaspora in Baghdad informed David Maimuni that he and his two sons, Ḥananel and Aaron, anathematized together with all the scholars of Babylon anybody who kept letters against Maimonides.[113]

By then the whole Jewish world was in uproar. The number of conflicting treatises and signatures of consent must have been prodigious but they have not come down to us. Among those lost, by an irony of history, is the excommunication of R. Solomon Petit by his scholar opponents, probably headed by David Maimuni, in Acre. From afar we have the testimony of the physician and philosopher Shem Tov. b. Joseph ibn Falaquera, who lived somewhere in Spain or southern France, who mentions the attack on Maimonides' book in 5050 (that is, 1290) by 'some of the Frenchmen', and that the exilarch of Damascus excommunicated them 'he and his court and all the communities of the Holy Land and of Acre . . . and the writings were sent to Barcelona and from there to us'.[114]

[113] Ibid. 76–7. [114] Appendix to *Mineḥat Kanaōth* (Pressburg 1838), 182–5.

Ibn Falaquera is probably referring to letters sent to Spain to the great luminary of the late thirteenth century, R. Solomon b. Aderet (Rashba). Answering a query of R. Solomon Abba Mari, Rashba mentions the controversy and that he was requested to intervene.[115] The letters contained almost a hundred signatures of those 'who wrote to me and this included a number of communities, who wrote openly and not in hiding ... even those who signed the first writing [in defence of Maimonides] apologized and I will not disclose their names.' As to his own stand, he is a great admirer of Maimonides, although opposed to his 'Greek wisdom'. He never intervened, as it was alleged, in France, and according to him, they certainly did not need his advice. There is nothing new in the material sent to him by Abba Mari 'because during the quarrel which was in Acre because of the *Guide* between the Nagid and his community (*ʿedah*) and the Rav R. Solomon Petit and his followers (*siʿah*) all of it was sent to me by the *nagid* Rabbi Levy [*sic*!][116] of blessed memory and all the signatures, and that of the other sect (*kat*) sent to me all their writings'. He answered the *nagid* and he answered the quest of the others. Unfortunately Rashba does not spell out what he suggested, but we may assume that he proposed to limit the study of some parts of the *Guide of the Perplexed*.[117] Thus, he claims, he established peace among the quarrelling parties. But peace was neither established nor imposed in Acre or anywhere else. Judaism, however, was never a monolithic or dogmatic religion—it was broad enough to find a place for an uneasy peace between the contending views.

Around September 1290, David Maimuni left Acre and took up his position again as the *nagid* in Egypt. This probably contributed to the abatement of the dispute. In any case, the days of the great Crusader centre were numbered. On 2 April 1291 the city came under siege by Sultan al-Malik al-Ashraf Kẖalil, and after forty days of fighting the city fell (18 May 1291). A general massacre ensued, and the Jewish inhabitants

[115] Published by Ad. Neubauer, 'Ergänzungen und Verbesserungen zu Abba Mari's Minhat Kanaut aus Handschriften', *Israelitische Letterbode* 4 (1878–9), 125–32.

[116] The text is rather obscure, but this seems to be the meaning. The answer was written after 1300 as the *nagid* is mentioned as deceased. B. Dinur (above, n. 95, p. 237) emends the text to mean that letters went out from the *nagid* and R. Levy who was allegedly one of the scholars of Acre.

[117] B. Dinur (above n. 95) 282 n. 51.

of the city were put to the sword with the rest of the population. Some, but probably very few, escaped, like R. Isaac of Acre who finally arrived in Spain.[118] Later he was to recall the burning of the synagogue in the city. Others were taken as captives to Egypt.[119] It is here that R. Joseph Yerūshalmi wrote a dirge on the fall of the city and an elegy on the death of his father, the grammarian Tanḥūm Yerūshalmi, who at one time lived in the Holy Land.[120] His son linked the news of the fall of the city and the death of his father's friends there as the cause which precipitated his decease. And so he noted in the heading: 'And his father died in Cairo on a Wednesday, the twenty-first of Tammūz in the year 5051 of Creation [i.e. 20 June 1291] . . . and this happened a few days after the arrival of the news about the massacre of the scholars and the destruction of their homes when the Ishmaelites captured the city.'[121] 'This was', he says, 'to all who heard about it a tragedy as terrible as the day of the ruin of Jerusalem'. The implications were spelt out by a late Jewish chronicler, Abraham Zacuto,[122] in his *opus magnum* on Jewish scholarship, the *Sefer Yuḥasīn* (Book of genealogies): 'Acre was ruined in the year 5050 (i.e., 1291) and the Just of Israel were killed therein in the four manners of death.'[123]

[118] R. Isaac of Acre was in Navarra. Cf. corrected text of the *Sefer Yūḥasin* as preserved in MS Bodl. 2202. See B. Z. Kedar in *Tarbiz* (H), 53 (1984), 405 and n. 72. The text is based on the lost *Sefer Divrei ha-Yamīm* (History) of R. Isaac of Acre. The latter noted the destruction of the synagogue in his Kabbalistic *Oṣar Ḥayim* (ibid. 406).

[119] Mentioned later by a Christian pilgrim. Cf. R. Röhricht, 'Ein niederrheinischer Bericht über den Orient', *Zeitschrift für deutsche Philologie* 19 (1886), 47.

[120] As already mentioned, the *cognomen* Yerūshalmi often denotes an inhabitant not of Jerusalem but of the Holy Land in general. On R. Tanḥūm, H. Shy wrote a thesis at the Hebrew University; see her short abstract 'Tanḥūm ha-Yerūshalmi: a Thirteenth-century Lexicographer and Biblical Exegete' (H), in *Jerusalem in the Middle Ages: Selected Papers*, ed. B. Z. Kedar and Z. Baras (Jerusalem 1979), 188–90.

[121] 'Elegies on Persecutions in Eretz Israel, Africa, Spain, Germany, and France' (H) ed. H. Shirman in *Qoveṣ 'al Yad* (Jerusalem, 1940), 62–4. Cf. Mann, *Texts* i. 436–7. Some facts emerge from under the heavy layer of rhetoric: the death of the scholars deprived the nation of a fountain of learning, people were killed in the prayer house, women who had learned Hebrew since birth (i.e. women with an excellent education) were taken captive.

[122] Abraham Zacuto produced the improved astronomical tables used by Columbus. Expelled from Spain, Zacuto served for a time at the court of John II of Portugal. Expelled again, he went to Tunis and then to Jerusalem and died in Damascus in 1515.

[123] [*Liber Jochassin*] *Sefer Yūḥasin*, ed. H. Filipowski, 88. He refers to the four modes of death imposed by the judgment of a court: stoning, burning, strangulation, and being put to the sword.

Epilogue

THE two-hundred-year Crusader domination came to an end at the time that major changes were taking place in the Near East. The most spectacular and important was the rise and establishment of the Mameluke power which for the next two hundred years was to dominate the destinies of the Levant.

The Christian episode was over, and the eastern coast of the Levant was once again cut off from Europe. True, the Mediterranean Sea remained open for trade and communication, but the European attempt to gain a foothold in the Levant had failed. For many long decades, however, there was fear of a new Crusade. The Mameluke rulers following the example started by Saladin and continued by some of his successors, embarked on a policy of laying waste the coastal cities, the possible disembarkation points of any new Crusade. The planning of Crusades, however, very seldom envisaged such disembarkation. Christian Europe had in mind a direct strike on the seat of power, on Egypt. Nevertheless, the fear of a Crusade seems to have had a traumatic effect on the Mamelukes.

Almost every city, from the castle of Darom in the south up to Antioch in Syria in the north, saw its fortifications razed and its population abandoning the coast. The main centres of population therefore now shifted to the mountainous regions of the interior.

The fate of the Jewish community followed the major changes in the pattern of settlement. Jewish communities still clung to Gaza in the south at the end of the caravan route which led from Egypt through Sinai to Palestine, but with this exception the Jewish communities were now to be found on the mountain ridge, from Hebron and Jerusalem in the south to Safad and Tiberias in the north. Slowly new communities were to emerge—like Safad which was to become an important centre of scribes in the fourteenth century. This obviously points to the existence of a population, and a wealthy one, for whom such copyists were working. New centres also appeared at this time in such other places as Bethsan in the Jordan Valley.

Pilgrimage and settlement were to continue throughout the fourteenth century, mainly from Spain and Italy, with a smaller trickle from Germany. A new nucleus of Jewish population came into being, the *musta'arabi*—those who spoke Arabic, the language of the country, as distinct from the European newcomers. None the less, the great revival of the Jewish communities was to be linked with the major migrations of Spanish Jewry that began at the end of the fourteenth century and were intensified over the next 150 years, that is, to the threshold of modern times and the rise of the Ottoman Empire.

Index

Aaron b. Meir 3n.
Aaron Halevy 54
'Abbasids 2, 4, 7, 35
Abī al-Kír Mubārakh 31
Abraham Abulafia 278–80, 285, *Book of Precepts* 279
Abraham al-Constantīnī 139, 140, 202
Abraham b. David of Posquière 151, 267
Abraham b. Solomon, the Yemenite 75
Abraham Ḥiyya 48; *Sefer Megillat ha-Megalleh* 48
Abraham ibn Abū Rabic'ah 280
Abraham ibn 'Ezra 141
Abraham ibn Tayyeb 235
Abraham Maimuni (son of Maimonides) 78, 79, 84, 86–7, 113, 114, 115, 120, 252, 265, 266n., 267n., 268–9, 270, 271–72, 280; *Wars of the Lord* 87, 268–9
Abraham of Tyre, *rosh ha-qahal* 52
Abraham, patriarch 23n., 25n.; well 213; *see also* Hebron
Abraham the dyer (of Jerusalem) 123
Abraham the Visionary (*ha-hōze*) 58, 117
Abraham Zacuto 291; *Sefer Yuḥasīn* 291
Abū al-Bahā b. Janāīm 50
Abū al-Fadl Sahl b. Jōsh'a b. Sha'aya 28, 29
Abū'l-Faraj 81
Abū Ḥureira, tomb 171
Abū al-Ḥuseīn b. Abū al- Kīr 58
Abū Sa'ad 31
Abū Sa'id al-Kutnāni 72
Abū Yūssuf Ya'aqūb al-Mansụr 73
Abū Zikrī 74n., 82–4
Abydos 12, 13
Abyssinians 28n.
Acco *see* Acre
Achard of Arrouaise 47, 48; *Tractatus super Templo Salomonis* 47–8
Acre 29, 34, 35, 42, 51, 58, 60, 61, 62, 65n., 66, 77, 79, 80, 83, 84, 85, 88, 91, 92, 95, 97, 103, 104n., 105, 106n., 113, 114, 116, 118, 119, 121, 124, 125, 142, 155, 156, 159, 161, 171, 181, 185, 195, 199, 215, 226, 231, 234, 235, 236, 237, 242, 244, 247–8, 249, 253, 254, 257, 258–92
  academies 106n., 121, 189, 231, 232
  'academy of Paris' 275–6
  cemeteries 248, 261
  churches: Mary Magdalen 263
    Convent of St John 263
    St George 263
    St Sergius 263
  fall of (1291) 291–2
  immigration to 103, 266–7, 273–4, 276
  Mount Musard 95, 103, 260, 262, 263
  pilgrimages to 188–9, 264–6
  ruga Judeaorum 103, 262–3
  tomb of Eleazar the Hasmonean 188
  upper and lower markets 261
  Venetian Quarter 103, 262
  Taqqanōth Ḥakhmei Acco 270–1, 273

Aden 193
Aegean islands 103, 193
al-Afdal, vizier 17, 26 n., 32, 41
al-Afdal 'Ali, Saladin's son 73, 83
Agnes of Scandalion 197
Aharon, tomb 250
'Ain al-Daulah Abī 'Aqil, ruler of Tyre 1 n.
'Ain-Jalūd 279
'Ain al-Zeitūn 56, 232, 244
Ajlun (Eglon) 250
'Akhbara 182, 232, 244
al-'Alawiya 56
Albert of Aix 25 n., 36, 40, 41, 43 n., 60 n.
Aleppo 44
Alexandria 26, 27, 28, 32, 61, 66, 74, 75, 79, 85, 87, 113, 125, 137, 216, 229, 270
'Alma 56, 117, 121, 197, 206, 220, 224, 232, 244
Amalric, count of Jaffa-Ascalon 108
Amalric (notary in Marseilles) 125
'Amūqa 55, 182, 185, 186, 220, 221, 224, 232, 244; tomb of Jonathan b. 'Uziel 186, 221
Anatoli b. Joseph of Lunel 52 n., 85, 88
Anna Comnena 22
Antioch 31, 33, 116, 193, 292
Apocalypse, Christian 9–10, 154, 161 n.; Jewish 6–7, 110, 222–3, 258–9; Muslim 11 n., 154; *see also* Messianism
Apulia 24, 31
al-Aqṣā Mosque *see* Jerusalem
Aragon 11
Arbel 181, 213, 215, 221, 225, 232, 244; synagogue of Nathai of Arbel 221; tomb of Dinah 225; tomb of Sheth b. Enosh 225
Armenia *see* Cilicia
Armenians 8, 99, 102, 200; *see also* Oriental Christians
Arnon River 206
'Arraba ('Araba) 182, 224, 244
al-As'ad 82
Ascalon 16, 26, 27, 28, 29, 30, 31, 33, 34, 42, 43, 46, 49, 50, 51, 60, 69, 70, 71, 72, 80, 92, 93, 116, 117, 185, 191, 196, 205; Jewish community 9, 14 n., 49–51, 70–1; Samaritan community 51, 117; Well of Abraham 187
Ascandranis, family from Barcelona 125
Ashdod (*Castellum Beroardi*) 185, 205, 249
Asher b. Yehiel (Rosh) 161 n., 245 n.
al-Ashraf Khalil, sultan 291
assises 95, 96, 106
Assuan 193
al-Athīmī 23
Atsiz, Seljuk commander 6, 8
Augustine St 25 n.
'Avarta 232, 238, 242
Ayalon, Valley (Val de Luna) 195–6, 200
Ayyūbids 81, 82, 85, 110, 128, 217, 251, 269
'Azata 185
'Azeiqa 185, 186
al-'Azīz, al-Malik 83

Baalbek 250
Bāb al Khalīl *see* Jerusalem, Jaffa Gate
Babylon, Jewish academies 2, 3, 111, 137, 177; *see also* Pumbedita; Sura
Badr al-Jamāli, Egyptian vizier 1 n., 35
Baghdad 1, 3, 4, 113, 193, 214, 215, 217, 283; academy of 207, 209, 289
Baibars, Muslim chronicler 90
Baibars, sultan 158
Baldric of Dol 24, 25, 40 n.
Baldwin I, king of Jerusalem 29, 30 n., 42, 47, 60
Baldwin II, king of Jerusalem 47 n.

Baldwin III, king of Jerusalem 107; *assise* of 50–1, 96n., 106
Banū Jarrah, bedouin tribe 15
Banyas (Pamyas, Paneas, Dan) 11n., 56, 85, 170, 182, 197, 206, 211, 214, 220, 226, 232; tomb of Iddo 184; altar of Jeroboam 206
Bar'am 182, 220, 221, 226, 232, 244; synagogue of Simeon b. Yohai 221, 244; tomb of Nahman Hatūfā 224; tombs of Queen Esther, Pinhas b. Yair, and Obadiah 226
Barak b. Avinoam, tomb 224
Barbastro 11
Barcelona 125, 126, 155, 272, 273
Bar Hebraeus 66
Bar Kokhba 49
Barqa 205
Baruk b. Isaac of Aleppo 44
Baruk b. Isaac of Worms 147; pilgrimage of 147n.; *Sefer ha-Terūmah* 147
Basra 193
Bat Galim *see* Haifa
bedouins 1, 81, 102
Beeroth *see* Bira, al-
Beirut 42–3, 62, 92, 116, 195, 198, 199, 226, 234, 235, 236, 248, 249
Beit Govrin *see* Beit Jibrin
Beit Jibrin 62, 196, 198, 203
Beit Nubā (Bethnoble, Nob) 62, 185, 186, 196, 204, 226
Belvoir 64
Benaciat b. Bonfils Destour (de Turribus) 125
Benedict of Peterborough 59, 60
Benjamin of Tudela 48, 51, 52, 56n., 58, 61, 62, 63, 105, 106, 116, 117, 122, 123, 124, 138, 139, 140, 171, 181, 218, 223, 242, 249, 256, 258; itinerary of 191–206
Bernard of Clairvaux 145, 146
Bernard of Narbonne 125
Bertrand of Tripoli 43n.
Bethel 219
Bethlehem 62, 131n., 180, 185, 186, 197, 203, 209, 218, 223, 233, 242
Bethnoble *see* Beit Nubā
Bethsan 122n., 195, 219, 224, 226, 293
Bilbais 14, 26, 50, 53, 71, 72, 74, 81, 82, 84, 85, 86, 90, 229; Ascalonites in 71
al-Birah 196, 197, 200, 204, 219, 238
Bīrya 56
Bnei Braq 205
Bohemia 207, 266
Bohemond III 102
Bohemond le Baube 199
Bonastruc de Porta *see* Nahmanides
Bonnat b. Bonfils 125
Bōtrūs ibn al-Rāhab 23
Bridge of the Daughters of Jacob (Jisr Banāt Ya'aqūb) 244, 250
Brittany 23, 78, 120
Burchard of Mt Sion 198, 235
Byblos *see* Jubail
Byzantine Empire 18, 35, 57, 60, 66, 68, 69, 122, 138, 154, 214, 215; Jewish communities 11–12, 13

Caesarea 15, 16n., 40n., 62, 185, 195, 199, 226; tomb of Ten Martyrs 189
Cairo 4, 8, 26, 27, 30, 32, 50, 52n., 53, 79, 80, 82, 117, 120, 272, 291; seat of Jerusalems Academy 111; *see also* Fustát
Caleb b. Jephunneh 130
Cana *see* Kfar Kana
'Capharnaum' 25, 195, 199, 225 and n.
capitatio, *see* poll tax, taxation
Carmoly, E. 227n.
Castellum Beroardi, *see* Ashdod
Castrum Cayphas, *see* Haifa

Caurole, (Caorle ? Veneto), bishop of 256
Champagne 228
Chosroes 60, 241
Church, councils: Third Lateran 104; Fourth Lateran 104; Jaffa 108
Cilicia 193, 194, 207
Clement IV, pope 155
Clermont, council 245n.
Clisson 120
Cluny 20
commenda 125
communes: in Acre 262; in Tyre 255–7; *see also* Genoa, Venice
community: autonomy 110–21; organization 116–21; ḥaber 16n.; ḥazan 16n.; *qahal* 116; rosh ha-qahal 106, 113, 114; rosh ha-gōla 3, 5, 113; *see also* Jerusalem Academy
Conrad of Montferrat 60, 254
Constantine (North Africa) 139
Constantinople 12, 193
conversion, to Christianity 254–5, 276; to Judaism 11n.
Copts 65n.
Corfu 193
Cosmas of Prague 25
Court of Burgesses 99
Court of the Market (*Cour de la Fonde*) 98, 99, 101; *see also* raīs, court of
Crimea 12n.
Crusade: First 1, 9–18, 19–45, 68, 154; 'Peasants' 11; Third 59–60, 67, 70, 75, 110, 115, 251, 254, 255, 258; Fifth 78n., 110
Cyprus 108n., 123, 125, 193, 226
Cyrus of Persia 68, 110

Daimbert, patriarch 35, 36–40
Dalātha *see* Daltōn
Daltōn (Dalātha) 56, 182, 220, 244; Holy Tombs 184
Damascus 6, 9, 22, 35, 52, 73, 78n., 80, 85, 98n., 113, 114, 117, 193, 197, 206, 209, 215, 217, 220, 221, 224, 235, 244, 249, 286, 288; seat of Jerusalem Academy 9, 111
Damietta 14, 26, 86
Damirah (Egypt) 53n.
Damsīs (Egypt) 53n.
Dan *see* Banyās
Daniel b. 'Azarya, exilarch 5
Daniel b. Solomon, exilarch 210
Dar'a 141, 250
Dardanelles 12
Darom 196, 292
David b. Daniel of Mosul, exilarch 5, 113, 115, 288
David b. Zakkai the Second of Mosul, exilarch 55
David, king, tomb of *see* Jerusalem
David Maimuni (grandson of Maimonides), *nagid* 114, 283–4, 284, 288, 289, 290, 291
dayyanim 3n., 11, 16n., 53, 54, 106, 111, 117; *see also* community
Dead Sea 62, 206, 212, 213, 215
dhimmis 2, 95; *see also* minorities
Dinah, tomb 220, 225, 227; *see also* Arbel
Dodanīm 185
Dome of the Rock *see* Jerusalem
Dominicans 155
Donin b. Jacob 231
Druzes 122, 199, 235

Ebles of Roucy 10n.
Ebyatar b. Elijah Hakkohen, *gaon* 13
Edessa 69n.
Edom 8, 48, 154, 199, 200
Efrat 186, 223; *see also* Rachel, tomb
Egypt 1, 2, 3, 5, 14, 16, 25, 26, 29, 30, 36, 37, 43, 45, 46, 50, 51, 52, 53, 58, 60, 66n., 70, 71, 78, 81, 83, 86, 87, 88, 89, 90, 91, 105, 111, 114, 115, 116,

117, 120, 124, 132, 138, 142, 148, 177, 178, 185, 186, 193, 205, 209, 216, 229, 230, 269, 283, 286, 291, 292; Karaites 27
Eileh ha-Massa'ōth 246–50
Ein Gedi 62
El'azar b. 'Arakh, tomb in Daltōn 184
El'azar b. 'Azaryah, tomb in Daltōn 184; in 'Alma 224
Eleazar the Hasmonean, tomb 188; academy of 189
Elḥanan of Dampierre 276
Eliezer b. Nathan 11
Elijah b. Solomon Hakkohen, *gaon* 56n., 184
Elijah b. Zekarya *dayyan* 81–2
Elijah of Acre 281
Elijah, prophet 12, 13; *see also* Mt Carmel
Elijah al-Raīs (b. 'Aqnīn) 72
Elijah's altar *see* Mt Carmel
Elijah's cave *see* Mt Carmel
Elonei Mamrei, *see* Mamrei Plain
Embriaci, Genoese dynasty 199
England 76, 107
Enoch 12n.
Ensisheim 153
Ephraim, tribe 141
Ephraim b. Shemarya 41n.
Ephraim Miṣri *see* Ephraim of Fusṭāt
Ephraim of Fusṭāt, *dayyan* 52, 53, 54, 117, 118; Ephraim Miṣri 52n.
Ephraim of Tyre *see* Ephraim of Fusṭāt
Epistle to Yemen, *see* Maimonides
Eschive, princess of Galilee 58
Esther, tomb 226
Li Estoire de Jérusalem et Antioch 24
Eusebius, *Onomasticon* 131n., 205
exilarch *see rosh ha-golah*
Ezekiel, prophet, tomb 210
Ezekiel Hakkohen the Galilean 59
Fāṭimids 1, 2, 3, 4, 6, 7, 9, 16, 18, 19, 20, 26n., 28, 32, 34, 35, 45, 93, 113, 169
Felix Faber 25n.
Ferrara 287
Floranza, Andalusia 150n.
France 10, 52, 69, 76, 77, 84, 86, 107, 117, 139, 148, 150, 151, 165, 191, 208, 209, 221, 228, 248, 274, 278, 282, 283, 284, 286, 290
Frederick II, emperor 90, 91, 177, 255
Fulk of Chartres 23n., 28n., 43n.
Fusṭāt 7, 8, 34n., 41n., 52, 53, 74, 85, 113, 148, 255; *see also* Cairo

Galdemar Carpenel 36, 38, 40
Galilee 3, 9, 16n., 18, 35, 36, 38, 49, 54, 55, 56, 58, 60, 64, 93, 101, 117, 121, 122, 170, 180, 181, 185, 186, 187, 196, 203, 211, 215, 217, 219, 224, 225, 232, 234, 237, 242, 247, 250, 251; communities of 54–60
gaon, head of the Jerusalem Academy 4, 5, 13, 111, 112; *see also* Jerusalem Academy; *gaon* of Tiberias
Gath 249
Gaul 36, 124
Gaza 16, 185, 186, 196, 216, 229, 249
Gebal *see* Jubail
Genizah 8n., 9, 22, 29, 43, 74, 79, 118, 131, 170, 273
Genoa 60, 103, 126, 199, 256
Georgians 200
Gerald of Sais 91
Germany 114, 138, 148, 150, 152, 162, 193, 281, 283, 284, 286, 287, 293
Gerona 277, 283
Gershom b. Joseph 86, 87, 120
Gesta Francorum 21, 28n.
Gibeah of Benjamin 238
Gibeah of Saul 204

Gibeon 200
Gilgal 212
Gilon of Toucy 20–1
Giscala *see* Gūsh Ḥalav
Godfrey of Bouillon 18, 19, 20, 21, 34, 35, 36, 38, 39, 40, 41
Gog and Magog 13 n.
Golan 36
Grand Gerin *see* Jenin
Greece 151, 193, 215, 231
Greek Orthodox 8, 65 n., 99, 102, 200, 261, 263; *see also* Oriental Christians
Guibert of Nogent 145 n., 146, 161 n., 245 n.
Guillaume Gros 125
Gūsh Ḥalav (Giscala) 55, 56, 78 n., 182, 220, 224, 232, 244
Guy of Lusignan, king of Jerusalem 60

Habakkuk, tomb of 219, 226, 232; *see also* Yaqūq
ḥaber 16 and n., 41, 111, 176; *see also* Jerusalem Academy
Ḥadrakh *see* Damascus
Hadrian, emperor 18, 46
Haggadah of the Birds 153 n.
Haggai, tomb of the prophet 241
Hai 219
Haifa 42, 181, 195, 199, 226, 236, 253; crusader conquest 35–40; Bat Galim 35, 236; cemetery 83 n., 199, 232, 253; *see also* Mt Carmel
hajj 132, 171, 210
Ḥalḥul 178, 218, 242; tomb of the prophet Nathan 218, 221; tomb of the prophet Jonah 223
Ḥanath 250
Ḥananya, head of the Academy 59
Ḥanīnā b. Horkenos, tomb 221
Ḥanīnā b. Yehuda 88; tomb in Safad 221
Hannah, mother of Samuel, tomb 186
Ḥaran 215
Har Ga'ash 185, 187, 215, 225; tombs of Joshua b. Nun and Caleb b. Jephunneh 211, 213, 225
al-Ḥarizi *see* Judah al-Ḥarizi
Ḥasidim (Ashkenaz) 149
Ḥasōr 16 and n., 43
Haute Cour 100
Hattin (Kfar Ḥiṭṭin) 181, 219, 232, 244; battle of 64, 92, 115, 254, 259; tomb of Jethro 219, 235; bucket of Miriam 244
Ḥayyim b. Ḥanael Hakkohen 147–8
ḥazanim 4, 79; *see also* Jerusalem Academy
Ḥazerim *see* Raffiah
'Head of the Diaspora' *see rosh ha-gōla*
Hebron 23, 40–2, 91, 130, 131, 170, 173, 180, 185, 196, 197, 199, 203, 211, 213, 215, 218, 222, 226, 233, 242, 279, 292; community of 40–2, 219; tombs of the patriarchs (Double Cave; Cave of *Machpelah*) 41, 130–1, 142, 177, 203, 212–13, 218, 219, 223, 242; pilgrimage to 142, 171, 173, 175, 177, 178, 185, 189, 212, 214, 217
Helbing 25
Herod 41, 224
Hillel and Shammai, tombs in Daltōn *see* Kfar Meron
Hillel b. 'Ali 26 n., 34 n.
Hillel b. Moses 114, 115
Hillel b. Samuel of Forli *see* Hillel of Verona
Hillel of Verona (Hillel b. Samuel of Forli) 272, 282 n., 285 n.
Hodaya b. Yesse, exilarch 84, 87, 88, 270
Holy Places 129, 169–250; *see also* Hebron; itineraries; Jerusalem; pilgrimages;

Tombs of the Ancestors; Tombs of the Just
Ḥoms 250
Honorius IV, pope 284n.
Hospitallers 60, 62, 102, 125, 200; *see also* military orders
Hugh of Fleuri 25
Hugh of Lusignan, king of Cyprus and Jerusalem 257

Ibelin *see* Yabneh
Ibn al-Athīr 28n., 51n., 93n.
Ibn al-Qalānisi 23
Ibn al-Yamani 83n.
Ibn Batriq (Eutyches) 60n.
Ibn Caspi *see* Joseph ibn Caspi
Ibn Faraj, son of Sa'id 263
Ibn Gabirol, Solomon 10, 141n.
Ibn Verga 75, 76, 79
Iddo, prophet, tomb of 184
Iftikhār al-Daulah 17, 19, 26, 28
immigration and settlement: Jerusalem 64–80, 149, 164; Acre 103, 266–7, 273–4, 276; opposition to 147–9; insistence upon 149–67; settlers 149–67; *see also* Acre; Jerusalem; pilgrimages
Indian Ocean 124
Innocent III, pope 254
Iraq 1, 3, 64, 115, 138, 207, 249, 250
Isaac b. Abraham of Sens 78, 79
Isaac b. Jacob ha-Lavan 208, 209
Isaac b. Mordecai 272
Isaac b. Samuel Cap 125, 126
Isaac b. Samuel the Spaniard, *dayyan* 43
Isaac b. Shem Tov 265, 272
Isaac Chelo 227n.
Isaac Luria (*Ari*) 277
Isaac of Acre 277, 279, 280, 283n., 291; *Meīrat Einayim*, 277; *Oṣar ha-Hayim*, 279
Isaac, patriarch *see* Hebron
Isaac Todros 277
Isaiah the Elder of Trani 264–5 *Psaq̄m* 264
Ishtori ha-Parḥi 204n., 276; *Kaftor va-Pheraḥ* 56n., 122, 131n., 135n., 150
Iskanderūna *see* Scandalion
Italy 46, 124, 138, 193, 282, 283, 287, 288, 293
Itineraries 130, 137, 140–1, 143, 169–250; general features 169–76; treatises: *Sefor Qabbalath Sạdiqei Eretz Israel* 176–84; itinery of Jacob b. Nathaniel 185–91; of Petaḥyah of Regensburg 206–15; of Samuel b. Samson 215–21; of Menahem of Hebron 221–8; of Judah al-Ḥarizi 228–30; Jacob the messenger of the Yeshiva of Acre 230–32; anonymous pupil of Nahṃanides (*Tōṣōth Eretz Israel* and *Eileh ha-Massa'oth*) 233–44

Jabalah 195, 199
Jacob b. Nathanel 58, 141; itinerary of 185–91
Jacob b. Samson of Sens 254, 273
Jacob of Segura 254; ident. with Jacob of Zagora (Zigura, Zigora) 273n.
Jacob ha-Ḥasid of Lunel 140
Jacob ha-Nazīr (the Hermit) 278
Jacob, patriarch 175; *see also* Hebron
Jacob the Messenger of Acre 275n.; itinerary of 231–3
Jacobites 96, 99, 200, 261, 263; *see also* Oriental Christians
Jaffa 34, 35, 195, 196, 197, 198, 205, 226, 235, 237; community 15–16; council of 108
James I of Aragon 155
James of Vitry 109
Jaujār (Egypt) 53n.
Jenin (Grand Gerin) 205, 237

Jericho 186, 250
Jeroboam, altar of 206; *see also* Banyās
Jerusalem 1, 2, 3, 4, 5, 6, 8, 9, 16, 17–18, 19–26, 27, 28, 29, 30, 31, 32, 33, 34, 42, 44, 46, 47, 48, 51, 63, 64, 66, 67, 68, 69, 70, 71, 72, 73, 74, 75, 78, 79, 80, 81, 82, 83, 84, 85, 86, 88, 89, 90, 91, 94, 97, 111, 115, 116, 117, 118, 123, 128, 129, 131, 132, 133, 134, 135, 138, 139, 140, 141, 142, 143, 145, 149, 150, 154, 156, 159, 169, 180, 182, 185, 186, 187, 190, 191, 195, 196, 197, 200, 201, 201–3, 209, 211, 213–14, 216, 217, 218, 220, 223, 227, 228, 229, 230, 232, 235, 237, 238, 240, 241, 247, 248, 251, 252, 253, 266, 267, 276, 292; crusader conquest (1099) 17–26; massacre 22–6, 30–1; Jewish Quarter (*Juiverie, Judearia*) 17–18, 21–2, 49, 65n.; *Samaritike* (Samaritan Quarter) 18; Christian Quarter 18; community: of Ascalon 69–71, 73, 75, 80, 117, 150; of France 69, 72, 75, 78, 82, 84, 86, 118, 150; of Maghreb 69, 71, 72, 73, 75, 150; of Yemen 73–5; of Egypt 18, 30, 72, 80–4, 138, 150; Karaites in 14, 18, 27, 28, 29, 51, 135, 138–9; Samaritans in 18; pilgrimages 132, 135, 138, 141, 142, 143, 172–3; Citadel (Tower of David) 19, 22, 23, 48, 123, 217, 240; Mt Zion 19, 139, 177, 180, 202, 223, 240; Mt of Olives 132n., 133, 172, 180, 213, 218, 220, 230, 238, 240; Temple Mount 22, 47, 91, 132, 133, 141, 143, 177, 180, 212–4, 217, 230, 238, 240, 247; Dome of the Rock (*Templum Domini*) 24, 47, 48, 143, 172, 201, 209, 240; al-Aqṣa (*Templum Solomonis*) 18, 177, 180, 200, 241n.; Western Wall (Wailing Wall) 201, 218, 223, 238; Stables of Solomon 201; Dome of the Chain 241n.; Temple of David 239; Tomb of David 130n., 139n., 141, 173, 202, 240; Tomb of Solomon 202; Tombs of the Kings 130n., 139n., 141, 173, 177, 202, 223, 233, 240; Tombs of the Prophets 141, 241; tomb of Absalom and Zacharia 180, 223, 240; Cave of the Lion 241; *Birket Banī Isrāīl* 201; Pool of Mamillah 241; Pool of Siloam 185, 202, 218, 238, 247; Brook of Kidron 201; Valley of Josaphat 180, 190, 201, 223; Valley of the sun of Hinnom 209, 238, 240; gates: David's (Jaffa) 19, 23n., 217; Zion Gate 22n., 91; Damascus Gate 18, 91; Josaphat 18, 201, 238; of the Chain 218; of Mercy (Golden Gate) 200, 201, 214, 223; churches: Holy Sepulchre 22n., 62, 190, 201, 209; St Mary in Valley of Josaphat 22n.; St Mary Magdalen 22n.; Hospital 209
Jerusalem Academy 2n., 3, 4–5, 13, 16, 17–18, 33, 111, 116, 117, 120, 176, 271; hierarchy 4–5; court 5; *haber* 16 and n., 41, 111, 176; *gaon* 4, 5, 13, 111; *semīkha* 271; right to fix calendar 2n., 3n.
Jesse b. Hezekiah, exilarch 97n., 113, 114, 286, 288
Jethro, tomb of *see* Hattin
Jezreel, Valley of 195, 237

al-jihād 146, 154
Jisr Banāt Ya'aqūb, *see* Bridge of the Daughters of Jacob
jizya, *see* poll tax
Joachimists 280
Jochebet, Moses' mother, tomb of *see* Mt Carmel
John of Brienne, king of Jerusalem 217, 255n., 264
John of Würzburg 62, 241
Jonah of Gerona 272, 273
Jonah, prophet 175, 211, 223; *see also* Ḥalḥul, Kfar Kana
Jonathan b. David Hakkohen of Lunel 76, 77, 217, 221
Jonathan b. 'Uziel, tomb in Amūqa 186, 221; in Daltōn 184
Jordan, River 205, 206, 214, 220, 224, 244
Joscelin of Scandalion 126
Joscius, archbishop of Tyre 254
Jose demin Yōqrat, tomb 224
Joseph, tomb 188, 219; *see also* Nablus
Joseph b. Baruk of Clisson 79–80, 267
Joseph b. Gershon Ṣarfatī 84, 87, 113, 270, 271
Joseph b. Nathanel 78
Joseph b. Solomon (of Safad) 279
Joseph b. Yeḥiel (Sire Délicieux) 274–5
Joseph ibn Caspi (Joseph of Argentière) 165–6; *Tam ha-Kesef* 165–6
Joseph Jerūshalmi 291
Joseph of Burgundy 254, 273 and n.
Joseph of Saintes (Soissons) 273 and n.
Joseph of Sens 281
Josephus Flavius 200
Joshiah b. Aaron 29
Joshua b. 'Ali 16
Joshua b. Nun 211, 212; *see also* Gilgal; Har Ga'ash; Timnath Seraḥ
Joshua b. Solomon 90
Jubail (Gebal, Byblos) 116, 195, 250, 281
Judaea 17, 49, 54, 170, 242
Judah *see also* Yehuda
Judah b. Aaron al-'Ammāni 79n., 89n.
Judah b. Nehōrai 58
Judah Halevy 52n., 141n., 143–6; tomb 206
Judah Hanassi 58, 140n., 205, 211, 278; tomb *see* Zippori
Judah al-Ḥarizi 48, 55n., 67, 68, 69, 72, 73, 75, 78, 79, 88, 110, 117, 134, 149, 225n., 228–30, 269; *Taḥkemoni* 67–8, 228–30; journey in the Holy Land 228–30
Judah ha-Ḥasid 208
Judas Iscariot 24, 25
judi 35
Jund Filastin 15
Justinian, emperor 106

Kabbalah 120, 139, 140; Kabbalists in Acre 277–80
Kabrī 52n.
Kadesh Naphtali 182, 197, 206, 224
Kaftor va-Pheraḥ, *see* Eshtori ha-Parḥi
al-Kāmil, al-Malik 90, 91, 177
Karaites 11n., 14, 18, 27, 28, 29, 30, 33n., 51, 135, 138–9, 172
Ke'īlah 199
Kfar Amūqa *see* Amūqa
Kfar 'Anan (Ḥananya) 56, 182, 185, 186, 219, 224, 232, 237, 244
Kfar Bar'am *see* Bar'am
Kfar Ḥananya *see* Kfar 'Anan
Kfar Ḥiṭṭin, *see* Hattin
Kfar Kana (Cana) 185, 211, 215, 244; tomb of prophet Jonah or sons of Jacob 175, 211
Kfar Manddi 244
Kfar Meron 55, 182, 185, 186, 196, 197, 211, 220, 224, 244;

Kfar Meron—*contd*
tombs of Hillel and Shammai 186, 187, 206, 221, 232, 234, 244; tomb of Simeon bar Yoḥai 220, 221, 232, 244
Kfar Nabartā, *see* Nabartā
Kfar Naḥum *see* 'Capharnaum'
Kfar Par'am 55, 182, 220, 244
Kfar Yehuda *see* Yehudiah
Khaibar 57
Khwarezmians 91, 251
Khazaria 12, 207
Khorasan 12n.
Kinnereth (Sea of Galilee) 206
Kishon, River (*Rivière de Caiphas*) 181, 236
Kurdistan 207

Laodicea, *see* Latakiah
Latakiah 102, 116, 195, 199, 249
Latrun 62–3, 195, 196
Lebanon 1, 6, 14, 35, 182, 247, 249
Legenda Aurea 25
legislation: crusader 94–102, 106; courts 97–100; *see also assises*; minorities
'Lenon' ('Linon') 10
León 10
Leshem 184
leuca, *see* measures
Livre des assises des bourgeois 99, 100, 108, 259–60
Lo Codi 106
Luban (Lubanum) 196, 197
Lunel 76
Lydda 62, 185, 186, 195, 196, 199, 205
Lyons 10

Madon 185, 186
Maghreb 31, 70, 71, 73, 269; *see also* Morocco
Maharam *see* Meir b. Baruk of Rothenburg
Mahomerie la Grande, *see* al-Bira
Mahomerie la Petite, *see* Qubeiba
Maimonides 10, 52, 53, 54, 61, 62, 77, 97n., 105, 108, 111, 113, 114, 117, 118, 119, 122, 130, 140n., 141, 148–9, 151, 157, 217, 248, 255, 265, 278; pilgrimage of 141–3; tomb in Tiberias 175, 248, 272n.; *Guide of the Perplexed* 78, 284–5, 287, 289–90; dispute over philosophical writings 265–6, 267, 272, 281–91
Mainz 152
Mameluks 128, 258, 264, 292
Mamrei, plain of (*Elonei Mamrei*) 213, 215; well of Abraham 213; well of Sarah 213
Manduel archives 124
Maon 181
Maronites 261; *see also* Oriental Christians
Marseilles 125, 164, 192–3, 265
Marsiglio Zorzi 103n., 255
Martin V, pope 285, 288
Maṣliaḥ b. Solomon Hakkohen 111n.
measures of distance: *parsa* (parasong) 197–8, 236n.; *leuca* 198; *mil* 232
Meborak, *nagid* of Egypt 16, 26
Mecca 210
Meggido 237
Meir Aldaby 161n., 245n.
Meir b. Baruk of Clisson 78, 79, 80, 267
Meir b. Baruk of Rothenburg (Maharam) 149n., 152–3, 162–4, 282
Meir b. Todros Halevy Abulafia 267–8
Meir of Carcasonne 52, 117
Meir 'Qasin', tomb in Tiberias 182, 232
Meir 'the Strangler' 210
Menaḥem b. Elijah 12
Menaḥem b. Perez of Hebron 175, 180–84; itinerary 221–28; Messianism 9–11, 66–8, 77,

141, 151, 154, 158, 161–2, 165–6, 222–3, 244–6; *see also* Apocalypse
Micah 206
mil, *see* measures
military orders 64, 101, 262; *see also* Hospitallers, Templars, Teutonic Knights
minorities 94–110; legal status of 94–100, 260–62; social position 100–10; *see also* legislation; Muslims; Oriental Christians
Miriam (sister of Moses) 244; *see also* Hattin
Miron, *see* Kfar Meron
Mizpah 204
Moab 171, 206
Modi'in 188n.
Mongols 165, 169n., 193n., 279
Monk of Lido 36, 37, 39n.
Mons Gaudii (*Montjoye*), *see* Nebī Samwīl
Montpellier 97n., 272, 273
Morea 274
Morocco 141, 142
Moses 99, 171
Moses b. Astruc 125
Moses b. Ḥisdai (of Tachau) 266
Moses b. Maimon, *see* Maimonides
Moses b. Naḥman, *see* Naḥmanides
Moses ha-Dar'iv 141
Moses of Acre 125
Mosul (Nineveh) 55, 207, 216, 217, 220, 221, 284, 286; people from in Acre 261
Mt Carmel 25, 35, 83, 178, 180, 181, 195, 199, 225, 232, 234, 236, 237, 253; cave and altar of Elijah 171, 175, 178, 180, 181, 231, 232, 234, 236; *see also* Haifa
'Mt Carmel', (near Tiberias), tombs of Jochebed and Zippora 181, 225 and n.
Mt Ebal 180, 237
Mt Gerizim 180, 238
Mt Gilboa 195, 196, 197, 200
Mt Musard *see* Acre
Mt Sinai *see* Sinai
Mt Tabor 262
'Mourners of Zion' (*Aveilei Ẓion*) 138–9
al-Mu'aẓẓam, al-Malik 83, 85, 86, 266
Mubārak, a slave 42
Muḥammed al-Nāṣir 73
Muḥrakah 236
al-Muqaddasi 121, 135
Musalam ben Abū Sahl 50
Mūsi b. Habba b. Salomon of Safad 57n.
Muslims 15, 22, 23, 24n., 25n., 39, 41, 42, 46, 47, 82, 85–6, 91, 94–100, 101, 102, 105, 106, 107, 108, 109, 121, 130, 135, 171, 174, 184, 187, 210, 220, 225, 234, 235, 236, 238, 240, 249, 252, 260, 276
al-Mustanṣīr 35
al-Muṭaīlib 81

Nabal the Carmelite 181
Nabartā (Nabartein) 55, 182, 220, 232
Nabartein *see* Nabartā
Nablus 50, 65, 178, 180, 185, 195, 196, 197, 200, 204, 225, 232, 237, 238, 247; council of 105; pilgrimages 185, 188, 219; tomb of Joseph 188, 219
nagid 16 and n., 26 and n., 41n., 43, 56, 113, 114
Naḥman Ḥatūfā, tomb 224
Naḥman of Regensburg 208
Naḥmanides 80n., 121, 131n., 147n., 152, 154–62, 163, 164, 165, 231, 232–50, 251–2, 253, 276–8; sermons 159–61; seal 253; tomb 234, 254
Naḥmanides, anonymous pupil of 233–50, 253–54
Nahōrai *see* Nehōrai
Naples 122
nasi, *see* exilarch

Nasir al-Dīn, caliph 217
Nasir-i-Khursau 35, 135
Nathai of Arbel 221
Nathan the prophet, tomb 221
Naveh, *see* Neveh
Nazareth 60, 237
Nebī Samwīl (Ramah, Ramathaim, *Mons Gaudii, Montjoye*) 17, 180, 196, 198, 203, 204, 219, 233, 237, 238; tomb 224, 238
Nebi Shu'ib, *see* Hattin
Nehōrai 58, 108, 140n., 278
Nehōrai the Jerusalemite 140
Nestorians 99, 261; *see also* Oriental Christians
Neveh (Nebo, Naveh, in Transjordan) 216n., 250
Nicaea 20
Nicholas IV, pope 272
Nicholas Donin 151
Nicosia 226
Nissim b. Moses of Marseilles 164–5
Nob *see* Beit Nubā
Normans 31
Nūr al-Daulah, emir 82
Nūr al-Din 69n., 115, 193, 206

Obadiah the prophet, tomb 228; *see also* Bar'am
'Obadya b. 'Ulah 114–15
Obadya the Norman 11n.
occupations 121–7: agriculture 121–2; crafts 122; dyers 122–3; glass-making 123–4; merchants 124–6; physicians 107–9; shipowners 124
Ogerio Ricci 256
Omar ibn al-Khatab 201
Oppenheim 152
Oriental Christians 15, 22, 46–7, 64–5, 82, 95–100, 101, 102, 104, 116, 121, 252, 256n., 260; *see also* Armenians; Greek Orthodox; Georgians; minorities; Nestorians; 'Syrians'
Ottomans 294

Pablo Christiani 155
Palestine Academy, *see* Jerusalem Academy
Palmaria 205
Pamias *see* Banyas
Paneas *see* Banyas
'Paphlangonians' 8 and n.
Par'am, *see* Kfar Par'am
Paris 20, 151, 273; academy of 49, 274
parsā, *see* measures
passagium 274n.
Pedro I of Aragon 10n.
Pedro III of Aragon 125–6
Persia 1, 3, 35, 37, 38, 57, 66n., 191, 249, 250
Perūshīm 138, 139
Petaḥyah of Regensburg (Ratisbon) 48, 58, 62, 105, 108, 117, 123, 139, 140, 171, 249; itinerary of 206–15
Peter of Blois 25 and n.
Peter of Scandalion 256
Peter Pennesinpa 257
Peter the Venerable 109
Petrus Alphonsi 25
Petrus Tudebodus 21
Philip II Augustus 260
Pierre Bellaygue 125
Pierre Gilles 125
Pierre Viadier 125
pilgrimages 128–67; character 128–37, 153, 171–73; pattern 137–40; ethnic origins of pilgrims 137–8; famous pilgrims 140–47; opposition to pilgrimages 147–9; *see also* itineraries
Pilgrim's Castle (Athlith) 257
Pinḥas b. Yair, tomb of 226
Pisa 35, 60, 125
Poland 207, 266
poll tax 255–6; *jizya* 65, 108, 256; *capitatio* 102–3, 256; *see also* minorities
Poulains 94

Prague 207, 208, 209
Prester John 193 n.
Prōd (Faradiyah) 232, 244
Provence 120, 124, 191, 277, 282, 284
Pumbedita 3, 111

Qadaq 250
qahal, *see* community
Qaqūn (Caco) 195
Qaṣr Ḥaifa, *see* Haifa
Qishon *see* Kishon
Qisma 55, 220
qivrei avōth, *see* Tombs of the Ancestors
qivrei Ṣadīqim, *see* Tombs of the Just
Qiyomia, tomb of Jose demin Yōqrat 224
Qubeiba (Mahomerie la Petite) 196
Qūṣ 74

Rabban Gamliel, tomb *see* Yabneh
Rabbenu Tam (Jacob b. Meir) 208
Rachel, tomb 131, 173, 180, 185, 186, 203, 209, 211, 212, 213, 215, 218, 223, 233, 242
Raḍi Abū'l Barakāt 82–3
rabbanim 72 n., 75 n., 79 n.,
Radulf of Caen 40 n.
Raffiaḥ 16
raīs, court of 97, 98; *see also* Court of the Market
Ramah *see* Nebī Samwīl
Ramah (Romi, Romā, in Galilee) 181, 204, 232, 244, 247
Ramallah 238
Ramathaim *see* Nebī Samwīl
Ramathaim Zophim 238
Ramerupt 209
Ramlah (Ramle) 3, 4, 5, 6, 8, 9, 15, 17, 18 n., 116, 195, 204; Karaite community 15
Ramle *see* Ramlah
Raqat *see* Tiberias
Rās Amās 181
Rashba (R. Solomon b. Adereth) 112, 277, 280–1, 282, 290
Rashi (R. Solomon of Troyes) 208–9
Ratisbon 207, 208, 209
Raymond of Aguilers 21
Raymond Martini 155
Raymond of Peñaforte 155
Raymond of St Gilles 19, 26
Raymond of Tripoli 58
Raymond Sultan 257
Rebecca (wife of Isaac) *see* Hebron
Red Sea 74
Reichert, V. E. 278–9
Rhineland 11, 12, 40 n.
Rhodes 25 n., 193
Ribaldo di Sarephia 126
Richard the Lionheart 70, 258, 260
Robert of Flanders 19
Robert the Monk 21
Robert of Normandy 19
Roger of Hoveden 60 n.
Romania *see* Byzantine Empire
Rome 18, 49, 69, 165, 193, 285, 287, 288
Romi (Romā) *see* Ramah
Rosh *see* Asher b. Yeḥiel
rosh ha-gōla (head of the Diaspora) 3, 5, 113; *see also* community
rosh ha-qahal (head of the community) 106, 113, 114; *see also* community
Rudolph of Habsburg, emperor 152
Rupert of Deutz 25 n.
Russia 131, 132, 207, 209

Sa'adya b. Berakhya 54
Sa'adya Gaon 3 n., 29
Sa'adya Hakkohen 75
Sa'adya *Ish Yemīni* 73–4
Ṣadoq b. Joshiah 33
Safad 55, 56, 57, 59, 64, 97, 220, 221, 224, 230, 232, 233, 247, 278, 279, 280, 286 n., 288,

Safad—*contd*
292; tomb of Ḥanīnā b. Horkenos 221
Sahl ben Maṣliaḥ 172
Ṣaīdā, *see* Sidon
St George *see* Lydda
St John, order of, *see* Hospitallers
Sakhnin 181
Saladin 24n., 64, 65, 66, 67, 68, 69, 70, 73, 74, 75, 81, 83, 86, 95, 209, 251, 254, 258, 259, 292; and the Jews 64–8
Salkhad 86
Salonika 12, 13, 132
al-Salt 250
Samanūd (Egypt) 53n.
Samaria 54, 170, 195, 215, 234, 235, 237, 242
Samaritans 18, 51, 99, 104, 106, 107, 237, 247, 261
Sambari, chronicle of 52n.
Sambation, river 279
Shamgar b. 'Anath, tomb 224; *see also* Tibnin
Samson b. Abraham of Sens 77, 78, 79, 80, 266, 268, 273; tomb 254, 267
Samuel b. 'Ali Hakkohen 207, 286
Samuel b. Samson 55, 76–7, 198; itinerary of 215–21, 228
Samuel, prophet 17, 238; *see also* Nebī Samwīl
Ṣarafand, *see* Sarepta
Samuel Hakkohen b. David (exilarch) 113, 289
Saragossa 272
Sarah, well of 213; *see also* Mamrei, Plain of
Sarepta (Ṣarafand, Zarephat) 195, 199, 242
Sarfith (Salfith) 242
Saure Rimous (Marseilles) 125
Scandalion (Iskanderūna) 126, 127
Scroll of Ebyatar 184
Schwabenspiegel 25
Schwarz, J. 194
Sebaste 195, 196, 197, 198, 200
Sefer Qabbalath Ṣadiquei Eretz Israel (*Qivrei Avōth*) *see* Itineraries
Sefer Yeṣīra 277
Seljuks 1, 2, 5–9, 15, 17, 32
Sepphoris *see* Zippori
serfs (*villani*) 101–2; *see also* slaves
Shalom b. Joseph of Ferrara 280n.
Shalom b. Levy 220
al-Shām 12, 115n., 121
Shamgar b. 'Anath, tomb 224
Shazōr 182, 224, 232, 244
Shechem *see* Nablus
Shefar'am (Le Saffran) 215, 237
Shemaiah and Avtalion, tombs *see* Giscala
Shem Tov b. Isaac of Tortosa 265
Shem Tov b. Joseph ibn Falaquera 290
Shem Tov the Spaniard of Léon 279; *Sh'arei Ṣedeq* 279–81
Sheth b. Enosh, tomb 225
Shī'ā 1, 38
Shiloh 180, 203, 204, 219, 232
Shlomo of Troyes *see* Rashi
Sicily 122, 125, 193, 280
Sidon 43, 62, 92, 94, 116, 122, 195, 199, 226, 234, 235, 236, 250
Simeon bar Yōḥai 220, 221, 244; *Prayer* 6–7; tomb *see* Kfar Meron; Bar'am
Simeon the Just, tomb 241
Simone Malocello 256
Sin ('Sinai', Tripoli) 249
Sinai 16, 71, 81, 92, 186, 230, 292
Sipht *see* Safad
slaves 24–5; captives 25–8, 31, 33, 46, 50n.
Sodom and Gomorrah 212, 213, 215, 250
Ṣofīm 238
Solomon, pools of 218
Solomon Abū'l-Barakāt 82, 84
Solomon b. Adereth *see* Rashba
Solomon b. ha-Yatōm, commentary to *Mashqin* (*Mō'ed qatan*) 130n.
Solomon b. Joseph Hakkohen 7, 8
Solomon b. Samson 11n.

Solomon b. Samuel ha-Ṣarfati *see* Solomon b. Samuel Petit
Solomon b. Samuel Petit 120, 278, 289, 285, 286, 287–8, 289, 290
Solomon b. Yehuda 41 n.
Solomon Hakkohen b. Moses Hakkohen 279
Solomon ibn Gabirol *see* Ibn Gabirol
Solomon of Montpellier 272
Solomon of Mosul 208
Solomon, *nasi* 29
Sonne, I. 222
Spain 10, 31, 48, 66 n., 120, 125, 126, 131, 144, 152, 155, 156, 157, 158, 192, 193, 229, 234, 266, 278, 279, 282, 290, 291, 293
Speyer 152
Strategius 241 n.
Ṣūfi 280
Sunbāt (Egypt) 53 n.
Sūrā academy of 3 and n., 111
Syrians 22 n, 65 n., 96, 98, 102, 107, 200, 261

Ta'anakh (Tannoch) 237
Taḥkemoni, *see* Judah al-Ḥarizi
Taīmin (Timnah) 196
Tam ha-Kesef, *see* Joseph ibn Caspi
Tanḥum Yerūshalmi 289
Tancred of Otranto 19, 24, 36, 38, 39, 40, 57
Tartary 207
taxation 102–4; *see also* poll tax
Tel-Keisān 253
Tel Keniseh ('Capernaum') 181 n.
Templars 60, 109, 125, 200, 241 n., 257; *see also* military orders
Temple Mount *see* Jerusalem
Temple of Solomon (al-Aqṣa) *see* Jerusalem
Teqo'a 178, 232, 242
Terah, 25 n.
Teutonic Knights 126, 262, 263; *see also* military Orders
Theodorich, pilgrim 25
Tiberias 9, 18, 36, 37, 57, 58, 59, 61, 91, 108, 117, 140 n., 178, 180, 181, 182, 184, 185, 187–8, 205, 215, 224, 225, 232, 242, 260, 288, 292; community of 57–8; Jewish market 57–8; *Ḥammei Tveryah* 224; tomb of Meir Qasịn 184, 232; tomb of R. Kahana 187; tomb of Maimonides 177, 182 n., 232, 248, 273 n.; academy in 3; *gaon* of 3; pilgrimages to 178, 180, 181, 182, 184, 185, 187–8, 219
Thoros, king of Cilicia 193
Tibnin (Teimin, Timnath(a), Toron) 182, 206, 224; tomb of Shamgar b. 'Anath 224
Timnath(a), *see* Tibnin
Timnath Seraḥ (Kfar Ḥeres) 180, 185, 242; tomb of Joshua b. Nun 180
Titus 24, 25 n., 48, 68 n., 200
Tobias of Thebes 13
Toledo 273
Tombs of the Ancestors (*Qivrey Avot*) 130–1, 141, 169–76, 191, 246
Tombs of the Just (*Qivrei ṣadīqim*) 106, 133 n., 135, 169–76, 191, 246
Tombs of the Patriarchs *see* Hebron
Toron de los Caballeros, *see* Latrun
Tosafists 77, 78, 79–80, 120, 147–8, 150–4, 208, 209, 226 n., 254, 267–9, 276
Tōsọ̄th Eretz Israel 80 n., 161–2, 233–50; *see also* itineraries, Naḥmanides, anonymous pupil of
Tractatus de inventione Sanctorum Patriarcharum 41–2
Transjordan 47, 91, 215, 249, 250
Tripoli 12, 13, 33, 34, 35, 193, 194, 195, 199, 247, 249
Troyes 209

Tustari, Karaite family 27n., 28, 31
Tyre 1n., 9, 33, 34, 37, 42, 43, 46, 49, 51, 52, 53, 54, 56, 60, 64, 92, 94, 97, 101, 103, 104, 105, 108, 111, 115, 118, 124, 126, 143, 184, 195, 226, 234, 235, 236; community 51–4, 117, 254–8; seat of Jerusalem's academy 9, 111; Jewish Quarter 255–6; Venetian Quarter 255–6; Genoese Quarter 256–7

Umayyads 35
Urban II, pope 146, 161n., 245n.
Urban IV, pope, 276
Usama ibn Munkidh 107
Ushā 215, 237

Val de Luna, *see* Ayalon, Valley of
Venice 35, 36 38, 39, 40, 103, 125, 255, 256, 262; *see also* communes
Vidal (Vital) Negrel 125
villani, *see* serfs
Vindicta Salvatoris 25
Volta, della, family 126

Walafrid Strabo 25
Warmundus, patriarch of Jerusalem, *pactum Warmundi* 255n.
Wars of the Lord, *see* Abraham Maimuni
Wasserburg 153
Wetterau 152
Wilbrand of Oldenburg 260n., 264
William of Tyre 47, 107, 108
William, prior of the Holy Sepulchre 92n.
Wipo 25
Worms 152, 153; *Book of Customs* 152–3

Yabneh (Ibelin) 171, 185, 186, 196, 197, 205, 211, 213, 215, 249; tomb of Rabban Gamaliel 171, 249
Yālū 196
Yaqūq (Ḥaquq) 182, 219; tomb of Habakkuk 219, 226, 232
Yeḥiel b. Elyaqīm, *dayyam* 88n.
Yeḥiel b. Isaac ha-Ṣarfatī Yerūshalmi 86, 87, 88, 89
Yeḥiel of Paris (Sire Vives) 150–2, 231, 274
Yehuda, *see* Judah
al-Yehudiyah (Kfar Yehūda) 250
Yeshivat Eretz ha-Tzvi, *see* Jerusalem Academy
Yeshivat Eretz Israel, *see* Jerusalem Academy
*Yeshivat Gaon Ya'*aqov, *see* Jerusalem Academy
Yemen 74, 138; Yemenites in Jerusalem 73–5
Yosei ha-Galīli, tomb 184; *see also* Daltōn

Zaru'a (Zore'a) 250
al-Ẓahir, caliph 18n.
Zarepath *see* Sarepta
Zar'in (*Petit Gerin*) 62, 196, 205
Zengi 64–5
Zephaniah, tomb (Mount Lebanon) 182, 249
Zippora, tomb 188; *see also* Mt Carmel
Zippori (Sepphoris) 130, 178, 180, 181, 185, 196, 205, 215, 232, 237, 244; tomb of Judah ha-Nasi 130n., 205, 211, 237